Social Studies for Secondary Schools
Teaching to Learn, Learning to Teach

Social Studies for Secondary Schools

Teaching to Learn, Learning to Teach

SECOND EDITION

Alan J. Singer

and the

Hofstra New Teachers Network
Hofstra University

LEA LAWRENCE ERLBAUM ASSOCIATES, PUBLISHERS
2003   Mahwah, New Jersey   London

**This book is dedicated
to the middle school and high school students
who spent so much time teaching us
how to become social studies teachers.**

Senior Acquisitions Editor:	Naomi Silverman
Textbook Marketing Manager:	Marisol Kozlovski
Editorial Assistant:	Erica Kica
Cover Design:	Kathryn Houghtaling Lacey
Textbook Production Manager:	Paul Smolenski
Full-Service Compositor:	UG / GGS Information Services, Inc.
Text and Cover Printer:	Victor Graphics, Inc.

This book was typeset in 12/14 Palatino, Bold, and Italic. The heads were typeset in Frutiger Bold.

Lawrence Erlbaum Associates, Inc., Publishers
10 Industrial Avenue
Mahwah, New Jersey 07430

Library of Congress Cataloging-in-Publication-Data

Singer, Alan J.
  Social studies for secondary schools : teaching to learn, learning to teach /
Alan J. Singer, and the Hofstra Social Studies Educators, Hofstra
University.—2nd ed.
    p. cm
  Includes index.
  ISBN 0-8058-4208-X (alk. paper)
  1. Social sciences—Study and teaching (Secondary)—United States.
I. Hofstra Social Studies Educators.   II. Title.

H62.5.U5S56 2003
300'.71'273—dc21   2002192825

Books published by Lawrence Erlbaum Associates are printed on acid-free paper, and their bindings are chosen for strength and durability.

Printed in the United States of America
10 9 8 7 6 5 4 3 2 1

Contents

Preface to the Second Edition

"This book gives me ammunition to defend my view of teaching."
Dean Bacigalupo, Lincoln Orens Middle School, Island Park, New York, member of
the Hofstra New Teachers Network

I want to thank Naomi Silverman and the editors of Lawrence Erlbaum and Associates for giving me the opportunity to produce a second edition of *Social Studies for Secondary Schools: Teaching to Learn/Learning to Teach*. The last five years (1997 to 2002) have been tumultuous times in our society, and secondary school social studies teachers have been asked to play a major role in helping students (our society's future leaders) understand events reshaping the country and the world. I have continued to work with the Hofstra Social Studies Educators (since renamed the New Teachers Network) (NTN) and these teachers' contributions greatly strengthen my approach to teaching and enrich this book. In their classrooms they have had to grapple with the attacks on the World Trade Center and the Pentagon, the U.S. response in Afghanistan and at home, and local issues in the New York metropolitan area such as charges of police brutality and racial profiling in minority communities, unequal school funding, and pressure to prepare students for standardized assessments.

Although I have not had the opportunity to return to the secondary school classroom on a full-time basis, I have been fortunate that members of the NTN have "lent" me their classrooms during Januarys and Junes to experiment with new lessons, activities, and approaches to teaching. These "guest appearances" have helped me remain in practice as a teacher, to field-test a Great Irish Famine curriculum guide for the State of New York, and to edit material for *Social Science Docket*, a joint publication of the New York and New Jersey Councils for the Social Studies. I hope that readers familiar with both volumes of this text find that I have continued to grow as a social studies teacher despite being stationed in a university teacher education program.

NEW IN THE SECOND EDITION

The structure of the book and most of the topics examined in this second edition remain the same as before, but every chapter has been updated and includes a number of new lesson ideas. These are especially designed to help new teachers address learning standards, work in inclusive settings, and promote literacy and the use of technology in social studies classrooms. I am pleased to see the new focus on document-based instruction and assessment in social studies, and I have worked with members of the NTN to develop sample activities that also can serve as tools for assessing student learning. Project or activity-based social studies instruction and multicultural education have been under ever-increasing attack by proponents of traditional educational practices, so I have sharpened my defense of both of these approaches to teaching throughout the book.

OVERVIEW

This book integrates discussions of educational goals and the nature of history and social studies with ideas for organizing social studies curricula, units, lessons, projects, and activities. Sections include lesson ideas developed by new and experienced middle school and high school social studies teachers. A major theme woven throughout the book is that what we choose to teach and the way we teach reflect our broader understanding of society, history, and the purpose of social studies education.

The book is intended as either a primary or support text in methods courses for undergraduate and graduate preservice social studies teachers. It should also be useful, however, for inservice training programs, as a reference for new social studies teachers, and as a resource for experienced social studies educators who are engaged in rethinking their teaching practice.

Part I, "Thinking about Social Studies," includes chapters that focus on philosophical issues such as the reasons for teaching and studying social studies (chap. 1), social studies goals and standards (chap. 2), and the design of social studies curricula (chap. 3). Part II, "Preparing to Teach Social Studies," is intended to be more practical. It examines strategies for planning social studies units (chap. 4) and lessons (chaps. 5 and 6) and includes many sample lesson ideas. These sections have new, extended discussions of inclusion and literacy. Part III, "Implementing Your Ideas," explores topics such as thematic and interdisciplinary teaching (chap. 7), a project approach to social studies (chap. 8), and assessing student learning and our own performance as teachers (chap. 9). It concludes with a guide to social studies resource materials and organizations (chap. 10). This part of the book has extended coverage of ideas for promoting literacy and the use of technology in social studies classrooms.

Every chapter addresses a broad question about social studies education. Sections within chapters begin with narrower questions that direct attention to specific educational issues. Chapters conclude with essays about related social studies topics. They also include sources for further reading, lesson "examples," and teaching, learning, and classroom activities designed to provoke discussion and illustrate different approaches to teaching social studies. Inserts labeled *Teaching Activities* are assignments and topics for discussion by students in university methods courses and social studies teachers. *Classroom*

Activities are sample lesson ideas designed for middle-level and high school students. Teachers and preservice teachers should experiment with some of these activities to see how they work and consider how they would use them in secondary school classes. *Learning Activities* are intended to be useful activities and important topics for discussion in both secondary school social studies classrooms and in university social studies methods courses. Activities are followed by four categories: Think it over, Add your voice to the discussion, Try it yourself, and It's your classroom.

GOALS AS AUTHOR AND TEACHER

I am an historian with a specialization in the social history of the industrial United States and a former high school social studies teacher. When I write about social studies, I generally use historical examples. I do not think this focus invalidates the points I raise about the social sciences, but I am prepared for criticism. I know this may sound heretical, but I do not think the specific content focus of a social studies curriculum should be the main concern; it is certainly not as important as taking a critical approach to any subject matter that is being explored. Social studies curricula need structure. Although my organizing preference is chronology, this is not a rule.

Many parts of this book are designed to hone in on points of contention. My intent is to promote dialogue between myself as author and you as reader. Literacy specialists call this active approach to examining a text and making meaning of it "reader response." I hope that new teachers think about the ideas I am raising and agree or disagree with me and with each other. If you disagree with my biases, criticize them. That is one of the overall goals of social studies education and a purpose of this book. It is how we get to be social studies teachers.

If you want to reach me, my address is Alan Singer, Department of Curriculum and Teaching, 113 Hofstra University, Hempstead, NY 11549. My e-mail address is catajs@hofstra.edu.

We have much to do if we are going to become social studies teachers who have some say in shaping the debates in our profession and active citizens who influence decisions in our society. So, let's roll up our sleeves and get to work.

ACKNOWLEDGMENTS

Alan J. Singer is the coordinator of the secondary school social studies program in the Department of Curriculum and Teaching of the Hofstra University School of Education. The Hofstra New Teachers Network (NTN) is a network of students and student teachers currently in the program, alumni, secondary school social studies teachers and administrators, co-operating teachers, field supervisors, and Hofstra faculty. NTN publishes a newsletter, sponsors two annual conferences, organizes support teams for new teachers, and promotes participation in teacher development activities.

Contributors to the second edition of *Social Studies for Secondary Schools* include Hofstra University teacher education students and graduates Christina Agosti-Dircks (Greenlawn, N.Y.); Lois Ayre (Garden City, N.Y.); Dean Bacigalupo (Island Park, N.Y.); Daniel Bachman (Massapequa, N.Y.); Jeannette Balantic (Ardsley, N.Y.); Jennifer Bambino (Carle Place, N.Y.); Pamela Booth; Michael Butler (Baldwin, N.Y.); Vonda-Kay Cambell (Valley Stream, N.Y.); Jennie

Chacko (Amityville, N.Y.); Lynda Costello-Hererra (Uniondale, N.Y.); Charles Cronin; Jennifer Debler (Baldwin, N.Y.); Henry Dircks (Bellmore-Merrick, N.Y.); Kenneth Dwyer (Oceanside, N.Y.); Robin Edwards (Levittown, N.Y.); Rachel Gaglione Thompson (Queens, N.Y.); Erin Hayden (Queens, N.Y.); Stephanie Hunte (Uniondale, N.Y.); Patricia Kafi (Lawrence, N.Y.); Laurence Klein (Queens, N.Y.); Robert Kurtz (Oyster Bay, N.Y.); Ken Leman (Brooklyn, N.Y.); Darren Luskoff (Mineola, N.Y.); Denise Lutz (East Meadow, N.Y.); Tammy Manor (Queens, N.Y.); Seth Margolin (Deer Park, N.Y.); William McDonaugh (Baldwin, N.Y.); Michael Pezone (Queens, N.Y.); Jennifer Palacio (Long Beach, N.Y.); Laura Pearson (Syosset, N.Y.); Lauren Rosenberg (Brooklyn, N.Y.); James Screven (Nassau County, N.Y.); Brendalon Staton (Hempstead, N.Y.); Richard Stern (Rockville Centre, N.Y.); Adeola Tella (Uniondale, N.Y.); Diane Tully (Island Park, N.Y.); Bill Van Nostrand (Connectquot, N.Y.); Cynthia Vitere (Harborfields, N.Y.). I am especially proud that many of my former students are now cooperating teachers and adjunct instructors in the Hofstra program.

Contributors also include Barry Brody (former assistant principal, Franklin K. Lane HS, Brooklyn, N.Y.), Sheila Hanley (assistant principal, James Madison HS, Brooklyn, N.Y.), Charles Howlett (cooperating teacher, Amityville, N.Y.), Rozella Kirchgaessner (high school staff developer, Queens, N.Y.), Andrea Libresco (teacher, Oceanside, N.Y., and Hofstra adjunct), John McNamara (curriculum coordinator, West Windsor–Plainsboro Regional School District, N.J.), Kevin Sheehan (social studies coordinator, Oceanside, N.Y.), and Cheryl Smith (cooperating teacher, Hicksville, N.Y.).

Mary Carter, Henry Dircks, Mary Hodnett (Hofstra adjunct and field supervisor); Andrea Libresco, Margaret MacCurtain (University College, Dublin); Cecelia Mariani (Valley Stream, N.Y.); David Morris (assistant principal, William Maxwell Vocational High School, Brooklyn, N.Y., and Hofstra adjunct); Rose Paternastro (Hofstra adjunct and field supervisor); Michael Pezone; and Leo Silverstone (Hofstra field supervisor) were involved in planning, discussing, and editing this book.

A committee of teachers including Dean Bacigalupo (Island Park, N.Y.); Kelly Delia (Hicksville, N.Y.); Richard DeLucia (New York, N.Y.); Kenneth Dwyer (Oceanside, N.Y.); Michael Ferrarese (Brooklyn, N.Y.); Joslyn Fiorello (Northport, N.Y.); Joseph Hartig (Hicksville, N.Y.); Kenneth Kaufman (Brooklyn, N.Y.); Steven Love; Jewella Lynch (Syosset, N.Y.); Michelle Maniscalco (Syosset, N.Y.); Tammy Manor (Queens, N.Y.); Seth Margolin (Deer Park, N.Y.); Daniel McKeon; Stephanie Morris; Laura Pearson (Syosset, N.Y.); Laura Peterson (East Rockaway, N.Y.); Kenneth Kapfar; Richard Stern (Rockville Centre, N.Y.); Nicole Theo (Islip, N.Y.); and Bill Van Nostrand (Connectquot, N.Y.) made suggestions to improve on the first edition of this book. Brian Messinger (Sewanaka, N.Y.) and Laura Vosswinkel were very effective graduate student assistants and did yeoman duty checking references on the Internet and proofreading manuscript.

Hofstra University School of Education and Allied Human Services faculty members Doris Fromberg, Selma Greenberg (deceased), Janice Koch, James Johnson, Maureen Miletta, Sally Smith, and Sharon Whitton made valuable contributions. Maureen Murphy, executive director of the New York State Great Irish Famine curriculum guide, and the English educator at Hofstra and S. Maxwell Hines, the Hofstra Science educator, deserve special recognition.

This book could not have been completed without support from the Hofstra

University Offices of Editing and Computer Services; the staff of the Curriculum Materials Center in Hofstra University's Axinn Library, especially Harriet Hagenbruch; the secretarial and administrative staff of the Hofstra University School of Education and Allied Human Services and the Department of Curriculum and Teaching; critical readings and suggestions by Dennis Banks (SUNY Oneonta), Kenneth Carlson (Rutgers University), Kathy Bickmore (University of Toronto), Stephan Thorton (Columbia University), and Pearl Oliner (Humbolt State University), and the invaluable assistance of Naomi Silverman and her staff at Lawrence Erlbaum Associates.

Judith Y. Singer, former director of the MLE Learning Center in Brooklyn and assistant professor of Elementary Education at Long Island University–Brooklyn Campus, was a full partner in the development of the educational philosophy and teaching approaches presented in both the first and second editions of this book. Our grown children, Heidi, Rachel, and Solomon, deserve special credit for years of ingenuity and patience as I experimented with them on approaches to teaching. Their willingness to continually argue with me has helped keep many a flight of fancy grounded in the reality of schools "as they are" while recognizing the potential of education "as it can be."

Introduction: Who Am I?

Overview

Trace the evolution of a social studies teacher
Consider the cultural, social, and historical nature of individual identity
Examine the roots of personal identity and its intersection with history
Explore reflective practice

Key Concepts

Identity, Cultural, Change, Experience, Competence, Experimentation

Essay

Questions about Identity

Used with permission of Seth Margolin.

Anybody who writes a book about teaching has to expect certain questions. Who are you? What have you studied? What is your experience? Will your ideas about teaching social studies be useful to me?

My name is Alan Singer. I am a white, male, husband, father, son, brother, college-educated, politically active, ethnic Jew, atheist, citizen of the United States, New Yorker, city dweller, sports fan, hiking and biking enthusiast, high school social studies teacher, college education professor with a PhD in U.S. history and a specialization in the organization of the coal miners' union.

Learning Activity: Ballad for Americans

Toward the end of the Great Depression and just before U.S. entry into World War II, the African American singer and political activist Paul Robeson performed the song "Ballad for Americans" (lyrics available on the web at http://www.cpsr.cs.uchicago.edu/robeson/links in a series of concerts across the country. It became so popular that in 1940 it was selected as the theme song for the Republican Party's national convention (Robeson, 1990). During the song, the chorus asks Paul Robeson to identify himself, and he responds that he is a member of every ethnic, religious, and occupational group in the United States and represents an amalgam of all the people who built America (LaTouche and Robinson, 1940). The song takes on particular importance in the contemporary United States as the country grows increasingly more diverse.

Try it yourself:
1. Who are you? Which groups of people are you a member of?
2. Explain how you became a member of each group.
3. How did different members of your family come to become "Americans"?

Add your voice to the discussion:
In the song "Ballad for Americans," Paul Robeson suggests that a large number of groups of people should be included in the history of the United States and our definition of what is an American. Do you agree or disagree with Paul Robeson? Explain the reason for your answer.

I grew up in a working-class community in the Bronx, New York, within walking distance of Yankee Stadium. Neither of my parents went to college, but I was always considered "college material." I attended one of New York City's academically selective public high schools, where I was a mediocre student. On the relatively rare occasions when I liked a teacher or a subject, I usually did well. More often, I just got by.

I have few memories of secondary school teachers or classes. I remember my ninth-grade algebra teacher. She was also my homeroom teacher and coach of the math team. I was on the math team, and she always made sure that I had money for lunch. If I did not, she lent it to me. I remember my tenth-grade social studies teacher because he gave students extra credit for bringing magazines to class and including pictures in their reports. I never got the extra credit because we did not have magazines in our house, and this was the era before copying machines made it possible to get pictures from the library. I was very bitter because, without the extra credit, I was kept out of the advanced placement history class. I remember my eleventh-grade U.S. history teacher because he challenged the class to find something incorrect or vague in the Declaration of Independence, which he considered to be the "greatest document ever written." I argued that the passage that states that "the People" have the right "to alter or to abolish" governments never spells out what percentage of the people are required for this kind of change. The teacher got me a copy of Carl Becker's book on the Declaration, in which Becker makes a similar point, and he discussed it with me (Becker, 1942).

I started college at the City College of New York (CCNY) in September 1967 partly because it was the thing to do after high school, partly because my parents said it would provide me with a "profession" and a middle-class standard of living, and partly because college meant a deferment from the war in Vietnam. When I thought about the future, I considered becoming a research scientist or maybe a lawyer. I never imagined myself becoming a secondary school teacher. How could I? I did not like high school the first time.

The years 1967–1971 were exciting times at CCNY and in the United States. Demonstrators protested against U.S. involvement in the war in Vietnam. The African-American community debated integration versus separation. Students were demanding the right to participate in the college decision-making process. In December 1967, I was arrested in a protest at Whitehall Street, the New York

City draft induction center immortalized by Arlo Guthrie in the ballad "Alice's Restaurant." I was charged with "obstructing pedestrian traffic" by standing on the sidewalk. The charges were later dropped. As a result of my arrest, which was unplanned, I emerged as a radical student leader and was elected to the student government.

My freshman, sophomore, and junior years were spent planning and protesting, working (in a cafeteria and as a taxi cab driver), traveling, and only occasionally attending classes. At the start of my junior year, I began to think about what I would do after I finished college. My long-term plan was to become a revolutionary. My short-term plan was to be employable. My father persuaded me to get my teaching credentials. After all, "anybody could teach."

At some point, and I am not sure when, I started to become a serious student. If I was going to change the world, I had to understand it. I began to read history, study, do research, and think about the world. I became a member of the United Community Centers, a community organizing group based in the working-class, largely minority community of East New York, Brooklyn. At the center, we worked with community youth, knocked on doors in the projects (public housing) raising money and discussing our ideas, distributed a community newspaper, organized people to participate in broader social movements, and operated a resident summer "sleep-away" camp. I spent my next five summers working in camp as a counselor, bus driver, and maintenance worker. Over thirty years later, I remain active in the center.

The education program at CCNY will surprise no one. After a series of disagreements between us in class, my first education professor said I should never become a teacher and recommended that I drop out of the program. The history of education professor lectured the class to sleep. The educational psychology professor was enamored with B. F. Skinner and Konrad Lorenz, so he spent all of his time discussing experiments with pigeons and geese. The social studies methods teacher was especially disappointing. His specialty was operating outdated audiovisual equipment, so we had workshops on each machine. At the end of his class, I swore I would never use an overhead projector in class, even if it meant permanent unemployment. But I did not really have to worry. The first time I worked in a school where I had access to an overhead projector was 1992.

Because of my reputation at City College as a troublemaker, I was exiled to student teach in an "undesirable" junior high school in the south Bronx. My cooperating teacher was starting her second year as a teacher. She was nice to the students but had little idea what to teach or how to organize a class. An adjunct in the School of Education was assigned to visit me three times.

My most memorable lesson as a student teacher was a mock demonstration in the classroom. We were studying Martin Luther's 95 theses. I met the students at the door and handed them flyers inviting them to come to a rally protesting against the injustices of the Roman Catholic Church. We yelled, sang protest songs, evaluated Martin Luther's demands, and then discussed similarities between protests against the authority of the Catholic Church in 1517 and against U.S. policy in Vietnam in 1971.

The draft remained a problem until the fall of 1971, when the law authorizing military conscription expired and the United States started its experiment with an all-volunteer army. My friends and

I had decided that if we were drafted, we would organize against the war in Vietnam from inside the military. I was terrified of this prospect and was tremendously relieved not to have to go into the army. One of the lessons that I always enjoy doing with students is examining where their lives, or the lives of people in their families, intersect with and are directly affected by historical events.

Classroom Activity: My Life and History

Try this exercise at the beginning of the semester. As a homework assignment, ask students to write about ways that their lives or the lives of friends or family members have been influenced (or changed) by historical events. This is a good homework activity because it gives students a chance to discuss their ideas with family members. As a follow-up in class, students can share their stories in groups, and the stories that groups find especially interesting can be read aloud to the class. After hearing the stories, students can discuss why they think these events took place. This discussion allows the class to formulate their own questions about history that can become the basis for organizing the term's work. Following are excerpts from essays by students who wrote about their experiences living in other countries.

Summer vacation in an Israeli prison

It was a hot and humid night on the West Bank in Palestine, where I was spending my summer visiting my grandparents. I was a 14-year-old boy looking for a good time, but what I got that night no one could have expected. I was on my way home from a cousin's house when I heard a truck pull up. Out of the truck came twelve Israeli soldiers. I was stunned and had no idea what to do. I began to walk quickly, hoping not to be bothered by the soldiers, but to my disappointment the soldiers stopped me. I had no identification with me, and a soldier asked me a question in Arabic. Before I could even answer him, they all began to beat me with clubs. I was in extreme pain and the blows to my head were so brutal that finally I fell unconscious. When I awoke, I found myself in the back of a military truck surrounded by soldiers. After three hours of driving, I was put in a prison. I was very scared, but one guy named Ali, another Palestinian-American, kept me straight. Ali was seventeen years old, and for the month that I was imprisoned he was like my brother.

It was the twenty-ninth day of our thirty-day sentence and Ali and I were hoping to get out the next day. We thought we could stay out of trouble for one more day, but avoiding these soldiers was nearly impossible. One of the soldiers kicked my food on the floor. I tried to keep cool, but I just could not anymore. I punched him in the face and he quickly fell to the ground. I jumped on him and continued to hit him. All of a sudden I heard a shot. I thought I was hit, but when I turned around, it was Ali who was bleeding. I ran right to Ali and held him in my arms. I stood silent in shock as I felt Ali's heartbeat get weaker and weaker on my chest until the beat just completely stopped and Ali was gone. A tear found its way down my check as I put Ali down on the ground.

I had trouble getting to sleep that night. I kept asking myself, "Why Ali?" I blamed myself for his death. Finally, I fell asleep. When I woke up in the morning, Ali's body was gone.

El Salvador—country in crisis

El Salvador is the smallest and most densely populated mainland country in the Western Hemisphere. Salvadorian politics are not easy to explain. During the 1970s, guerrilla bands formed among the peasants because of their frustration at unfairness and the hopeless situation under which they lived. The guerrillas are both men and women, and they can be children or even senior citizens. Sometimes they wear bandannas over their faces to hide their identities from the military. If guerrillas are captured, they will be tortured to release the names of their friends. The military is willing to kill innocent people so they can get their hands on the person that they want to catch.

In 1979, when I was five years old, the Catholic Church decided to take an active role in politics in El Salvador. Archbishop Romero and Father Grande decided that the Catholic Church had to help people get a better life while they were still in this world.

My family was extremely religious. Every Sunday, without fail, we put on our best clothes and went to a mass in San Salvador that lasted about two hours. During one mass, I feel asleep. I woke up about 45 minutes later to the sound of gunshots. I was still sleepy, but I remember that my aunt scooped me up and we left the church. Later, I woke up on the living room floor at home. Only then did I learn what had happened at church. Archbishop Romero had preached that people had to oppose the government of El Salvador. In the middle of the sermon, he was assassinated by military officers. They killed the archbishop in cold blood in a holy place in front of all the worshippers, and the government claimed that the murderers were justified!

Think it over:
What questions do you have about the events described in the stories told by these students?

Try it yourself:
Write an essay about the way that your life or the life of someone in your family has been influenced (or changed) by historical events.

It's your classroom:
What would you do if students did not believe these stories or were upset by them?

Although I liked student teaching, I still did not plan to become a teacher. An unanticipated result of my changed attitude toward studying was that I was accepted into the U.S. history doctoral program at Rutgers University and offered a teaching assistantship. Suddenly I was in graduate school and was going to be both a scholar and a revolutionary. During the next few years, I learned that coffee house intellectualizing, academic revolutionary theorizing, and long lonely hours of library research were not all that appealing. What I liked most was teaching history classes. When I completed my coursework and passed my written and oral exams, I resigned my assistantship and became a substitute teacher in a middle school in Brooklyn. Within a few months, I had my own Language Arts and Reading program, but then New York City went bankrupt and thousands of teachers were laid off. My name was placed on a list that remained frozen until 1978.

During the next few years, I got married, started a family, began work on my doctoral dissertation about coal miners, subbed, drove a truck, drove a bus for the New York City Transit Authority on the midnight shift, and worked at the center and the summer camp. It was in camp that I learned how to become a teacher. I figured out that the keys to working with young people were treating them as human beings, listening to their concerns, and finding ways to connect what I was interested in with who they are and their interests. Teaching requires interaction, students and teachers working together, and developing shared classroom goals. Otherwise, I might be talking, but I would not be teaching and they would not be learning.

In the fall of 1978, I made my semi-annual call to the New York City Board of Education to see if my list had been "unfrozen." They said "no," but three days into the school year a high school contacted me and said I had been appointed to work there. Finally, I was a social studies teacher and now I wanted to be one. The school that I was assigned to had serious academic, discipline, and attendance problems, and my first few years as a teacher were very hard. Many teenagers from low-income public housing projects with high crime and unemployment rates were zoned into the school. Attendance was erratic, fighting was frequent, and teachers were often just as glad when the kids did not show up. During my first semester, I had a ninth-grade modified (low reading level) global studies class the last period of the day. The class had 42 students, 38 of them boys. None of the students had a lunch period, and all of the boys had gym the period before they came to me. When I asked the department chair what I could do to teach the class, she answered, "Nothing!"

I wanted to be a good teacher and I worked at it. I had students in my tenth-grade economics class analyze the Board of Education budget report. We prepared our own recommendations, and then we testified at government budget hearings. The students were so excited that they organized a school club so they could remain involved with public issues when they were no longer in my class. Two years later, the club helped organize a rally against educational budget cuts at New York City Hall that involved approximately 5,000 people.

During the first three years, my lessons were largely hit or miss. Sometimes it seemed like I had the entire class in the palm of my hand and I could do no wrong. On other days, the students acted like I was not even present. The worst part was that I could not predict when lessons would work or why. I read a book called *The Last Unicorn* by Peter S. Beagle; it captured the way I felt about my teaching. It

is the story of a hapless young magician who is trying to save unicorns from extinction. Sometimes he finds that he has great magical powers, but then, inexplicably, the magic is gone. The magician eventually realizes that humans cannot control magic. It comes only when there is a great need. During those years, I frequently felt that I was that hapless magician. I was always hoping for the magical lesson, but I never knew when it would appear (Beagle, 1968).

Part of the problem during those early years was of my own making. I believed that I knew better than everybody else about how to manage a classroom, organize a curriculum, and connect with teenagers, so I would not take any advice. I had to think everything through for myself and continually reinvent the wheel. Another part of the problem is that, even when you work at becoming a teacher, it takes between three and five years of hard work, planning, and practicing for the things you want to happen in a lesson to happen on a consistent basis.

Finally after experimenting and failing and experimenting again, I learned how to organize lessons centered on the interests and concerns of my students, rather than simply on what I would like to have discussed. More and more of the lessons worked. The need for magic disappeared.

As I became more competent in lesson planning and more confident in my performance as a teacher, I found I was able to appreciate the competence of other people more and learn from them. I was also able to experiment much more. I developed integrated thematic units, long-term group projects, and cooperative learning activities. I worked on motivations, transitions, promoting student discussions, and improving written expression. I tried to develop new means of assessing what my students had learned and what I had taught. Eventually I was able to move myself out from the "center" of every lesson. I eased up my control over the class and created more space for my students to express their voices.

At the same time that I matured as a classroom teacher, I completed my doctoral dissertation on the transformation of consciousness among bituminous coal miners in the 1920s. At first glance, the topic might seem narrow and distant from my teaching, but in my dissertation I was actually examining one of the same questions I was exploring in the classroom: How do people (coal miners, community residents, or high school students) develop fundamentally new perceptions of their world and their place in it?

Over the years I learned along with my students, and much of this book is an effort to share what they have taught me. However, I remain committed to many of the goals I struggled for as a young revolutionary in college in the 1960s and as a community organizer in the 1970s. My primary goal as an educator continues to be empowering young people so that they can become active citizens and agents for democratic social change. I recognize that the most effective way to empower students is to encourage them to think about issues and to help them learn how to collect, organize, analyze, and present information and their own ideas. If I can encourage them to think and act,

the habit of thinking and acting will stay with them long after I am just a dim memory. If they agreed with an idea only because I presented it in class and they wanted to identify with me, they will just agree with someone else's idea the next year.

Because of these beliefs, I am a strong supporter of state and national learning standards that encourage document-based instruction; the ability of students to locate, organize, and present information; critical thinking; and the promotion of literacy in the content area subjects.

I consider myself both a "transformative" and a "democratic" educator, and I believe that the full package that I offer here is consistent with radical notions of education developed by contemporary thinkers such as Paulo Freire, Maxine Greene, and Henry Giroux and progressive ideas championed by John Dewey and his students. Paulo Freire argues that the role of the transformative educator is to help students pose and explore the problems that impact on their lives so they can develop "critical consciousness" about the nature of their society and their position in it (Freire, 1970). Henry Giroux calls on transformative educators to allow students to explore their lived experiences, locate themselves culturally, dissect their personal beliefs and the dominant ideology of their society, and confront established power relationships (Giroux, 1992).

Learning Activity: Another Brick in the Wall

Michael Pezone is a high school teacher and a mentor teacher in the Hofstra New Teachers Network (NTN). He uses lyrics from the song "Another Brick in the Wall (Part 2)" (lyrics available on the web at http://pinkfloydhyperbase.dk) by the British rock band Pink Floyd to provoke his students into thinking about who they are, how school affects them, what education is and should be, and why the world is the way that it is. The song focuses on the alienation of students in schools and accuses teachers of contributing to their oppression (Waters, 1979).

It's your classroom:
1. What popular song, if any, would you use to begin this discussion? Why would you select this song?
2. How would you respond to a colleague who thinks that using a song like this in class turns the kids against school and teachers?

I am a democratic educator in the traditions of Maxine Greene (1988) and John Dewey (1916; 1927/1954; 1938/1963). I share Greene's beliefs that democratic education must be based on acceptance of the plurality of human understanding, experience, and ideas, and that freedom represents a process of continuous individual and collective struggle to create more humane societies; it is neither a commodity that can be hoarded by a limited number of individuals nor a right institutionalized by governments and enjoyed by passive citizens. I share Dewey's understanding that the primary classroom responsibility of the teacher is to create democratic learning experiences for students and his commitment to educating an "articulate public" capable of fighting to extend human freedom. I have learned a lot about implementing Deweyan ideas in the classroom from the work of Alfie Kohn (1986) and George Wood (1992), who discuss the importance of building democratic communities where students are able to express and explore ideas and feelings.

I hope you see the impact of their work on my ideas about teaching and social studies, but it is not necessary to buy the entire package for this book to be useful. I think most readers, regardless of whether they agree with my broader goals, will find valuable and challenging ideas that will enable them to enrich social studies curricula in their classrooms.

Time is an incredibly valuable commodity for teachers; we never have enough of it. There are always papers to mark, lessons to plan, tests to design, departmental responsibilities, students and parents to meet with, school-imposed deadlines, and assorted emergencies. A job that is supposed to be over at 3 PM and to include regular days off and extended vacation time has a way of stretching until it fills every waking moment.

I have been lucky to have time to reflect on my teaching and write this book. After 13 years in a New York City high school classroom, I was offered a position at Hofstra University as a social studies educator. Working with people who wanted to become teachers gave me the chance to become a more conscious teacher and to root my practice in educational theory. I began to think about many of the ideas about teaching, social studies, and adolescents that I had come to accept, and the things that I just did year after year. Hofstra also gave me the opportunity to go back to high school teaching so I could test out what I had been talking about. Since that time I have been a strong proponent of both "reflective practice," the systematic and ongoing evaluation of our work as classroom teachers, and "action research" on our classroom practice to better assess what our students are actually learning.

Over the years, I have experimented with different ways to begin the semester by involving students in exploring social studies and its implications for their lives. Sometimes I change my introductory lessons because they are not working the way I want them to work. Sometimes

I give them a particular twist for a special course. Sometimes I change them because I like to experiment with new ways of doing things or with an idea someone has shared with me.

Let me confess at the outset that I believe nothing is ever completely new in teaching, especially teaching social studies. We are always recycling ideas and materials "borrowed" from other teachers (ideas and materials that they also "borrowed" from someone else). As you play around with some of the ideas and lessons introduced in this book and as you invest in yourself and your students, I think you will discover that rethinking your own lessons and recycling other people's lessons are two of the things that help to make teaching social studies so exciting.

In the 1955 movie *Blackboard Jungle* (Brooks), Glenn Ford portrays an English teacher working in a tough urban high school who explains his desire to be a teacher as an attempt to do something "creative." He tells his university mentor, "I can't be a painter or a writer or an engineer. But I thought if I could help to shape young minds, sort of sculpt lives—and by teaching I'd be creating." The character's pedagogy is a bit dated. Students certainly play a much more active role in their own learning, or refusing to learn, than this statement suggests. I love watching the movie, however, and I think these sentiments capture the spirit I want to convey here.

On the first day(s) of class (whether I am teaching social studies in a secondary school or a university), I usually have four goals:

- I want to introduce the class to what I mean by social studies.
- I want to help students discover why the social studies are important in

understanding who we are as individuals and members of groups.
- I want to help students begin to define social studies questions they would like to explore during the course.
- I want to begin the process of creating a supportive democratic classroom community where young people (of any age) will work together in an effort to understand the nature of our world.

One successful opening lesson is asking students to answer this question: Who am I? I use this lesson on a number of different academic levels, ranging from middle school through graduate school, although, of course, I structure it differently for different age groups. Sometimes I ask students to make a list of at least ten things about themselves. Sometimes I ask students to write a paragraph about who they are. Sometimes I introduce the activity by saying, "We all belong to different kinds of groups. Some of these groups we are born into. Some of these groups we are placed in. Some of these groups we join voluntarily. Make a list of all of the groups that you belong to." When I start this way, students usually ask for an example of a group. I try to throw the question back to the students and have them come up with suggestions.

Whichever way I begin, I always have students write something. I find that writing helps people focus their thoughts. It allows time for thinking about, organizing, and editing ideas. It also ensures that every student has something he or she can contribute to discussion. When everybody has written something, I usually have students come together in small groups to examine the similarities and differences in their responses. I also ask groups to look for categories that can be used to organize the different ways that people in the class define themselves.

Classroom Activity: Who Am I?

I have students complete one of these exercises. In class, we discuss why they describe themselves in these different ways, and I ask them why they think these categories and groups are important. I try to get them to think about how their identities are defined, whether people have to be defined in these ways, and whether their identities are set for life. We use the conversation about our identities to formulate questions about the nature of our society and what we should learn about in class.

- Each of us thinks about ourselves in a number of different ways. Suppose you had to describe yourself in a letter to someone who does not know you. Think about who you are and then write a letter to introduce yourself. In your letter, include a minimum of ten (or twenty) things about yourself.
- All of us belong to many different groups or categories of people. Some groups we choose to join. Some groups we are born into. Some groups other people place us in. Examples of groups or categories that you may belong to include a school club or the group that consists of all people who are female. Make a list of all the different groups or categories to which you think you belong. Try to think of ten to twenty groups or categories.
- Interview the student sitting next to you. Find out as much as you can about the person and how he or she describes himself or herself. In what way is this person like you? In what way is he or she different?

Try it yourself:
Select one of the identity exercises and complete it yourself.

It's your classroom:
Would you share your autobiography with your students. Why or why not?

While people are working in their groups, I am very busy. I travel from group to group, asking questions that help students uncover patterns and understand the reasons for the characteristics and categories they have selected. I usually carry a notepad and jot down some of their ideas so I can refer to them during full class discussion. Eventually, I have to make judgments based on how the small-group discussions are progressing. At some point, I want the class to become a committee of the whole. I also have to decide how to start discussion in the larger group. Sometimes I simply ask a group to report on its discussions, and this broadens into a full class exploration of the individual, social, and historical nature of the way we identify ourselves. Other times I have the class "brainstorm" a list of the different characteristics or categories people have used to describe themselves. We list their ideas on the board and then try to find ways of grouping them.

Most students primarily focus on either personality, interests, or physical appearance when they list the characteristics that define them. However, their lists also include references to social categories such as voluntary group memberships (clubs), family relationships (they are sons or daughters, mothers or fathers, sisters or brothers), occupational roles (student, worker), and broad categories based on their gender, race, religion, and ethnicity. Many students like to include their species: human being.

In the discussion that follows, we use the lists to explore how people see themselves, the ways that societies see people, and the ways that people are both similar and different. We discover many things about who we are and the nature of identity.

Some of the characteristics and categories are very individual and particular, whereas others are much broader and include many people. Some group memberships are voluntary, but people are born into other groups or placed in them by their society. We choose some definitions of who we are, but other definitions are imposed on us by the community where we live. Some categories appear to be unchanging, whereas others seem to change on a regular basis.

From this discussion of who we are, the class begins to explore where we come from: that we have histories as individuals and as members of social groups. Sometimes students also begin to talk about how they would like things to be and how they can achieve their goals. By the end of the lesson, students begin to realize that studying social studies helps them understand themselves, their social relationships, and the nature of their world. The lesson creates a reason for them to explore the things the class will examine during the course of the semester.

I did not invent this activity; it is "borrowed" and then reworked to fit my classes and the way that I like to teach. At the center's summer camp in 1971, the campers and staff held a "Convention of Minorities," in which we explored the histories and cultures of different racial and ethnic groups in the United States. During the "convention," campers ranging in age from seven to seventeen began to formulate and discuss three interrelated questions: Who am I? Where do I come from? Where do I want to go? I have never forgotten these discussions and the way that they involved such a racially, culturally, religiously, and chronologically diverse group in exploring social studies issues.

Essay: Questions about Identity[*]

The New York City subway system does not have a very good image in the national media, but New Yorkers actually use it to get to and from work and to visit family and friends. In many ways, the subway system is New York's "great equalizer." There is one class of service (some would say uniformly bad), and "strap-hangers" from all walks of life and ethnic groups are squeezed together during rush hours, jostled on its platforms, and share the aggravation of its periodic delays.

During our subway journeys, a favorite "strap-hanger" pastime, especially when the cars are too crowded to read the newspaper, is guessing the identity and making up stories about fellow riders. One morning, as I traveled to work, the man sitting directly across from me in the car was an Orthodox Jew, probably a Hasid. He was wearing a black suit, coat, shoes, and fedora, and had a long beard. Sharing his seat was a young African-American man, dressed for Wall Street with a stylishly sharp suit, brown wing tips, and short tight dreadlocks. Also in our section of the subway car was an Asian couple, a Latina woman with features that suggested Native-American ancestors and Andean or Central American origins, and a middle-aged African-American male with a Malcolm "X" baseball cap.

On that morning, I wore a broad-brimmed Ecuadorian felt hat and a woolen Colombian poncho. But I do not think anyone here would argue that my clothing on that particular day makes me a member of the Andean Ecuadorian cultural community. I speak neither Spanish nor any of the native Andean languages. I was born in New York City, and all of my grandparents were immigrants from Eastern Europe.

*Other versions of this essay were presented at the 1992 annual meeting of the American Educational Research Association and were published in the fall 1992 issue of *Democracy and Education* (Ohio University School of Education).

Learning Activity: Lens to the Past

People have a tendency to view the past through the lens of the present. It is one of the major reasons that we need to study history. Secondary school students frequently assume that people from their ethnic background or social group lived like them and always held the same relative position in American society. Over the years, I have looked for newspaper articles from the past that illustrate the experiences of people with the same ethnic identity as students in my classes. Discussion of these articles brings people like them into the historical process and helps students reconsider who they are, where they come from, how their ethnic group has been affected by events in the United States, and how its position has changed.

Try it yourself:

Of what ethnic groups are you a member? How were these groups treated in the past? Find a newspaper article or primary source document that illustrates the position of one of these groups in American society during another historical period.

It's your classroom:

How would you respond to students who do not understand why they have to learn about "them"?

But what about the rest of my traveling companions? Who were these people on that subway car, and how do we know? Will the people on that subway car always identify the way they do now, or will they change the way that they identify over the course of their lifetimes? Is cultural identity something that is historically and socially determined, is it something that individuals are free to choose and repeatedly change, or is it some combination of both of these factors?

The complexity of human cultural identity raises many other questions for social studies educators. When we teach about culture, are we teaching about something that is distinct and decidedly different for each individual, community, and society, or is human experience similar enough so that, despite diversity, people end up doing a lot of things the same way or for the same reasons? Personally and professionally, I believe that cultures are similar enough so that people can understand each other, empathize with each other, and learn from each other, but I am willing to accept that this is an idea that is subject to discussion and debate.

Another important question is this: What factors define the boundaries of a culture? Are boundaries scientifically defined, or are they arbitrary? In the natural world, there is a wide range of biological differences within many species, but each species, by definition, forms a distinct reproductive community. In the cultural world, boundaries are not so clear. Should individuals be

obligated to accept specific patterns of behavior to qualify for group membership, and, if so, who decides on the formula? Must cultures be "ethnically" based, or can they be primarily rooted in race, class, religion, geography, or ideology? I suspect that our definitions will always be somewhat arbitrary, and that cultures are best defined by varying combinations of factors at different historical periods and for differing human groups.

Third, is it meaningful to say that every human difference defines a distinct culture? Are gays a culture, or women, or teachers, or youth, or are they subgroups within cultures? I am not happy with the idea that groups of human beings must be labeled a distinct culture to be respected and included in our curricula. Whatever their opinions on these questions about cultural identity, I think people will agree that the questions must be addressed as we try to create social studies curricula.

The relationship among race, culture, and identity is another particularly difficult area to define. For example, do African Americans have a distinct culture? Certainly, significant aspects of what has been identified as African-American "culture" are shared with the rest of the peoples of the United States, and some differences are only temporary and superficial, primarily differences of style. Yet the roots of racial discrimination and oppression in the United States are deep, and I believe they have shaped the kind of long-term group historical experience that creates cultural distinctiveness.

However, I also recognize that cultural formation is a historical phenomenon, and cultural groups are neither permanent nor unchanging. I have a friend who came to the United States from Trinidad as a child. Is she Trinidadian? Caribbean? African American? American? African? Her own self-conception has changed over the years, and I suspect that her current answer is not a permanent one.

I would argue that, at this time, as a result of some of the same historical forces, White Americans do not form a single cultural group. Traditional White ethnic communities still have some sense of distinct cultural identification, especially when ethnic differences are reinforced by class-based experiences. With the long-term decline in European migration to the United States after 1920, however, increasing access to secondary and higher education, and the general homogenization of society through exposure to mass media, that identification is becoming less distinct; as a result, White American "culture" is in the process of becoming more uniform.

Classroom Activity: Family Artifacts

Most people, especially people who are members of the dominant groups in a society, assume their own culture is the norm. They absorb it from their families and the media while they grow up. Unless they are exposed to other cultures, they live their lives without really thinking about who they are and the ways that they do things. One way to help students begin to think about cultural identity and the values, ideas, and practices of their own cultures is to have them bring a family artifact to class. Students can present their artifacts to the class and explain their origins and why they are important to their families. The class can compare artifacts from different cultures and use them to begin an exploration of cultural similarities and differences.

In variations of this activity, Cynthia Vitere (NTN) has high school students bring in family artifacts, which are circulated around the room anonymously. Student teams examine the artifacts and speculate about cultures of origin. After teams report hypotheses to the class, the students who brought in the artifacts discuss their actual significance to their families. Rachael Gaglione Thompson (NTN) and Laurence Klein (NTN) have students in their middle school classes use the family artifacts to organize a Museum of Immigration. Sometimes parents and grandparents come to class to explain customs and holidays, model clothing, and prepare food.

Try it yourself:
Bring an artifact to class that shows something about the cultural background of your family.

If anything, I think the nature of these questions makes it clear that, in a society such as the United States, social studies curricula can never be permanent. They need to be growing, changing, evolving things, just like culture and identity.

I would like to conclude with a challenge. I think social studies educators need a new metaphor to describe the United States. I frequently ask students and teachers whether they think the United States is more like a melting pot or a salad bowl. We always have great discussions and generally end up deciding that it has some attributes of each image. Some people have assimilated into the melting pot, blending into the American stew while adding their own particular "spice." Other groups, either by choice or as a result of discrimination and exclusion, have remained separate and more distinct.

If we want to develop new social studies curricula and a new multicultural conception of the United States, I think we also need to develop a new metaphor. We need a metaphor that allows for both cultural identity and cultural change; a metaphor that describes the past while pointing the way for the future. I have been toying with the idea of a kaleidoscope, but I am not sure, What do you think?

Classroom Activity: Cartoon Metaphors

These cartoons are from a lesson on European immigration to the United States from 1880–1920. They can be used in either middle school or high school.

Try it yourself:
1. Which metaphor best illustrates your vision of American society? Why?
2. Design a cartoon presenting your pictorial metaphor for the United States today.

REFERENCES

Beagle, P. *The Last Unicorn*. New York: Viking, 1968.

Becker, C. *The Declaration of Independence*. New York: Knopf, 1942.

Brooks, R. dir. *Blackboard Jungle*. MGM, 1995.

Dewey, J. *Democracy and Education*. New York: Macmillan, 1916.

Dewey, J. *The Public and Its Problems*. Athens, Ohio: Swallow Press, 1927/1954.

Dewey, J. *Experience and Education*. New York: Collier/Macmillan, 1938/1963.

Freire, P. *Pedagogy of the Oppressed*. New York: Seabury, 1970.

Freire, P. *Pedagogy of Hope*. New York: Continuum, 1995.

Giroux, H. *Border Crossings: Cultural Workers and the Politics of Education*. New York: Routledge, 1962.

Greene, M. (1988). *The dialect of freedom*. New York: Teachers College Press.

Kohn, A. *No Contest: The case against Competition*. Boston, Mass.: Houghton Mifflin, 1986.

LaTouche, J., and E. Robinson. *Ballad for Americans*. New York: Robbins Music Corporation, 1940.

Robeson, S. *The Whole World in His Hands*. New York: Citadel Press, 1990, 117–18.

Waters, R. "Another Brick in the Wall (Part II)." Pink Floyd Music Publishing/Unichappel Music. In *#1 songs from the 70's & 80's*. Winona, Minn.: Hal Leonard Publishing, 1979.

Wood, G. *Schools That Work*. New York: Dutton, 1992.

I

Thinking about Social Studies

1
Why Teach Social Studies?

Overview

Define history and the social sciences

Examine theories about the role of history and the social sciences for creating knowledge and understanding our world

Explore the similarities, differences, and relationships between the disciplines included in social studies

Discuss the significance of social studies in secondary education

Key Concepts

Multiple Perspectives, History, Social Science, Social Studies, Geography, Anthropology, Political Science, Sociology, Philosophy, Economics, Psychology

Questions

Why Teach Social Studies?
Why Study History?
What Does It Mean to Be a Historian?
What Is History?
What Are Historical Facts?
How Does an Historian Study History?
Is the Study of History Scientific?
Are There Laws in History?
What Are the Goals of Historians?
What Is the Relationship between History and Social Science?
What Do We Learn from the Social Science Disciplines?

Essays

What Social Studies is All About
Are We Teaching "Greek Myths" in the Global History Curriculum?

WHY TEACH SOCIAL STUDIES?

The song "This Land Is My Land" (1956, lyrics available on the web at http:www.arlo.net/lyrics) has become a popular standard at public school assembly programs in the United States. It is difficult to imagine that it was written by Woodrow Wilson "Woody" Guthrie, a formerly unemployed and homeless Okie who was involved in left-wing political causes during a career that spanned from the 1920s through the 1950s. Guthrie spent his youth in Oklahoma, absorbing the culture and music of hoboes, farm laborers, and hillbillies before joining the great dust-bowl migration to the U.S. west coast. In California, he was an active supporter of the labor movement and the Communist Party (Blum, 1990: 284–85). Many of Guthrie's songs celebrate the United States, but in a way that questions the fundamental inequalities he witnessed in our society. A simple statement like "this land is your land, this land is my land," which says that the nation belongs to everyone, challenges a world where some people have great wealth and limitless opportunity while others are impoverished, discriminated against, and disempowered. In stanzas that rarely appear in school productions, Woody's political message is much more explicit. For example, one stanza openly challenges the idea of private property (Seeger, 1985: 160–62).

Removing Woody Guthrie and his music from their historical and political contexts changes the meaning of his songs and ignores what he tried to achieve during his life. However, when teachers provide a context for Guthrie's songs, it opens up the possibility for broad discussions of the social, economic, and political nature of U.S. society, including philosophical explorations of morality, individual action, and social justice. Providing a context that broadens people's understanding of our world and gets us to question our assumptions about it is a primary reason to study and teach history and the social sciences or, in the lexicon of education, the social studies.

According to the National Council for the Social Studies (NCSS, 1994):

> Social studies is the integrated study of the social sciences and humanities to promote civic competence. Within the school program, social studies provides coordinated, systematic study drawing upon such disciplines as anthropology, archeology, economics, geography, history, law, philosophy, political science, psychology, religion, and sociology, as well as appropriate content from the humanities, mathematics, and natural sciences.

> The primary purpose of social studies is to help young people develop the ability to make informed and reasoned decisions for the public good as citizens of a culturally diverse, democratic society in an interdependent world.

Because of the complexity of our world and because of a democratic society's dependence on thoughtful, informed, active citizens, the social studies are multidisciplinary and interdisciplinary. Social studies teachers are the intellectual imperialists of secondary education. Everything is included in our subject's domain. To be taught in schools, however, social studies has to be organized into curricula with calendars, units, and lessons that include goals, content, and concepts that (1) promote academic and social skills, (2) raise questions, (3) provoke disagreements, (4) address controversial issues, (5) suggest connections, and (6) stimulate action.

Adding to the difficulty of defining and teaching social studies are the political implications of many curriculum choices. For example, in January 1995, the U.S. Senate voted 99 to 1 to reject National History Standards that were prepared by the National Center for History in the Schools with participation from the NCSS, the Organization of American Historians (OAH), and the American Historical Association (AHA). The Senate resolution claimed that the standards, which were written under a grant from the federally funded National Endowment for the Humanities, promoted historical understandings that failed to provide students with a decent respect for the contributions of western civilization to the development of the United States. The sole dissenting vote was cast by Senator Bennett Johnston, a Democrat from Louisiana. Johnston opposed the resolution as being an inadequate repudiation of the proposal (Rethinking Schools, 1995: 7).

The dispute over the National History Standards (discussed in Chapter 3) is just the tip of a very large iceberg. Within the social studies are ongoing curriculum debates pitting supporters of multicultural versus traditional European-centered curriculum; advocates of a focus on historical content versus champions of history as a process of discovery (inquiry-based learning); organizations that want history at the center of any curriculum and groups that prefer a broader social science perspective; celebrators of America's glories versus critics of its inconsistencies; political historians versus social historians versus economic historians versus feminist historians; and people who want teachers to play a strictly neutral role in classroom discussions against those who argue that claims for neutrality mask support for the status quo.

Many of these debates, especially those on multiculturalism (discussed at greater length in chapter 3), were re-ignited following the attacks on the World Trade Center in New York and the Pentagon in Washington, D.C., on September 11, 2001. Chester E. Finn Jr. accused proponents of multiculturalism of shortchanging patriotism (Hartocollis, 2001a: A32). Lynne Cheney, wife of Vice President Richard Cheney and chairman of the National Endowment for the Humanities from 1986 to 1993, denounced educators who wanted U.S. schools to expand efforts to teach habits of tolerance, knowledge, and awareness of other cultures (Hartocollis, 2001b: 9). Diane Ravitch, a former official in the federal Department of Education, charged that "multiculturalism, as it is taught in the United States, . . . teaches cultural relativism because it implies that 'no group may make a judgment on any other.' "

Even when politicians keep their distance from the schools, social studies teachers by themselves are a contentious lot. I think that this is the way it should be. How can we teach students to value ideas and knowledge and to become participants in democratic decision making if we hide what we believe? Sometimes the best way to include students in discussions is for teachers to express their opinions and involve classes in examining and critiquing them.

WHY STUDY HISTORY?

When our children were younger, my wife and I sang a song with them by Robert Clairmont called "The Answers" (Engvick, 1965: 38–39). In this song, a child questions a lamb, a goat, a cow, a hog, a duck, a goose, and a hen about the origin of the world and records their responses: quack, honk, oink, and moo. The idea of copying down responses from barnyard animals seemed so ridiculous that we all used to laugh. Unfortunately, writing down meaningless answers to what are potentially such wonderful questions goes on in social studies classrooms across the United States. For far too many students, social studies means copying from the board.

As a witness during his libel suit against the *Chicago Tribune* in July 1919, Henry Ford is quoted as saying, "History is more or less bunk" (Seldes, 1966: 253). Ford's statement was probably just part of an effort to collect from the newspaper, but he possibly also understood the power of history if it got into the wrong hands: the hands of the automobile workers in his factories, ordinary citizens, or people who disagreed with his economic and political views. History gives us both the information and the means for understanding our world. History is the past, and it is the human effort to study, understand, and utilize the past to help us make choices about, and to shape, the future. History is neither bunk nor moo, despite what Henry Ford or the cow may have said.

If we are going to teach students about history and the social sciences, we have to have some idea what each discipline includes. I am referring not only to information about the past and present—that part is laid out effectively in textbooks—but also to ideas about how practitioners of these disciplines work, insights into the motivation of people and societies, opinions about the way the world operates and changes, and theories about the connections among past, present, and future.

A number of historians have shaped my thinking about the meaning of history (the past) and the use of history (the field of study). Much of the discussion in this section is based on my reflections on the work of two historians, E. H. Carr, an historian of modern Russia and the Soviet Union in the 20th century, and Stephen Jay Gould, a paleontologist who is also an historian of science. Their ideas on the meaning of history are much more developed than mine, and I strongly recommend that social studies teachers examine their work. I first read E. H. Carr's book, *What is History?* (1961), as a graduate student in the early 1970s. When I reread it while preparing this chapter, I was surprised to discover how much of an impact it had had on my thinking about history. Carr introduced me to the idea of thinking about the past and present as part of a continuum that stretches into the future. He believes that concern with the future is what really motivates the study of the past.

I enjoy reading Stephen Jay Gould's books and articles for a number of reasons. Gould asks interesting historical and scientific questions, has the ability to

connect what appear to be narrow issues with sweeping global concerns, and uses philosophical and literary metaphors to create mental images that illustrate complex ideas. In his writing, especially *Wonderful Life* (1989), he demonstrates how a point of view directs our questions and allows us to see things that we might otherwise miss.

Wonderful Life is the story of 525-million-year-old fossils discovered at a rock quarry in the Rocky Mountains near the British Columbia–Alberta border. Known as the *Burgess Shale*, they are possibly the oldest soft body animal fossils in existence. When they were first collected in the early part of the 20th century, evolution was considered a gradual, incremental process, so scientists assumed

Author at the Burgess Shale Quarry

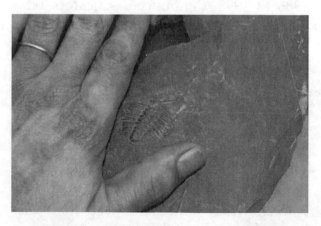

Close up of a 500-million-year-old trilobite.

they were similar to animal families (phyla) that survive today. Since that time, scientists have become aware of numerous catastrophic extinctions in the distant past and have developed a new understanding of the evolution of life. This theory, called *punctuated equilibrium*, posits long periods of stability followed by relatively rapid change. When the Burgess Shale were reexamined from this new perspective in the 1970s, scientists realized that these were entirely different life forms with no contemporary descendants. I was actually inspired by the book and the theory of punctuated equilibrium to make the trek to the fossil site, a trip that included a 10-hour guided mountain hike through Yoho National Park.

A good example of Gould's approach to historical study is his effort to explain William Jennings Bryan's apparent shift from progressive to conservative during the course of his career (1991: 416–31). Bryan was a Midwestern Populist who ran unsuccessfully for U.S. President as a Democrat in 1896, 1900, and 1908. He also served as Secretary of State under Woodrow Wilson. In the 1920s, Bryan was a leader in the campaign to prevent the teaching of evolutionary biology in the schools, and he served as the prosecuting attorney in the 1925 *Tennessee v. Scopes* ("Monkey") trial.

In the *Age of Reform and Anti-Intellectualism in American Life*, Richard Hofstadter (1955) used Bryan's opposition to evolution to support his position that U.S. agrarian populism was an anti-intellectual revolt against modernity and a reason to reject radical reform movements in general. Gould reexamined Bryan's ideas and developed a different explanation for his political positions. According to Gould, Bryan, along with many of his contemporaries, incorrectly identified Darwinian evolution with the biological determinism and racism of 19th- and 20th-century Social Darwinism. Bryan campaigned against the teaching of evolution because, as a progressive, he considered it a dangerous ideology that undermined democracy and justified imperialism, war, and the exploitation of farmers and workers.

Teaching Activity: What Does It Mean to Be a Historian?

Historians are faced with an infinite number of potential facts and have to decide which ones are historically significant. Examine the following headlines from *The New York Times* and notes based on the articles. You need to decide whether these are important historical facts and whether there are historical explanations that connect any of the articles.

Headline: "Where Arab Militants Train and Wait" (August 11, 1993)

According to Hamid Gul, a retired Pakistani general who was responsible for providing $3 billion in U.S. money and weapons to Afghan anticommunist guerrillas, the guerrilla army included large numbers of Islamic militants from other parts of the Arab world. According to Western intelligence officials, among the militants trained and armed in Pakistani refugee camps were a number of the radicals later convicted of bombing the World Trade Center in New York City and of other bomb plots in the United States.

Headline: "One Man and a Global Web of Violence" (January 14, 2001)

Nine months before the attacks on the World Trade Center in New York and the Pentagon in Washington, D.C., an article described Osama bin Laden and his goals and supporters. In the early 1980s, while Islamic groups were fighting a Soviet invasion of Afghanistan with support from the Central Intelligence Agency, bin Laden was considered a man the West could use.

However, around 1987, he began to take aim against what he considered "the corrupt secular governments of the Muslim Middle East and the Western powers." By January 2001, U.S. officials considered him responsible for masterminding the 1998 bombings of two U.S. embassies in Africa that killed more than 200 people and suspected him of involvement in the October (2000) bombing of the destroyer *Cole* in Yemen, which killed 17 sailors.

Headline: "U.S. Spied on Its World War II Allies" (August 11, 1993)

According to newly declassified documents, the United States operated an enormous and previously unknown spy network aimed at our allies during World War II. It included reports on General Charles DeGaulle, leader of the free French forces, Belgium, Greece, Mexico, China, and Switzerland, as well as information from Germany and Japan. Documents from the Soviet Union were not made public; however, information on our Soviet allies is contained in some of the other reports. Communications with Latin American governments show that, toward the end of the war, the United States was working to develop a united front to oppose the Soviet Union in the postwar world. The files also contain a memorandum from a German diplomat indicating that leaders of the Japanese army were willing to surrender more than three months before the United States dropped nuclear bombs on Hiroshima and Nagasaki, even if the terms were hard.

Headline: "Arthur Randolph, 89, Developer of Rocket in First Apollo Flight" (January 3, 1996)

An obituary for Arthur Randolph appeared in *The New York Times* in 1996. When he died, Randolph was living in Hamburg, Germany. He had left the United States and returned to Germany in 1984 after the U.S. Justice Department accused him of working thousands of slave laborers to death while he was the director of a German factory that produced V rockets during World War II.

Randolph, who was the project manager for the Saturn rocket system used on Apollo flights, was 1 of 118 German rocket scientists who were secretly brought to the United States after the war. At the time he entered the United States, Randolph was considered an ardent Nazi by the U.S. military and a war criminal by both West German and U.S. officials.

Try it yourself:

1. In your opinion, what motivated U.S. actions in each case?
2. Develop an historical explanation that connects the information from the articles. Explain your hypothesis.

Think it over:

1. Do you consider the information contained in these headlines and summaries important historical facts? Why?
2. In your opinion, can historians make sense of historical facts without also developing theories of historical explanation? Explain your views.

It's your classroom:

1. Would you use these articles in a middle school or high school class? Why? How?
2. Would you express your views during the course of discussion? Why?

Teaching Activity: Defining History

- Lord Acton (Sir J.E.E. Dalberg), 1896: "It [*The Cambridge Modern History*] is a unique opportunity of recording . . . the fullness of the knowledge which the nineteenth century is about to bequeath. . . . Ultimate history we cannot have in this generation; but . . . all information is within reach, and every problem has become capable of solution" (Carr, 1961: 3).
- Sir George Clark, 1957 (Introduction to *The New Cambridge Modern History*): "Historians . . . expect their work to be superseded again and again. They consider that knowledge of the past has come down through one or more human minds, has been processed by them. . . . The exploration seems to be endless, and some impatient scholars take refuge in skepticism,

or at least in the doctrine that, since all historical judgments involve persons and points of view, one is as good as another and there is no objective historical truth" (Carr, 1961: 4).

- E. H. Carr (1961: 111): "Scientists, social scientists, and historians are all engaged in different branches of the same study: the study of man [*sic*] and his environment, of the effects of man on his environment and of his environment on man. The object of the study is the same: to increase man's understanding of, and mastery over, his environment."
- Lawrence "Yogi" Berra, Hall of Fame catcher and former manager of the New York Yankees and Mets, during the 1973 National League pennant race (1989: 6–7) "It ain't over til it's over".

Add your voice to the discussion:
Which of these four quotes (or other statements of your choice) comes closest to your view of history? Explain your answer.

WHAT IS HISTORY?

Frequently it is confusing when a term is used in more than one way, especially when it is used to describe related concepts. In essays discussing political battles over the teaching of evolution and creationism in public schools, Stephen Jay Gould (1983: 253–62) explains that scientists since Charles Darwin have used the word *evolution* to mean both the fact that life on earth changes over time as new species develop and to describe theories such as natural selection that explain how and why these changes take place. Gould believes that the dual meaning of evolution as both fact and theory has either been misunderstood or misused by advocates of creationism, who dismiss the fact of evolution as just one among a number of possible theories.

The definition of *history* is even more complicated because it refers to a number of different but related concepts. If we accept E. H. Carr's view that historians, along with scientists and social scientists, are engaged in an active process of asking questions, seeking out information, and forming explanations that enable society to understand and master our environment, what we commonly refer to as *history* actually includes a series of distinct but related ideas: (1) events from the past—"facts,"

(2) the process of gathering and organizing information from the past—historical research, (3) explanations about the relationships between specific historical events, and (4) broader explanations or "theories" about how and why change takes place. History is the past, the study of the past, and explanations about the past.

Other factors adding to the complexity of studying history are the differing experiences and ideas of historians from different societies and the fact that historians are trying to understand an incomplete process that continues to take place around them. In 1896, living in a world where European—especially British—cultural, economic, and political dominance in world affairs seemed unshakable, Lord Acton argued that ultimate history, the ability to know and explain everything of importance, was within our grasp. Two horrific world wars and numerous revolutions that shook the confidence of European society, changed the situation, however. While Acton and his colleagues possessed certainty, Sir George Clark, a successor of Acton as an editor of *The Cambridge Modern History*, was overwhelmed by the difficulty of establishing an objective account of history and accepted that historians would continually reinterpret the past. Clark recognized that every generation and community answers certain questions (What happened in the past? How does it shape the present and future?) based on new research and experiences and different ideological explanations about human actions and social change.

Yogi Berra is a former baseball player, not a historian, who is well known for apparent malapropisms (misstatements) that manage to capture meaning in imaginative ways. Berra is supposed to have made the statement, "It ain't over til it's over," when besieged by sports writers who wanted him to explain the failure of the New York Mets to capture a pennant before the season was over or the race was even decided. Berra could not explain the team's defeat because he still was not convinced that they were going to lose.

Historians have a similar problem. Identifying history as the past arbitrarily breaks up an ongoing process that includes the present and extends into the future a process that is incomplete and difficult to evaluate.

During the last two centuries, numerous theories about the importance of history and numerous explanations of historical change have been stated. I think social studies teachers and students need to think about and discuss these theories and this question: What is history? Andrea Libresco, a former high school teacher, argues that one of our major goals as social studies teachers should be to undermine students' certainty about past events and to help them understand that, if anything, history is messy.

Learning Activity: Reading History and the Social Sciences

Over the years, I have tried to read at least one "serious" book during the winter breaks and another each summer. Usually they are works of fact, either a monograph directed at experts in a field, a book written for a popular audience, essays, and collections of lectures; sometimes they are historical fiction.

Eric Hobsbawn is probably my favorite historian. *The Age of Extremes: A History of the World, 1914–1991* (1994) is a comprehensive survey of the twentieth century in which Hobsbawn attempts to explain the development of the modern world. I also recommend *On the Edge of the New Century* (with Antonio Polito, 2000) and *On History* (1997), collections of essays that examine historical interpretation and controversial issues.

Eric Foner has written numerous books on U.S. history. In *The Story of American Freedom* (1998), Foner offers a thematic overview of the history of the United States as he discusses the evolution of the meaning of freedom.

Dava Sobel writes about the history of science for a popular audience. In *Galileo's Daughter* (1999), she uses letters written to Galileo by his daughter as the basis for understanding his ideas and accomplishments, conditions in 17th century Italy, and the role of the Roman Catholic Church in that era. In *Longitude* (1993), her focus is on efforts to develop a reliable method for determining a ship's location while at sea. Sobel uses these efforts as a lens to examine the impact of technological change, naval history, British imperial policy, and the broader relationship between science and society.

In the social sciences, Jared Diamond's *Guns, Germs, and Steel: The Fates of Human Societies* (1997) won a Pulitzer Prize and is eminently readable. He makes a powerful case for the role of geography in shaping history and provides plenty of material that is easily translatable into classroom activities. Amartya Sen is a Nobel Prize–winning economist concerned with social justice. His book, *Development as Freedom* (1999), argues that advancing private profit should not be the primary engine of an economic system in a democratic society. Cornell West has written widely on race in the contemporary United States. Many of his best essays are collected in *Race Matters* (1993).

In recent years I have been especially moved by the historical fiction of Denise Giardina. *Storming Heaven* (1987) and *The Unquiet Earth* (1992) explore the struggle of Appalachian coal miners to survive under difficult conditions, organize unions, and establish their humanity. Her novel *Saints and Villains* (1998) is the story of Dietrich Bonhoeffer, an anti-Nazi Lutheran theologian who was executed because of participation in a plot to assassinate Adolph Hitler.

Add your voice to the discussion:

1. List three books from history and/or the social sciences that influence the way you think about the world and social studies.
2. Why did you choose these books?
3. How do they influence your thinking?

WHAT ARE HISTORICAL FACTS?

Many social studies teachers, feeling pressure to prepare students for standardized exams, present their classes with long lists of key facts to memorize. I call this the "Dragnet School of Social Studies Education." Dragnet was a 1950s television series in which police inspector Joe Friday would greet a prospective witness with the request, "Just the facts." The idea that the goal of history is the collection of an enormous volume of information can probably be traced back to Aristotle in ancient Greece and certainly was behind the encyclopedia movement of the 18th century French Enlightenment. In recent years, E. D. Hirsch, Chester Finn, Diane Ravitch, and Allan Bloom have championed this approach to social studies.

One problem with this view of history is that not everyone agrees on which facts are important to include when analyzing the past. While researching U.S. history, I become engrossed in the sports pages of old newspapers. During the summer preceding the New Orleans General Strike of 1892, Dan Brouthers of Brooklyn and Clarence Childs of Cleveland battled for the National League batting title, but it was Boston, the first team to win more than 100 games in a season, that won the pennant. Babe Ruth hit 60 home runs the same summer that worldwide protests

were being held against the scheduled execution of Sacco and Vanzetti. These are interesting facts, but do they have historical significance? Are they historical facts? If we dismiss the Bambino as historically insignificant, what about barely remembered U.S. presidents such as William Henry Harrison, James Garfield, Chester Arthur, or Warren G. Harding? It is certainly possible that future generations will be uninterested in the administrations of Gerald Ford, Jimmy Carter, Ronald Reagan, George H. Bush, Bill Clinton, and George W. Bush. What establishes them as historically important? What about events or individuals who fail to make the newspapers or textbooks? Does that automatically mean they were unimportant in their time and for all time?

The Parthenon on the Acropolis in Athens. Should it be viewed as a crowning achievement of a society experimenting with democracy or as a symbol of imperialist ventures and slave labor? How did the people who did the labor view its creation?

I do not believe there are any independent objective criteria for establishing a particular event or person as historically important. The status of a fact rests on its importance in explaining the causes of events that interest historians and societies. The Italian historian Benedetto Croce (Carr, 1961: 23) argued that essentially all history is contemporary history because people read the past and decide on what is important in the light of current problems and issues. The attitude of U.S. historians toward the 19th-century presidency of Andrew Jackson is an example of this at work. During the New Deal, Jackson's presidency was cited as an historical precedent for democratic participation and a reformist spirit. However, since the Civil Rights movement of the 1960s, Jackson's ownership of enslaved Africans and attacks on the rights of native peoples have led to a reevaluation of his role in U.S. history.

Weighing the historical importance of facts is also a problem because they are continually screened through the decades and centuries. Historians are forced to draw major conclusions based on limited information that was preselected by contemporaries, considered important by earlier generations of historians, or survived because of fortuitous accident. For example, our picture of life in ancient Greece and the belief that it was the inspiration for modern democracy is unduly influenced by what we know about a very small group of free male citizens living in the city-state of Athens.

Recognizing that facts take on meaning within the context of explanations, and that the historical record is, at best, incomplete, does not mean that all facts carry the same weight and that all interpretations are equally valid. Within the historical craft, accuracy is an obligation, interpretations must be supported by evidence, and evidence is subject to review. U.S. historian Carl Becker argued that the facts of history do not exist for any historian till he [sic] creates them (Carr, 1961: 23). If we want our students to become historians, we need to involve them in deciding which facts are important for understanding history and what criteria to use when making decisions, instead of focusing our efforts on providing them with lists of someone else's important facts.

Classroom Activity: A Worker Reads History by Bertolt Brecht*

Who built the seven towers of Thebes?
The books are filled with names of kings.
Was it kings who hauled the craggy blocks of stone?
And Babylon, so many times destroyed,
Who built the city up each time?
In which of Lima's houses,
That city glimmering with gold, lived those who built it?
In the evening when the Chinese wall was finished
Where did the masons go? Imperial Rome
Is full of arcs of triumph. Who reared them up? Over whom
Did the Caesars triumph? Byzantium lives in song,
Were all her dwellings palaces?
And even in Atlantis of the legend
The night the sea rushed in,
The drowning men still bellowed for their slaves.
Young Alexander plundered India.
He alone?
Caesar beat the Gauls.

Was there not even a cook in his army?
Philip of Spain wept as his fleet
Was sunk and destroyed. Were there no other tears?
Frederick the Great triumphed in the Seven Years War. Who
Triumphed with him?
Each page a victory,
At whose expense the victory ball?
Every ten years a great man,
Who paid the piper?
So many particulars.
So many questions.

Think it over:

What point is Brecht making in this poem? Do you agree or disagree with him? Why?

It's your classroom:

How could this poem be used to promote a discussion of the nature of history?

* Bertolt Brecht and H. R. Hays (1947). *Selected Poems*. New York: Harcourt, Brace, Jovanovich, p. 108. Reprinted with the permission of the Brecht Estate and the publisher, Routledge, New York.

HOW DOES A HISTORIAN STUDY HISTORY?

The role of theory or point of view in the study of history is sharply debated, yet crucial for understanding how historians know what they claim to know. Most social studies teachers would argue that students should get their facts straight before they worry about interpretation. I am not sure most practicing historians agree.

According to E. H. Carr (1961), a frequent assumption is that a "historian divides his (*sic*) work into two sharply distinguishable phases or periods. First, he spends a long preliminary period reading his sources and filling his notebooks with facts: then, when this is over, he puts away his sources, takes out his notebooks, and writes his book from beginning to end" (32–33). The idea that research should be completed before analysis begins is rooted in the dominant empiricist ideas of late 19th-century Europe. I think these ideas are epitomized in the research methods of Sherlock Holmes, Sir Arthur Conan Doyle's fictional Victorian-age detective.

Doyle explains Holmes' approach to problem-solving in the story "A Study in Scarlet" (1890). According to Sherlock Holmes, the only way to remove bias from research is to make scientific deductions based on accurate observations. Holmes advises his friend Dr. James Watson that, "It is a capital mistake to theorize before one has data. Insensibly, one begins to twist facts to suit theories, instead of theories to suit facts" (Hardwick, 1986: 32).

I love to read the Holmes adventures, but I challenge anyone to employ this method to understand the world, solve mysteries, or study the past. Despite the assertion that his conclusions are induced from empirical evidence untainted by point of view, Holmes simply does not recognize his own assumptions. When Watson is struck by his ignorance of literature, philosophy, astronomy, and politics, Holmes defends himself by arguing that the human brain is an attic with limited space, and he does not want to crowd it with information that "would not make a pennyworth of difference to me or to my work" (Hardwick, 1986: 24–25). To discard information as irrelevant, Holmes must have a point of view about causality that lets him know which facts to ignore and what needs to be stored for later reference. In "Silver Blaze" (1892), Inspector Gregory asks Holmes, "Is there any point to which you would wish to draw my attention?" When Holmes answers, "To the curious incident of the dog in the night-time," a puzzled Gregory says, "The dog did nothing in the night-time." Holmes replies, "That was the curious incident" (Hardwick, 1986: 79). Without assumptions (theories) about the behavior of dogs, Holmes would have missed this "curious incident" altogether.

Nowhere are Holmes assumptions more apparent than in his views about women. In "A Scandal in Bohemia" (1891), Holmes claims to have discovered a series of truths about women. They "are naturally secretive, and they like to do their own secreting." During emergencies, a woman's instinct is "to rush to the thing which she values most. It is a perfectly overpowering impulse." A "married woman grabs at her baby" while "an unmarried one reaches for her jewel-box" (Hardwick, 1986: 54). Poor Sherlock is so committed to the idea of objectivity that he cannot even see his own biases.

When E. H. Carr describes his own research, he explains that data gathering and analysis "go on simultaneously. The writing is added to, subtracted from, reshaped, canceled as I go on reading. The reading is guided and directed and made more fruitful by the writing: the more I write, the more I know what I am looking for, the better I understand the significance and relevance of what I find. . . . I am convinced that . . . the two processes . . . are, in practice, parts of a single process." Historians are engaged in a "continuous process of molding facts to interpretation and of interpretation to the facts. . . . The historian without facts is rootless and futile; the facts without their historian are dead and meaningless" (Carr, 1961: 32–35).

Teaching Activity: Sherlock Holmes

Add your voice to the discussion:
1. How do you evaluate Sherlock Holmes' approach to understanding our world?
2. Do you agree or disagree with E. H. Carr's concept of writing history? Why?

Think it over:
Was the job of the historian presented to you in high school or college? How was it explained?

It's your classroom:
1. How can Carr's view be used to shape a social studies curriculum?
2. Is it possible to present Carr's view of history to secondary school students in a useful way? Explain how you would do it.

IS THE STUDY OF HISTORY SCIENTIFIC?

Early in his career as a philosopher and mathematician, Bertrand Russell hoped for the development of a mathematics of human behavior as precise as the mathematics of machines (Carr, 1961: 71). However, the prevalence of contingent factors (accidents and uncontrolled or unanticipated incidents) and the recognition that individual points of view and cultural assumptions strongly influence what historians see have made Russell's dream highly unlikely. Meanwhile, the possibility of objective and predictive history has been popularized by science fiction writers. In high school, I devoured the Foundation series, where Isaac Asimov developed the science of psychohistory. However, even Asimov's psychohistorians had to contend with "The Mule," an unexpected mutant who threw off all of their calculations.

When most of us think of real science, we think of people in white coats, usually men, operating sophisticated machinery and running carefully controlled experiments in sterile laboratories (e.g., images from Michael Crichton's *The Andromeda Strain*, 1969, and *Jurassic Park*, 1990). According to the scientific method taught in high school, scientific experiments require a formal hypothesis to be tested, a predicted and quantifiable outcome, control over the immediate environment, the ability to regulate variables, and assurance that the same result will be obtained each time the experiment is replicated. Historians can never conduct this kind of experiment. They do not control events which happened in the past, are known incompletely, are much too complex, and are never repeated in exactly the same way, or people. They cannot remove a Lenin or Hitler from the historical equation and play back the 20th century, and they are not very successful at predicting specific historical events (the collapse of the Soviet Union or the election of particular candidates).

Significantly, many sciences do not have this kind of control either. Evolutionary biology, geology, and astronomy all have a historical dimension and a breadth of field that cannot be contained within a laboratory. Extinct species cannot be resurrected to see if they would survive under different circumstances (despite the premise of Crichton's novel), earthquakes cannot be replayed for closer observation, the big bang will not be repeated, at least not for many billions of years, and no one seems very good at predicting the weather.

The level of control and precision in the "laboratory sciences" is also exaggerated.

You might remember that in high school chemistry, certain processes occurred only when an experiment took place at standard temperature and pressure (STP). Although the notion that a particular range of temperature (between the freezing and boiling points of water) and a specific pressure (sea level on Earth) defines what is normal may be useful, it is also arbitrary. High-altitude cooking in Denver, Colorado, differs from sea-level cooking in New York City because the boiling point of water is lower; as a result, recipes have to be changed. In fact, it is only in a limited number of locations that water even occurs in its liquid form. What we see as the standard on Earth is not standard for the rest of the universe.

In addition, as scientists work with increasingly smaller and faster subatomic particles and charges, the certainty of Newtonian laws has been replaced by the uncertainties of quantum mechanics, relativity, and chaos theory. According to Werner Heisenberg, a German scientist writing in the 1920s, when scientists examine a physical or chemical process, their observations and measurements interfere with and change what is taking place; they can never know exactly what was happening before they intervened. The classical scientific method still has value, but we need to remember that it can only be applied in its traditional rigor under special and limited circumstances (Hawking, 1988: 53–61).

The question for us is, how can any historical science where contingency is always a factor, including human history, be scientific?

Stephen Jay Gould (1989: 277–91; 1991: 385–401) argues that the historical sciences have their own appropriate scientific methods based on constructing narratives of events that allow us to locate patterns, identify probable causes, and create broader explanations and encompassing theories. Historical explanation uses specific events to describe general categories and general categories to explain specific events. For example, labeling a group of events as social revolutions means they have similar qualities that historians and social scientists can identify in other locales and eras, and that these qualities explain human actions and point to new, potentially revolutionary situations.

However, if the label proves to be too inclusive or of little use in predicting revolutionary situations, new general categories and explanations must be sought. Historians and other historical scientists also search for evidence that defies our explanations and forces us to redefine them.

Gabriel Kolko's *The Triumph of Conservatism* (1963), uncovered significant corporate support for federal regulation of business and stimulated a reconceptualization of the Progressive Era in U.S. history. Because history and the historical sciences do not rely on experiments that can be replicated in other laboratories, they also require a different form of verification. The ultimate check on the historian is the marketplace of ideas where explanations are debated and analyzed, and colleagues are convinced that interpretations explain the data, are logical, are consistent with other things that we know, and provide possibilities for new explanations and further research.

Classroom Activity: Steps to Revolution

FIG. 1.1   Used with permission of Pamela Booth.

Try it yourself:

1. Which step was most important in causing the American revolution? Why?
2. When was a backward step no longer possible? Why?

ARE THERE LAWS IN HISTORY?

Historians, historical scientists, philosophers, politicians, and theologians look for causes, patterns, and laws in nature and history. However, that may be where their agreement stops.

In the 16th century, Protestant theologian John Calvin presented the doctrine of predestination. Calvin argued that the fate of every individual human being, born and yet to be born, was predetermined by God at creation. All events past, present, and future were already fixed. Current Christian millennialists continue to embrace these beliefs as they prepare for Armageddon, a battle between the forces of good and evil, final divine victory, judgment day, and ultimate rapture. To some extent, a notion of predestination, although not as dramatic and couched in scientific terminology, is also implied in the ideas of contemporary genetic determinists and sociobiologists.

In the 18th century, philosophers and scientists increasingly viewed the universe, the natural world, and the social world as Newtonian machines operating according to scientific laws. The astronomer Pierre-Simon La Place, who coined the term *celestial mechanics*, claimed that if anyone could identify the position and motion of every particle of matter in the universe, knowledge of natural law would permit that person to predict all future history (Gould, 1995: 26). Montesquieu argued that "there are general causes, moral or physical, which operate in every monarchy, raise it, maintain it, or overthrow it, and that all that occurs is subject to these causes" (Carr, 1961: 114).

Predetermination or determinism entered the 19th century in the philosophy of Georg W. F. Hegel, who viewed humans as actors in events they did not understand or control in a world moving forward under its own spiritual dynamic toward the achievement of a "Universal History." Hegel discounted human free will and argued, "The great man of the age is the one who can put into words the will of his age, tell his age what its will is, and accomplish it" (Carr, 1961: 68). In recent years, Francis Fukuyama (1992: 59–69) has championed Hegelian philosophy. He argues that, with the collapse of the Soviet Union and the triumph of the West, humanity has achieved "the end of history," and human beings are now freed from the forces that had propelled development in the past.

In my opinion, the dominant intellectual forces of the 19th and early 20th centuries were Karl Marx, Charles Darwin, and Sigmund Freud. Each of these thinkers presented a different image of history and historical change. Marx claimed to stand Hegel on his head, locating the dynamic element of historical change in the economic law of motion of modern society. In Marx's view, new social systems emerged as the result of inherent economic, social, and political conflicts among social classes existing in earlier societies. As a result of Darwin's work explaining the evolution of life on earth, his name became associated with the ideas of history as continuous, gradual, and progressive change in society. Both Marxist and Darwinian progressive ideas have been associated with a sense of historical inevitability. In contrast, Freudian psychology added an element of the irrational to history, which won adherents, especially after European and U.S. experiences during the two world wars of the 20th century.

Social studies teachers have many questions to think about as we involve our students in the study of history:

1. Do individual events have identifiable and understandable causes?
2. Are these causes single or multiple? If there are multiple, are some causes more significant than others?
3. Are there patterns in history? If so, what are they? What causes them?
4. Do natural laws determine what happens in history? If so, what are they? What are their origins?
5. Are individuals and groups able to make choices based on free will, or are they subject to historical and social forces beyond their control?
6. Is the future predetermined, or is it contingent on accident and unpredictable incident? Can individual or group action influence the course of the future? Would the world be different if Hitler had died at childbirth?
7. With sufficient information about the past and present, will historians be able to predict the future?
8. Is there a goal or purpose to history?

Learning Activity: The Nature of History

For the want of a nail the shoe was lost. For want of a shoe the horse was lost. For the want of a horse the rider was lost. For the want of a rider the battle was lost. For the want of a battle the kingdom was lost—And all for want of a horseshoe-nail.
—Benjamin Franklin, Maxims . . . Prefixed to Poor Richard's Almanac (1758) in Burton Stevenson (1952: 2041).

Try it yourself:
1. In your opinion, what lesson does this proverb express? In your opinion, what does the author believe about the nature of history?
2. Draw a picture illustrating your view of the nature of history.

WHAT ARE THE GOALS OF HISTORIANS?

All historians try to make sense out of the past, but many also have other goals. The issue here is whether these other goals are valid. For example, must historians remain impartial, objective, and apolitical, or can history legitimately be used to achieve political or social goals and support moral judgments? In *The Education of Henry Adams*, 19th century U.S. historian Henry Brooks Adams (Seldes, 1966: 40) argued, "No honest historian can take part with—or against—the forces he has to study. To him even the extinction of the human race should be merely a fact to be grouped with other vital statistics." However, during the American Civil War, the same historian dismissed the idea of impartiality and wrote, "The devil is strong in me. . . . Rebellion is in the blood, somehow or other. I can't gone on with out a fight" (41).

Point of View

In *The Disuniting of America: Reflections on a Multicultural Society*, Arthur Schlesinger Jr. (1992) decried the political uses and distortions of history in authoritarian countries and by people in the United States he described as *ethnic chauvinists*. Schlesinger was particularly concerned with what he described as efforts to define "the purpose of history in the schools" as "therapeutic" (80). However, in the same book, Schlesinger supported the use of history to promote patriotism. He argued that "a nation denied a conception of its past will be disabled in dealing with its present and future. As a means of defining national identity, history becomes a means of shaping history" (45–46). Why is it wrong to use history to develop a sense of self-worth among African American children but right to use it to build national unity? Schlesinger denounced his opponents in the name of objective and impartial history while ignoring the possibility that he also had biases and a political agenda.

Is it unacceptable for historians to try to establish the legitimacy of their points of view? Or is it a more serious problem when historians deny that their conclusions are influenced by their ideologies and, as a result, the conclusions go unexamined?

During the Enlightenment, Denis Diderot praised Voltaire, writing that "other historians relate facts to inform us of facts. You relate them to excite in our hearts an intense hatred of lying, ignorance, hypocrisy, superstition, tyranny; and the anger remains even after the memory of the facts has disappeared" (Zinn, 1970: ix). During the 19th century, Karl Marx argued that, although "philosophers have . . . interpreted the world differently . . . the point is to change it" (Carr, 1961: 182–83). Even Schlesinger (1992) believes that "honest history is the weapon of freedom" (52).

All of these statements seem consistent with the social studies goals of promoting critical thinking and active citizenship. Perhaps a political agenda is a virtue for an historian, a social studies teacher, and students in a social studies class.

NEW TEACHER'S DEBATE "POINT OF VIEW"

Two new social studies teachers, Richard Stern and Bill Van Nostrand, edited this section of the book for its second edition. One day in class they started to argue about whether a teacher should express her or his point of view in class. Bill stated that "as a ninth grade global history teacher, I discovered that students will sometimes agree with whatever I say, just because I said it. That is why I try not to express my opinions in class. It automatically gives students a one-sided view of the past and prevents them from drawing their own conclusions. When I withhold my opinion, they are more likely to think critically." Richard responded: "Our lessons are always shaped by our opinions whether we, or our students, are conscious of it or not. Any teachers who claim they are keeping their opinions out of their lessons are just not telling the truth. I think it is more honest to state your opinions openly. It opens up a teacher's views for critical examination by a class and helps students understand how an informed opinion must be supported by evidence."

Add Your Voice to the Discussion:

Who do you agree with, Bill or Richard? Why?

Moral and Political Judgments

Does the study of history provide information and explanations that can be used to make moral and political judgments about the past and present and hopes for the future? Of course. I think that is one of the main reasons that people are interested in history. Does that give historians special authority to make moral and political judgments? In this case, not only do I think the answer is no, but also I think historians have an obligation to slow the rush to judgment. First, because historians are accustomed to studying societies within specific social and chronological contexts, they tend to reject applying absolute universal moral standards of right and wrong. Second, because they are aware that "it ain't over til it's over," historians are sensitive to the need to reevaluate the past based on new findings, ideas, and historical developments.

Innumerable efforts have been made to define moral standards throughout human history. I suspect that every country that ever went to war considered itself the aggrieved party and argued that right was on its side. The U.S. expansion into the Great Plains and to the west coast of North America was considered "manifest destiny," or God's will. However, its growth was achieved at the expense of numerous small Native American nations that were nearly exterminated.

Some 18th- and 19th-century British philosophers, in an effort to counter the arbitrary nature of many political and economic judgments, argued that decisions should be evaluated based on whether they provided the greatest good for the greatest number (Mill, 1963). At first glance, this seems like a reasonable equation, but it is difficult to apply. The enslavement of millions of Africans made possible the development of North America and financed the European commercial and industrial revolutions. Was it justified? Frederick Engels called history "the most cruel of all goddesses" because those called on to pay the price of progress are rarely the people who receive its benefits (Seldes, 1966: 240).

Furthermore, judgments change as events unfold. In 1910, an historian studying the impact of Bismarck on Germany and Europe might have praised the Iron Chancellor's political agenda and organizational skill. The same historian, reevaluating events after 1945, however, would be inclined to notice destructive tendencies that had been missed in the earlier study. Future developments in China and Eastern Europe, economic depression in Western economies, or communist success in other parts of the world may lead to a reevaluation of a system that was largely discredited with the collapse of the Soviet Union. Historians have the same right as anyone else to make judgments, but they also have a professional responsibility to question them. Eric Hobsbawn, author of *The Age of Extremes* (1994), is an excellent example of a contemporary historian who consciously applies a point of view to understand the past and who uses understandings about the past to draw tentative conclusions about the present and to raise questions about the future. If Yogi Berra is right, maybe only the future holds the key to understanding the past.

Teaching Activity: Goals of Historians

Combatants in war often claim that God is on their side. Following the attacks on the World Trade Center and the Pentagon, President George W. Bush concluded a public statement explaining air strikes against targets in Afghanistan by saying, "We will not waver, we will not tire, we will not falter and we will not fail. Peace and freedom will prevail. Thank you. May God continue to bless America." (*The New York Times*, October 7, 2001, B6)

Osama bin Laden, a Saudi-born dissident accused of masterminding the attacks, responded, "I swear to God that America will not live in peace before peace reigns in Palestine, and before all the army of infidels depart the land of Mohammed, peace be upon him. God is the Greatest and glory be to Islam." (*The New York Times*, October 7, 2001, B7)

Try it yourself:
In their statements, both George W. Bush and Osama bin Laden called on God for strength and support. How do you respond to their invocation of God for their causes? Explain.

It's your classroom:
How would you respond to a student who claims that "God is on the side of the United States"?

Add your voice to the discussion:
1. In your opinion, should historians strive for impartiality or seek to establish particular theories or points of view? Why?
2. In your opinion, should historians be involved in making moral and political judgments about the past and about contemporary societies? Why?

WHAT IS THE RELATIONSHIP BETWEEN HISTORY AND THE SOCIAL SCIENCES?

The social sciences started to develop as areas of study during the European Enlightenment of the 17th and 18th centuries when new scientific approaches were applied to understanding the ways that societies were organized and people made decisions. For an essay in an undergraduate European intellectual history class at City College in the 1960s, my instructor asked us to discuss this topic: "To what extent were later Enlightenment thinkers Newtonian?" Sir Isaac Newton believed that the physical universe obeyed natural laws that could be described with mathematical precision. The teacher wanted us to examine efforts by thinkers such as John Locke, Thomas Hobbes, and Adam Smith in Great Britain, Voltaire, Montesquieu, Diderot, and Rousseau in France, and Benjamin Franklin, Thomas Jefferson, and James Madison in the United States to adapt Newton's view of the physical world so they could develop a calculus describing the world of human interrelationships.

The social sciences—political science, sociology, economics, geography, anthropology, and psychology—emerged as individual disciplines during the 19th century, coinciding with efforts to explain mass social upheavals, the development of industrial society, and the need of growing European nation-states to gather and organize statistical information and manage complex economic, political, and social systems. During this period, social scientists formulated research questions about areas of society that had previously been ignored and developed new methodologies for study. Important theorists such as Auguste Comte, Emile Durkheim, David Ricardo, John Stuart Mill, Karl Marx, Herbert Spencer, and, later, Sigmund Freud changed the way we understand ourselves and our world. By the late 19th and early 20th centuries, the different disciplines were institutionalized in the United States and Europe with their own university departments and professional organizations. The American Historical Association (AHA) was founded in 1884, the American Political Science Association in 1903, the American Sociological Association in 1905, and the

National Council of Geography Teachers in 1914.

Twentieth-century movements for expanded government intervention in economies and regulation of society, whether called *progressivism, bureaucratization, technocracy, fascism,* or *socialism,* increased the importance of the social sciences. In the United States, the Great Depression and the New Deal—government-industry partnership during World War II—and the influence of British economist John Maynard Keynes contributed to an expanding role for the social sciences in managing the capitalist economic system and in measuring the impact of economic development and government-sponsored social programs on the general population.

Generally, the social sciences have distanced themselves from the study of history by focusing on analysis of contemporary events, rigorous application of social theory and research methods, and the "scientific objectivity" of their findings. At the dedication of a new social science research building at the University of Chicago in 1929, economist Wesley Mitchell argued that the social sciences represented the victory of the "man of facts" over the "man of hunches" (Smith, 1994). John Merriam, president of the Carnegie Foundation, believed that many of the highly contested issues of the era would "melt away" as soon as social scientists had collected sufficient data to objectively resolve social policy debates. Many economists and political scientists concentrated on designing mathematical descriptions and models of society. Some sociologists and psychologists distinguished their fields from history and philosophy by identifying them as behavioral sciences. Although boundaries remained between the disciplines, areas of study continued to overlap. In recent years, historians have increasingly incorporated the theories, methodologies, and insights of the social sciences while many social scientists have added an historical dimension to their work. In addition, there have always been social scientists such as sociologists Robert Lynd, Gunnar Myrdal, and C. Wright Mills who reject the possibility of total objectivity and believe that their research should support progressive political goals (Smith, 1994).

In the United States, the importance of history and the social sciences in education has roots in the early national period. Benjamin Rush, a physician in colonial America who represented New York at the Continental Congress and signed the Declaration of Independence, argued that education was vital to the development of citizenship. Thomas Jefferson was an early champion of including history and geography in a basic education. During the 19th century, history, geography, and civics tended to be independent subjects, with history gradually supplanting geography as the dominant influence on curriculum.

The idea of social studies as a comprehensive secondary school subject, including history and the social sciences, was a product of the move toward rationalizing and standardizing education during the Progressive era at the start of the 20th century. In 1912, the National Education Association created the Committee on the Social Studies to reorganize the secondary school curriculum. The committee, with representatives from different social science disciplines and educational constituencies, issued a report in 1916 that defined the social studies as "those whose subject matter relates directly to the organization and development of human society, and to 1 man [sic] as a member of social groups" (U.S. Bureau of Education, 1916: 9). The committee also established that the preparation of citizens was the primary goal of the social studies. In a preliminary statement, Thomas Jesse Jones, chair of the committee, claimed that "high school teachers of social studies have the best opportunity ever offered to any social group to improve the citizenship of the land" (9). The committee's focus on citizenship education is not surprising, given the Progressive era's concern with the assimilation of millions of new eastern and southern European immigrants to the United States, especially as the country prepared for possible involvement in the Great War being fought in Europe.

The National Council for the Social Studies (NCSS) was founded in 1921, with the support of the national historians' organization as a response to the NEA–sponsored report and as an effort by historians to assert the central role of their field in social studies. From 1925 to 1975, NCSS served as the NEA's department of social studies. The relationship between the AHA and the NCSS continued until 1935, when the NCSS became an advocate for a broader definition of the social studies. One of the organization's most important activities was publication of the journal *Social Education*, which expanded its influence in shaping social studies curricula (NCSS, 1995).

Although the debate over citizenship education versus discipline-based instruction and the relative importance of different subject areas continues, since the end of World War II, secondary schools have generally integrated history and the social sciences into a multiyear, history-based social studies curriculum. Although economics and political science are often assigned specific courses in the social studies sequence, geography, sociology, anthropology, psychology, and philosophy are usually taught within the confines of other subject areas or in elective courses. In the last decade, however, social science requirements for teacher certification, especially knowledge of geography, government, and economics, have been increased as part of the general push to raise educational standards.

WHAT DO WE LEARN FROM THE SOCIAL SCIENCE DISCIPLINES?

Geography

The focus of geography in secondary education is generally on the location of cities, states, countries, continents, natural resources, major land formations and bodies of water, international boundaries, and interconnecting routes. One of its more important functions in social studies curricula is academic skill development, through map reading and design, and the creation and analysis of information on charts and graphs. Geography is also used to help students develop their ability to observe, organize, and analyze information presented in pictures, slides, and videos.

As an academic discipline, the importance placed on geography in secondary education has had peaks and valleys, and it now seems to be increasing.

In the early national era, geography, not history, tended to be the main focus of what is now called the *social studies*. In a physically expanding, largely agrarian nation that also depended on international trade, a subject that focused on map skills, international and domestic trade routes, and land formations had more concrete value than stories of great deeds by heroic figures from the past. However, as the study of history became associated with explanation and nation building during the 19th and 20th centuries, geography was eclipsed. In social studies classes, geography continued to provide students with information that teachers believed they needed to memorize, but curricula were organized around history.

In recent decades, four factors have contributed to a resurgence of geography within the social studies: (1) focus on global interdependence, including increased attention to the non-Western world, its contributions to world history and culture, and its role in contemporary world affairs, (2) concern for the impact of environmental issues, such as pollution, resource depletion, and global warming, on the quality of human life, (3) the importance of understanding global demographics and population diversity, and (4) as a result of the work of Jared Diamond (mentioned earlier in the chapter), increased attention to the idea of geographical causality (e.g., accidents of geography have a major impact on cultural and historical development). Geography, although still generally taught within the context of history or current events, has become crucial for defining and comparing regions of the world; understanding the relationship between people and place; examining the migration of people, plants, and animals; explaining ways that the physical world influences human development; and exploring the ways that human development has changed the physical world.

An example of an area in which geography enriches our understanding of history is the study of the impact of the post-Colombian exchange that, among other things, brought crops including sugar cane to the Americas and potatoes to Eurasia and Africa. Results of the introduction of potatoes into Ireland included concentration on one-crop agriculture, a rapid increase in population from approximately 1.5 million people in 1760 to 9 million people in 1840, a devastating potato famine between 1845 and 1852, and the death or emigration of millions of people (Hawke and Davis, 1992).

Geography also contributes to the interdisciplinary nature of the social studies by introducing understandings drawn from the natural and physical sciences about climate, agriculture, and the use of resources such as air, water, and land. These topics are particularly important when preparing students to participate in decision making as active citizens.

Sample Geography Lesson Ideas

1. Map or Globe: Which Is More Accurate?

Compare the island of Greenland and the continent of Africa on a globe and on a standard Mercator projection map. On the map, they are roughly the same size. On the globe, Africa is considerably larger. Which is a more accurate representation of the relative sizes of Greenland and Africa? Why? If students cannot resolve the issue through discussion, try the following demonstration.

a. With a magic marker, draw a line representing the equator on a grapefruit and mark the poles.

b. Slicing through the poles with a knife, cut the grapefruit into six sections.

c. Have student volunteers eat the grapefruit and return the peel (be sure to provide napkins).

d. Flatten the peels and lay them out so the lines of the equator are touching. What happened when we tried to reproduce a three-dimensional sphere, the earth (the grapefruit), as a two-dimensional map? Why is Greenland larger on the map? Which is a more accurate representation of the Earth, the map or the globe? Why?

Adapted From Dircks, (2002).

2. Ecological Disasters: Acts of Nature or Acts of People?

The world is a changing place. The Sahara Desert is expanding into the Sahel region of Africa. Flooding threatens human life and property along the Mississippi River in the United States and the Ganges River in Bangladesh. Forests have disappeared in Northern India and Haiti. Are these changes caused by acts of nature or acts of people? The simple activity that follows illustrates the importance of preserving marsh lands to minimize the devastation caused by flooding.

a. Place a dry sponge in an open plastic container. This represents the marshlands along the banks of a river. Slowly pour in a measured amount of water. This represents spring floods caused by snow melting in the Mississippi River's watershed area. The sponge expands and absorbs the water.

b. Wring out the sponge and pour the water back into a measuring container.

c. Replace the sponge with something the same size and shape that is nonporous (e.g., a plastic container filled with sand, a block of wood sealed with paint and weighted down so it doesn't float). This represents economic development (e.g., the construction of shopping centers that pave over the marshlands).

d. Slowly pour the same measured amount of water into the plastic container. A devastating flood sweeps across the landscape.

3. Where Would You Build the City?

Draw a map showing mountains, two branches of a river meeting, a coastline, and other natural features. Have students discuss where they would build a city and why. Compare the areas they choose to areas around selected cities throughout the world.

4. How Do We Define a Region?

Many geographic subdivisions (e.g., some national boundaries, or lines of longitude and latitude) are arbitrary. Others have a historical or cultural logic that is not apparent at first glance. For example, what is the Middle East? Allow students to look at a map, and have the class brainstorm the names of countries they believe should be included in the region. List all the countries on the board. When the list is complete, examine the suggestions, discuss their similarities and differences, decide on criteria for including countries in the region, and define the Middle East.

5. How Did Agriculture Spread in the Ancient World?

Spread of Fertile Crescent Crops

Era	Location
before 7000 B.C.	Fertile Crescent
7000–6000 B.C.	Asia Minor, Egypt, Crete, Greece, Caspian Sea, Persia
6000–5000 B.C.	Central Europe, Iberian and Italian Peninsulas
5000–2500 B.C.	Northern and western Europe

Source: Adapted from Jared Diamond, (1997). *Guns, Germs, and Steel*, New York, Norton, p. 181.

a. Locate the different areas on a map.

b. How long did it take for agriculture to travel from the Fertile Crescent to northern and western Europe?

c. In your opinion, how did agriculture spread from region to region?

Teaching Activity: Geography in the Curriculum

Add your voice to the discussion:
Do you think geography should be integrated into a history-based social studies curriculum or taught as an independent subject? Why?

It's your classroom:
Would you use these geography activities as is? Would you modify them? Would you discard them? Why?

Anthropology

Franz Boas, one of the founders of modern anthropology, described it as the study of the growth and development of human cultures, human inventions, materials, spiritual and artistic creations, institutions, relationships, beliefs, values, and practices. As anthropologists delved deeply and systematically into the way of life of different peoples and compared different cultures, they contributed to ongoing debates about human nature. There are (a) anthropologists who argue that human cultures develop primarily as responses to similar basic needs and diverse environments, (b) supporters of the idea that human genetic makeup determines cultural development, and (c) researchers who stress the individual and contingent nature of societies.

Generally, anthropologists draw conclusions about the development of culture from studies of small, traditional societies where they can make in-depth observations of entire communities and account for outside influences. They also examine the artifacts, or material culture, of societies that no longer exist. In earlier decades, anthropologists looked for relatively isolated communities. However, in today's world, these communities are extremely rare. The best known anthropological study is probably Margaret Mead's (1973) work about adolescence on the Samoan Islands in the southern Pacific. Mead spent nine months living with the people of Pago Pago, and observed the experiences of adolescent girls as they prepared to enter adulthood. Her study demonstrated that the rite of passage in this society was less stressful than in western industrial societies. She concluded that the western concept of adolescence, rather than being rooted in the nature of human development, was a product of cultural experience.

In the secondary school social studies curriculum, anthropology is generally integrated into and expands the study of history.

In regional studies, anthropology helps students focus on the range of human diversity and the similarities and differences in the ways that societies around the world organize to survive and prosper. A global history class can compare naming ceremonies in European Christian societies with similar practices among the Yoruba people of West Africa, or they can examine why, in both traditional Japanese society and among the Kikiyu people of East Africa, newborn babies were not considered fully human. A United States history class can study Native American spirit masks and students can design and create masks that express their own struggles or beliefs (see chapter 8).

Anthropology draws attention to the transformation of cultural practices as people migrate and adapt to new worlds. Students can explore cultural diffusion by examining the influence of traditional West African religious beliefs, like Vodun from Benin, on the practice of Christianity in many communities in the Americas.

The analysis of artifacts extends human history further back into the past so that prehistoric societies and even the cultures of our prehuman ancestors can be examined. It makes it possible for students to examine and compare the development of different civilizations, and to explore topics like the contributions of women to husbandry, agriculture, and metallurgy, and the origins of family patterns and religious beliefs.

Anthropological approaches like the examination of material culture (artifacts) and community rituals enrich social history. Pictures of clothing can be used to illustrate social stratification in colonial America and pre-Revolutionary France. Hand tools and crafts can be used to demonstrate technological development in societies. In the book, *The Souls of Black Folk* (1961), W. E. B. DuBois examined the religious music of 19th-century southern African Americans to explore their ideas and the impact of racism on their lives. In *The Making of the English Working Class* (1963) E. P. Thompson traced the changing political consciousness of preindustrial British workers by analyzing popular and protest music.

An anthropological approach also introduces major debates into the social studies curriculum. Boaz and Mead believed that anthropologists had to get as close as possible to a society in order to understand it from the inside from the perspective of its members. However, Marvin Harris, who has written a series of books that explain anthropological puzzles such as food taboos and belief in witchcraft, argues that an anthropologist can never understand a society from within. His theory of cultural materialism ignores why people believe they are doing something. Instead, his focus is on the ways that different practices either support or interfere with the survival of a community. The idea of studying people by entering into cultures has been challenged for other reasons as well. Patrick Tierney (2001) argues that efforts to study the Yanomami people of the Venezuelan and Brazil rainforest were really a form of unwarranted interference that introduced new diseases and social turmoil into their culture and transformed the way they lived.

Another sharp debate in anthropology, which must also be addressed by multiculturalists, is over the issue of cultural relativism. For example, how should Western societies respond to cultures and religions that deny women what they consider to be basic human rights? On the other hand, do societies that reject capital punishment as a violation of human rights have the right, or even the responsibility to interfere with countries that execute people?

☺📖☺ ☎ ☹ 💻☺ ✏☺ 🔔☹

Should anthropologists go

"inside the box" in order to

understand a society?

☺📖☺ ☎ ☹ 💻☺ ✏☺ 🔔☹

Can anthropologists better ☺ ➡

understand cultures by ☹ ➡

observing them from ☺ ➡

"outside the box"? ☺ ➡

📖 v 🖥️💻☺✂✏☜◐🔳📖

📄🔢🔣☜◐♦☀⚡🎏➜✦❄✝✿☾

🌑🎴✿∏©♥Ω≠÷∅√$+%

Sample Anthropology Lesson Ideas

Participant/Observers "Inside the Box"

Andrea Libresco (NTN) has students observe the cultural practices and mores of their classmates and keep observational logs. Students can also observe family customs and rituals, and develop hypotheses that explain different practices. A possible topic is eating rituals and practices. Items that are considered good to eat, cooking practices, and even utensils vary from culture to culture and environment to environment. Through systematic observation of family members and note-taking, students can discover and record:

What we eat and what we don't eat.
How we produce (or obtain) what we eat.
How we prepare what we eat.
How we eat.
When we eat.
Who we eat it with.
What we think about what we eat.

Isomo Loruko—Yoruba Naming Ceremony

Patricia Kafi (NTN) is a native of Nigeria. According to Patricia, among the Yoruba people of Nigeria, an entire community participates in naming a new baby (Kafi, 1998). In their culture a name is not just a name. It tells the circumstances under which a child was born. There are names for just about every situation. Sometimes a new name is even created. A name can also tell group or family history. It is always selected by family elders. Yoruba people celebrate the naming ceremony when a child is seven days old.

At the traditional ceremony, people bring the child symbolic gifts like spices, sweets, and water, which represent hope for the future. The pen and a book, especially the Bible or the Koran, are fairly recent additions to the ceremony. As with many other aspects of Nigerian life, the items used as well as the ceremony itself, vary depending on the ethnic group and family preferences. The theme they share in common is that the birth of a child is a time of great joy and celebration for the entire family and community.

Isomo Loruko, the Yoruba Naming Ceremony, can be reenacted in a global history class and used to stimulate discussion comparing Yoruba culture with the traditions observed by students in the class and the importance of tradition for families and communities. Many of the ingredients used in this version of the Yoruba Naming Ceremony are difficult to find in the United States so other items can be substituted. For example, vegetable oil can be used instead of palm oil. When acting out the ceremony in a classroom, use fruit juice instead of wine.

Ingredients: Fruit juice, water, palm oil or vegetable oil, honey, bitter kola and kola nut (unsweetened baker's chocolate), whole peppercorns (or a clove of garlic), dried fish (preferably catfish), pen, book.

Participants: Elder (Agba), Mother (Iya), Father (Baba), Grandmother (Iya-iya: mother's mother), Grandfather (Baba-baba: father's father), Aunt (Aburo-iya: mother's younger sister), Uncle (Egbon-baba: father's older sibling), Honored Guests (Alejo Pataki) (5), Community members.

Elder (Agba): We are gathered here today because Fola and Ayinde have brought us a new life. We have brought certain gifts today to use in this naming ceremony, and we ask our ancestors to bless these things. We thank our ancestors for this addition to the family. We ask our ancestors to join us and bless this child. May the names given today enhance this child's life.

Community: Ase (so it shall be).

(Traditionally, each of the items used in the ceremony is rubbed on the child's lips. Today, for health reasons, the mother of the child tastes the food items instead of the infant.)

Mother (Iya): We offer wine to our ancestors as libation so that they might join us today in blessing this child.

Community: Ase (so it shall be).

Father (Baba): Water (omi) has no enemies because everything in life needs water to survive. It is everlasting. This child will never be thirsty in life and like water, no enemies will slow your growth.

Community: Ase (so it shall be).

Grandmother (Iya-iya): Palm oil (epo) is used to prevent rust, to lubricate and to massage and soothe the body. May this child have a smooth and easy life.

Community: Ase (so it shall be).

Grandfather (Baba-baba): The bitter kola (orogbo), unlike most other kolas, lasts a very long time. This child will have a very long life.

Community: Ase (so it shall be).

Aunt (Aburo-iya): Kola nut (obi) is chewed and then spit out. You will repel the evil in life.

Community: Ase (so it shall be).

Uncle (Egbon-baba): Honey (oyin) is used as a sweetener in our food. Your life will be sweet and happy.

Community: Ase (so it shall be).

Honored Guest (Alejo Pataki) 1: Peppers (ata) have many seeds within its fruit. May you have a fruitful life with lots of children.

Community: Ase (so it shall be).

Honored Guest (Alejo Pataki) 2: We use salt (iyo) to add flavor to our food. Your life will not be ordinary, but it will be filled with flavor, happiness and substance.

Community: Ase (so it shall be).

Honored Guest (Alejo Pataki) 3: The fish (eja) uses its head to find its way in water, no matter how rough the water is. You will find your way in life and never drown, even through tough times.

Community: Ase (so it shall be).

Honored Guest (Alejo Pataki) 4: The pen (biro) is very important today because it can be used for both good and evil. You will not use the pen for evil and no one will use it for evil against you.

Community: Ase (so it shall be).

Honored Guest (Alejo Pataki) 5: This book (iwe) contains the word of (God, philosophy, and science, etc.). May you be God smart and book smart. May God be with you as you follow in God's path.

(The last two items (pen and bible) are new additions to the ceremony).

Community: Ase (so it shall be).

Elder (Agba): We will now name this child together. I want you all to repeat the names after me so that this child can hear them. The names are [Abejide (male), Ifeoluwa (female)] Balogun.
(*The last name is the surname. The class should select a given name for the child.*)
Community: [Abejide (male), Ifeoluwa (female)] Balogun!
(*This is followed by prayers and celebration for the rest of the day.*)

Teaching Activity: Anthropology in the Curriculum

Add your voice to the discussion:
1. Should anthropologists enter a community and study its members even if it means potentially interfering with their way of life?
2. Should societies challenge the cultural practices and religious beliefs of other groups whom they consider in violation of basic human rights? Explain.
3. Do you think anthropology should be integrated into a history-based social studies curriculum, or taught as an independent subject? Why?

Think it over:
What customs in the United States parallel the Yoruba naming ceremony?

Try it yourself:
Study eating practices, or other rituals, in your family.

It's your classroom:
Based on your experience with the eating practices activity, how do you think it would work with middle school or high school students? Why?

Political Science

Political science examines who makes decisions in societies (power and citizenship), how they are made (government), rules and procedures for enforcing decisions (laws), and the impact of decisions on societies (justice and equity). The study of political science often includes philosophical queries, and examines the values, dilemmas, choices, and broader belief systems (ideologies) that shape political decisions. It is closely related to the social science disciplines of sociology and economics.

In secondary school social studies curriculum, separate political science courses generally focus on the principles (e.g., representative democracy), institutions (e.g., the Presidency), and processes (e.g., electoral politics) of the U.S. government and current U.S. social issues. Because a major goal is the development of the knowledge, skills, and habits of mind required for active citizenship, a recent trend has been to encourage student involvement in participatory citizenship projects like voter registration and lobbying. Many schools offer electives or include thematic social studies units on aspects of the American legal system. Political science is also integrated into the global studies curriculum, where major themes include comparing decision-making and government in contemporary societies and in different historical eras.

FIG. 1.2   Cartoon Dialogue
Used with permission of Pamela Booth.

Sample Political Science Lesson Ideas

1. Political Cartoon Dialogues

Mike Pezone provides students with political cartoons with empty dialogue boxes. Students add their own dialogue ideas, which are acted out in class. Mike uses political cartoons clipped from newspapers or from cartoon collections. Useful sources are books by Herbert L. Block (Herblock), Fred Wright, and Bill Mauldin, which include cartoons dating back to the 1940s. Many political cartoons are available at http://www.NewYorktimes.com/diversions/cartoons. The Library of Congress has a Herblock exhibit at http://www.loc.gov/loc/lcib/0010/herblock.html.

a. Complete the empty cartoon dialogue box.
b. What is a good title for your cartoon?
c. What is the main idea you want to present? Why?

2. Hidden Government

One of the topics in a government class is the hidden government (parts of the government that are not mentioned in the U.S. Constitution). This unit can include an examination of the evolution of the Cabinet, the growing responsibilities of presidential and congressional advisory committees, and the often secret role of lobbyists and political action committees. This activity involves students in using mathematical information supplied by a chart to draw social studies conclusions. It can be completed by individuals or small groups. The questions are designed to direct students to locate information, help them use the information to describe what is taking place, encourage them to draw conclusions about the impact of this information on the country, and stimulate them to form opinions that they can support with data from the chart and with other information they have learned.

Who Influences Government Decisions?

Table 1.1 shows companies with political action committees that are among the 10 largest contributors to congressional campaigns as reported to the Federal Election Commission (FEC). This information is available under the Federal Freedom of Information Act.

a. Which of the companies in Table 1.1 gave the largest percentage of its contributions to Democratic candidates in 1993–1994? What was that percentage?
b. Which of the companies in Table 1.1 gave the largest percentage of its contributions to Republican candidates in 1995? What was that percentage?
c. Which of the companies in Table 1.1 had the largest increase in contributions to the Republicans from 1993–1994 to 1995? How large was the increase?
d. Describe the trend (pattern) shown in the reports to the Federal Election Committee in 1993–1994 and 1995.
e. In your opinion, how do you explain the change reflected in these statistics?
f. Do you think this change is positive or negative? Why?

g. In your opinion, should a list of contributors and the amount they contributed be made available to the constituents of elected officials? Why?

h. In your opinion, should large corporations be allowed to give donations to political candidates? Why or why not?

TABLE 1.1
Contributions to House and Senate Candidates

Company	Years	Percent to Democrats	Percent to Republicans
United Parcel Service	1993–1994	51%	48%
	1995	31	69
AT&T	1993–1994	59	41
	1995	40	60
Northup	1993–1994	56	44
	1995	24	76
RJR Nabisco	1993–1994	47	53
	1995	21	77
Philip Morris	1993–1994	61	39
	1995	22	78
General Electric	1993–1994	60	40
	1995	28	70

3. Philosophical Issues: The Responsibility of Government and People

"When it shall be said in any country in the world, my poor are happy; neither ignorance nor distress is to be found among them; my jails are empty of prisoners, my streets of beggars; the aged are not in want, the taxes are not oppressive . . . ; when these things can be said, then may that country boast of its constitution and its government."—Thomas Paine (Foner, 1945: 446)

a. What is the main idea that Thomas Paine raises in this quote?

b. According to Paine, are the poor responsible for their own condition? Do you agree or disagree with him? Why?

c. In your opinion, do individuals who are successful in a society have an obligation to change rules that leave some people at a disadvantage? Why or why not?

d. Draw a political cartoon that presents your views on these issues.

Teaching Activity: Political Science in the Curriculum

Add your voice to the discussion:
Do you think political science should be integrated into a history-based social studies curriculum or taught as an independent subject? Why?

Try it yourself:
How would you answer the questions in these political science activities?

It's your classroom:
Would you use these political science activities as is? Would you modify them? Would you discard them? Why?

Behavioral Sciences

Sociology and psychology are often called *behavioral sciences*. Sociology examines human relationships and institutions in complex contemporary societies. Its goal is to establish theories that explain events, activities, and ideas about human interaction and group behavior. It often overlaps psychology, which examines the motivation and behavior of individuals. In secondary school social studies, insights and topics from sociology and psychology are usually included in courses that focus on government, citizenship, and current issues. They can also be incorporated into units on recent history. Some schools offer upper-level social studies electives in these fields.

Social inequality—and its impact on individuals and social groups—is an area where political science, philosophy, sociology, and psychology overlap. For a research report and in-class discussions focusing on current issues, students can examine how different social scientists view the problem of social inequality in the United States and the relationship among inequality, racism, and crime.

For example, Herbert Gans (1995) argues that poor and minority people are unfairly labeled as *dangerous* and *different*, and this allows the majority in our society to blame them for social problems that are beyond their control. As a result, programs that are supposed to assist poor people receive little public support and are frequently designed to punish them. Manning Marable (1983) believes that racism and inequality persist because they benefit segments of U.S. society. Cornel West (1993) is concerned that racism and inequality debilitate people so that it becomes difficult to rebuild communities, families, and the lives of individuals.

Sample Sociology and Psychology Lesson Ideas

1. Student Surveys

Students can conduct surveys that examine the attitudes, beliefs, and practices of other students or of community residents. Studies can focus on a specific target population, or they can compare different groups. Individuals, teams, or classes identify the goals of the study and research questions, define subject populations, construct questionnaires, interview subjects, analyze data, draw conclusions, and report findings. Topics can include the following:
"Opinions on the impact of music lyrics on the ideas and values of teenagers."
"Evaluations of community institutions (e.g., schools)."
"Ideas about community or national issues (e.g., abortion rights)."

2. Illegal Drug Use in the United States: Crime and Punishment, 1993

It is illegal to possess or sell cocaine in any form in the United States. However, the law provides different punishments, depending on whether the drug is powdered or in crystal (crack) form. The legal penalties for crack cocaine, which is the primary variety used in African American communities, are much stiffer than the penalties for powdered cocaine. Examine Fig. 1.3 and answer the questions that follow.
a. Approximately what percentage of the people in each group are African American?
   Population of the United States _____
   Drug users in the United States _____
   Arrests for drug possession _____

      Convicts of drug possession _____
      Imprisoned for drug possession _____
  b. Describe the pattern illustrated by the information in Fig. 1.3.
  c. What conclusions can you draw based on the information in Fig. 1.3?
  d. What questions do you have based on your examination of this data?
  e. In your opinion, do these figures result from social inequality and racism? Explain your
     answer.

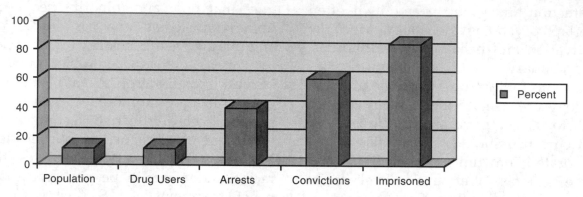

FIG. 1.3 Drug Use and Possession in the United States: African Americans as Percentage of Each Group

---

Teaching Activity: Sociology and Psychology in the Curriculum

Add your voice to the discussion:
Do you think sociology and psychology should be integrated into a history-based social studies curriculum or taught as independent subjects? Why?

Try it yourself:
How would you answer the questions in these sociology and psychology activities?

It's your classroom:
Would you use these sociology and psychology activities as is? Would you modify them? Would you discard them ? Why?

Economics

Economics examines how societies produce and distribute the goods and services that people, communities, and nations need to survive. Because economic recommendations impact sharply on government policies, they involve some of the most controversial issues in the social sciences. Economists are engaged in disputes over the merits of different economic systems, including communist and socialist centrally managed economies, capitalist economies where planning decisions are made by private corporations in the pursuit of profits, and various mixed economies that attempt to balance private and public interests. Within all of these societies, economists address problems related to depression, inflation, unemployment, government subsidy of business, tax policy, and social service budgets. Economics-related controversies extend into the school curriculum; teachers often disagree over the relative importance of mathematical models for describing economic systems and whether what are described as natural economic laws are actually human creations.

In many high schools, economics is taught as a separate subject. As in political science (government) classes, the curriculum tends to describe the way U.S. institutions are supposed to function. Other major economic topics include the impact of technology on society, global trade, and economic interdependence; the environmental impact of economic decisions; the role of government in managing modern economies; relationships between privately owned corporations and workers; acquisition and use of scarce resources; and individual investment strategies. Some social studies programs offer electives or thematic units through which students learn business and occupational skills.

Sample Economics Lesson Ideas

1. What Do People Need to Survive?

For an introductory lesson on economics, individual students list what they believe people need to survive. The entire class brainstorms a list on the board and evaluates ideas. In a follow-up lesson, students discuss how these items are made (produced) and acquired (distributed) in our society.

2. Look at the Labels

An important economic concept is global interdependence. Students examine labels in their clothes to discover where items were manufactured. For homework, they can examine major appliances in their homes.

3. Describing the Soccer Ball

Students toss a soccer ball around the class. When a student catches the ball, he or she tells the class one piece of information about the ball. Terms are listed on the board. Eventually, one of the students mentions where the ball was manufactured. Often it was made in a Third World nation where factories use child labor. Students discuss whether this is important to know when they purchase a product.

4. "Natural Economic Laws"

In 1776, Scottish philosopher Adam Smith introduced the idea that a market economy is a self-regulating machine whose rules are unchangeable scientific laws rooted in the nature of human behavior. In the United States, the idea that the role of government is to support these natural laws was succinctly expressed in a 1925 speech by President Calvin Coolidge, who believed, "The business of America is business." These ideas reenter public discussion whenever politicians and economists argue against government efforts to rectify economic imbalances and in favor of letting the economic mechanism work out its own irregularities.

Students should consider whether economic development in the United States and the world economy are the results of natural law or of a series of business, government, and individual decisions that can be altered to produce different results, including a cleaner environment and a more equitable distribution of wealth.

5. Mortgage Interest Deductions: Is the System Fair?

The U.S. government allows individuals and corporations to deduct certain expenses from their income when calculating federal income tax payments. One of the most common tax deductions for individuals is the interest payment on home mortgages. This tax break has broad popular support, even among advocates of a flat tax that would eliminate most other deductions. Examine Table 1.2 and answer the questions that follow.

TABLE 1.2
Mortgage Interest Deductions on Federal Income Taxes

Annual Income	Percent of All Tax Returns	Percent of Total Savings on Mortgage Deductions	Average Savings per Person
Under $10,000	18.5%	Less than 1.0%	$258
$10,001–$20,000	19.1	Less than 1.0%	411
$20,001–$30,000	15.9	1.5	514
$30,001–$40,000	12.8	3.8	721
$40,001–$50,000	9.1	6.3	944
$50,001–$75,000	13.8	22.0	1,265
$75,001–$100,000	5.7	21.9	2,183
$100,001–200,000	4.1	27.6	3,511
$200,001 and over	1.1	16.5	8,348

Source: The New York Times, January 12, 1996, D1.

a. What percentage of income tax returns are for incomes less than $10,000?
b. Which income bracket receives the largest percentage of total savings on mortgage tax deductions?
c. Which income bracket receives the largest per person savings?
d. What percentage of income tax returns are for incomes over $100,000?
e. What is the total percentage savings for incomes over $100,000?
f. Based on Table 1.2, are mortgage tax deductions equitable to all taxpayers? Why?
g. In your opinion, why do mortgage interest tax deductions have broad support, even though the benefits are distributed this way?
h. Changes in economic policies can have broad repercussions. In what ways could an end to mortgage income deductions change the U.S. economy?
i. In your opinion, are deductions such as the mortgage interest tax deduction, a product of natural economic laws, or political and economic decisions to benefit particular groups and industries? Explain the reasons for your answer.

6. Mr. Block Learns about Workfare

During the early years of the 20th century, the Industrial Workers of the World had a cartoon series in its labor union newspaper featuring the character "Mr. Block." Mr. Block's head is made of wood so he never understands what is going on until it is too late. Fig. 1.4 reintroduces Mr. Block in a contemporary setting.
a. Describe what is happening in the cartoon.
b. What is the main idea presented by the cartoonist?
c. Do you agree or disagree with the point of view of the cartoonist? Why?
d. Explain a possible solution to Mr. Block's problem.
e. Create a cartoon that illustrates your ideas about a problem facing the U.S. economy.

FIG. 1.4   Mr. Block Learns about Workfare
Used with permission of Pamela Booth.

Teaching Activity: Economics in the Curriculum

Add your voice to the discussion:
Do you think economics should be integrated into a history-based social studies curriculum or taught as an independent subject? Why?

Try it yourself:
How would you answer the questions in these economics activities?

It's your classroom:
Would you use these economics activities as is? Would you modify them? Would you discard them? Why?

Essay 1: What Social Studies is All About

The undergraduate section of the secondary education social studies methods class at Hofstra University is a small group. There are 11 students, 7 females and 4 males. I asked students to introduce themselves, including their name, major, place in the program, and how they identify themselves ethnically and culturally. It is an interesting group of students more diverse than many of my previous classes at this suburban university. One woman is a Caribbean American whose parents are from Jamaica in the West Indies. One woman was born in Medellin, Columbia. One of the men and one of the women are from Greek American families. Their parents are immigrants and they speak Greek at home. Two women identified themselves as Italian American. One of the male students is a Russian immigrant who arrived in the United States when he was a preteenager. Three White students, two women and a man, described themselves as Americans from many

different backgrounds. Two of these students are in their late twenties, the man and one of the women. All of the students in the class are history majors. Eight are seniors; three are juniors.

I began the second part of the lesson by distributing a 1927 newspaper article about a teenage girl named Aurora D'Angela, and I asked the students to answer questions based on the article (Johnstown Tribune, 1927). Aurora D'Angela was a teenage Italian immigrant who was arrested during a demonstration in Chicago protesting against the impending execution of Sacco and Vanzetti. I use this article in my teaching because many of the high school students on Long Island come from Italian American families, but they have not really thought about what that means. They live in a culturally isolated time warp, with little sense of who they are, where they come from, or how their culture and history are similar or different from anyone else's. They have little sense of how the world today differs from the past. I find that this story promotes discussion and gets them to ask questions.

While the students were answering the questions, I circulated around the room looking at what they were writing. This gave me some idea about what they were thinking, and it helped me organize my thoughts and formulate questions. Sometimes I wrote down notes on a memo pad.

We began a discussion by brainstorming about events in the United States during the 1920s. Our list included prohibition; international isolation; "between the wars"; the Scopes ("monkey") trial; an economic boom followed by depression; anti-immigrant feelings and quotas; prejudice against Catholics, Jews, and African Americans; and, of course, the Sacco and Vanzetti trial. Three students confessed that they did not know who Sacco and Vanzetti were, so two students gave a pretty complete account. They included charges that the court was biased against Sacco and Vanzetti because they were immigrants, Catholics, and political radicals.

One of the students who explained the Sacco and Vanzetti case to the class identified herself as an Italian American. She remembered learning about this case in high school. I asked her why this story had stuck with her. She said that her grandparents were Italian immigrants and that the treatment of Sacco and Vanzetti always struck her as unjust and as anti-Italian: "It hit me in the gut."

Another student, who also identified herself as Italian American, now remembered reading a statement by Vanzetti to the court. She spoke about the problem these two immigrant men had had expressing themselves during the trial because of their limited English.

One of the Greek students spoke up. She explained that the problem of discrimination against people who have trouble with English still continues. She told a story of how her father had been to court, how difficult it was for him because of language, and how her older sister had had to go and help him to make sure he was treated fairly.

One woman, who had been quiet for much of the period, explained the importance of making it possible for teenagers to identify with what went on in the past. She said it was important to her that the newspaper story was about a teenager who was a female and an immigrant. She identified with this girl. She knew girls like her.

I asked another woman who identified herself as "part Italian" whether she thought it was significant that Aurora was Italian. She answered that "Italian kids on Long Island don't think of themselves in this way so much anymore. They really didn't know about what their families had gone through. They need to learn about this." Two students added that they do not remember ever learning about people like themselves, "ordinary people," in school.

At this point, our discussion shifted. I asked, group members if they thought that the demonstration in Chicago in 1927 could be compared to any demonstrations today. The Caribbean American student said that people associate this type of demonstration today with African Americans. She gave protests in Crown Heights, Brooklyn, and Los Angeles as examples of current protests. The Russian immigrant strongly objected to this comparison. He argued that "looting is different from protesting." Other students thought he was exaggerating the differences. There was a lot of disagreement in class.

Learning Activity: Attitudes Toward Immigrants

1. Nicolas Vanzetti was tried in Massachusetts twice, first for bank robbery and then for murder. In the first trial, Webster Thayer, who was the judge in both cases, told the jury: "This man, although he may not have actually committed the crime . . . , is nevertheless morally culpable, because he is the enemy of our existing institutions" (Boyer and Morais, 1955: 226).

2. The following quotes were made by two Congressmen during the debate over immigration quotas in December 1920.
   Congressman James McClintic, Democrat Oklahoma: "I say the class of immigrants coming to the shores of the United States at this time are not the kind of people we want as citizens in this country" (Congressional Record, 1921: 177).

   Congressman Lucian Parrish, Democrat Texas: "We should stop immigration entirely until such a time as we can amend our immigration laws and so write them that hereafter

no one shall be admitted except he be in full sympathy with our constitution and laws"
(Congressional Record, 1921: 180–81).

It's your classroom:
1. How could you use these quotes to promote student discussion of conditions facing immigrants to the United States during the 1920s?
2. What questions would you ask your class? Why?
3. Would you connect discussion of these quotes with current debate about immigration? Explain the reasons for your answer.

Teaching Activity: Student Voice

It's your classroom:
You are the teacher and you have to make a decision. Are these personal statements by students taking us off on tangents, or are they making it possible for us to better understand the issues in the Sacco and Vanzetti case and the situation facing immigrants to the United States? What do you think? What do you decide?

Teaching Activity: Ordinary People

It's your classroom:
1. Would you include the history of ordinary people in social studies curricula? Why or why not?
2. If you would, how would you do it?

I asked whether people thought Aurora should have been arrested for protesting. The Greek American man identified himself as a "traditionalist" from a "strict family." He argued that if Aurora had broken the law, she should be punished, no matter how much she felt Italians were discriminated against. "Breaking the law is wrong in all cases." Another student thought that protesters should not be arrested: "They have a constitutional right to protest." She believed that contemporary protests and the Sacco and Vanzetti protests of the 1920s were similar. "It is important for students to recognize this. It will help them deal with their prejudices today."

One student questioned whether the report that Aurora and the other protesters were rioting was true. I asked her what made her suspicious of the accuracy of the article. She responded that the article credited the "United Press" as its source. "If a reporter witnessed the events and wrote the story, he would have had a by-line. This story was probably from a police account." I asked the group, "If the account comes from a police report, does that make it inaccurate"? There was scattered uncertainty. I asked if anyone ever had a

reason to doubt the police version of a story. One of the Italian American women became very agitated. She began to tell the story of a visit she made to another college: "The police broke up a beer blast on campus and started arresting participants and then beating them. When other students gathered, the police started attacking, beating, and arresting people in the crowd. They marched in full riot gear, and I was terrified. A young man near me was grabbed, beaten, and arrested. I narrowly escaped. We tried contacting the media, but they didn't come. It was a police riot, but the whole incident was covered up by the press." When she finished, other students began to recount experiences that made them skeptical about a police account. They wanted to read what other witnesses had to say before they made any judgments.

At this point, I asked the group to step back so we could examine what we had done. I asked if any students could remember a free-flowing discussion like this on a social studies issue in either high school or college. No one could. All they remember about social studies classes is lectures and notes.

When I asked, "What made our discussion possible?" the following were given:

"We had the article as a starting point."

"You gave us time to answer questions and write down our ideas so we could have something to contribute."

"It was the first meeting of the class, but you knew our names. It seemed like you cared about what we were saying."

"You asked us to speak louder so everyone could hear."

"You asked us 'What do you mean?' and then you gave us a chance to think and explain more. You didn't guess what we were thinking and repeat it for the class."

"When _____ interrupted, you asked him to wait so _____ could finish her idea."

"The discussion connected to things we knew about, things from our experience. We talked about our religions and families. We used what we knew to help us understand the past."

"These are important things that concern us."

"We went back and forth between the past and the present. We used our knowledge from today to understand the past and the past to increase our knowledge about today."

As a summary question, I asked the group if members thought this was an important discussion for a high school social studies class. One student argued it was because we "had talked about a lot of important things and we reached agreement about the importance of this historical event."

I asked, "What if we hadn't reached agreement; would it still be an important discussion?"

There was a broad consensus that it would be. People in the class said they had gotten a chance to think about different sides of an issue and to express their views. They had not just expressed their views, however; they felt my questions had, pushed them to use evidence from history and their lives to support their ideas.

In recent years I have modified this lesson. Before we discuss Aurora D'Angela, I ask students to complete an activity sheet, "Foreign Criminals In New York," designed for use in an 11th grade U.S. history class. It is based on an article from a magazine called *The North American Review*. I have also used the activity sheet in workshops with high school students before a discussion of stereotypes about different ethnic groups.

Teaching Activity: Breaking the Law

Add your voice to the discussion:
1. Is breaking the law wrong in all cases? What do you think? Why?
2. Should we always accept statements from people in authority? What do you think? Why?

It's your classroom:
1. How would you handle student skepticism about authority?
2. How would you respond to these questions if they were raised by students in your classroom?

Teaching Activity: Student Discussions

Add your voice to the discussion:
Think about your secondary school experiences as a student, observer, and teacher. In your opinion, can this kind of discussion take place in a middle school or high school social studies classroom? Should it? What do you think? Why?

FOREIGN CRIMINALS IN NEW YORK

By Police Commissioner Theodore A. Bingham

When the circumstance is taken into consideration that eighty-five percent of the population of New York City is either foreign-born or of foreign parentage, and that nearly half of the residents of the five boroughs do not speak the English language, it is only a logical condition that something like eighty-five out of one hundred of our criminals should be found to be of exotic origin. It is not astonishing that with a million (a) _____ in the city (one-quarter of the population), perhaps half of the criminals should be of that race.

The crimes committed by the (b) _____ are generally those against property. They are burglars, firebugs, pickpockets and highway robbers—when they have the courage; but, though all crime is their province, pocket-picking is the one to which they seem to take most naturally.

Among the most expert of all the street thieves are (c) _____ boys under sixteen, who are being brought up to lives of crime. Many of them are old offenders at the age of ten. The juvenile (d) _____ emulates the adult in the matter of crime percentages, forty percent of the boys at the House of Refuge and twenty-seven percent of those arraigned in the Children's Court being of that race. The percentage of (e) _____ children in the truant schools is also higher than that of any others.

Although, while the (f) _____ are outnumbered in New York by the (g) _____ by two to one, the (h) _____ malefactor is by far the greater menace to law and order. For more than ten years, wherever a few (i) _____ laborers have gathered together, whether it be at work on a railroad, or in a mine, or on a farm or an irrigation ditch, or in the vineyards of the Pacific slope, the desperadoes of the race have fastened themselves upon the honest and industrious. In New York, presumably the very center of Western civilization, crimes of blackmailing, blowing up shops and house and kidnapping of their fellow countrymen, have become prevalent among (j) _____ residents of the city to an extent that cannot much longer be tolerated.

The audacity of these desperadoes is almost beyond belief. Arrested for crimes that, proved against them, might given them capital punishment or life terms of imprisonment, they will obtain bail and return to the scene of their depredations to jeer at and threaten their victims.

(k) _____ children come next after the youthful (l) _____ in the percentage of arraignments in the Children's Court and commitments to the truant schools and the House of Refuge—the lower rounds of the ladder of crime. They are 20 percent of the total brought into the court, and 10 percent of those at the House of Refuge. There are no figures available as to percentages of commitments to the truant schools.

Year the article was written _____

Answers: (a)–(e), (g), (l), Hebrews (Jews); (f), (h)–(k), Italians. Year: 1908.

Essay 2: Are We Teaching "Greek Myths" in the Global History Curriculum?

In March 2001, *The New York Times* (Broad, 2001: F1) reported that a submerged robot, searching the bottom of the Mediterranean Sea off of the island of Cyprus, had found the remains of an ancient Greek vessel. The research team identified it as a Hellenistic trader carrying a shipment of wine between Rhodes and Alexandria. They estimate that it sank 2,300 years ago in the era of Alexander the Great.

The discovery supports the idea that in the ancient world, the Mediterranean Sea was a giant highway for transporting products, peoples, and cultures from one site to another. This supported the process of cultural diffusion and contributed to the growth of early empires. In *The Odyssey*, Homer claimed that the Greek hero Odysseus sailed a similar route from Crete to North Africa. That voyage would have taken place about 1300 B.C. The Greeks were not the only prolific sailors of this era. During the thousand-year period before the consolidation of the Mediterranean world under Roman rule, the Phoenicians regularly sailed between the Middle East and Carthage in present-day Tunisia and as far as Spain.

This find is of major historical significance because the isle of Rhodes is about 200 miles north of the wreck, near the coast of present-day Turkey. Alexandria, Egypt, is an additional 200 miles south of the wreck in North Africa. The trip necessitated navigating across open water away from the sight of land.

The research team is continuing to search the region, hoping to uncover a Minoan shipwreck. The Minoans were seafarers who ruled an empire in the eastern Mediterranean and Aegean Seas from the island of Crete between 2,500 and 1,200 B.C. This period is known as the *Bronze Age* because it predates the manufacture of iron tools and weapons in the Mediterranean region. No Minoan ship from this period has ever been recovered.

The subheading of *The Times* article was "Accidental Find Lends New Credence to Greek Tales of Sailing Feats." This statement is the crux of the issue that I address in this essay. Do social studies teachers present history "backward" when our starting point is Greek accomplishments? If the Mediterranean was truly a highway in this period, the likelihood is that it was dominated by the era's military, economic, and cultural superpowers, Egypt on the Nile River and Sumeria or Babylon in Mesopotamia (the Fertile Crescent). Greece, at best, would have been a peripheral trading partner. If Greece was at the margins and Egypt and Mesopotamia were at the center of cultural and technological advancement in this period, are social studies teachers presenting "Greek myth" as history when we attribute the origin of "Western Civilization" to ancient Greece?

The significance of the Nile and Fertile Crescent civilizations in early human cultural development and the power of cultural diffusion are well established. To cite a recent example, Jared Diamond (1997) shows that agricultural and animal husbandry emerged in the Fertile Crescent and spread to the Nile River Valley more than 10,000 years ago (8,500 B.C.). Eventually, this "food

package" and the sedentary way of life based on it spread throughout the Mediterranean world. Diamond traces a similar route for the spread of writing systems. Starting about 5,000 years ago (3,200 B.C.), the systems develop in Mesopotamia and Egypt (later, but independently, in China around 1,300 B.C. and Meso-America in 600 B.C.) and diffuse across the globe. Other cultural developments in the ancient Mediterranean world followed a similar pattern of dispersion. Pottery first appears in the Nile Valley and Mesopotamia about 7000 B.C., metallurgy about 4,000 B.C., formal governments about 3,700 B.C., and iron tools about 900 B.C. Since the historical record makes it virtually impossible to decide whether a development first emerged in Egypt or Mesopotamia, they are considered as a single point of origin.

Given the early achievements of Mesopotamia and Egypt, why the unbalanced focus on ancient Greece in history textbooks and social studies classrooms?

There are three general answers to this question. Historians and teachers often focus on ancient Greece because they perceive Greek civilization as fundamentally different (as somehow more "western") from the civilizations that preceded it or existed at the same time and they believe this difference produced the modern world as we know it. Historian Peter Burke (1998: 2) calls this view the "Grand Narrative of the rise of Western civilization: a triumphalist account of Western achievement from the Greeks onwards in which the Renaissance is a link in the chain which includes the Reformation, the Scientific Revolution, the Enlightenment, the Industrial Revolution, and so on." Within this framework, Houghton Mifflin's high school text, *History of the World* (Perry, 1990), reports that "the earliest civilizations that grew up on the Greek islands developed a unique culture. Although these people were conquered by foreign invaders, many of their traditions endured. Greek ideas would come to have a powerful influence on the politics, thought, and art of Europe and the Western Hemisphere. For this reason, Greece is known as the "cradle of Western civilization" (71).

Is there sufficient evidence to document historical continuity from ancient Greece to the modern era? Diane Ravitch and Abigal Thernstrom (1992) edited a collection called *Democracy Reader* that includes classic and modern speeches, essays, poems, declarations, and documents on freedom

An earlier version of this essay appeared in the Winter–Spring 2002 issue of *Social Science Docket*, published by the New York and New Jersey Councils for the Social Studies.

and human rights. In the book, Ravitch and Thernstrom try to support a thesis championed by Harvard sociologist Orlando Patterson (1991), who argues that we can trace the history of democratic ideals as an essential component of western philosophy from ancient Greece to the modern world. An examination of the table of contents raises an interesting problem, however. The book contains no documents for the 1,500-year period between Aristotle's *The Politics* (written circa 320 B.C.) and Thomas Aquinas' *Summa Theologia* (written about 1250 A.D.). Even if the ancient Greek city-states possessed a system with recognizably democratic elements, it is exceedingly difficult to establish a direct political or intellectual connection between societies separated by more than 1,500 years of history. In fact, Greek texts were largely unknown in Europe prior to the Crusades and survived only because they were preserved by Arab scholars.

A second explanation for the unbalanced focus on ancient Greece is that we in modern societies can see ourselves in its art, literature, philosophy, and ideologies. Classical Greek sculpture appears realistic rather than symbolic or exotic. Socrates and Plato sound as if they could be giving interviews on C-SPAN. Athens seems the model for democratic society, and martial Sparta reminds some of 20th century totalitarian societies or Star Trek's Klingon Empire. Even their gods, with soap-opera-like battles and love affairs, remind us of our own passions and conflicts.

Are we reading more into Greek culture and history than actually can be supported by the historical record? Are we seeing what is there or what we want to see? Let me offer two examples that illustrate what I mean. The first is an example of seeing what is not there: an ancient philosopher championing modern democratic values. The second is an example of ignoring what is clearly there: a different attitude toward sexual mores.

The popular conception is that Socrates was a Greek philosopher and teacher persecuted and then executed by an authoritarian government for questioning leaders and pursuing the search for truth. Unfortunately, the historical record is not so clear cut. In *The Trial of Socrates* (1988), I. F. Stone concluded that Socrates was actually involved in an attempt by the oligarchy to undermine efforts to broaden representation in Athenian government.

A second issue, rarely addressed because of our culture's homophobia, is the Greek attitude toward same-sex sexual relationships. According to M. I. Finley (1963: 123–25), Aristotle believed that true friendship was possible only between equals, hence

impossible between men and women. Bisexuality was common, especially among the upper class, where men and women were expected to seek both physical and spiritual companionship from people of the same gender. Sexual relations between adult men and younger boys was a feature of military elites in Sparta and Thebes and among the nobility in Athens. This aspect of ancient Greek culture is missing from most high school textbooks.

Probably the most comprehensive effort to read the present into the past is the celebration of Greek "democracy." According to Houghton Mifflin's *History of the World* (Perry, 1990: 86–87), "Democracy, which had been developing in Athens over many years, reached its peak under the leadership of Pericles. He opened all political offices to any citizen. He paid jurors so that poor citizens as well as the wealthy could serve. Athens had a direct democracy—that is, all citizens had the right to attend the Assembly and cast a vote." In the next paragraph, however, we learn that "Athenian democracy was far from complete. Citizens had time for public service largely because they owned slaves. . . . Most residents of Athens were not citizens and had no say in government. . . . Women, too, had no political rights." In fact, during the era of Pericles, the population of Athens was about 450,000 people, and less than 10 percent were adult male citizens with the power to vote. About 18 percent of the population were foreign born with no legal rights, and 55 percent of the residents of Athens were enslaved. Athenian "democracy" was so restricted in scope and in time (the age of Pericles lasted about thirty years), that students should consider whether it can legitimately be labeled democratic at all.

A third explanation for the focus on ancient Greece as the source of Western Civilization is *Eurocentrism*: the effort to center history on European societies and to minimize the contributions of non-European "others." For example, the debate over the relationship between Egypt, Mesopotamia, and Greece in the ancient world is highly charged. Claims by Afrocentric authors that Egypt was the source of Greek civilization, that ancient Egyptians were "Black Africans," and that this history has been hidden by mainstream "White" institutions in order to strip people of African ancestry of their proper place in history have been challenged by essays in most of the major historical and archeological journals (Lefkowitz, 1992: 440–60; Pounder, 1992: 461–64; Lefkowitz and Rogers, 1996).

I want to sidestep the debate over whether ancient Egyptians were "Black Africans" because

I believe it takes us away from the more important issue of Egyptian influence on Greek culture and development. We will probably never know for certain the skin color or genetic heritage of ancient Egyptians. Their art is largely symbolic, and I suspect that the colors used to portray people were selected from pigments available to artists, not because of the subjects' skin color. Most likely, since ancient Egypt was a crossroads civilization, it was a genetically and culturally blended society with diverse people who probably did not place the same significance on race as we do in the United States today.

Much of the debate over the relationship between Egypt, Mesopotamia, and Greece is in response to the work of Martin Bernal (1987; 1991; 2001 with D. Moore), who has published two volumes of a proposed three-volume collection called *Black Athena: The Afroasiatic Roots of Classical Civilization*. Bernal marshals extensive evidence to present a detailed case for Egyptian and Semitic (Middle Eastern) contributions to Greek culture during the Bronze Age (prior to 1100 B.C.) based on an examination of religion, art, mythology, language, and artifacts. Among other things, he provides powerful arguments for the origins of the Hercules legend and the Sphinx in ancient Egypt.

The ancient world is not my area of expertise as either a teacher or historian, so I cannot evaluate Bernal's documentation. What I find most interesting are the concessions made by his opponents. Among his more vocal critics, Molly Myerwitz Levine (1992) accepts some of Bernal's claims about Bronze Age influence but argues that they are not at the core of what we identify as classical Greece—its art, politics, and philosophy.

In an essay titled, "Did Egypt Shape the Glory That Was Greece?" John Coleman, a classicist from Cornell University, presents an alternative historical scenario to Bernal's and concludes that "recognizing that Greek civilization was influenced from abroad and made use of previous advances in mathematics and science, . . . is a far cry from asserting that it had Afroasiatic roots" (1996: 281). Coleman claims that all scholars recognize the contributions of Egypt and the Middle East to the ancient Greek world, especially to Minoan or Crete civilization, and argues that the dispute with Bernal is primarily a matter of degree.

According to Coleman's narrative, cultural contact between the Aegean and Egypt started in the early Bronze Age, around 2100 B.C., as a result of migration and trade. Crete needed to import tin, a major ingredient in the manufacture of bronze, which was lacking in the Aegean world. The widespread diffusion of pottery from 2100 to 1725 B.C. shows increasing contacts between Greece and Egypt. During this period, Minoan culture, which was shaped by its contacts with Egypt, exerted a powerful influence on the developing mainland Greek societies. Later, with the decline of Crete, Mycenaean (or mainland Greek societies) took over the trade connections with Egypt. We know less about Greece between 1100 and 750 B.C., but after 750 B.C., Greek soldiers were used as mercenaries in Egypt and, according to Coleman, there is a "flood of influence on all Greek arts and crafts from Egypt" (296). These conclusions are supported by an exhibit, "Crete-Egypt: Three Millennia of Cultural Interactions," which I visited at the Herakleion Archaeological Museum in Crete. It contains 527 artifacts that demonstrate interaction between the two Mediterranean peoples. Some of the exhibit can be viewed at the museum's web site (http://www.culture.gr/2/21/211/21123m/e211wm01.html).

I find Coleman's statement balanced and reasonable and believe that it establishes a significant relationship that was ignored before the Bernal work. It is in sharp contrast to what is currently taught in secondary schools. Houghton Mifflin's *History of the World* (Perry, 1990) section on Minoan civilization reports that they were "seafaring traders, exporting wine, honey, and olive oil to Egypt, Asia Minor, Syria and Greece" (71) but ignores any Egyptian influence on Crete or Greece. After the collapse of Crete, Egypt plays no further role in Greek history until Alexander the Great conquers it. The chapter on ancient Egypt (34–42) reports that Egypt traded with other civilizations in the Mediterranean region including Crete but does not identify the Greek world or discuss any cultural exchange between the two civilizations. The spread of Greek culture through Alexander's conquest of the Mediterranean world, known as *Hellenization*, is presented as a major accomplishment of ancient Greece that stimulated trade, science, philosophy, and cultural diffusion. Should conquest and forced assimilation into the Greek world be presented uncritically? Would similar conquests and assimilations be viewed that way if they took place today? The much celebrated Hebrew revolt under the Maccabees (the story of Hannukah) about 170 B.C. was a response to efforts by Greek rulers to enforce Greek culture, law, and religion in ancient Israel (Johnson, 1987: 102–7).

The celebration of ancient Greece's role within the "Grand Narrative" of the Western world is reinforced in standard interpretations of the European Renaissance, which define the era as a rebirth of classical Greek and Roman civilization (Thompson, 1996). According to Burke (1998), "the major innovators of the Renaissance presented—and often perceived—their inventions and discoveries as a return to ancient traditions after the long parenthesis of what they were the first to call the Middle' Ages" (2). Houghton Mifflin's text credits Italian humanists, especially Petrach of Florence, with reading ancient texts and "rediscovering knowledge that had been lost or forgotten" (1990: 327).

Even if Renaissance innovators believed that social change was a result of the rediscovery of ancient traditions, that does not mean that it actually happened that way. In *Worldly Goods: A New History of the Renaissance* (1996: 12), Lisa Jardine presents a materialist interpretation of the period, arguing that the celebrated culture of the European Renaissance was the result of a "competitive urge to acquire" stimulated by the growth of trade, cities, and a new affluent, secular elite. She believes that "Early Renaissance works of art which today we admire for their sheer representational virtuosity were part of a vigorously developing world market in luxury commodities" (19).

Why would this increasing affluent, secular world claim spiritual and intellectual descent from classical Mediterranean civilizations? The answer is related to the power of religious authority in that era. The Roman Catholic Church was threatened by competing religions and new world views and brutally resisted change. Framing new ideas and discoveries as a rebirth of knowledge from classical Greco-Roman and Biblical eras was necessary for survival. In Florence, where the European Renaissance first emerged, major religious authorities attacked the study of "pagan authors" as an impediment to salvation, and humanists were forced to defend the texts as compatible with church teachings (Burke, 1998: 31–32). In the end, Church and secular authorities preferred to credit Aristotle and Ptolemy with the origin of civilization rather than acknowledging the role of contemporary Moslems and Jews.

Debates over ideas during the European Renaissance were not just intellectual exercises. In the early 13th century, Pope Innocent III launched a crusade to crush heresy in southern France that resulted in the slaughter of tens of thousands of people (O'Shea, 2000). After warring against its Islamic population, Spain's Roman Catholic monarchs expelled Jews and in 1477 established the Inquisition. Under Torquemada, the third Grand Inquisitioner, more than 2,000 people were burned at the stake for suspicion of rejecting Catholic religious orthodoxy (Thompson, 1996: 509). Noted Renaissance artists and scholars were not immune from suspicion or attack. In 1516, Leonardo da Vinci, whose actions and work were frequently impious and who made no pretense of connection with classical antiquity, fled the Italian peninsula and sought sanctuary from King Francis I of France (Thompson, 1996: 147–58). In 1633, Galileo was tried for heresy by the Holy Office of the Inquisition in Rome for challenging the Ptolemaic system and asserting that the Earth traveled around the Sun (Sobel, 1999: 273–78).

Where does this leave social studies teachers? We need to reconceptualize both the "grand narrative" of Western Civilization presented in global history and the way we teach social studies. Instead of presenting the past as a series of facts and truths to be memorized and celebrated, teachers should engage students in a critical examination of different explanations of the past and present. The Global History curriculum can be organized so students explore essential historical questions (Wiggins and McTighe, 1998: 28–32; Singer, 1999: 28–31), including these: What were the origins of Western Civilization? Was there only one origin? Was Athens or any ancient society democratic? Does conquest make a leader (Alexander) great? What are the costs of cultural diffusion and assimilation? How does democracy emerge? How do societies change? Why do societies accept and promote myths about their past?

REFERENCES AND RECOMMENDATIONS FOR FURTHER READING

Bernal, M. *Black Athena: The Afroasiatic Roots of Classical Civilization. Vol. 1, The Fabrication of Ancient Greece, 1785–1985.* New Brunswick, N.J.: Rutgers University Press, 1987.

Bernal, M. *Black Athena: The Afroasiatic Roots of Classical Civilization. Vol. 2, The Archeological and Documentary Evidence.* New Brunswick, N.J.: Rutgers University Press, 1991.

Bernal, M., and D. Moore. *Black Athena Writes Back: Martin Bernal Responds to His Critics.* Durham, N.C.: Duke University Press, 2001.

Berra, Y., with T. Horton. *Yogi: It Ain't Over. . . .* New York: Harper & Row, 1989.

Bingham, T. "Foreign Criminals In New York." *North American Review*, September 1908.

Broad, W. "In an Ancient Wreck, Clues to Seafaring Lives." *The New York Times*, March 27, 2001.

Burke, P. *The European Renaissance, Centres and Peripheries*. Oxford, United Kingdom: Blackwell Publishers, 1998.

Blum, J. "Guthrie, Woody (1912–1967)," in M. Buhle, P. Buhle, and D. Georakas, eds., *Encyclopedia of the American Left*. New York: Garland, 1990.

Boyer, R. and Morais, H. (1955). *Labor's Untold Story*. New York: Cameron.

Carr, E. H. *What Is History?* New York: Vintage, 1961.

Coleman, J. E., 1996. 'Did Egypt Shape the Glory That Was Greece?', in: Lefkowitz, M. R., & MacLean Rogers, G., eds., *Black Athena revisited*, Chapel Hill & London: University of North Carolina Press, pp. 280–301.

Congressional Record. *3rd session, 66th Congress, Vol. LX–Part 1, December 6, 1920–January 6, 1921*. Washington DC: Government Printing Office, 1921.

Crichton, M. *Andromeda Strain*. New York: Knopf, 1969.

Crichton, M. *Jurassic Park*. New York: Knopf, 1990.

Diamond, J. *Guns, Germs, and Steel: The Fates of Human Societies*. New York: Norton, 1997.

Dircks, H. "Using Geography to Integrate Science and Social Studies." *Social Science Docket*, (Winter–Spring 2002): 34–36.

DuBois, W. E. B. *The Souls of Black Folk*. New York: Fawcett, 1961.

Engvick, W., ed. *Lullabies and Night Songs*. New York: Harper & Row, 1965.

Finley, M. (1963). *The Ancient Greeks*. London: Chatto & Windus.

Foner, E. (1998). *The Story of American Freedom*. New York: Norton.

Foner, P. ed. *The Complete Writings of Thomas Paine*. New York: Citadel Press, 1945.

Fukuyama, F. *The End of History and the Last Man*. New York: The Free Press, 1992.

Gans, H. *The War against the Poor: The Underclass and Antipoverty Policy*. New York: Basic Books, 1995.

Gardiner, P., ed. *Theories of History*. New York: The Free Press, 1959.

Giardina, D. *Storming Heaven*. New York: Norton, 1987.

Giardina, D. *The Unquiet Earth*. New York: Ballantine, 1992.

Giardina, D. *Saints and Villains*. New York: Ballantine, 1998.

Gould, S. J. *Hen's Teeth and Horse's Toes*. New York: Norton, 1983.

Gould, S. J. *Wonderful Life*. New York: Norton, 1989.

Gould, S. J. *Bully for Brontosaurus*. New York: Norton, 1991.

Gould, S. J. *Dinosaur in a Haystack*. New York: Harmony Books, 1995.

Hardwick, M. *The Complete Guide to Sherlock Holmes*. New York: St. Martin's Press, 1986.

Hartocollis, A. "Campus Culture Wars Flare Anew over Tenor of Debate after the Attacks." *The New York Times*, September 30, 2001.

Hartocollis, A. "Lynne Cheney Disputes Official's Call for More Teaching of Multiculturalism." *The New York Times*, October 10, 2001.

Hawke, S. D., and J. E. Davis. *Seeds of Change: The Story of Cultural Exchange after 1492*. Menlo Park, Calif.: Addison-Wesley, 1992.

Hawking, S. W. *A Brief History of Time: From the Big Bang to Black Holes*. New York: Bantam Books, 1988.

Hobsbawn, E. *The Age of Extremes: A History of the World, 1914–1991*. New York: Pantheon.

Hobsbawn, E. *On History*. New York: The New Press, 1997.

Hobsbawn, E., with Polito, A. *On the Edge of the Century*, New York: The Free Press, 2002.

Hofstadter, R. *The Age of Reform*. New York: Random House, 1955.

Hofstadter, R. *Anti-Intellectualism in American Life*. New York: Random House, 1962.

Jardine, L. *Worldly Goods: A New History of the Renaissance*. New York: Doubleday, 1996.

Johnson, P. *A History of the Jews*. New York: Harper and Row, 1987.

Johnstown Tribune "Chicago Girl Urges General Protest Strike," 1.

Kafi, P., and A. Singer. "Isomo Loruko: The Yoruba Naming Ceremony." *Social Education Middle Level Learning Supplement*, January 1998.

Kolko, G. *The Triumph of Conservatism: A Reinterpretation of American History, 1900–1916*. New York: The Free Press, 1963.

Lefkowitz, M. "The Use and Abuse of Black Athena." *American Historical Review*, April 1992.

Lefkowitz, M., and Rogers, G. *Black Athena Revisited*. Chapel Hill, N.C.: UNC Press, 1996.

Levine, M. 1992, 'Review Article: The Use and Abuse of Black Athena', *American Historical Review*, 97, 2: 440–464.

Marable, M. *How Capitalism Underdeveloped Black America*. Boston: South End Press, 1983.

Mead, M. *Coming of Age in Samoa*. New York: American Museum of Natural History, 1973.

Mill, J. S. *The Six Great Humanist Essays of John Stuart Mill*. New York: Washington Square Press, 1963.

National Council for the Social Studies. *Curriculum Standards for Social Studies: Expectations of Excellence, NCSS Bulletin 89*. Washington, D.C.: NCSS, 1994.

National Council for the Social Studies (November/December, 1995). *Social Education*, 59 (7), passim.

O'Shea, S. *The Perfect Heresy*. New York: Walker, 2000.

Patterson, O. *Freedom*. New York: Basic Books, 1991.

Perry, M. *History of the World*. Boston: Houghton Mifflin, 1990.

Perry, M. *History of the World*. Boston, MA: Houghton Mifflin, 1990.

Pounder, R. "Black Athena 2: History without Rules." *American Historical Review*, April 1992.

Ravitch, D., and A. Thernstrom, eds. *The Democracy Reader*. New York: HarperCollins, 1992.

Schlesinger, A., Jr. *The Disuniting of America: Reflections on A multicultural Society*. New York: Norton, 1992.

Seeger, P. and Reiser (1985). *Carry It On!*. New York: Simon and Schuster. *Rethinking Schools*, Spring 1995, 9 (3).

Seldes, G., ed. *The Great Quotations*. New York: Lyle, Stuart, 1966.

Sen, A. *Development as Freedom*. New York: Knopf, 1999.

Singer, A. "Teaching Multicultural Social Studies in an Era of Political Eclipse." *Social Education* 63, no. 1 (1999).

Smith, M. *Social Science in the Crucible: The American Debate over Objectivity and Purpose, 1918–1941*. Durham, N.C.: Duke University Press, 1994.

Sobel, D. (1993), *Longitude*. New York: Walker.

Sobel, D. *Galileo's Daughter*. New York: Walker, 1999.

Stevenson, B., ed. *The Home Book of Quotations*. 6th ed. New York: Dodd, Mead, 1952.

Stone, I. F. *The Trial of Socrates*. New York: Doubleday, 1988.

Thompson, B. *Humanists and Reformers: A History of the Renaissance and Reformation*. Grand Rapids, Mich.: Eerdmans, 1996.

Tierney, P. *Darkness in El Dorado*. New York: Norton, 2001.

U.S. Bureau of Education *Report of the Committee on Social Studies*. Washington, D.C.: Government Printing Office, 1916.

West, C. *Race Matters*. Boston, Mass.: Beacon, 1993.

Wiggins, G., and McTighe, J. *Understanding by Design*. Alexandria, Va.: ASCD, 1998.

Zinn, H. *The Politics of History*. Boston: Beacon Press, 1970.

2

What Are Our Goals?

WHY HAVE GOALS?

The first written homework assignment for preservice teachers in my social studies methods class is to prepare notes in outline form for a chapter from an 11th-grade U.S. history textbook. At the next class meeting, we compare chapter outlines. Generally, they range in length from one to eight typed pages. To open up discussion, I ask "Which outline is a more appropriate model to use with students in a high school social studies class?"

There is always a wide range of opinions. One position is that the more notes a student takes, the better. "This way they know something." "Facts are important." "They won't have to go back and study from the book for the test."

A number of the preservice teachers "confess" that they do assignments like these because they are required to, but they do not really think about the material. They skim, they copy a phrase, they skim some more. Information goes directly from book to paper without being processed by the brain. When they were in secondary school, they handed in the work and they got good grades, but they did not learn much social studies. According to one participant, "People who were considered 'good students' in high school—this is how they got by."

Some of the people in the class admit that in high school they were "bad students." They tried to do the work, but if they saw no point in it, they got bored, stopped handing in assignments, and learned to live with the consequences.

Sometimes the preservice teachers challenge the idea of note taking at all. They charge that it is always a mechanical assignment. "It's not designed to teach students anything, just to prepare them for tests." "Teachers use assignments like these to sort students out, label them, and justify grades. They have nothing to do with social studies." "If the assignments are too long, I just don't do them."

Other discussants defend the idea of assigning high school students to take notes on chapters if the note taking has clear goals and the assignments are both flexible and manageable. "Students need to decide which information is more important and how to organize it so it is useful to them." "When I take notes

I write down the things that make sense to me and help me remember. I keep my notes short. When I study, if I don't remember something, I can always look in the book again."

The concluding point of nearly every discussion like this one is that teachers have to be clear about their long-term goals and short-term objectives when they give students assignments and that students need to understand, or even participate in defining the goals and objectives. Are we just trying to memorize facts, or are we learning how to gather, organize, and use information? Depending on the goals and objectives, chapter notes look very different.

As social studies teachers, each of us has a variety of educational goals; some are widely shared, some are individual, and some are hotly contested. In addition, we have short- and long-term subject-specific goals. Our assignments and lessons need to take all of these goals and objectives into account. Maxine Greene, whom you will meet later in this chapter, describes this process of consciously and continually rethinking our teaching practice as being "wide awake." John Dewey, whom we will also meet later, calls this "reflective practice."

This chapter introduces different types of goals and objectives: broad pedagogical goals that reflect our teaching philosophies; conceptual and content goals for understanding history and the social sciences (examined again in chap. 3); skills goals: social studies, general academic, and social skills that students need so they can process information and work with other people (examined again in chaps. 5 and 6); and personal goals for our own professional growth. In this chapter, I also discuss my goals and the educational and social studies theorists I found useful in shaping them.

PEDAGOGICAL GOALS: ARE WE TEACHING SUBJECT MATTER OR STUDENTS?

In secondary school social studies classrooms across the United States, teachers who consider themselves subject area experts believe they impart vital information to their classes in a clear and logical fashion. In these classrooms, it is the responsibility of individual students to decide whether they learn it. This view of social studies education is supported by popular writers such as E. D. Hirsch (1987), Chester Finn and Diane Ravitch (1987), and Allan Bloom (1987), who bemoan declining academic standards while compiling lists of "facts" that students should know at each grade level. What I call the "Dragnet School of Social Studies Education" (lecturing the facts) is frequently referred to as the *transmission model*. It is a teacher-centered approach to classroom practice; teaching is defined as organizing and presenting information to essentially passive learners. Brazilian educator Paulo Freire (1970) describes it as the "banking method."

Advocates of the transmission model in secondary schools usually consider university lectures the most efficient format for presenting students with information. Many practitioners are quite entertaining and skilled at holding student attention. To modify the approach for use in high schools and junior high schools, they adjust for lower levels of student interest, skills, and maturity. They also allow class time for academic skill development, especially in lower-track classes. In their upper-level honors and advanced placement classes, where teachers are free to exercise their expertise, however, they pitch their "chalk and talk" toward a "college-level" audience.

By this point, you know that I have many problems with this approach to teaching. Memorizing long lists of facts is not the way that historians understand our world, and passive listening is not the way that most students learn. Concentration on streams of facts is not even a good lecture technique. The best lecturers pull their audiences into their arguments, and they think about ideas together. Philosophically, the transmission model supports the beliefs that (1) knowledge is a scarce resource, (2) learning ability is unevenly distributed throughout the population, and (3) the goal of teachers should be to invest in people with the greatest potential and sort out those who cannot do the work. This approach to education serves a stratified society that is based on competition for resources but not committed to either learning or democratic values.

I support a model for teaching based on an alternative view of how people learn and a different set of educational and social goals. Inquiry-based social studies education centers on student questions and research and on student–student and student–teacher interaction. In an inquiry-based classroom, teachers work with students to organize learning experiences and then join with students in exploring the world and making meaning out of what they discover. Academic and social skills develop as students become historians and social scientists; students understand the meaning of citizenship and community because they experience democratic relationships; and success in teaching is measured by what students learn.

Supporters of the transmission model sometimes accept "hands-on" social studies as appropriate for middle school students who are experiencing the transition from the seemingly unstructured experiential learning of elementary school to the disciplined academic learning of high school. However, I argue that structured experiential learning is the most effective way to teach social studies on every level. My middle and high school lesson and unit recommendations differ in skill difficulty and conceptual sophistication but not in basic structure or philosophy. Both are based on student activities; lessons are organized around primary source document analysis, and units include long-term individual and group projects.

Teaching Activity: Models of Social Studies Learning

Add your voice to the discussion:
1. Which of your secondary school social studies teachers influenced your views of social studies education the most? Why?
2. What happened to you in classrooms you didn't like? Why?
3. What most strongly motivated you to learn? Why?

WHO ARE OUR STUDENTS, AND HOW DO WE CONNECT TO THEM?

In an interview with the editor of *Rethinking Schools* (1994), U.S. historian Howard Zinn explained that he "started studying history with one view in mind: to look for answers to the issues and problems I saw in the world around me. By the time I went to college I had worked in a shipyard, had been in the Air Force, had been in a war. I came to history asking questions about war and peace, about wealth and poverty, about racial division" (150).

I think that Paulo Freire, who has worked in adult literacy programs in Third World communities since the 1950s, would argue that Howard Zinn was motivated to read the word (to study books) because he wanted to read (understand) the world. Freire (1995) believes that there is a dynamic interactive relationship between increasing academic literacy and the desire to understand and change the world around us.

Freire's insight into the way people learn is supported by similar findings in history, psychology, and education. Chapter 1 described a reciprocal relationship between research and the development of historical understanding and theories. Early childhood educators and educational psychologists including Lucy Calkins (1983), Lev Vygotzky (Reiber and Carton, 1987), and Loris Malaguzzi, the founder of an internationally acclaimed early childhood program in Reggio Emilia, Italy (Gandini, 1993: 4–9), find the same dynamic at work as young children explore the world around them and learn to read. In their teaching autobiographies, Septima Clark (1986) and Myles Horton (1990) argued that freedom schools in the U.S. south during the civil rights movement of the 1960s successfully promoted literacy because they built on the struggle of African Americans to win the right to vote.

The careers of Freire, Clark, and Horton demonstrate that intense and complex learning is possible when motivated adults are helped to draw connections among their life experiences, social concerns, political points of view, and academic knowledge and skills. However, the question remains whether connecting the study of the word with study of the world will also motivate (1) 13-year-old, 7th-grade boys from affluent suburban communities who are yeasting with hormones, (2) self-effacing young women in 11th-grade classes who behave in school and do all their work but whose interests are elsewhere, or (3) angry students whose lives are overwhelmed by feelings of oppression and with the difficulty of dealing with prejudice, poverty, and urban (or rural) violence. How do teachers convince these students to invest in school and learn social studies?

Many educators have grappled with ways to reach students in the classroom, suggesting strategies for changing the ways that teachers teach, the content of the curriculum, and classroom relationships. Lev Vygotsky, working in the 1920s and 1930s in the Soviet Union, was concerned that educators were often trapped by narrowly conceived and universally applied ideas about human social and psychological development and, as a result, had rigid views about appropriate learning strategies. Vygotsky recognized that students are strongly influenced by the social and historical circumstances of their lives; he believed that, to stimulate academic learning, educators had to "scaffold," or build on the individual and social experiences of students and what they already knew about the world (Newman and Holtzman, 1992; Berk, 1994).

The idea that teachers should respond to individual differences in the ways that students learn is also a crucial component of Howard Gardner's theory of multiple intelligences. Gardner (1987: 187–93) disputed the ideas that human intelligence can be accurately summarized with one reference point and that all people learn in essentially the same fashion. He suggests seven types of intelligence possessed by students in a variety of combinations:

linguistic, logical-mathematical, spatial, body-kinesthetic, musical, interpersonal (social), and intrapersonal (reflective). Gardner argues that curricula and teachers must "recognize and nurture all of the varied human intelligences, and all of the combinations of intelligences," so that schools and societies are able to appropriately address "the many problems that we face in the world."

Advocates of curriculum reform, especially since the 1960s, frequently argue that relevance—drawing connections between school learning and life experience—is crucial for motivating students to learn, particularly in social studies. For example, Howard Zinn recommends that teachers organize curricula so that students "go back and forth and find similarities and analogies" between the past and present (1994: 150). Henry Giroux (1983; 1992) believes that curriculum should be organized so that students are continuously involved in examining their lived experiences. According to Giroux, this makes it possible for students to understand the relationship between their ideas and cultures and the ideology and culture of the broader society. Peggy McIntosh (1983) wants teachers to involve students in creating curricula that include everyone and in critiquing earlier forms of instruction and the social theories behind them.

Nel Noddings (1992) and Alfie Kohn (1986) take different approaches in motivating students, focusing on the nature of classroom community rather than particular subject content. Noddings proposes a feminist approach to education based on an ethic of caring and concern for others, the acceptance of a wide range of human differences, and the nurturing of individual student strengths. Kohn believes that academic and social competition among students is inherently destructive.

He emphasizes cooperative instruction as the basis for creating supportive, democratic learning environments.

Gloria Ladson-Billings (1994) integrates these approaches in what she calls culturally relevant pedagogy. Concerned with both curriculum content and classroom organization, Ladson-Billings believes that teachers must familiarize themselves with the "home" cultures of students and adjust both the subject matter and their classroom practice so that students feel their lives and sensitivities are included in what is taking place. Ladson-Billings' specific research area is on successful approaches to teaching African American students; she argues that a culturally relevant pedagogy is especially important when students come from communities outside the cultural mainstream.

Drawing on my understanding of these educators (Vygotsky, Gardner, Giroux, McIntosh, Noddings, Kohn, and Ladson-Billings), it seems that if we start with the assumption that our primary responsibility is to teach students rather than to teach specific subject matter, social studies teachers must be knowledgeable about who our students are emotionally, socially, and academically and need to address issues related to race, class, gender, cultural differences, prior preparation, and student interest in our classrooms and curricula. It means we have to adjust our teaching to meet the individual and collective needs of our students.

The issue in classrooms is not really relevance; essentially, any topic can be made relevant if teachers establish a context for student understanding. For example, I began lessons on famine-era Irish immigration in the 1840s by asking students to discuss contemporary attitudes toward immigrants in the communities where they live.

One of my pedagogical goals is to reach every student in every classroom every day. I do not have all of the answers about how to do this, and I am not even sure that it is possible, but I do know that the starting point is accepting responsibility for what students learn and always asking this question: Who are my students and how do I connect to them?

Teaching Activity: Heterogeneous or Homogenous Grouping?

Many schools assign students to social studies classes based on their performance on exams, their perceived intelligence or talent, parental pressure, or teacher recommendation. Supporters of homogenous grouping (tracking) argue that it allows teachers to focus on the specific academic needs of the students in their classes. In theory, homogenous grouping benefits students on every academic track while preparing them to succeed in a competitive society where rewards are distributed based on achievement.

Supporters of heterogeneous grouping respond that tracked classrooms are inherently inequitable, reinforce social divisions, and injure students. The experience of being tracked teaches students to believe that intelligence is innate, people are fundamentally different, and some are incapable and undeserving of rewards. Tracking encourages competition and increases the resentment of others. Denied experiences with diverse groups of young people, students never learn to work with people different from themselves. Students in lower tracks believe that they are born inferior and are destined to fail. They develop low self-esteem, give up trying to learn, and many drop out of school. Students in upper tracks are hurt as well. Many become lonely and alienated. Others grow anxious. They feel that they are always being tested and that eventually their inadequacies will be exposed. Instead of enjoying learning, they fear that they will be thrown out of the upper track and, thus, let down their parents. Even the students who respond to the competition and do well are vulnerable. When, like any ordinary human being, they stumble, their entire self-image is subject to question. One result of tracking is that even the best students experience school as an oppressive, stressful place.

Think it over:
1. What track were you assigned to in secondary school?
2. What was your relationship with students in other tracks?
3. What was the impact of tracking on your learning and on your life?
4. Thinking back, could your school have been organized differently? How?

Add your voice to the discussion:
Where do you stand on the issue of heterogeneous versus homogenous grouping in social studies classes? Why?

WHAT USE IS EDUCATIONAL THEORY?

In *Sometimes a Shining Moment: The Foxfire Experience*, Eliot Wigginton (1985), who helped promote the project approach to teaching (discussed in chap. 8), discussed his reaction as he began to reread John Dewey after a number of years of secondary school teaching. Wigginton was amazed that "all of those discoveries I thought I had made about education, Dewey had elucidated into complete clarity fifty years and more before." He asked, "Why didn't I hear what Dewey et al. were saying when I was first introduced to them?" (281).

Wigginton's comments underscore the importance, but inaccessibility, of educational theory for many teachers. While in preservice teacher education programs, we lack the practical experiences that make ideas meaningful. Later, little time is structured into the school year to read, systematically explore issues with other teachers, or conduct action research on classroom practice. We feel pressured to develop our practical competence rather than develop theoretical understanding—to teach while wearing educational blinders. Just as our students do, we end up learning so we can pass the test.

I got lucky during the 1992–1993 school year when I was able to return to the high school classroom after a two-year leave of absence as a preservice teacher-educator at Hofstra University. In my social studies classes, I had the opportunity to systematically experiment with the ideas, theories, and teaching methods discussed in my teacher education classes, especially the work of John Dewey, Paulo Freire, and Maxine Greene. Their work, and the work of some of the other people discussed in the next two sections, gave me a new appreciation for the value of educational theory in directing teaching practice. I include a brief introduction to their ideas in this book so that each new generation of social studies teachers does not have to reinvent every wheel.

Teaching Activity: Educational Theory

In *Experience and Education*, John Dewey (1938) wrote that, unless teachers base "educational plans and projects" on theories of how people learn, they are "at the mercy of every intellectual breeze that happens to blow" (51). In high school, we call these intellectual breezes the gimmick of the month—miracle cures that somehow fail to make much of a difference.

Add your voice to the discussion:
In your opinion and based on your experience, should social studies teachers study educational theory? When? Why?

HOW CAN WE TEACH DEMOCRACY?

In his November 19, 1863, address at the dedication of the Gettysburg National Cemetery, Abraham Lincoln defined democracy as "government of the people, by the people, for the people" (Stern, 1940: 786–87). John Dewey's progressive educational philosophy was concerned with the need to educate people for life in such a society. Key concepts for Dewey (1938) were experience, freedom, community, and "habits of mind." Dewey believed there was an "organic connection between education and experience" (25); that effective teachers are able to connect the subject matter to the existing experience of students and then expand and enrich their lives with new experiences.

According to Dewey, students learn from the full spectrum of their experiences in school, not just the specific thing they are studying in class. They learn from what they are studying, how they are studying, who they are studying with, and how they are treated. In racially segregated or academically tracked classes, students learn that some people are better than others. In teacher-centered classrooms, they learn that some people possess knowledge and others passively receive it. When teachers have total control over classrooms, even when they are benevolent or entertaining, students learn to accept authoritarianism. During his career, Dewey continually examined the experiences educators need to create for students so they become active participants in preserving and expanding government of, by, and for the people.

For Dewey, the exercise of freedom in democratic societies always involves education. He identifies freedom with "power to frame purposes" or achieve individual and social goals. This kind of freedom requires a probing, critical, disciplined "habit of mind." It includes intelligence, judgment, and self-control, qualities that students never acquire in classrooms where they are subject to external controls and are forced to remain silent. In progressive schools that use a Deweyan approach, students engage in long-term thematic group projects from which they learn to collectively solve problems, and classrooms become democratic communities where "things gain meaning by being used in a shared experience or joint action."

In the social studies, Harold Rugg became a leading advocate for Dewey's educational theories. Rugg (NSSE, 1923: 1–20) argued, "Not the learning of texts, but the solving of problems is what we need. . . . For the pupil to think, he [*sic*] first must be mentally blocked and thwarted until he is obsessed with a desire to clear up the matter; he must also have at hand data, the facts on all sides of the issue, before he can think constructively on it; and third, he must be practiced in deliberations on situations that are somewhat similar. . . . Only those who are trained through five, ten, twelve years of practice in deliberation will tend to use critical judgment about contemporary problems."

Traditionally, Dewey's ideas have been implemented in small, private elementary schools, where student populations tend to be academically and socially well prepared for school. Recently, however, under the leadership of Ted Sizer, the Coalition of Essential Schools (CES) has championed Deweyan principles in public secondary education. CES promotes smaller schools where students feel connected to a learning community and argues that, in terms of curriculum content, "less is more." Coalition schools encourage students to be active learners and researchers and teachers to be their co-learners and coaches. The most noted participants in the CES are the Central Park East Secondary Schools in New York City, where Deborah Meier (1995) and her colleagues were recognized for creating democratic classroom communities where working-class and poor, urban, and minority youth have achieved a high level of academic success. Can social studies teachers teach democracy? If Dewey is right, this can happen only in classrooms where students experience democracy.

Learning Activity: Decision Making in a Democratic Classroom

Sojourner Truth was an African American woman and a former slave who was active in the women's rights movement of the 1850s. Her participation was frequently challenged by White activists who did not want woman's suffrage associated with abolitionism in the public's mind. At the 1851 Akron, Ohio, women's rights convention, Sojourner Truth delivered one of the most famous speeches in U.S. history. Truth could neither read nor write; however, a report on her address and the audience's response was included by Frances Gage, president of the convention, in her reminiscences. In her report, Gage presented readers, as best as she could, with Sojourner Truth's accent, syntax, and grammar. Her version of the speech has been edited and re-edited numerous times over the years.

The first version that follows is by Frances Gage (Stanton, Anthony, and Gage, 1889: 116) and was published in *History of Woman Suffrage, Vol. 1*. The second version is adapted from an attempt to modify and modernize the language for use in a high school classroom (Millstein and Bodin, 1977: 116–17). The third version is from Diane Ravitch's *The American Reader: Words That Moved a Nation* (1990: 86–87). In the original Gage version, Sojourner Truth refers to herself and other African Americans as "niggers." Ravitch changed the word to Negroes. Other editors have substituted Blacks or Africans.

Which version should we use in our classes? If we use Gage's original text, how do we handle the painful impact of certain words on many people? Should we remain committed to historical accuracy? Should we follow Dewey's lead and involve students in making these decisions?

1. Frances Gage's version of Sojourner Truth's speech

"Wall, chilern, whar dar is so much racket dar must be somethin out o' kilter. I tink dat 'twixt de niggers of de Souf and de womin at de North, all talkin' 'bout rights, de white men will be in a fix pretty soon. But what's all dis here talkin' 'bout? . . . Den dey talks 'bout dis ting in de head; what dis dey call it? ['Intellect,' whispered someone near.] Dat's it, honey. What's dat got to do wid womin's rights or nigger's rights? If my cup won't hold but a pint and yourn holds a quart, wouldn't ye be mean not to let me have my little half-measure full?"

2. Edited version of Sojourner Truth's speech

"Well, children, where there is so much racket there must be something out of kilter. I think that between the niggers of the South and the women of the North, all talking about rights, the white men will be in a fix pretty soon. But what's all this here talking about? . . . Then they talk about this thing in the head; what do they call it? ['Intellect,' whispered someone near.] That's it, honey. What's that got to do with women's rights or nigger's rights? If my cup won't hold but a pint and yours holds a quart, wouldn't you be mean not to let me have my little half-measure full?"

3. Diane Ravitch version

"Well, children, where there is so much racket there must be something out of kilter. I think that 'twixt the Negroes of the South and the women of the North, all talking about rights, the white men will be in a fix pretty soon. But what's all this here talking about? . . . Then they talk about this thing in the head; what do they call it? ['Intellect,' someone whispers.] That's it, honey. What's that got to do with women's rights or Negro's rights? If my cup won't hold but a pint and yours holds a quart, wouldn't you be mean not to let me have my little half-measure full (20)?"

Think it over:

Which version of Sojourner Truth's speech would you prefer to use? Why?

It's your classroom:

1. Would you involve your students in deciding which version to use? Why?
2. If you decide to do so, how would you involve them?
3. What would you say and do if their opinions were divided along racial lines?

SHOULD TEACHERS ENCOURAGE STUDENTS TO WORK FOR SOCIAL CHANGE?

> "The tree of liberty must be refreshed from time to time, with the blood of patriots and tyrants. It is their natural manure."—Letter from Thomas Jefferson to Col. William S. Smith, 1787 (Feder, 1967: 45).

Thomas Jefferson believed that, in a democratic society, teachers do not really have a choice about encouraging students to work for social change. According to Jefferson, freedom and republican government rest on two basic principles: "the diffusion of knowledge among the people" (Seldes, 1966: 368) and the idea that "a little rebellion now and then is a good thing." (Feder, 1967: 45) Jefferson supported the right to rebel because he recognized that the world was constantly changing. The crucial question was not whether it would change but the direction of change. Education was essential so that ordinary citizens could participate in this process, defending and enhancing their liberties.

In the United States, there has frequently been a close connection between advocacy for mass public education and demands for expanding democracy, social equity, and political reform. For example, in the mid-19th century, Horace Mann championed public education because he believed that the success of the country depended on "intelligence and virtue in the masses of the people" (*The New York Times*, 1953: 29). He argued, "If we do not prepare children to become good citizens, . . . then our republic must go down to destruction."

John Dewey (1939) saw himself within this intellectual tradition. He believed that democratic movements for human liberation were necessary to achieve a fair distribution of political power and an "equitable system of human liberties." However, criticisms have been raised about limitations in Deweyan approaches to education, especially the way they are practiced in many elite private schools. Frequently, these schools are racially, ethnically, and economically segregated, and therefore efforts to develop classroom community ignore the spectrum of human difference and the continuing impact of society's attitudes about race, class, ethnicity, gender, social conflict, and inequality on both teachers and students. In addition, because of pressure on students to achieve high academic scores, teachers maintain an undemocratic level of control over the classroom. Paulo Freire addressed both of these issues; he calls on educators to aggressively challenge both injustice and unequal power arrangements in the classroom and society.

Paulo Freire was born in Recife in northeastern Brazil, where his ideas about education developed in response to military dictatorship, enormous social inequality, and widespread adult illiteracy. As a result, his primary pedagogical goal was to provide the world's poor and oppressed with educational experiences that make it possible for them to take control over their own lives. Freire (1970, 1995) shared Dewey's desire to stimulate students to become "agents of curiosity" in a "quest for . . . the 'why' of things" (1995: 105) and his belief that education provides possibility and hope for the future of society. Freire believes, however, that these can be achieved only when students are engaged in explicitly critiquing social injustice and actively organizing to challenge oppression.

For Freire, education is a process of continuous group discussion (dialogue) that enables people to acquire collective knowledge they can use to change society. The role of the teacher includes asking questions that help students identify problems facing their community (problem posing), working with students to discover ideas or create symbols (representations) that explain their life experiences (codification), and encouraging analysis of prior experiences and of society as the basis for new academic understanding and social action (conscientization) (Shor, 1987).

In a Deweyan classroom, the teacher is an expert who is responsible for organizing experiences so that students learn content, social and academic skills, and an appreciation for democratic living. Freire is concerned that this arrangement reproduces the unequal power relationships that exist in society. In a Freirean classroom, everyone has a recognized area of expertise that includes, but is not limited to, understanding and explaining his or her own life, and sharing this expertise becomes an essential element in the classroom curriculum. In these classrooms, teachers have their areas of expertise, but they are only one part of the community. The responsibility for organizing experiences and struggles for social change belongs to the entire community; as groups exercise this responsibility, they are empowered to take control over their lives.

Teaching Activity: Defining a Freirean Curriculum

Add your voice to the discussion:

1. Should students participate in defining the curriculum? Why or why not? To what extent?
2. In your opinion, do all people have an area of expertise that can be integrated into the curriculum? Explain your answer.

HOW CAN CLASSROOM TEACHERS EMPOWER STUDENTS?

I agree with Freire's concern that teachers address social inequality and the powerlessness experienced by many of our students. I also recognize that it is difficult to imagine secondary school social studies classrooms where teachers are responsible for covering specified subject matter organized directly on Freirean principles. Maxine Greene (1993a; 1993b; 1993c), an educational philosopher who advocates a "curriculum for human beings" integrating aspects of Freire, Dewey, and feminist thinking, offers ways for teachers to introduce Freire's pedagogical ideas into the classroom.

Greene believes that, to create democratic classrooms, teachers must learn to listen to student voices. Listening allows teachers to discover what students are thinking, what concerns them, and what has meaning to them. When teachers learn to listen, it is possible for them and students to collectively search for historical, literary, and artistic metaphors that make knowledge of the world accessible to us. In addition, the act of listening creates possibilities for human empowerment; it counters the marginalization experienced by students in school and in their lives, it introduces multiple perspectives and cultural diversity into the classroom, and it encourages students to take risks and contribute their social critiques to the classroom dialogue.

Greene's ideas are especially useful to social studies teachers. Just as historians discuss history as an ongoing process that extends from the past into the future, Greene sees individual and social development as processes that are "always in the making." For Greene, ideas, societies, and people are dynamic and always changing. She rejects the idea that there are universal and absolute truths and predetermined conclusions. According to Greene, learning is a search for "situated understanding" that places ideas and events in their social, historical, and cultural contexts.

Greene believes that the human mind provides us powerful tools for knowing ourselves and others. She encourages students to combine critical thinking with creative imagination in an effort to empathize with and understand the lives, minds, and consciousness of human beings from the past and of our contemporaries in the present. She sees the goal of learning as discovering new questions about ourselves and the world, and this leads her to examine events from different perspectives, to value the ideas of other people, and to champion democracy.

Learning Activity: Creative Imagination and Literature

Because of her continuous search for metaphors that illuminate meaning, Maxine Greene's interests are interdisciplinary. She examines the sciences, social sciences, art, and history, and argues that literature allows us to explore imagination with the least constraints, to ignore superficial detail, and to focus on the greater reality. In her work, she examines the ideas of fictional characters such as James Joyce's Stephen Dedalus, Albert Camus' Tarrou and Dr. Rieux, and the mother in Toni Morrison's *Beloved*.

As a high school teacher, I used Mark Twain's Huck Finn (1996), Okonkwo from Achebe's *Things Fall Apart* (1996), and the title character from Katherine Paterson's *Lyddie* (1991) in a similar way.

Try it yourself:

Select a character from a work of literature from the past. How do the ideas, experiences, and relationships of this character help you understand that society and era?

It's your classroom:

1. As a social studies teacher, do you believe these insights would be useful to students in your class? Why?
2. What characters from literature would you introduce to middle school students? High school students? Why?

HOW DO TEACHERS TRANSLATE EDUCATIONAL THEORY INTO SOCIAL STUDIES PRACTICE?

During the Great Depression, striking Harlan County, Kentucky, coal miners sang the song "Which Side Are You On?" (lyrics available on the web at http://www. geocities.com/Nashville/3448/whichsid. html). In a book he coauthored with Paulo Freire, Myles Horton (1990) of the Highlander School argued that educators, like the miners, cannot be neutral. He called neutrality "a code word for the existing system. It has nothing to do with anything but agreeing to what is and will always be. It was to me a refusal to oppose injustice or to take sides that are unpopular" (102).

James Banks (1991; 1993), an educational theorist whose focus is on the development of social studies curriculum, shares the ideas that "knowledge is not neutral," and that "an important purpose of knowledge construction is to help people improve society." Although Banks is a strong advocate of a multicultural approach to social studies, he argues that a "transformative" curriculum depends less on the content of what is taught than on the willingness of teachers to examine their own personal and cultural values and identities, to change the ways they organize classrooms and relate to students, and to actively commit themselves to social change.

The main ideas about education and society at the heart of the philosophies of Dewey, Freire, Greene, Horton, and Banks are that society is always changing; knowledge is not neutral—it either supports the status quo or a potential new direction for society; people learn primarily from what they experience; active citizens in a democratic society need to be critical and imaginative thinkers; and students learn to be active citizens by being active citizens. Assuming that we agree with these ideas, we are still left with these questions: How do we translate educational theory into social studies practice? What do these ideas look like in the classroom?

I know many excellent secondary school social studies teachers who work hard to connect to the ideas and lives of their students and who try to teach based on these understandings. None of them, including myself, however, has created a model transformative classroom. It may simply be that, although the educational goals discussed so far provide a vision of a particular kind of classroom, transformative education, like history, is part of a process that is never finished. This section concludes with examples from social studies classrooms where teachers and their students are engaged in struggles to build transformative learning communities.

Addressing Racism in Brooklyn, New York

As a middle school social studies teacher in Crown Heights, Brooklyn, and as an African American male, Don Murphy found that building a transformative classroom community meant he had to deal with the impact of racism on the lives of his African American, Caribbean, and Latino/a students. In an article in the New York City teachers' union newspaper, Murphy (1991) reported that his "students wanted to talk about racism. They needed to talk about it—they face it every day. They have little close interactions with white people. They can't walk into Kings Plaza Mall without being watched like criminals, or onto a subway car without white people moving away" (9a).

As a result of their experiences, many of Murphy's students expressed anti-White and anti-Jewish sentiments. As a teacher, his choices were to ignore their statements and continue with an academic examination of bias, moralize in class against prejudice, use his authority to silence students, or find ways that he and the class could examine their own biases as they analyzed the formation and continued existence of racism in our society. Murphy decided to make the active examination of racism the center of his class's social studies curriculum and the vehicle for creating a transformative classroom community.

In response to student bitterness during discussion of the enslavement of Africans, Murphy challenged them to "concoct a plan for enslaving whites," an idea they gradually rejected because of the kind of people they would become in such a slave society. After this activity, students became interested in examining beliefs that justified other forms of exploitation, including their own ideas about gender, sexual orientation, ethnic and religious groups, and themselves.

Eventually, the class studied Nazi anti-Semitism and the Holocaust in Europe. Murphy selected the topic because he wanted students to understand the oppression of other groups and because of tense relationships that existed between local African American and Hasidic Jewish communities. Students viewed documentaries, read and discussed *The Diary of Anne Frank*, and made posters that compared the Holocaust with the Middle Passage and the Nazis with the Ku Klux Klan. One young man wrote in his journal: "(I) started thinking of all the things I used to say, 'Heil Hitler' to the Jews and now I know what it feels like."

Murphy believes that combining "the opportunity to articulate and honor their personal experiences" with an open examination of racism in a variety of forms and settings helped his students develop empathy for the "suffering of others, and a universal, humanist perspective." This was a crucial step in the development of a transformative classroom community. Social studies made it possible to develop community while community enhanced the ability of students to learn social studies.

Creating Equality and Democracy in Portland, Oregon

William Bigelow (1988; 1990; Rethinking Schools, 1994) and Linda Christensen (2000) are social studies and English team teachers who taught together at Jefferson High School in Portland, Oregon. Linda and Bill attempted to systematically incorporate Freirean educational principles into their teaching practices and wrote about their classroom experiences on a regular basis for the educational newspaper *Rethinking Schools*.

Linda and Bill describe their classrooms "as a center of equality and democracy" where students are engaged in "an ongoing, if small, critique of the repressive social relations of the larger society" (Bigelow, 1990: 437). They use literature and history "as points of departure to explore themes in students' lives and then, in turn, use students' lives to explore history and our society today." Their goal is to have students become "social researchers, investigating their own lives." Among the history books they recommend are Howard Zinn's *A People's History of the United States: 1492–Present* (1999) and Ronald Takaki's *A Different Mirror* (1993).

Linda believes that it is a mistake for teachers to ignore the toll the outside world exacts on students. She begins the semester by having students interview each other to establish that their identities and questions are at the center of the curriculum. Readings are selected to explore the issues that students raise. One semester,

when Jefferson High School students were caught up in a storm of violence plaguing Portland, she had her class read *Thousand Pieces of Gold* by Ruthann Lum McCunn (1981). The novel includes an uprising by Chinese peasants who rampage through the countryside. Some of the outlawed peasants organize into bandit gangs in which they recreate relationships that were lost when their families were destroyed. As her students read about these Chinese rebels, they discussed conditions in their own communities. As they better understood their own lives, they began to recognize what was happening in the Chinese society they were studying.

Bill (Rethinking Schools, 1994: 158–59) frequently has his students become "textbook detectives." They learn about different interpretations of historical events and then examine standard textbooks to see how these events are presented. A major topic is the coverage of Christopher Columbus and descriptions of Native American people. Bill's goal is to have students question their assumptions about the past and examine why certain interpretations have become standard beliefs. To encourage student activism, Bill has his students present their findings in teach-ins for other classes in the school.

A valuable learning activity that both Bill and Linda (Christensen, 2000: 134) employ "to promote student empathy with other human beings" is the interior monologue. For an interior monologue, students imagine the thoughts of a character in history, literature, or life during an event that they are studying. Linda and Bill believe that this activity develops social imagination, which allows students to connect with the lives of people "with whom, on the surface, they may appear to have little in common." Students read their dialogues out loud in class, which allows the entire group to discuss their observations and arrive at new understandings about history.

One of the things I enjoy about Linda and Bill is their willingness to discuss the difficulties they have as secondary school teachers with a commitment to transformative education. They describe how they struggle with their students to build supportive and democratic learning communities, to become intellectually and emotionally aware of their own choices and prejudices as European Americans and middle-class professionals, and to be engaged social activists. They recognize how difficult it is to relinquish a teacher's control over the curriculum, their uncertainties when student decisions push classes into uncharted waters, and their concern that after all of their efforts, a cohesive classroom community might not emerge.

Learning Activity: The Intersection of Life and History

Try it yourself:
1. Interview someone about his or her life. Where does the person's life intersect with broader historical events? How has history shaped the person? How has he or she shaped history?
2. Select a character from a work of literature or from history. Describe a specific historical moment in which this person lived or participated. Write an interior monologue about his or her thoughts at this time.

Think it over:
Do you think these activities have validity in a social studies classroom? Why?

Defending Student Rights in Queens, New York

Michael Pezone (New Teachers Network) shares Linda Christensen's and Bill Bigelow's emphasis on creating classrooms where students are able to expose their ideas, feelings, and academic proficiencies in public without risking embarrassment or attack and being pressed into silence. Students in his classes at Law, Government and Community Service Magnet High School frequently write position papers on controversial issues and deliver them in class where they are discussed as the basis for social action.

During the fall 2001 semester, in response to the destruction of the World Trade Center, the New York City Board of Education required all public schools to lead students in the Pledge of Allegiance at the beginning of each school day and at all schoolwide assemblies and school events. Mike's students were confused about the law governing behavior during the flag salute and concerned with defending the first amendment rights of fellow students. They contacted the New York Civil Liberties Union to clarify legal issues and learned that participation was not required by law. They decided to monitor both the compliance with the directive's requirement that the Pledge of Allegiance be recited each day and the freedom of dissent. They also circulated a questionnaire in the school that asked students about their opinions on the issues, encouraged students to behave respectfully and responsibly during the pledge, informed them of their legal right not to participate, and asked them to report violations of the law. The results of the student survey and student comments were later distributed in the school's magazine.

Participating in Local Government

In my high school social studies classes, I have promoted transformative goals through direct student involvement in social action projects as part the State of New York's "Participation in Government" curriculum. In New York City, periodic budget crises, ongoing racial and ethnic tension, and the need for social programs in poor communities have provided numerous opportunities to encourage students to become active citizens. Class activities have included sponsoring student forums on controversial issues, preparing reports on school finances and presenting them as testimony at public hearings, writing position papers for publication in local newspapers, and organizing student and community support for a school-based public health clinic.

During each activity, social studies goals included making reasoned decisions based on an evaluation of existing evidence, researching issues and presenting written and graphic information, exploring the underlying ideas that shape our points of view, giving leadership by example to other students, and taking collective and individual responsibility for the success of programs.

Becoming Community Volunteers

Adeola Tella, Michael Maiglow, and Jennie Chacko of the New Teachers Network were middle school social studies teachers working in an inner-city community with students with serious academic problems. To promote student literacy and responsibility, they enlisted their students as multicultural literacy volunteer's to read with four-year-olds from a neighboring day care center.

When the project was introduced to the classes, some of the students insisted that "we should be paid to volunteer." However, each eventually decided to volunteer "to do something important," and 100 percent of the students returned signed permission slips allowing them to visit the preschool program. To prepare for their role, students studied international and American folk tales and practiced reading aloud to each other. They also rewrote some of the stories as plays and performed them wearing plastic masks and using giant puppets.

Adeola and Jennie report two student comments that underscore the importance of the project for their middle school students. Nearly every year when the project is introduced, one student will ask in surprise, "Why are you asking us? Do they know we aren't good students?" Later, after a visit to the day care center, an excited student will say, "This was special. They really looked up to us."

A number of members of the New Teachers Network have pursued similar goals through community improvement projects. Christina Agosti-Dircks has involved her classes in community cleanups and fund-raising for homeless families. Darren Luskoff's students assisted in a food kitchen while studying hunger and famine. Laurence Klein has middle school students read to the elderly. Each of these teachers reports these projects are particularly successful in integrating students with a broad spectrum of academic levels, including students with educational disabilities.

The Mifflin International School in Columbus, Ohio, has made student involvement in community projects an integral part of its thematic social studies curriculum (Crook, 1994). Seventh graders walk to raise money to combat hunger around the world, and eighth graders work in a community kitchen.

WHAT DOES A CLASSROOM BASED ON TRANSFORMATIVE PRINCIPLES LOOK LIKE?

Democratic classroom communities based on transformative principles are not easy to build, but they are essential if we want to engage students in wanting to learn social studies and to prepare them for active citizenship in democratic societies. Consider the following:

- One of my favorite African American spirituals is "Freedom Is a Constant Struggle" (lyrics available on the web at http://www.lib.virginia.edu/speccol/exhibits/music/lrg_html/FCS.html). Freedom is not something people achieve and then have forever; it is something that people continually work for and must always re-create. I look at a democratic classroom community in the same way. It is a long-term ongoing process of construction and reaffirmation. Democratic classroom communities are not finished products.
- In democratic classroom communities, students learn to respect themselves and each other. Communities provide students with emotional support so they can trust the group and take intellectual and social risks. For these communities to develop, teachers must play active roles. They must model what it means to develop a point of view and must

support a position with evidence and what it means to listen and learn from others.

- Student voice (written and oral expression of their ideas) is crucial to social studies learning for at least two reasons. Sharing ideas is the way that people, especially historians and social scientists, check their theories about the world. In social studies classrooms where teachers define their role as the transmitter of information, students never learn to evaluate ideas, create metaphors that express connection and understanding, share differences of opinion, arrive at consensus or respectful disagreement, experience intellectual and social decision making, or become critical and imaginative thinkers. In addition, social studies teachers cannot assume that students are making the intellectual connections that we make or that we would like them to make. If we do not learn to listen to our students, we cannot know what they are thinking and we cannot create experiences that help them examine their beliefs and discover new ideas.
- Academic knowledge by itself, even knowledge of social struggles against racial and gender prejudice, does not enable students to reconsider their basic ideas and values and the way they act toward others. Most students primarily learn from reflection on what they experience, not from what teachers say. Social studies curricula must provide experiences that enable students to discover the parallels between school learning and life.
- Teachers need to encourage student leaders who can engage their peers to take responsibility for community

learning and create new levels of understanding. Leadership and responsibility are crucial to community, citizenship, and social change.

- The type of activities discussed here can create conflict among students in the class, students and their teachers, and teachers in a school. Conflict and conflict resolution are inherent to the community process; they cannot be avoided and should not be ignored. They help us focus in on differences, make our ideas clear, and demonstrate that multiple perspectives are genuinely respected. Paulo Freire argues that "conflicts are the midwife of consciousness."

Of course, this chapter is based on my goals as an educator and activist, my experiences as a social studies teacher with a commitment to transformative education, and discussions with teachers, preservice teachers, and high school students. As you think about the type of social studies teacher you want to become, you may agree with all of these ideas, disagree with some of them, or reject the entire package. Whatever type you choose, however, you should consciously do so based on your educational goals and your ideas about history and the social sciences.

HOW ARE GOALS REFLECTED IN DIFFERENT APPROACHES TO TEACHING SOCIAL STUDIES?

Although models for social studies teaching vary depending on goals, teaching approaches do not fit into neat compartments. The transmission model is often associated with demands for increased classroom control, social assimilation, and political conservatism, but it also has supporters who want to ensure that academic knowledge is available to working-class and minority students who have traditionally been denied access to a rigorous education. Similarly, educators with points of view across the political spectrum can adapt the inquiry method and student-centered approaches. Who is included in a social studies curriculum, which documents and ideas are introduced for examination by teachers, and whether activities focus on individual achievement or group struggles can differ sharply from classroom to classroom.

Although advocates for a transformative approach to teaching social studies tend to support similar classroom goals and practices, there are no rules that guarantee consistency. Some transformative social studies teachers do minimal advanced planning because they want students to take the initiative in class. I prefer to overplan lessons. I bring extra documents and activities to class and decide what to include, shift to another day, or drop based on class discussion and student questions. Because this approach involves many options, I can teach a lesson five times and may never include the same materials.

WHAT ARE THE TRADITIONAL ACADEMIC GOALS IN SOCIAL STUDIES?

Careful advanced planning helps me integrate short- and long-term content, conceptual, and academic and social skills goals into my teaching. In secondary school social studies classes, students are expected to (1) develop their ability to examine and explain historical and social science concepts and understandings, (2) utilize information from history and the different social science disciplines, (3) develop the academic and analytical skills necessary to discover information on their own, make reasoned decisions, and present their ideas, and (4) enhance the social skills needed to share ideas and work with others.

Social Studies Concepts and Understandings

Social studies concepts are overall organizing categories. I compare them to the "folders" used to store computer files. They suggest relationships among people, ideas, and events that allow students to make meaning of, sort, and remember information. Understandings are main ideas about a topic that describe the relationships and patterns. For example, actions have consequences in both everyday life and in the historical arena. When a teenage woman consciously violates the family curfew, she anticipates conflict with her parents and decides that the risk is worth the reward. Similarly, a large country that invades a smaller neighbor understands that it risks provoking a response from that country's allies.

Several systems identify key social studies concepts and understandings. In general, these systems share the belief that students should reexamine basic ideas from different vantage points throughout a curriculum. The approach developed by

the National Council for the Social Studies (1994), calls concepts *thematic strands*. Aspects of at least one strand, preferably multiple strands, should be explored in each social studies lesson.

In another approach, the State of New York, Department of Education (1987) organizes its secondary school social studies program to teach and reinforce 15 overarching concepts in grades 7–12.

Within these general categories, both the NCSS and State of New York recommend that social studies students examine specific historical and social science relationships, patterns, and conclusions.

A problem with both the NCSS and the State of New York strategies is that they present social studies concepts as neutral principles that are independent of broader historical explanations or theories. In a social studies curriculum that encourages students to view the world through a critical lens, other basic concepts need to be included. For example, individuals and societies are not just interdependent; relationships are often exploitative. Secondary school students need to examine concepts such as injustice, racism, and imperialism and to decide when they are operating. Although continuity and change are significant concepts, students also need to examine different theories about change and to compare concepts including progress, reform, reaction, and revolution.

NCSS Thematic Strands

The 10 NCSS thematic strands are as follows (available on the web at http://www.ncss.org/standards/stitle.html):

Culture: Ways that human groups learn, create, and adapt to meet their fundamental needs and beliefs they develop to explain the world.

Time, Continuity, and Change: Ways that human groups locate themselves historically.

People, Places, and Environments: The influence of geography on human cultures and history.

Individual Development and Identity: Relationships between the ways that people perceive themselves and their membership in social groups.

Continued

Individuals, Groups, and Institutions: Roles played by social institutions such as schools and families in a society and their impact on individuals and groups.

Power, Authority, and Governance: Ways that individuals and societies make decisions about rights, rules, relationships, and priorities.

Production, Distribution, and Consumption: Ways that individuals and societies make decisions about the things people need to survive and how they will be provided.

Science, Technology, and Society: Methods and tools used by people to produce and distribute what they need and want within an economic system.

Global Connections: The increasingly important and diverse relationships between societies.

Civic Ideals and Practices: The relationship between the expressed beliefs of a society and the implementation of these beliefs in actual practice.

New York State Social Studies Concepts

The 15 New York State concepts follow:

Change: The basic alterations in things, events, and ideas over time.

Choice: The ability of people and societies to continually decide among alternatives.

Citizenship: Membership in comminutes that influence people's behavior and provide them with both rights and responsibilities.

Culture: Ways that human groups learn, create, and adapt, to meet their fundamental needs and beliefs that they develop to explain the world.

Diversity: Different approaches that people and societies develop to address similar human concerns.

Empathy: Understanding diverse people and societies by identifying similarities between aspects of your own life and the experience, behavior, and responses of others.

Environment: Natural and humanmade elements in the world around us.

Identity: Definition of yourself as an individual who is a member of different social groups.

Interdependence: The reliance by people in a society, or by societies, on each other for mutually beneficial interactions.

Human Rights: Inalienable rights that exist prior to and independently of political systems and nation-states.

Justice: The idea that the citizens of a nation-state are entitled to participation in its political system, equitable laws that are administered without bias, and protection of their basic human rights.

Political System: The ways that groups of people make and implement decisions in a nation-state or a subdivision.

Power: The ability to influence or determine decisions in a society.

Scarcity: The conflict between unlimited human needs and wants and limited natural and human resources within an economic system.

Technology: Methods and tools used by people to produce and distribute what they need and want within an economic system.

NCSS Thematic Strand on Culture

The NCSS thematic strand on culture includes the following understandings:

Human cultures are similar. They all include systems of beliefs, knowledge, values, and traditions that influence individual and group behavior.

Each human culture is unique because people view the world from different vantage points.

Cultures are dynamic. They change to accommodate new beliefs, ideas, and conditions.

Religious beliefs and political ideals influence other aspects of a culture.

Language is an important ingredient for expressing cultural values and practices.

Continued

> Cultures change through adaptation to new environmental and social conditions, assimilation of group members into other cultures, diffusion of cultural practices through cross-cultural interaction, and cultural dissonance between different groups of people.

Teaching Activity: Concepts, Understandings, and Controversies

Translating broad concepts into specific content understandings and lesson plans introduces controversy into social studies curricula. Examine the example that follows.

- *Concept: economic system.* The decision-making process related to and the production and distribution of the goods and services that people in a society need to survive and/or prosper.
- *Understanding.* In a managed capitalist economy such as the United States, a drop in the official unemployment rate below approximately 6 percent has led to increased inflation, a decline in the value of money, and decreased confidence in political leaders.
- *Controversies.* Is unemployment a result of uncontrollable market forces or conscious economic policies that benefit business and people with secure jobs at the expense of a significant minority of the population? Is it fair to pursue economic policies including cutting government budgets for social service programs and tightening credit, which disproportionately injure the poor and members of racial and ethnic minorities?
- *Lesson design.* Examine a graph showing the relationship between inflation and unemployment, a statement by the head of the Federal Reserve system explaining a decision to raise interest rates, and a political cartoon showing the president calling on poor African American children to become "inflation fighters."

Try it yourself:

1. List five understandings that you think high school students should learn about the U.S. economic system.
2. Why do you consider these understandings important?
3. How would you introduce these understandings into lessons?
4. What controversies are related to at least one of these understandings?

Academic and Social Skills

The term *social studies skills* covers a broad range of classroom activities and goals. For example, National History Standards (discussed in Chapter 3) focus on five historical thinking skills that "students should be able to do to demonstrate their understandings and to apply their knowledge in productive ways. . . . These thinking skills are the process of active learning" (National Center for History in the Schools, 1994: 7). They include chronological thinking, historical comprehension, historical analysis and interpretation, historical research, and historical issue analysis and decision making. The National Standards for Civics and Government describe similar academic capacities but identify them as intellectual and participatory skills. According to these standards, students should be able to acquire, describe, explain, and evaluate information, arrive at and defend conclusions that are based on evidence, and take action based on their conclusions (Center for Civic Education, 1994).

In its Curriculum Standards for Social Studies, the NCSS (1994: 148–49) offers a comprehensive list of "essential skills for social studies." Skills for acquiring information are divided into reading, study, research, and technical skills, and each of these sections has numerous subdivisions. For example, reading skills include comprehension, vocabulary, and rate of reading, and comprehension is redivided into 12 distinct activities that students should be able to perform (e.g., "use picture clues and picture captions to aid comprehension"). Other broad skill categories include organizing and using information (thinking, decision making, and metacognitive skills), interpersonal relationships (personal and group interaction skills), and social and political participation. As a demonstration of their social and political participation skills, secondary school students are expected to be able to (1) keep informed on issues that affect society, (2) identify situations in which social action is required, (3) work individually or with others to decide on an appropriate course of action, (4) work to influence those in positions of social power to strive for extensions of freedom, social justice, and human rights, and (5) accept and fulfill social responsibili-ties associated with citizenship in a free society.

All of these approaches argue that content and conceptual learning in social studies does not take place in isolation. Students learn about history, government, and society; to really learn about them, they must develop literacy, numeracy, and oral and written communication skills; analytical abilities; and the capacity to work independently and with others. Social studies students need skills for (1) getting information: observing, listening, reading, researching, and measuring, (2) using information: thinking, evaluating, organizing, questioning, creating, and evaluating hypotheses, (3) expressing information and ideas: writing, explaining, and discussing, and (4) developing interpersonal and group relations: cooperating, sharing, empathizing, democratic community building, and decision making.

It is important to remember that developing academic and social skills requires planned instruction by the teacher and considerable practice by the students. Skills must be integrated into specific lessons and carefully and systematically woven throughout a social studies curriculum.

Teaching Activities: Including Academic Skills in Social Studies Lessons

Literacy and numeracy are basic skills in all academic subjects. In social studies, students need to use language and numbers to acquire and present information. Individual and team activities can be integrated into most lessons.

Mathematical skills:
1. What is the title of the graph in Fig. 2.1?
2. What year is this information from?
3. What percentage does the entire circle represent?
4. Which country is the largest producer of oil?
5. What percentage of world production comes from that country?
6. Which countries are members of OPEC?
7. What percentage of world oil production comes from OPEC nations?
8. In your opinion, how can decisions made by OPEC affect other countries?

Writing skills:
Use pictures of artwork from different eras to encourage students to write. Students write brief essays describing pictures, explaining what they thought an artist was trying to portray, and

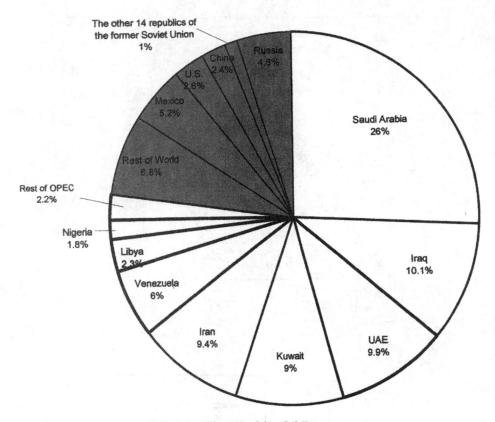

FIG. 2.1   The World's Oil Reserves.
From *Oil and Gas Journal*, December 30, 1991.

discussing what the pictures illustrated about an historical period. Images of many famous paintings are available on the web at WebMuseum, Paris (http://www.ibiblio.org/wm/paint).

Map skills:
1. What year is it in the map in Fig 2.2?
2. What section of the current United States is shown in Fig. 2.2?
3. Use the compass to figure out the direction a person travels going from Boston, Massachusetts, to Albany, New York.
4. In what direction does the Hudson River flow?
5. Use the map key to estimate the distance from New York, New York to Richmond, Virginia.
6. In your opinion, why are most of the cities in the British colonies in North America near the Atlantic Ocean?

Teaching Activity: Context, Content or Skills

Add your voice to the discussion:
Do you think social studies teachers should incorporate basic mathematical and literacy skills in social studies lessons? Why?

Think it over:
Are you comfortable teaching basic mathematical and literacy skills? How would you prepare yourself to teach them?

It's your classroom:
Select one of the two activities described here. How would you integrate this activity into a lesson?

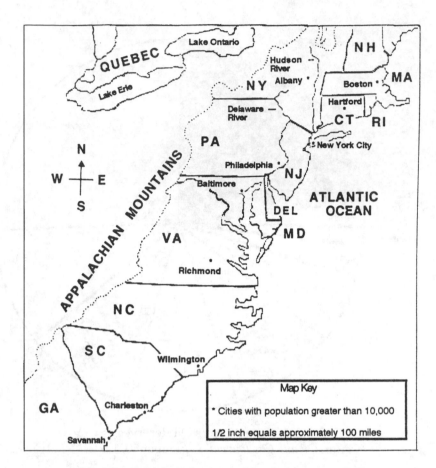

FIG. 2.2   British Colonies in North America, 1770.

HOW DO TEACHERS INTEGRATE ACADEMIC GOALS INTO CLASSROOM PRACTICE?

One of the most successful examples of integrating social studies concepts, understandings, and academic and social skills into classroom practice that I have been involved with was a group project with elementary school children in the after-school program at the MLE Learning Center in Brooklyn. The group and its teacher used a traditional African American folktale, "The People Could Fly" (from a collection of folktales, *The People Could Fly*, "retold" by Virginia Hamilton, 1985), to learn about the desire of people for freedom. In the story, enslaved Africans are working in a cotton field in the American south. When the master and overseer whip a young mother who is too tired to continue working, an old man tells her magic words so that she can fly away to Africa.

After reading the folktale, the group decided to rewrite it as a play and perform it for the rest of the school. It was an interracial group of young people, and an important part of the project was the discussion of how to cast the roles in the play. Members discussed how the roles were related to each other and decided not to use race as a criteria for casting because "that's not the way we are at the Learning Center."

Since seeing their performance and discussing it with them, I have had teams of students at different grade levels rewrite and perform this story and others from the same collection. I always have them discuss how they want to cast the play. Teams have made different decisions; one even made giant puppets to play the master and overseer while students played "the people who could fly." The discussion of casting has always made possible discussion of student views on slavery, oppression, and freedom, as well as their feelings about race relations in their schools and our contemporary society.

Example: Seventh-Grade Lesson Outline for "The People Could Fly"

- *Lesson aim*: How did African Americans express their desire for freedom?
- *Concepts*: Freedom, slavery, culture, racism, justice.
- *Content*: Learn about the song "Go Down Moses," the story "The People Could Fly," the conditions for enslaved Africans on cotton plantations in the American South, and the religion of enslaved Africans, and their efforts to build community.
- *Academic skills (class)*: Analyze a reading passage. Discuss meaning of a play. Discuss casting and racism. Write a story about freedom.
- *Social skills (group)*: Work together to create a production. Arrive at consensus decision about casting. Present production and decision.
- *Social skills (class)*: Participate as an audience and in discussion. Share writing.
- *Understandings/Main ideas*: Throughout human history, people have found ways to express their desire for freedom. Enslaved African Americans (slavery) used stories, songs, and religious practices (culture) to express their desire for freedom. Although racial tension continues in our society today, overt discrimination (racism) is both illegal and considered unacceptable (justice).
- *Activities*:
  1. Read and discuss the song "Go Down Moses" (lyrics available on the web at http://www.acronet.net/~robokopp/usa/gomoses.htm)
  2. Have the student cooperative learning team perform "The People Could Fly."
  3. Initiate class discussion(s) of the play, casting decisions, racism, and freedom.
  4. Write a story that explains why freedom is important to you.

Teaching Activity: Including Goals and Understandings

Think it over:
In your opinion, is it necessary to include goals and understandings in a lesson outline? Explain the reasons for your answer.

Try it yourself:
Take a story from a folktale collection and rewrite it as a play. What concepts and understandings could you teach using this folktale?

It's your classroom:
Would you use the lesson outline presented here as is, modify it, or discard it? Explain the reasons for your answer.

WHAT ARE THE STATE STANDARDS?

As you have moved through your teacher certification program, you quickly discovered that everybody in the United States (the media, politicians, parents, and teachers) is worried about higher standards and the assessment of student learning. It seems as though every educational organization has its own published list of what children should know and every political unit (city, county, or state) has its own standardized tests that students are expected to pass, but there is very little public discussion of exactly what we mean by *standards*. Most experienced social studies teachers I know respond to the call for higher standards by saying that this is the same thing we always do.

I think the general public finds the call for higher standards confusing because the word means different things in different contexts. In track and field, the *standard* is the record performance that other athletes try to surpass. In baseball, it is the Yankees with a century of accomplishment. In basketball and golf, it is identified with one player, Michael Jordan or Tiger Woods, but everybody cannot be like Mike, Tiger, or the Yankees, and that is the problem with using the top performer as a measure or standard.

In education, *standards* can best be described as goals, the things we hope all students will achieve, the things we plan for them to achieve. Achieving standards is not a competition. In theory, in a well-run classroom with effective teaching strategies, every student should be able to obtain the goals.

Most state departments of education now publish general and subject-related learning standards on the web. The State of New York, where I work, offers elementary, intermediate, and commencement (high school graduation) standards in each subject area, but not unit or lesson plans. Teachers, departments, schools, and districts are expected to develop their own strategies for achieving the standards. Student achievement and the success of social studies programs are measured by comprehensive tests administered in 5th, 8th, 10th, and 11th grades.

Links to social studies curriculum, standards, and assessments for many of the states and for major national organizations are available on the web at http://www.indiana.edu/~ssdc/stand.htm. Most open with a statement of purpose defining the goals for social studies education. The introduction to the K–12 social studies quality core curriculum in the State of Georgia (http://www.glc.k12.ga.us/qstd-int/ancill/sstudies/in-ss.htm) identifies the "primary purpose of Social Studies education" as helping students to become "productive and responsible citizens." To achieve this goal, "The Social Studies curriculum enables students to develop the ability to make informed decisions that balance concern for individual interests and the public good in a culturally diverse and interdependent world." The three principal elements of Georgia's social studies standards are "knowledge (what students need to know about various social sciences and related disciplines), skills (what students should be able to do with acquired knowledge and skills), and values." The social studies standards then offer teachers a matrix that correlates the content, concepts, skills, and values to be taught at different grade levels.

State department of education social studies standards around the country tend to be organized around two models. One model, thematic strands, similar to those produced by the NCSS (available on the web at http://www.socialstudies.org/

standards), focus on broad concepts. Content is primarily offered to provide examples of what should be taught in different classes. The other model, content-based approaches to standards, similar to those developed by the National Council for History in the Schools (available on the web at http://www.sscnet.ucla.edu/nchs/), which generally provides lists of information and definitions of terms, grouped either chronologically or thematically, that students should master at different grade levels. These models have a broad area of overlap, and both approaches expect students to develop appropriate academic skills. Published standards, whether offered by state departments of education or national social studies organizations, vary widely as to the amount of sample lessons, activities, and assessments they provide to teachers. I think it is useful to look more closely at an example of each of these approaches to standards at greater depth. While I prefer the thematic approach, standards that I have examined offer a teacher enough leeway that I believe I could be comfortable adapting my style of teaching to the requirements of either set of standards.

The State of Michigan's social studies standards are an example of a primarily thematic or conceptual approach. Michigan's social studies curriculum is "designed so that students meet 25 standards that are indicators of responsible citizenship. These standards, expressed as attributes we envision for our graduates, are the intended results of students' experience with the curriculum. Students make continuous progress toward meeting the standards at each level of schooling. All of the standards are pursued at every grade level of the curriculum from kindergarten to graduation. Although the standards refer to areas of knowledge and skill that no one ever masters completely in a total sense, benchmarks are established for each to designate clearly what students are expected to know and be able to do" at different grade levels.

Strands I–IV focus on different content areas (history, geography, economics, government). Strand V and VI address skill acquisition (inquiry, information processing, research, and the communication of ideas), and Strand VII emphasizes the values of citizenship in a democratic society.

MICHIGAN OVERVIEW OF SOCIAL STUDIES CONTENT STRANDS

(http://www.cdp.mde.state.mi.us/MCF/ContentStandards/SocialStudies/default.html)

Strand I. Historical Perspective

Students use knowledge of the past to construct a meaningful understanding of our diverse cultural heritage and to inform their civic judgments. A rich historical perspective begins with knowledge of significant events, ideas, and actors from the past. That knowledge encompasses both our commonalities and our diversity exemplified by race, ethnicity, social and economic status, gender, region, politics, and religion. Meaningful understanding of the past involves the integration of historical knowledge and thinking skills. Neither historical knowledge nor thinking develops independently of the other. If our decisions in contemporary life are to be guided by knowledge of the past, we must learn to engage in historical reasoning, to think through cause-effect relationships, to reach sound historical interpretations, and to conduct historical inquiries. Over time and in varying contexts, students develop an increasingly sophisticated historical perspective by drawing upon the following fields of historical thinking.

Continued

Standard I.I Time and Chronology

All students will sequence chronologically the following eras of American History and key events within these eras in order to examine relationships and to explain cause and effect: The Meeting of Three Worlds (beginnings to 1620); Colonization and Settlement (1585–1763); Revolution and the New Nation (1754–1815); Expansion and Reform (1801–1861); Civil War and Reconstruction (1850–1877); The Development of the Industrial United States (1870–1900); The Emergence of Modern America (1890–1930); The Great Depression and World War II (1929–1945); Post War United States (1945–1970); and Contemporary United States (1968–present). Chronological thinking is at the very heart of historical reasoning. Without a clear sense of historical time we are bound to see events as one great tangled mess. Events must be sequenced in time in order to examine relationships among them or to explain cause and effect.

Standard I.2 Comprehending the Past

All students will understand narratives about major eras of American and world history by identifying the people involved, describing the setting, and sequencing the events. Reading accounts of human events with understanding requires recognition of chronological sequence—the beginning, middle, and end of a story. Comprehension also requires identification of the characters involved, the situation or setting in which the narrative takes place, and the sequence of events through which the story unfolds, including the initiating event(s) and the results.

Standard I.3 Analyzing and Interpreting the Past

All students will reconstruct the past by comparing interpretations written by others from a variety of perspectives and creating narratives from evidence. History is not a succession of facts marching to a settled conclusion. Written history is a human construction and conclusions about the past are tentative and arguable. Documents, eyewitness accounts, letters, diaries, artifacts, photos, historical sites, and other fragments of the past are subject to analysis and interpretation. Credible reconstruction of the past draws on a variety of records and compares interpretations that reveal more than one perspective on events. One can engage in "doing history" by assessing historical narratives written by others or by creating a narrative from evidence that has been compiled, analyzed, and interpreted.

Standard I.4 Judging Decisions from the Past

All students will evaluate key decisions made at critical turning points in history by assessing their implications and long-term consequences. At critical turning points in history, we sometimes encounter key decisions that were made at the time. By entering personally into such moments, we can confront important issues of an era. When revisiting these issues, we can analyze the interests and values held by those caught up in the situation, consider alternative choices and their consequences, assess the ethical implications of possible decisions, and evaluate the decision made in light of its long-term consequences revealed in the historical record.

A *Historical Perspective* includes the ability to sequence chronologically the eras of American history and key events within these eras in order to examine relationships and to explain cause and effect; constructing and interpreting timelines of people and events in the history of Michigan and the United States; characterizing eras in United States history; comparing interpretations written by others from a variety of perspectives and creating narratives from evidence; using primary and secondary records; challenge arguments of historical inevitability by formulating examples of how different choices could have led to different consequences; and selecting contemporary problems in the world and composing historical narratives that explain their antecedents.

Michigan's Social Studies Strand II, the *Geographic Perspective*, has five standards that explore the following themes: Diversity of People, Places, and Cultures; Human/Environment Interaction; Location, Movement, and Connections; Regions, Patterns, and Processes; and Global Issues and Events. Strand III, the *Civic Perspective*, is designed to make it possible for students to "use knowledge of American government and politics to make informed decisions about governing their communities." Five standards explore the purposes of government; the ideals of American democracy; democracy in action, including decision making, consensus building, and conflict resolution; the functioning of American government and politics; and the role of the American government in world affairs. In Strand IV, the *Economic Perspective*, students acquire knowledge of the production, distribution, and consumption of goods and services to make personal and societal decisions about the use of scarce resources. Standards focus attention on individual, household, and business choices; the government's role in the economy; economic systems; trade; and development.

Strands V and VI focus on the acquisition of social studies–related academic skills. Under the Inquiry strand, students learn to "use methods of social science investigation to answer questions about society." This component includes development of information-processing skills, including learning to "acquire information from books, maps, newspapers, data sets, and other sources, organize and present the information in maps, graphs, charts, and time lines, interpret the meaning and significance of information, and use a variety of electronic technologies to assist in accessing and managing information." Students also learn to "conduct investigations by formulating a clear statement of a question, gathering and organizing information from a variety of sources, analyzing and interpreting information, formulating and testing hypotheses, reporting results both orally and in writing, and making use of appropriate technology." Under the Public Discourse and Decision Making strand, students learn to "analyze public issues and construct and express thoughtful positions on these issues." This component includes the ability to identify and analyze an issue and to participate in group discussion as well as competence in written persuasion. The final social studies strand is Citizen Involvement, which requires that students "act constructively to further the public good" and includes "responsible personal conduct."

The State of New Mexico's Curriculum Framework in Social Studies, which takes a more content-based approach, is actually adapted from the Massachusetts State Department of Education's History and Social Science Curriculum Framework. It provides Social Studies Content Standards, Benchmarks, and Performance Standards that "describe the disciplinary content and skills students should learn at specific grade levels" and "serve as the basis for statewide assessment of student learning."

New Mexico's Social Studies Content Standards, Benchmarks, and Performance Standards are organized within a spiraling framework so that skills and course content at each grade level increase in complexity and important topics, texts, and documents are continually reexamined. Content Standard 1 is history. Under this standard, students are expected "to identify important people and events in order to analyze significant patterns, relationships, themes, ideas, beliefs, and turning points in New Mexico, United States, and world history in order to understand the complexity of the human experience."

In seventh grade, students compare and contrast the contributions of the civilizations of the Western Hemisphere (e.g., Aztecs, Mayas, Toltecs, Mound Builders) with the early civilizations of the Eastern Hemisphere (e.g., Sumerians, Babylonians, Hebrews, Egyptians) and their impact upon societies; describe the characteristics of other indigenous peoples that had an affect on New Mexico's development; explain the significance of trails and trade routes within the region; describe how important individuals, groups, and events impacted the development of New Mexico from 16th century to the present (e.g., Don Juan de Oñate, Don Diego de Vargas, Pueblo Revolt, Popé, 1837 Revolt, 1848 Rebellion, Treaty of Guadalupe Hildago, William Becknell and the Santa Fe Trail, Buffalo Soldiers, Lincoln County War, Navajo Long Walk, Theodore Roosevelt and the Rough Riders, Robert Goddard, J. Robert Oppenhiemer, Smokey Bear, Dennis Chavez, Manuel Lujan, Manhattan Project, Harrison Schmitt, Albuquerque International Balloon Fiesta); explain how New Mexicans have adapted to their physical environments to meet their needs over time; and explain the impact of New Mexico on the development of the American West up to the present.

In eighth grade, students compare and contrast the settlement patterns of the American Southwest with those in other regions of the United States, analyze New Mexico's role and impact on the outcome of the Civil War, explain the role New Mexico played in the U.S. participation in the Spanish American War, and analyze how people and events of New Mexico have influenced U.S. and world history since statehood.

In 9th through 12th grades, students compare and contrast the relationships over time of Native American tribes in New Mexico with other cultures; analyze the geographic, economic, social, and political factors of New Mexico that impacted U.S. and world history; analyze the role and impact of New Mexico and New Mexicans in World War II; analyze the impact of the arts, sciences, and technology of New Mexico since World War II; and explain how the state's history represents a framework of knowledge and skills within which to understand the complexity of the human experience. Similar lists of topics, events, and people are provided for each grade level for U.S. and world history.

**NEW MEXICO CURRICULUM FRAMEWORK
SOCIAL STUDIES GUIDING PRINCIPLES**

(http://www.sde.state.nm.us/resources/index.html)

A list of what high school students in New Mexico are expected to learn about U.S. history follows.

The impact and changes that Reconstruction had on the historical, political, and social developments of the United States.

The transformation of the U.S. economy and the changing social and political conditions in the United States in response to the Industrial Revolution, including innovations in technology, evolution of marketing techniques, changes to the standard of living, the rise of consumer culture, the rise of business leaders (e.g., John D. Rockefeller, Andrew Carnegie) and their companies as major forces in America, development of monopolies and their impact on economic and political policies (e.g., laissez-faire economics, trusts, trust busting),

Continued

the growth of cities (e.g., influx of immigrants, rural-to-urban migrations, racial and ethnic conflicts that resulted), efforts of workers to improve working conditions (e.g., organizing labor unions, strikes, strike breakers), the rise and effect of reform movements (e.g., Populists, William Jennings Bryan, Jane Addams, muckrakers), the conservation of natural resources (e.g., the Grand Canyon; Yellowstone; Anasazi ruins at Mesa Verde, Colorado; National Reclamation Act of 1902), and progressive reforms (e.g., the national income tax, direct election of senators, women's suffrage, prohibition).

The expanding role of the United States in the world during the late 19th and 20th centuries including causes for a change in foreign policy from isolationism to interventionism, causes and consequences of the Spanish American War, expanding influence in the Western Hemisphere (e.g., the Panama Canal, addition of the Roosevelt Corollary to the Monroe Doctrine, the "Big Stick" policy, "Dollar Diplomacy"), events that led to U.S. involvement in World War I, U.S. rationale for entry into World War I and impact on military process, public opinion and policy, U.S. mobilization in World War I (e.g., its impact on politics, economics, and society), the U.S. impact on the outcome of World War I, and the U.S. role in settling the peace (e.g., Woodrow Wilson, Treaty of Versailles, League of Nations, Senator Henry Cabot Lodge, Sr.).

The major political, economic, and social developments that occurred between World War I and World War II including social liberation and conservative reaction during the 1920s (e.g., flappers, prohibition, the Scopes trial, Red Scare), causes of the Great Depression (e.g., overproduction, underconsumption, credit structure), the rise of youth culture in the "Jazz Age," the development of mass/popular culture (e.g., rise of radio, movies, professional sports, popular literature), human and natural crises of the Great Depression (e.g., unemployment, food lines, the Dust Bowl, western migration of Midwest farmers), changes in policies, role of government, and issues that emerged from the New Deal (e.g., the WPA, Social Security, challenges to the Supreme Court), and the impact of changing demographics on traditional communities and social structures.

The role of the United States in World War II including reasons the United States moved from a policy of isolationism to involvement after the bombing of Pearl Harbor, events on the home front to support the war effort (e.g., war bond drives, mobilization of the war industry, women and minorities in the workforce), and major turning points in the war (e.g., the Battle of Midway, D-Day Invasion, dropping of atomic bombs on Japan).

The development of voting and civil rights for all groups in the United States following Reconstruction including the intent and impact of the 13th, 14th, and 15th Amendments to the Constitution; segregation as enforced by Jim Crow laws following Reconstruction; key court cases (e.g., *Plessy v. Ferguson, Brown v. Board of Education of Topeka, Roe v. Wade*); roles of and methods used by civil rights advocates (e.g., Martin Luther King, Jr., Malcolm X, Rosa Parks, Russell Means, César Chávez); the passage and effect of the voting rights legislation on minorities (e.g., 19th Amendment, role of Arizona Supreme Court decision on Native Americans and their disenfranchisement under Arizona constitution and subsequent changes made in other state constitutions regarding their voting rights [New Mexico 1962], 1964 Civil Rights Act, Voting Act of 1965, 24th Amendment); the impact and reaction to the efforts to pass the Equal Rights Amendment; and the rise of Black Power, Brown Power, the American Indian Movement, and the United Farm Workers.

The impact of World War II and the Cold War on U.S. foreign and domestic policy including the origins, dynamics, and consequences of the Cold War tensions between the United States and the Soviet Union; the new role of the United States as a world leader (e.g., Marshall Plan, NATO); the need for and establishment and support of the United Nations; the implementation of the foreign policy of containment, including the Truman Doctrine and Red Scare (e.g., McCarthyism, House Un-American Activities Committee, nuclear weapons, arms race); external confrontations with communism (e.g., the Berlin Blockade, Berlin Wall, Bay of Pigs, Cuban Missile Crisis, Korea, Vietnam); Sputnik and the space race; images of 1950s affluent society; political protests of Vietnam Conflict (War); and counterculture in the 1960s.

Continued

The impact of the post-Cold War Era on U.S. foreign policy including the role of the United States in supporting democracy in Eastern Europe following the collapse of the Berlin Wall, new allegiances in defining the new world order, and the role of technology in the information age.

The way U.S. history represents a framework of knowledge and skills within which to understand the complexity of the human experience including perspectives that have shaped the structures of historical knowledge and ways historians study the past and explain connections made between the past and the present and their impact.

Essay 1: What We Should Teach*

The graduate section of the social studies methods class at Hofstra University has 31 students who plan to become middle school or high school social studies teachers. The size of the class can make discussion difficult; this is a group of people who like to talk, but I still have them sit in something that approximates a circle. As students enter the room, I hand them a three-question "surprise quiz." The first question is multiple choice. The second and third questions require brief written responses.

After students complete the quiz, I break the class into groups of four designed so there are students who made different choices in each group. I give the groups very general instructions:

Examine your points of agreement and disagreement. Try to resolve your differences.

While the students deliberate, I join one group at a time. One issue that keeps reappearing is whether the land should be considered America before it was named America. This generally leads students to discuss the question, What is America? I find myself asking roughly the same questions in each group. Did the voyage of Columbus bring about such a major change that there is basic discontinuity between what existed before and after the voyage? Can we agree on a set of criteria that we can use to evaluate the Native American's contribution to American history?

Classroom Activity: When Does American History Begin?

1. In What year(s) did American history begin?
   - 40,000–20,000 B.C.: People first migrate from Asia across the Bering land bridge.
   - 985–1000 A.D.: Vikings from Scandinavia explore the western North Atlantic.
   - 1492 A.D.: The first voyage of Christopher Columbus occurs.
   - 1565 A.D.: Spanish settlement is established at St. Augustine in Florida.
   - 1607 A.D.: The first permanent British settlement is made at Jamestown, Virginia.
   - 1619 A.D.: The first enslaved Africans are brought to Jamestown.
   - 1620 A.D.: Pilgrims arrive in what will become Massachusetts.
   - 1776–1783 A.D.: The Declaration of Independence is followed by a successful war for separation.
   - 1787–1789 A.D.: The Constitution is written and a new government is formed.
   - 1861–1865 A.D.: The U.S. Civil War is fought.
     Another date/event _____
2. Why do you select this event?
3. Would your answer be different if the question had asked, What year(s) does U.S. history begin? Why?

---

*Names of participants are changed in this essay.

Try it yourself:
Which date would you select? Why?

Add your voice to the discussion:
Do you believe that a question such as this has a "right answer?" Why?

It's your classroom:
1. How could you use this activity to promote discussion in a high school classroom? Why?
2. How would you resolve disagreements among students? Why?

After reassembling as a full class, groups report on their discussions. The first group agreed on the migration of nomadic peoples from Asia as the start of American history. One group member explains, "We shouldn't just define things in European terms. People were here before the arrival of the Europeans. It is important for students to know about their cultures." A student from another group thinks that including the native peoples is carrying the idea of American history to an illogical extreme. He counters, "Why not just start with the continent's geological formation? It had existence independent of people."

This comment opens up a wide-ranging discussion. Donald argues that the voyage of Columbus is the single most important event setting off conquest, migration, and change. It defines what comes after it. Another student adds that the idea of America does not even exist until it is named by a German mapmaker based on the accounts of Vespucci and Columbus.

A woman in the class interrupts. She says she was uncertain about her answer, but "in a real sense, what we know of as America doesn't start until the Declaration of Independence." Someone says we have to consider whether "America would be America if there had been no native Americans." Cathy responds that "there were crucial native contributions that made it possible for the Europeans to survive and prosper. This meant they had to be included."

Darlene says the question for her is "What do we choose as important in U.S. history for students to understand? We cannot include everything." She believes that "American identity and experience as we know it really starts with British settlement," but she recognizes that this is her opinion, not something that can be presented as historical fact. One of the men adds, "How can we call it American history before the European arrival? The earlier nomadic people who settled here were important, but not crucial." He concludes,

"America begins with the Declaration of Independence." Jean agrees that the Europeans had learned many things from the Indians, but she believes that the crucial developments took place somewhere between the British settlement and independence. Harvey adds that "the British remained British in India; in the United States they became American. This is what has to be explored."

Anthony believes that "American history starts at different times in different localities. It isn't one uniform nation until after the Civil War. Maybe that is the starting point." Tom says he feels that the key is identity: "When did Americans identify as a separate and distinct people?" Alice feels that this idea also contains problems: "America is pluralistic; there are still some people that don't share this common identity. We define everything by the experiences of White Anglo-Saxon males. But that's not the way it is."

Bart insists that, as teachers, we have a responsibility "to teach students the facts," but Sharon counters, "What are the facts? What if we don't agree on the facts?" Carol adds, "Students need to discover the facts for themselves, to form their own opinions and to listen to each other." Marie suggests letting students debate a question such as "When does American history begin?" Bart still is not satisfied. "Students don't know anything yet. They have to learn the facts first. How can they decide when American history begins and who contributed?"

Lisa says that there are no right answers to some questions: "The key goal is to get students to think and explore the different answers about what makes America 'America'. They need to form opinions based on the information they have available to them. Then as they get new information they can rethink their opinions. It isn't useful to talk about right or wrong answers."

At this point, I enter the discussion. I ask the class, "Are all answers equally good?" Jim responds, "We have different interpretations of when American history begins because we have different concepts of America, as a place, a people, an idea, a continent. We need to help students develop criteria to evaluate answers. This is part of what they are learning; it's what historians do."

We spend the rest of the time trying to establish criteria to decide if the pre-Columbian experiences of the native peoples should be considered part of American history. Most of us conceptualize history as a single timeline of events. I suggest that it might be more useful to think of history as a river with a number of different tributaries. The native contributions are one of the tributaries; so are the European and African contributions. Students can examine the past and try to decide how large or important a stream it is.

One student asks, "Are you saying that African history is also part of the river? It must be a very small part." At this point the class erupts into discussion again. Anthony outlines the triangular trade and the importance of African labor in creating the wealth of the Americas. Jim argues that the profits from the slave trade financed the Industrial Revolution in Europe. Cathy says, "You're stretching the point. They were brought as slaves. How much can they be credited for these developments?" Marie asks, "Should we include everybody? How do we include the newest immigrants?" Darlene answers, "Why not at least include the kids in our classes? Show where their families entered the stream." Someone else asks what the state wants us to teach, but it is already 10 minutes past the end of the class time. These issues will have to be part of other discussions.

Teaching Activity: History Is a River

Add your voice to the discussion:
What do you think of this metaphor, "History is a river with a number of different tributaries?" Why?

It's your classroom:
Teachers are always making choices. Which experiences would you include in the "American River?" Which would you emphasize? Why?

Teaching Activity: The Tree of Liberty

After studying the United States Constitution, I have students create posters that illustrate their views about the fundamental nature of American society. They identify its roots, trunk, branches, leaves, and fruit. We hang the posters on the wall, and each student makes a presentation to the class. Often the images are profoundly different. For example, should racism and/or freedom be considered "roots"? How much "bitter fruit" should be included on the tree?

Add your voice to the discussion:
Create your own symbolic "Tree of Liberty." What do you include? Why?

It's your classroom:
Would you use an assignment similar to this one in your class? At what grade level? Explain.

Essay 2: What Are the Essential Questions?

As a high school social studies teacher, I distributed newspapers and news magazines to teams of students in my 11th grade U.S. history classes at the start of the semester. The student teams were assigned to select five articles that they believed reported on important issues facing the United States in the contemporary world. Teams had to write down the headlines of the articles and their reasons for selecting them. At the end of the period, students listed the topics of the articles on the board, and I asked at least one group to report on its deliberations.

On the second day, the rest of the groups reported. After the presentations, students categorized the issues facing the United States, identified underlying problems raised by the news articles, and discussed questions they wanted to answer during the year. Articles on racial discrimination, sexual harassment, and police brutality led to questions such as, Can the United States become a more just society? Topics including welfare reform, health care, unemployment, tax breaks, and crime promoted students to ask, What is the responsibility (or job) of government? Other questions developed by students have included these: Should the United States be the world's police force? and Is technology making the world a better place? Essential questions can be placed on poster boards and hung prominently around the room. Students took pride in the questions they came up with, and the project

increased their willingness to participate in class and furthered our exploration of social studies and history.

During the course of the school year, student-generated questions, especially about social justice and the responsibility of government, led to other "big" questions and provided a focus for studying about the past, understanding the present, and deciding how to engage the future. The key to the "essential question approach" is to respect student questions and to encourage student voices. Teachers in the New Teacher Network (NTN) have used this same approach successfully in global history, economics and U.S. government classes.

Kenneth Dwyer (NTN) recommends the following questions developed by Kevin Sheehan and the social studies department in Oceanside, New York, for use in global history classes. Teachers at Oceanside also assemble a packet of documents for each unit that students examine and use to discuss one of these questions.

OCEANSIDE HIGH SCHOOL'S ESSENTIAL QUESTIONS FOR GLOBAL HISTORY

What is civilization?
To what extent are civilized societies uncivilized?
Is contemporary civilization superior to civilizations of the ancient world?
Is geography destiny?
How do societies change?
Is cultural diffusion a positive or negative force in world history?
Do advances in technology really improve society?
Is the diffusion of ideas more powerful than the diffusion of goods?
Was imperialism an inevitable consequence of industrialization and nationalism?
Is nationalism a positive or negative force?
Can wars be prevented?
Can political revolutions achieve their goals?
Do people control governments, or do governments control people?
Does the world's diversity make for a stronger planet or lead to inevitable conflict?
Is the world today a better world than the world in previous ages that we studied?
Can the world learn to live without global conflict in our lifetimes?
Will the world be able to more successfully deal with its problems in the coming century?

Join the Discussion:

1. What questions would you add to the list?
2. Which questions would you drop or modify? How?

Similarly, Maureen Murphy, the English education coordinator at Hofstra and I organized the New York State Great Irish Famine curriculum guide (Murphy and Singer, 2001) to address a

series of essential questions in global history. For example, in 1861, Irish nationalist John Mitchel charged that "no sack of Magdeburg, or ravage of the Palatinate ever approached the horror and dislocation to the slaughters done in Ireland by mere official red tape and stationery, and the principles of political economy. . . . The Almighty sent the potato blight, but the English created the famine" (287).

Whether or not one agrees with Mitchel's accusation about British policy in Ireland during the Great Irish Famine, his statement contains a number of key ideas about Irish, British, and world history. The sack of Magdeburg, a German Protestant city, by the forces of the Catholic League—which included Italy, France, and Spain—in 1631 was part of the Thirty Years War in Reformation Europe. The ravaging of the Palatinate, also in Germany, by the forces of Louis XIV of France from 1688–1697 was more directly related to imperial ambition during an era of European colonial expansion. Both of these conquests, as well as the British conquest and rule of Ireland, force students and historians to consider human motivation and behavior during times of war; the legitimacy of religions and religious leaders who urge war to promote or enforce beliefs; and the relationship between large powers and their smaller, vulnerable neighbors. Significantly, these are all major questions confronting the world today: the Balkans and central Africa (war), Southwest Asia and Afghanistan (religion), and the U.S. role in the Americas (use of power). In addition, Mitchel is asking us to explore causality in history, the workings of a laissez-faire political economy, the nature of bureaucracy, and collective responsibility for government action (or inaction).

One small quote unleashes a slew of major issues and powerful questions.

An essential questions approach to Irish and world history uses current events to help high school students and teachers frame and examine complex and controversial questions about the contemporary world and uses these questions to direct their examination of the past. It draws on Grant Wiggins's work on social studies teaching methods, Paulo Freire's belief that education must involve students in posing and examining questions about the problems facing their own communities, and the *Handbook on Teaching Social Issues* by the National Council for the Social Studies.

Wiggins argues that teachers should present students broad questions without simple answers that are reintroduced over and over throughout the curriculum. For social studies, he suggests questions such as these: Is there enough (e.g., food, clothes, water) to go around? Is history a story of progress? When is law unjust? Who owns what and why? We have students develop their own questions about the past, present, and future. We recommend starting the school year with teams of students searching through newspapers and selecting articles they believe report on important issues facing the contemporary world. Teams categorize the issues, identify underlying problems, and formulate the questions they want to answer. Their big questions are placed on poster boards, hung prominently around the room, and referred to continuously.

ESSENTIAL QUESTIONS FROM THE NEW YORK STATE GREAT IRISH FAMINE CURRICULUM

The Great Irish Famine Curriculum started with a few thematic questions. However, it was designed so that new questions would continually be introduced as students explored global history. These 12 essential questions emerged when teachers field-tested the Great Irish Famine curriculum in secondary school social studies classes.

Can a small thing or event transform the world?

What role does religion play in human history?

How does technology change the way people live and work?

Are famines more often acts of nature or the result of decisions by people with power?

What are the consequences of ethnic prejudice?

What is the responsibility of government in times of disaster?

What is the responsibility of the media when it reports the news?

What are the responsibilities of individuals when faced with injustice or calamity?

What causes imperialism?

What are human rights?

Continued

What is genocide?
Can individuals and groups shape the future?

Try it yourself:

Select three of the essential questions from this list and write a brief essay expressing your views.

At workshops with high school teachers, participants generally express three major concerns with an essential questions approach to social studies curriculum. They worry about the need to prepare students for standardized tests, the problem of establishing historical truth when multiple voices and controversial positions are introduced into discussion, and their ability as teachers to conduct an open and civil classroom discourse if sharp conflicts emerge.

I find that the problem of preparing students for standardized exams is the easiest to address. On most standardized tests, students do not pass or fail because of the specific social studies content presented in class or in textbooks. Students do well on these examinations when they are engaged by discussion in class, understand the general social studies concepts integrated into the curriculum, and have adequate reading and writing skills. No specific piece of information is ever absolutely crucial.

In 14 years as a high school social studies teacher, I never taught a specific lesson on the collapse of the Ottoman Turkish Empire (although I did discuss the Armenian genocide with students). Students need to understand both the positive and negative effects of nationalism and modernization, and they should examine the global impact of World War I, but they can examine these historical concepts and events while looking at Germany, Italy, Russia, Eastern Europe, Africa, China, India, or Turkey. They can touch on them again when they discuss post-World War II Kenya, Vietnam, Iran, China, or Algeria. It is both impossible and undesirable for students to memorize extensive details about each place on earth and its history. An engaged student is much more likely to be successful in school and in life than is someone who passively copies volumes of notes from the board.

The debate over what makes something true is much more difficult to resolve, and I do not have a simple solution. The dispute over what constitutes truth is not new; the meaning of truth and the possibility of acquiring it have been debated throughout world history, especially in Western intellectual traditions. For example, according to the multivolume *Great Books of the Western World* (Adler, 1952: 915), a collaboration between the University of Chicago and the *Encyclopedia* Britannica, "the great issues concern whether we can know the truth and how we can ever tell whether something is true or false. Though the philosophers and scientists, from Plato to Freud, seem to stand together against the extreme sophistry or skepticism which denies the distinction between true and false or puts truth utterly beyond the reach of man, they do not all agree on the extent to which truth is attainable by men, on its immutability or variability, on the signs by which men tell whether they have the truth or not, or on the causes of error and the means for avoiding falsity" (915). While Aristotle argued that we should accept theories as true "only if what they affirm agrees with the observed facts," many of our students and many of our colleagues probably would agree with Augustine and Spinoza that "God is the warranty of the inner voice which plainly signifies the truth" (920). If these noted philosophers could not decide whether something is true or not, why should students take our word that what we say is true and what they believe is false? Perhaps one of our essential questions should simply be, What is truth?

I am not suggesting an everything-goes attitude or that every statement about the past is equally valid. However, what social studies teachers need to acknowledge is that we are much less certain than we like to pretend and that we are also susceptible to being trapped by comforting myths. Instead of insisting that students accept one version of immutable facts, we need to help them become practicing historians and social scientists who weigh evidence, evaluate theories, and work collectively to establish and continually reevaluate criteria for understanding our world.

Discussion of essential questions requires introducing historical topics (e.g., government policy during famines, the African Slave Trade or the European Holocaust) and points of view that have the potential to produce sharp conflict in social studies classes. Teachers are often concerned that they will not be able to control classroom discussions, but conflict is not necessarily bad; it can be a creative force that pushes people to delve more deeply into issues and to find evidence to support their opinions. Control, on the other hand, is not necessarily good, especially when it stifles intellectual freedom and student voice.

Heated discussion, if it is going to be productive, requires that people listen to each other and respond to one another's ideas. In my experience, this happens more effectively in a democratic community than it does in an authoritarian, teacher-controlled environment. For a social studies curriculum based on an examination of essential questions and controversial issues to be effective, students need to feel related to each other and to their teachers and must have respect for other people and their intelligence, even when there is disagreement about the validity of particular ideas. Students need to engage in dialogues rather than debating to win and need to see themselves as part of a shared quest to study and understand the world (Pezone and Singer, 1997: 75–79).

REFERENCES AND RECOMMENDATIONS FOR FURTHER READING

Achebe, C. *Things Fall Apart*. Portsmouth, N.H.: Heinemann Educational Books, 1996.

Adler, M. ed. *Great Books of the Western World*, Vol. 3. Chicago: Encyclopedia Britannica, 1952.

Banks, J. "A Curriculum for Empowerment, Action and Change." In *Empowerment Through Multicultural Education*, ed. C. Sleeter, Albany, N.Y.: SUNY Press, 1991, 125–142.

Banks, J. "The Canon Debate, Knowledge Construction, and Multicultural Education." *Educational Researcher* 22, no. 5 (1993): 4–14.

Berk, L. "Vygotsky's Theory: The Importance of Make-Believe Play." *Young Children*, November 1994, 30–39.

Bigelow, W. "Critical Pedagogy at Jefferson High School." *Equity and Choice* 4, no. 2 (1988), 14–19.

Bigelow, W. "Inside the Classroom: Social Vision and Critical Pedagogy." *Teachers College Record* 91, no. 3 (1990), 437–46.

Bloom, A. *The Closing of the American Mind*. New York: Simon and Schuster, 1987.

Calkins, L. *Lessons from a Child: On the Teaching and Learning of Writing*. Exeter, N.H.: Heinemann Educational Books, 1983.

Center for Civic Education. *National Standards for Civics and Government*. Calabasas, Calif.: CCE, 1994.

Christensen, L. *Reading, Writing, and Rising Up*. Milwaukee, Wis.: Rethinking Schools, 2000.

Clark, S. *Ready from Within: Septima Clark and the Civil Rights Movement*. Navarro, Calif.: Wild Trees Press, 1986.

Crook, J. "The Social Studies Teacher as Curriculum Creator: Reflections on Teaching Middle School Social Studies." In *Reflective Practice in Social Studies, NCSS Bulletin No. 88*, ed. E. W. Ross. Washington, D.C.: National Council for the Social Studies, 1994.

Dewey, J. *Democracy and Education*. New York: Macmillan, 1916.

Dewey, J. *Experience and Education*. New York: Collier/Macmillan, 1938/1963.

Dewey, J. *Freedom and Culture*. New York: G. P. Putnam's Sons, 1939.

Feder, B. *Viewpoints: USA*. New York: American Book Company, 1967.

Finn, C. Jr., and D. Ravitch. *What Do Our 17-year-olds Know? A Report on the First National Assessment of History and Literature*. New York: Harper and Row, 1987.

Freire, P. *Pedagogy of the Oppressed*. New York: Seabury, 1970.

Freire, P. *Pedagogy of Hope*. New York: Continuum, 1995.

Gandini, L. "Fundamentals of the Reggio Emila Approach to Early Childhood Education." *Young Children,* November 1993, 4–9.

Gardner, H. "Beyond IQ: Education and Human Development." *Harvard Educational Review* 57, no. 2 (1987).

Giroux, H. *Theory and Resistance in Education: A Pedagogy for the Opposition.* South Hadley, Mass.: Bergin and Garvey, 1983.

Giroux, H. *Border Crossings, Cultural Workers and the Politics of Education.* New York: Routledge, 1992.

Greene, M. "Diversity and Inclusion: Towards a Curriculum for Human Beings." *Teachers College Record,* 95, no. 2 (1993a), 211–21.

Greene, M. "Reflections on Post-Modernism and Education." *Educational Policy* 7, no. 2 (1993b), 106–11.

Greene, M. "The Passions of Pluralism: Multiculturalism and Expanding Community." *Educational Researcher* 22, no. 1 (1993c), 13–18.

Hamilton, V. *The People Could Fly American Black Folktales,* New York: Alfred A. Knopf, 1985.

Hirsch, E. Jr. *Cultural Literacy: What Every American Needs to Know.* Boston: Houghton Mifflin, 1987.

Horton, M., and P. Freire. *We Make the Road by Walking.* Philadelphia: Temple University Press, 1990.

Horton, M., with J. Kohl, and H. Kohl. *The Long Haul: An Autobiography.* New York: Doubleday, 1990.

Kohn, A. *No Contest: The Case against Competition.* Boston: Houghton Mifflin, 1986.

Ladson-Billings, G. *The Dreamkeepers: Successful Teachers of African American Children.* San Francisco: Jossey-Bass, 1994.

McCunn, R. *Thousand Pieces of Gold.* San Francisco: Design Enterprise, 1981.

McIntosh, P. "Interactive Phases of Curricular Re-Vision: A Feminist Perspective." Working Paper No. 124. Wellesley, Mass.: Wellesley College Center for Research on Women, 1983.

Meier, D. *The Power of Their Ideas: Lessons for America from a Small School in Harlem.* Boston: Beacon, 1995.

Millstein, B., and J. Bodin, eds. *We the American Women: A Documentary History.* Chicago: Science Research Associates, 1977.

Murphy, D. "Teaching the Hard Lessons of Racism." *United Federation of Teachers Bulletin,* September 30, 1991, 9a.

Murphy, M., and A. Singer. "Asking the Big Questions: Teaching About the Great Irish Famine and World History." *Social Education,* September 2001, 286–91.

National Center for History in the Schools. *National Standards for United States History: Exploring the American Experience.* Los Angeles: NCHS, 1994.

National Council for the Social Studies. *Expectations of Excellence: Curriculum Standards for Social Studies. NCSS Bulletin 89.* Washington, D.C.: NCSS, 1994.

National Society for the Study of Education. Twenty-Second Yearbook. Bloomington, Ill.: Public School Publishing Co., 1923.

Newman, F., and L. Holtzman. *Lev Vygotzky: Revolutionary Scientist.* London: Routledge, 1992.

New York State Department of Education. *9 & 10 Grade Global Studies Syllabus.* Albany, N.Y.: State Department of Education, 1987.

The New York Times. "Horace Mann." September 15, 1953.

Noddings, N. *The Challenge to Care in Schools.* New York: Teachers College Press, 1992.

Noddings, N. "Social Studies and Feminism." *Theory and Research in Social Education* 20, no. 3 (1992), 230–41.

Paterson, K. *Lyddie.* New York: Puffin Books, 1991.

Pezone M., and A. Singer. "Empowering Immigrant Students Through Democratic Dialogues." *Social Education* 61, February 1997.

Ravitch, D. *The American Reader: Words That Moved a Nation*. New York: HarperCollins, 1990.

Reiber, R., and A. Carton, eds. *The Collected Works of L. S. Vygotsky*. Vol. 1, *Problems of General Psychology*. New York: Plenum, 1997.

Rethinking Schools. *Rethinking Our Classrooms: Teaching for Equity and Justice*. Milwaukee: Rethinking Schools, 1994.

Seldes, G., ed. The Great Quotations. New York: Lyle Stuart, 1996.

Shor, I. "Educating the Educators: A Freirean Approach to the Crisis in Teacher Education." In *Freire for the Classroom*, ed. I. Shor. Portsmouth, N.H.: Heinemann Educational Books, 7–32, 1987.

Shor, I., and P. Freire. *A Pedagogy for Liberation: Dialogues on Transforming Education*. South Hadley, Mass.: Bergin and Garvey, 1987.

Stanton, E., S. Anthony, and M. Gage, eds. *History of Woman Suffrage*, Vol. 1. Rochester, N.Y.: Charles Mann, 1889.

Stern, P., ed. *The Life and Writings of Abraham Lincoln*. New York: Modern Library, 1940.

Takaki, R. *A Different Mirror*. Boston, Mass.: Little, Brown, 1993.

Twain, M. *Adventures of Huckleberry Finn*. New York: Oxford University Press, 1996.

Wigginton, E. *Sometimes a Shining Moment: The Foxfire Experience*. New York: Anchor/Doubleday, 1985.

Zinn, H. *A People's History of the United States: 1492–Present*. New York: HarperCollins, 1999.

3

How Do You Plan a Social Studies Curriculum?

Overview

Define curriculum
Evaluate teacher decision making
Examine the components of a social studies curriculum
Participate in current curriculum debates
Explore curriculum options
Develop social studies curriculum calendars

Key Concepts

Curriculum, Directed Experience, Reflection, Hidden Curriculum, Standards, Curriculum Calendar

Questions

What Is a Curriculum?
How Does a Curriculum Help Teachers Make Decisions?
Why Was the Debate on National History Standards So Heated?
How Are Social Studies Curricula Organized?
How Do You Plan and Use a Curriculum Calendar?

Essays

Teaching Global History
Multicultural Social Studies

WHAT IS A CURRICULUM?

A curriculum is a long-range plan for achieving content, concept, academic skill, and social goals. It helps social studies teachers decide how to organize units, lessons, and activities for their classes. The most effective curricula offer teachers a range of options rather than fixed guidelines. They provide direction for classroom decisions while allowing for continuous reevaluation and are open to

change in response to student needs, new ideas, and classroom developments.

John Dewey (discussed in chap. 2) believed that understanding the relationship between learning and human experience is fundamental for developing classroom curriculum. Dewey wanted teachers to direct learning by organizing experiences for students and by encouraging them to reflect on these experiences. In a real sense, in a Deweyan school, curriculum is everything that happens to students and helps them make meaning out of their lives. In these schools, all aspects of the program are continually evaluated because they all impact student learning. In most secondary schools, however, curriculum is much more narrowly defined. In these schools, *curriculum* refers to the content knowledge teachers are expected to convey to students in a particular subject area. Although broader subject-related concepts and specific academic skills may be included in prescribed guidelines, most of these curricula are text and test directed, and student recall of information is what is valued. Many of these curricula even attempt to eliminate the decision-making role of teachers by providing "teacher-proof" lessons.

Michael Apple, a contemporary educational theorist, is highly critical of this narrow view of curriculum. He claims that much of what takes place in traditional content-centered programs is based on an unstated and assumed "hidden curriculum." In *Ideology and Curriculum* (1979), Apple shows how a hidden curriculum shapes subject content, classroom relationships, and teacher practice in ways that limit a teacher's choices, suppress critical thinking by students, and train people to accept without question the social status quo.

In social studies classrooms, the hidden curriculum includes the encouragement of highly stratified competitive relationships among students, the authoritarian position held by many teachers, and the passive nature of most learning, which reinforce, and are reinforced by, unquestioned assumptions about the nature of society. For example, social and ideological conflict are generally presented as negative factors that undermine societies, and consensus is promoted as a paramount social virtue. Even when conflicting views are examined in social studies classes, students are usually offered only a narrow spectrum of officially condoned choices.

If Dewey and Apple are correct, although an official curriculum may be narrowly defined, the actual classroom curriculum continues to be everything that happens to students. The issue for social studies teachers is whether we act openly and consciously examine hidden curriculum assumptions or we allow them to operate in the shadows.

Teaching Activity: What Was Life Like in Colonial New York City?

This excerpt from my teaching journal illustrates the dynamic three-way interrelationship that I believe should exist among a teacher's classroom decisions, student involvement in learning, and a long-range social studies curriculum. It describes the graduate social studies methods class for preservice teachers, although I have taught similar lessons as part of an 11th-grade U.S. history curriculum. A lesson such as this one can take alternative directions in different classes. When I prepare, I organize optional document-based material, either printed on the same activity sheet or a separate sheet, which I present in response to student questions.

From Alan's teaching journal:

The class examined a map of New York City (New York Historical Society, n.d.: 25) drawn in 1813, but showing the layout of the city in the 1740s. Students were divided into small groups (three or four members) who were asked to identify "interesting or puzzling" aspects of the map. When the groups reported back to the class, three things stood out in their comments.

The northernmost boundary of the city in the 1740s was a wall near what we now call Canal Street. New York City in the era prior to the American Revolution was a village at the tip of Manhattan Island, a small fragment of the city we know today.

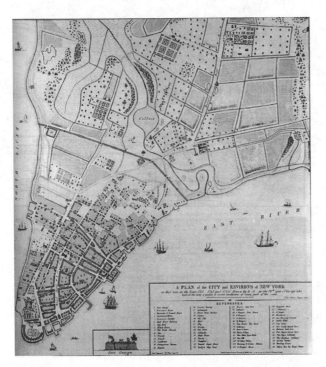

Reprinted from *America Begins in New York*: *The Peopling of New York City: A Teacher's Resource Manual* by permission of the New York City 100 Collaborative Project, The New York Historical Society and the Board of Education of the City of New York.

Although many streets retain the same names over two centuries later, some familiar streets and landmarks have different names. The North River of colonial America is now known as the Hudson River.

Each group of students located labels and symbols on the map that they could not explain. In the discussion that followed, students commented that New York City in the 1740s was very different from the way they envisioned it when they casually read about the past. During the discussion, we examined three of the perplexing labels and symbols just north of the city's wall; a "collect," a tiny gibbet or gallows with a hanging body, and a picture of a small fire. Once they realized that there were streams entering and leaving the collect, students quickly figured out that it was a reservoir. However, the gallows, which were labeled, "Plot Negro Gibbeted," and the fire, which was labeled "Plot Negro's burnt here," did not have easy explanations. A number of students were surprised to learn that Africans and slavery existed in New York City during this period.

In response to student speculation about the symbols, I distributed a letter that Robert Hunter, Royal Governor of New York and New Jersey, sent to the Lords of Trade in London in 1712. The letter described a slave revolt that took place in the city on April 6, 1712, and detailed the punishment of the rebels. During the revolt, a fire was started and "nine Christians were killed, and about five or six wounded" by the Africans. After the uprising was suppressed, six of the rebels committed suicide and 21 were executed. "Some were burnt, others hanged, one broke on the wheel, and one hung alive in chains in the town, so that there has been the most exemplary punishment inflicted that could be possibly thought of" (Berkin and Wood, 1987: 20).

After students read the letter, I asked if they thought the Africans should have been executed for rebellion and murder. A number of students raised their hands. A white male student opened discussion by arguing that laws are laws, and people who break them should be punished. Other students, all white, agreed with his statement.

A male student, one of the few African Americans in the class, claimed that the people who were executed were "freedom fighters." He argued that, at worst, they should have been treated as defeated soldiers: "They should not have been punished in these ways."

A white male student, not the original speaker, accused him of looking at the events described in the letter "from the perspective of today." He believed that high school students had to "understand events the way they were intended and understood in the past." A white female student raised whether we want our students to learn that "issues of right and wrong are relative or are universal." Toward the end of the discussion, I asked whether students thought we could understand the motivation of either the Africans or the British officials, and then I called on nonvolunteers.

The class argued over these issues for nearly 20 minutes without reaching a consensus. We ended with these questions: Can historians place themselves "in the shoes" of other people?

Should historians judge people from the past? Is there a universal morality? How important was slavery in shaping New York and the other British northern colonies?

As a summary activity, I referred to the previous lesson, in which we discussed the Mayflower Compact and a statement by Diane Ravitch (1990a: 3) that this document showed that "the settling of America began with an idea. The idea was that the citizens of a society could join freely and agree to govern themselves by making laws for the common good." I asked whether our discussion of slavery in 18th-century New York City made them reconsider their earlier reactions to Ravitch's statement. Student response was heated; speakers disagreed with each other, with what they perceived to be my views, and with Ravitch.

Add your voice to the discussion:
1. How should we define *curriculum*?
2. In your opinion, is there such a thing as a "hidden" curriculum? Why or why not?
3. In your opinion, is there a "hidden" curriculum in the classroom described here? Explain your answer.

Think it over:
Compared with the South and the Caribbean, there were relatively few enslaved Africans in the northern British colonies. The existence of slavery in the North could be acknowledged in a few sentences. In your opinion, does this topic merit major focus in the secondary school social studies curriculum? Why or why not?

Try it yourself:
1. Reexamine the Teaching Journal excerpt. Identify between five and ten decisions made by the teacher prior to and during the course of the lesson.
2. What goals are reflected in these decisions?
3. Would you have made similar choices? Why or why not?

It's your classroom:
In a high school classroom, would you spend a class period on this lesson? Why or why not?

HOW DOES A CURRICULUM HELP TEACHERS MAKE DECISIONS?

Teaching involves choices that are based on our goals as teachers, our understanding of our students and their academic and social needs, and our efforts to achieve the goals spelled out in a course outline. Ideally, a curriculum helps teachers visualize a broader picture, allowing us to focus on what we are teaching today within a context of what we will examine with our students tomorrow, the next week, the next month, and at the end of the school year. A curriculum helps teachers understand the relationship between lessons and to build on activities, understandings, and skills over the course of time. It also helps us examine the ramifications of our choices. If in November a teacher decides to spend an extra day on the Bank Controversy during the Jackson administration, it could mean that in June the class will not have time to discuss the impact of the Vietnam War on U.S. society.

Curriculum choices and changes can also be on a much grander scale. In fall 2001, in response to the destruction of the World Trade Center in New York and the Pentagon in Washington and to the war in Central Asia that followed, many social studies teachers revamped their course outlines. Some simply infused more current events into class discussions and assignments. Others shifted or emphasized discussion of fundamental social studies concepts such as nationalism, imperialism, isolation, globalization, democracy and justice and focused more attention on geographic content and map-reading skills. This kind of shift is easier when a teacher has a sense of the year as a whole and focuses on themes and essential questions rather than on the accumulation of discrete content.

The excerpt from my teaching journal in the previous learning activity illustrates both the intricacy of and some of the controversy involved in social studies curriculum decisions. The curriculum of that class included everything that took place: the documents, the discussion, the questions, and even the sequence of the speakers. For example, if I had called on the student who identified the Africans as freedom fighters at the beginning of the class, the period probably would have had a very different dynamic.

Does a teacher's effort to direct class discussion through questioning and the selection of participants to speak she or he has mean that an undemocratic hidden curriculum? I do not think so. Having goals is not the same as having a hidden curriculum if teachers are conscious of their choices and are willing to examine and reevaluate them along with their students and colleagues.

In this graduate seminar, I had a considerable amount of freedom of choice as a teacher and a two-hour period in which to work. A reasonable question is this: How much freedom is there to promote critical discussions and create democratic classrooms in traditionally organized middle schools and high schools? Based on my experience, I think it is both possible and desirable to achieve these goals in secondary school social studies classes.

Among other things, whatever the test preparation pressures placed on teachers in secondary schools, they also have many more days to work with students. This lesson does have a relatively narrow content focus, but it introduces broad social studies themes about racism and social justice that can be built on in future lessons. In addition, it gives students an opportunity to work in groups and engage in a full class dialogue, and it encourages students to act as historians as they develop their map and document analysis skills. Although secondary school students bring less content background with them to social studies classes, they tend to be more flexible and willing to experiment with the way learning is organized and are responsive to being treated as thinking human beings whose opinions are valued.

I believe every decision I made during this class, what I intended to happen, what developed as a result of student initiatives, and even what did not happen, are all aspects of the curriculum: things to be examined, considered, and used to direct classroom experience in future lessons. Take a look at 20 of the decisions I made prior to and during the lesson. See whether we understand what happened in the same way.

DECISIONS, DECISIONS, DECISIONS

Decision 1: Time. My secondary social studies methods classes meet 14 times. In the methods class, this lesson is also used to introduce a document-based or inquiry model for teaching social studies and to examine lesson goals. In my annual high school U.S. history calendar, I use a full lesson period to introduce slavery in the northern British colonies: one lesson out of approximately 160 teaching classes (this does not count days that are reserved for tests, review, and clerical tasks). I focus on New York because it draws a connection between slavery in the past and the place where my students live.

Continued

Decision 2: Goals. My goals in this lesson in both high school and in the secondary methods class include establishing roots of contemporary racism in the colonial era; introducing slavery as a national, rather than a regional, issue; questioning the idea that one theme (e.g., expanding democracy), characterizes U.S. history; developing individual map-reading and document analysis skills; promoting cooperative social skills; encouraging students to listen to and respond to each other and to respect differences of opinion; and promoting discussion of broader historical and philosophical issues as part of social studies learning.

Decision 3: What to include. Based on my goals, the materials I had available, and my previous experience teaching about this topic, I organized a document analysis and class discussion lesson around slave rebellions in New York City in 1712 and 1741.

Decision 4: What to leave out. I decided not to focus on other aspects of daily life in colonial New York. Daily life would be a focus in lessons about colonial Williamsburg and Massachusetts.

Decision 5: Choosing documents. I selected documents for the lesson: the 1813 map showing New York City in the 1740s, the letter written by Robert Hunter, and excerpts from the trial of people accused of plotting a 1741 slave rebellion. I decided that these documents provided an historically "accurate" picture of racial issues in colonial New York.

Decision 6: Preparing documents. I edited and adapted the documents instead of using them in their original form. I decided not to include specific questions at the end of the reading passages.

Decision 7: Introducing lesson. I decided to use a "generic" broad aim that signaled place and time but did not identify the aspects of life in New York City we would actually be examining in class. I wanted the class to "discover" the existence of slavery in the north.

Decision 8: Group, team, or individual work. I decided to have students examine the maps in temporary work groups instead of in semipermanent cooperative learning teams or as individuals. I decided that students would read the letter individually and discuss it as a full class.

Decision 9: Instructions to students. Instead of providing detailed instructions for the map analysis and drawing attention to particular features of the map, I decided to make the assignment open ended. Students were asked to identify what they found interesting or puzzling.

Decision 10: Changes over time. Examining similarities and differences between past and present is a major social studies theme. However, although the changes in the city over time are noted during the lesson, they are not explored in detail.

Decision 11: Labels and symbols. After the initial discussion, I directed student attention to the specific labels and symbols I wanted to discuss: the "gibbet" and the "fire." I included the "collect" because of widespread student interest.

Decision 12: Directing discussion. I opened discussion of the letter by Robert Hunter with an opinion question (Do you think the Africans should have been executed?) rather than a question about the information presented in the letter. My goal was to draw students into a discussion by connecting their views on law and order and justice with the events from 1712.

Decision 13: Multiple perspectives. In my teaching journal I noted that the students who initially support the execution are White, whereas the student who calls the rebels "freedom fighters" is African American. During this discussion, I decided not to ask whether students thought that the racial identity of students in class influenced the way they viewed the past. When I reconsidered this decision after the class, I decided that I wanted to organize another lesson where the discussion would allow me to raise this question.

Decision 14: Calling on students. At the start of the discussion, I decided to call on volunteers rather than allowing individuals to speak at will. A number of students signaled that they wanted to open up the discussion, including the African American student who identified the Africans as freedom fighters. Based on previous discussions in class, I anticipated his point of view, and I made the decision to have other students speak before I called on him. I was concerned that if he presented his ideas first, some of the White students would hesitate to express their ideas and discussion would close down.

Continued

Decision 15: Nondirective discussion. I decided to permit prolonged student discussions of how to view events in the past and the nature of values instead of focusing the discussion entirely on slavery in colonial America.

Decision 16: Eliminating 1741. The decision to allow broader discussion of history and philosophy meant that we would not examine documents about and discuss the trial of people accused of plotting a slave rebellion in 1741. After class, I decided not to include this material in another lesson.

Decision 17: Student participation. In an effort to include everyone in the discussion, I asked whether students thought we could understand the motivation of either the Africans or the British officials, and I decided to call on nonvolunteers.

Decision 18: Closure. The discussion ended with continued disagreement and a series of questions for future investigation and discussion rather than with consensus.

Decision 19: Summary and application. Rather than directly reviewing what we had discovered about New York City in the 18th century, I decided to place the lesson in the context of a discussion about the nature of American society that began the previous week.

Decision 20: Homework. In a high school class, I might have assigned work prior to the lesson to provide students with background information and a general context for the discussion. I might also assign a follow-up written assignment requiring students to summarize their views on the issues raised in class.

Teaching Activity: How Representative Is a Primary Source Document?

A key question teachers must consider when organizing lessons around the analysis of primary source documents is whether a document is representative of an era or a group of people. Should social studies students be presented a quote that offers biblical defense of slavery in the United States, a patriotic song, a political cartoon representing a minority point of view, a terrorist or a dictator's justification for his or her actions, or a selection from a personal memoir such as *The Diary of a Young Girl* by Anne Frank (1995), which tells the story of one adolescent girl?

As a student teacher, Stephanie Hunte (NTN) wanted students in her 10th-grade global history class to explore the roots of Nazi ideology in 19th-century German nationalism. She provided them an excerpt from a poem written in 1878 by someone she identified as a "popular German poet." Stephanie located the poem in *Source Records of the Great War, Vol. 1* (Horne, 1931: 89) published by the American Legion. In the introduction to the collection, the editors wrote that "the German character" includes "vain and reckless arrogance in power" and that German society stood in opposition to "the sunlight of democratic civilization." The editors did not provide the title of the poem, the name of the poet, or a source for the fragment.

During class, a student asked, "How do we know if this poem is the view of one person or represents the German point of view? Didn't other ideas exist in Germany also?" As a result of the student's question and class discussion that followed, Stephanie decided to drop this poem from the lesson.

Add your voice to the discussion:
1. Do you consider this poem an acceptable primary source for a high school social studies class? Explain your answer.
2. When teachers select "representative" documents for students to examine in class, are we editing the past and deciding in advance what students will discover? Explain your views.

Think it over:
How would you have addressed the student's questions?

It's your classroom:
How would you decide which documents to use in a document-based inquiry lesson?

WHY WAS THE DEBATE ON NATIONAL HISTORY STANDARDS SO HEATED?

Arguing that there is space within a traditional social studies curriculum for teachers to expand classroom democracy and critical discussion by students does not mean that it is easy and can be done without generating conflict within a class, the department, or the school. The best recent example of how difficult it is to modify a social studies curriculum is the political explosion that followed the release of voluntary "national history standards" in October 1994. According to the U.S. Department of Education (1994, N.P.), the purpose of "content standards" in different subject areas was to "define what all students should know and be able to do." They describe the knowledge, skills, and understandings that students should have in order to attain high levels of competency in challenging subject matter. In addition, performance standards identified expected "levels of achievement in the subject matter" and the ways that students would "demonstrate their competency in a subject." The Department of Education and most advocates for national standards stressed that they were not proposing mandatory curriculum guidelines with lesson plans. Even if general standards were adopted, it would remain the job of state committees, school districts, and individual teachers to decide what was taught in the classroom and how it would be done.

The idea of developing national educational standards in social studies and other subject areas was fueled during the 1980s by concern that U.S. secondary school students trailed their foreign contemporaries in academic performance. National standards were endorsed by the Republican Bush administration at a national governors' conference in 1989, and in 1994 they were included in GOALS 2000 legislation signed by Democratic President Bill Clinton.

At first glance, the creation of broad voluntary national standards sounds like an activity appropriate for classroom teachers familiar with what is taught in different secondary school subjects on a daily basis. However, the development of national standards for social studies quickly became a contested battleground involving academics, public and private funding agencies, politicians, and competing professional organizations. As a result of pressure from historians, the social studies were divided into different fields: The National Center for History in Schools wrote history standards, the National Council for Geographic Education wrote geography standards, the Center for Civic Education wrote civics and government standards, and the National Council for Economic Education wrote economics standards. Meanwhile, the National Council for the Social Studies independently created a separate set of standards that integrated history and the social sciences.

When the U.S. and world history standards were released by the National Center for History in Schools, they included suggested approaches to the study of history, statements outlining broad historical themes, lists of topics to analyze, and suggestions for how some of the themes and topics could be examined in social studies classes. Although critics generally ignored the broader themes and topics, the classroom suggestions quickly became a lightning rod for conservative discontent with public education, multiculturalism, immigration, ethnic identity movements, a declining U.S. economy, and "eroding family values." The standards were widely denounced in the popular media; a columnist for *U.S. News and World Report* (Natale, 1995: 18–23) charged that they placed "Western civilization . . . on a par with the Kush and the Carthagians," and they were overwhelmingly rejected by the U.S. Senate.

Initially, the historians and educational groups who developed the history standards vigorously defended them at professional conferences and in social studies publications. The Organization of American Historians dedicated an entire theme issue of its magazine for secondary school teachers to a discussion of the standards

---

Teaching Activity: What Did the United States Purchase in 1803?

Controversy about historical issues frequently intensifies as curricula become more specific. For example, according to an 11th-grade textbook by Jordan, Greenblatt, and Bowes, *The Americans: A History* (Evanston, Ill.: McDougal, Littell & Co., 1992: 234–35):

"In 1800 Napoleon Bonaparte of France persuaded Spain to return the Louisiana Territory it had received in 1762. . . . Then news of the secret transfer leaked out, Americans reacted with alarm. . . . Jefferson decided to see whether he could resolve the problem by buying New Orleans and western Florida from the French. He sent James Monroe to join . . . the American ambassador in Paris. Before Monroe arrived, however, Napoleon had abandoned his vision of an empire in America. . . . So, in 1803, he offered to sell the entire Louisiana Territory to the United States."

National Standards for United States History, Grades 5–12 (1996a: 94, available on the web at http://www.sscnet.ucla.edu/nchs/standards supports this perspective on the Louisiana Purchase. It says that students should be able to "demonstrate understanding of the international background and consequences of the Louisiana Purchase," which includes "analyzing Napoleon's reasons for selling Louisiana to the United States, comparing the arguments advanced by Democratic Republicans and Federalists regarding the acquisition of Louisiana," and "analyzing the consequences of the Louisiana Purchase for United States politics, economic development, and race relations, and describing its impact on Spanish and French inhabitants."

Neither the text nor the standard has students examine this question: What did the United States purchase in 1803? Despite European imperial pretensions, however, neither France nor Spain occupied or controlled the area they identified as Louisiana. In reality, it was occupied and controlled by dozens of Native American nations who never recognized foreign sovereignty over their traditional lands. What the United States purchased was France's "claim" to this territory, but it had to wage decades of war against native peoples before it established control.

Add your voice to the discussion:
Was U.S. expansion west an act of imperialism? If so, did the ends justify the means? Explain your answers.

Think it over:
Should a discussion of these issues be introduced in middle school and high school social studies classrooms? Why or why not?

It's your classroom:
1. What do you think we should teach about the Louisiana Purchase? Why?
2. How would you teach it? Why?

(Nash, 1995). Spokespeople for the National Center for History in Schools (Thomas, 1996) stressed that the standards were voluntary and accused critics of a "disinformation campaign." In response to charges that references to "McCarthyism and the rise of the Ku Klux Klan put too much emphasis on failings in our nation's history," they responded that "these episodes demonstrate for students the strength of the democratic system to protect itself, as long as concerned and vigilant citizens use the power of its institutions to turn back such assaults." They also argued that "situating European history within its global context does not 'diminish' Western history. On the contrary, students are likely to gain a far better understanding of the relationship of European to world developments if the framework for their studies is the human community as a whole."

As the attacks continued, politically important proponents of national educational standards distanced themselves from the history proposals. Diane Ravitch, an Under Secretary of Education during the Bush administration, and Albert Shanker, former president of the American Federation of Teachers, both favored revising the history standards so that their "flaws" could be eliminated.

In April 1996, the National Center for History in Schools issued a new single-volume of revised national history standards. *The New York Times* (Thomas, 1996) noted that, based on recommendations by two review panels, the revised standards eliminated "their most criticized feature: the examples of classroom activities." The review panels wanted the teaching examples dropped because of concern that they invited students "to make facile moral judgments."

The new standards minus the teaching suggestions were almost as widely acclaimed as the original draft was condemned. Christopher T. Cross, president of the Council for Basic Education, declared that "the revised history standards are excellent. The UCLA National Center for History in the Schools has listened well to the criticisms of the earlier documents, has made substantial improvements throughout, and created a new document that will serve schools well as a guide to improving the teaching of U.S. and world history."

Diane Ravitch and Arthur Schlesinger Jr. celebrated the changes in an article for *The Wall Street Journal* (Ravitch and Schlesinger, 1996). They praised the removal of references to Mansa Musa's African Empire, the Ku Klux Klan, Senator Joseph McCarthy, and numerous obscure people who, they believe, had been included because they were non-White, nonmales. Ravitch and Schlesinger felt that the revised edition correctly focuses on "America's developing democratic tradition, the movement from exclusion to inclusion. . . . While attention is rightly directed to our nation's troubled history of racial, ethnic and religious tension, these issues are now placed within the context of the nation's continuing quest to make our practices conform to our ideals" (14).

If I read the initial criticisms and the later praise correctly, the first versions of the national history standards were rejected because they moved beyond broad generalities and discussed the ideas and information that teachers would present in social studies classes. The teaching suggestions were unacceptable because they involved students in examining fundamental assumptions about history, U.S. society, and world civilizations, exactly what I believe social studies is supposed to be about in a democratic society.

Has the United States been engaged in a "continuing quest to make our practice conform to our ideals," or have the country's ideals frequently been subjects of sharp disagreement (e.g., slavery, women's rights, reproductive freedom, immigration quotas)? Changes in practice are frequently the result of long-term struggles. Should the view that there is an evolving national consensus be assumed, or should multiple views be presented to students so they can sift through evidence and explanations to formulate their own interpretations?

Teaching Activity: Can a Social Studies Curriculum Be Nonpolitical?

"A nation denied a conception of its past will be disabled in dealing with its present and its future. As the means of defining national identity, history becomes a means of shaping history. The writing of history then turns from a mediation into a weapon. 'Who controls the past controls the future,' runs the Party slogan in George Orwell's *1984*; 'who controls the present controls the past.' "—Arthur Schlesinger Jr. (1992: 46)

Add your voice to the discussion:
In your opinion, can social studies curricula be nonpolitical? Explain your answer.

Think it over:
As a beginning teacher, how do you explain your curriculum choices?

It's your classroom:
How do you make it possible for your students to become critical thinkers prepared for active citizenship in a democratic society?

HOW IS A SOCIAL STUDIES CURRICULUM ORGANIZED?

I hope that you have not been scared away from becoming a social studies teacher by the political conflict over curriculum. In my experience, most of this conflict does not trickle down into the classroom; even when it does, responsible, student-centered teachers who are prepared to explain their curriculum decisions usually have a considerable amount of free space in which to maneuver. In any case, although social studies includes everything, everything cannot be included in a year-long social studies curriculum. A curriculum needs a focus and basic organizing principles. This section examines general strategies for organizing social studies curriculum.

Who Decides What Is Taught?

The U.S. Constitution does not mention education. It is a responsibility reserved for individual states, which can approach it in a variety of ways, including how to develop and promote social studies curricula. For example, California provides local school districts with a formal social studies curriculum and financial incentives to adopt it. Texas tries to mandate its curriculum through centralized control over the approval of textbooks. New York State gives local school districts broad freedom to develop their own curriculum guidelines but expects teachers to prepare students for standardized final examinations in global studies and U.S. history and government. Within all of these approaches, secondary school social studies departments take the basic guidelines and translate them into curriculum calendars; individual teachers use the calendars to develop daily lesson plans and student projects.

What Are the Models for Social Studies Curriculum?

The National Council for Social Studies (NCSS) advocates teaching an integrated social studies curriculum, including anthropology, economics, geography, history, philosophy, political science, psychology, and sociology. The NCSS (1994) argues that an integrated interdisciplinary approach is the best way "to help young people develop the ability to make informed and reasoned decisions for the public good as citizens of a culturally diverse, democratic society in an interdependent world" (vii). The organization's curriculum guidelines, including *Charting a Course: Social Studies for the 21st Century* (1989) and *Expectations of Excellence: Curriculum Standards for Social Studies* (1994), stress purposeful and experiential learning over course content. According to *Expectations of Excellence*, to promote civic competence, a social studies curriculum must "foster individual and cultural identity along with understanding of the forces that hold society together or pull it apart; include observation and participation in the school and community; address critical issues and the world as it is; prepare students to make decisions based on democratic principles; and lead to citizen participation in public affairs" (159).

These goals require a curriculum that promotes knowledge of diverse subjects, the ability to integrate ideas from different disciplines, democratic values and beliefs, thinking skills, and social and civic participation skills. *Charting a Course*

emphasizes that

> content knowledge from the social studies should not be treated merely as received knowledge to be accepted and memorized, but as the means through which open and vital questions may be explored and confronted. Students must be made aware that just as contemporary events have been shaped by actions taken by people in the past, they themselves have the capacity to shape the future (3).

Advocates of content-focused teaching tend to prefer a history-based curriculum (Evans, 1989). When Diane Ravitch endorsed the revised "national history standards," she contrasted them to "our current national curriculum of mushy, insubstantial social studies." Lynne V. Cheney, while chair of the National Endowment for the Humanities, argued that the idea of social studies is so broad that it includes "everything from driver education to values clarification" (Cheney, 1987: 9).

The National Council for History Education (Reinhold, 1991; Cornbleth and Waugh, 1995) successfully recruited prominent university historians—including Gary Nash of UCLA, Eric Foner and Kenneth Jackson of Columbia, and Mary Beth Norton of Cornell—to a campaign to have history "occupy a large and vital place in the education of the private person and the public citizen." The organization's greatest success was in California, where the state's department of education developed curriculum guidelines based on a statement from the California History–Social Science Framework (Berenson, 1993) that "history is the discipline best able to integrate the social sciences, literature, and the humanities into a coherent whole for the purposes of K–12 education." This curriculum uses a heavily chronological content focus to teach U.S. and world history in Grades 7–12.

Alternative approaches for organizing social studies curricula include thematic (examined in chap. 7) and project-based (examined in chap. 8) approaches that can focus on either history or social studies. The project-based approach actively involves students as historians and social scientists and engages them in hands-on activities and research. In recent years, it has been identified with the Coalition for Essential Schools and Brown University. Advocates of a thematic approach to social studies include the National Issues Forum (McKenzie and Hellenman, 2002), which publishes booklets that present multiple perspectives on controversial issues; Jerome Bruner (Dow, 1992), a child psychologist who helped develop *Man: A Course of Study* (*MACOS*), a middle grades curriculum that integrated anthropology and biology; Mortimer Adler (1982), author of *The Paieda Proposal*, who argued that the in-depth exploration of selected topics leads to more substantive learning than broad surveys; and ethnic nationalists, who believe that students should concentrate their studies on the history and culture of their own ethnic groups. The NCSS, in *Charting a Course*, endorsed the general idea of a thematic curriculum "selective enough to provide time for extended in-depth study" (4).

Which Version of History?

Even if history is placed at the center of a social studies curriculum, the problem still remains: Which version of history? In the 1990s, there were major public battles over the reenactment of a slave auction at Colonial Williamsburg (was it insensitive to African Americans?) (*The New York Times*, 1994a; 1994b), the symbolic importance of the Alamo (does it represent Anglo imperialism in Texas?), a Smithsonian exhibit commemorating the

50th anniversary of the end of World War II (was the nuclear bombing of Hiroshima justified?), and the Holocaust in Europe during World War II (did Nazi efforts to exterminate Eastern European Jewry constitute a unique historical event?).

In June 2000, in an opinion essay in *The New York Times*, Eric Foner, a past president of both the American Historical Association and the Organization of American Historians, challenged historians and teachers to rethink the way we think about and teach about slavery in the United States, especially slavery and the Northern states. According to Foner, "Much of the North's economic prosperity derived from what Abraham Lincoln, in his second inaugural address, called 'the bondman's two hundred and fifty years of unrequited toil.'" Foner argued that "when New York's history is taught in public schools, the city's intimate link with slavery should receive full attention (29)."

Nel Noddings (1992), a feminist educator, calls for sweeping reorganization of social studies curricula because of their overwhelmingly male context. She recommends introducing women's culture into social studies by focusing on social interaction and human relationships, family and community building, the role of love and caring in different cultures, and movements for world peace. As an example of how the male cultural bias shapes social studies curriculum, she cites the career of Emily Greene Balch, winner of the Nobel Peace Prize in 1946, whose work is ignored because in our society, peace is not valued as much as war. The question of which version of history should we teach issue is discussed in greater detail in one of the essays at the conclusion of this chapter.

Teaching Activity: Facts or Thinking Skills?

Among advocates of a history-based curriculum, there is continuing disagreement whether its focus should be on historical facts or historical thinking skills.

- Lynne V. Cheney (1987: 5–6) is concerned that current social studies curricula focus too much on " 'process': the belief that we can teach our children *how* to think without troubling them to learn anything worth thinking about, the belief that we can teach them *how* to understand the world in which they live without conveying to them the events and ideas that have brought it into existence. . . . Dates and names are not all that students should know, but such facts are a beginning, an initial connection to the sweep of human experience."
- E. D. Hirsch (1993: 19) wants social studies teachers to teach a content-based core curriculum that replaces learning skills with content goals. Hirsch believes that problem-solving skills depend on a wealth of relevant knowledge; kids already "possess higher order thinking skills . . . what these students lack is not critical thinking but academic knowledge."
- Gary Nash (National Center for History in the Schools, 1996b) counters, "The study of history involves much more than the passive absorption of facts, dates, names and places. History is at its essence a process of reasoning based on evidence from the past."

Add your voice to the discussion:
Do you believe social studies curricula should focus more on the absorption of facts or on a process of reasoning? Why?

HOW DO YOU PLAN AND USE A CURRICULUM CALENDAR?

Whatever the content of a curriculum or its concept and skills goals, its value for social studies teachers and their willingness to follow it depend on whether it provides a useful lesson schedule, or curriculum calendar, and classroom materials. Curricula are usually organized by grade level, and annual calendars are subdivided into units (discussed in chap. 4), lessons (discussed in chap. 5), and activities (discussed in chap. 6). Strategies to introduce, develop, and reinforce content, concepts, and academic and social skills are woven throughout the calendar.

The State of New York uses an expanding horizons social studies curriculum based on three principles: (1) young children learn about the world by examining ever larger "circles" or "communities" and by comparing what they find with what they already know about themselves and their social relationships (e.g., self | family | school | neighborhood | city | state | nation | world), (2) as students mature intellectually and socially, they will discover new meaning and develop enhanced skills by reexamining familiar topics, and (3) to prepare students for life in a multicultural society and world, social studies curricula must examine the history and cultures of a broad spectrum of people and civilizations.

From kindergarten through third grade, the New York social studies curriculum moves from self to family, school, community, and world community as children compare the similarities and differences among people and cultures. U.S. history is formally introduced in Grade 4 and is studied in greater depth in Grades 7 and 8 and again in Grade 11. World history, divided into the history of the western hemisphere and the eastern hemisphere, is introduced in Grades 5 and 6 and is studied in greater depth in Grades 9 and 10. The U.S. government and its political and economic systems are explored in Grade 12. Students are expected to pass a standardized statewide final examination in global studies at the end of Grade 10 and in U.S. history after Grades 8 and 11. Using this guideline as a starting point, each school district establishes its own curriculum calendars.

CALIFORNIA SOCIAL STUDIES COURSE AND SEQUENCE

(available on the web at http://score.rims.k12.ca.us/standards/grade7.html)

The state of California's social studies curriculum is considered a model history-based social studies curriculum.

Grade 5: United States History and Geography: Making a New Nation

Students study the development of the nation up to 1850, with an emphasis on the people who were already here, when and from where others arrived, and why they came. Students learn about the colonial government founded on Judeo-Christian principles, the ideals of the Enlightenment, and the English traditions of self-government. They recognize that ours is a nation that has a constitution that derives its power from the people, that has gone through a revolution, that once sanctioned slavery, that experienced conflict over land with the original inhabitants, and that experienced a westward movement that took its people across the continent. Studying the cause, course, and consequences of the early explorations through the War for Independence and western expansion is central to students' fundamental understanding of how the principles of the American republic form the basis of a pluralistic society in which individual rights are secured.

Grade 6: World History and Geography: Ancient Civilizations

Students expand their understanding of history by studying the people and events that ushered in the dawn of the major Western and non-Western ancient civilizations. Geography is of special significance in the development of the human story. Continued emphasis is placed on the everyday lives, problems, and accomplishments of people; their role in developing social, economic, and political structures; as well as in establishing and spreading ideas that helped transform the world forever. Students develop higher levels of critical thinking by considering why civilizations developed where and when they did, why they became dominant, and why they declined. Students analyze the interactions among the various cultures, emphasizing their enduring contributions and the link, despite time, between the contemporary and ancient worlds.

Grade 7: World History and Geography: Medieval and Early Modern Times

Students study the social, cultural, and technological changes that occurred in Europe, Africa, and Asia in the years A.D. 500–1789. After reviewing the ancient world and the ways in which archaeologists and historians uncover the past, students study the history and geography of great civilizations that were developing concurrently throughout the world during medieval and early modern times. They examine the growing economic interaction among civilizations as well as the exchange of ideas, beliefs, technologies, and commodities. They learn about the resulting growth of Enlightenment philosophy and the new examination of the concepts of reason and authority, the natural rights of human beings and the divine right of kings, experimentalism in science, and the dogma of belief. Finally, students assess the political forces let loose by the Enlightenment, particularly the rise of democratic ideas, and they learn about the continuing influence of these ideas in the world today.

Continued

Grade 8: United States History and Geography: Growth and Conflict

Students study the ideas, issues, and events from the framing of the Constitution up to World War I, with an emphasis on the U.S. role in the war. After reviewing the development of America's democratic institutions founded on the Judeo-Christian heritage and English parliamentary traditions, particularly the shaping of the Constitution, students trace the development of U.S. politics, society, culture, and economy and relate them to the emergence of major regional differences. They learn about the challenges facing the new nation, with an emphasis on the causes, course, and consequences of the Civil War. They make connections between the rise of industrialization and contemporary social and economic conditions.

Grade 9: Elective Courses (No state standard or mandated content)

Grade 10: World History, Culture, and Geography: The Modern World

Students in grade 10 study major turning points that shaped the modern world, from the late 18th century through the present, including the cause and course of the two world wars. They trace the rise of democratic ideas and develop an understanding of the historical roots of current world issues, especially as they pertain to international relations. They extrapolate from the U.S. experience that democratic ideals are often achieved at a high price, remain vulnerable, and are not practiced everywhere in the world. Students develop an understanding of current world issues and relate them to their historical, geographic, political, economic, and cultural contexts. Students consider multiple accounts of events in order to understand international relations from a variety of perspectives.

Grade 11: United States History and Geography: Continuity and Change in the 20th Century

Students study the major turning points in U.S. history in the 20th century. Following a review of the nation's beginnings and the impact of the Enlightenment on U.S. democratic ideals, students build on the 10th grade study of global industrialization to understand the emergence and impact of new technology and a corporate economy, including the social and cultural effects. They trace the change in the ethnic composition of U.S. society, the movement toward equal rights for racial minorities and women, and the role of the United States as a major world power. An emphasis is placed on the expanding role of the federal government and federal courts as well as the continuing tension between the individual and the state. Students consider the major social problems of our time and trace their causes in historical events. They learn that the United States has served as a model for other nations and that the rights and freedoms we enjoy are not accidents but the results of a defined set of political principles that are not always basic to citizens of other countries. Students understand that our rights under the U.S. Constitution are a precious inheritance that depends on an educated citizenry for their preservation and protection.

Grade 12: Principles of American Democracy (1 Semester) and Economics (1 Semester)

Add Your Voice to the Discussion:

1. Do you have questions about or disagreements with any of these course descriptions? Explain.
2. As a teacher, would you prefer a mandated content or the ability to make your own curriculum decisions within broad guidelines? Explain your views.

Sample 11th-Grade Curriculum Calendar

In my experience, the most useful curriculum calendars give teachers a sense of how an entire year looks while leaving plenty of room for collective departmental decisions and individual teacher choices based on developments in their classes. A curriculum calendar is an evolving document designed to meet specific program needs rather than a precise model to be copied. When I started at Franklin K. Lane High School in 1982, the department began the year with the exploration and settlement of the New World by Europe and ended the first semester with 1865 and the conclusion of the Civil War. Later we shifted the semester break to 1877 and the end of Reconstruction. A 1989–1990 calendar divided the academic year at the presidential election of 1896.

As the social studies department curriculum committee redesigned Lane's U.S. history calendar, we tried to take the following into account:

- New York City has semiannual reorganization in high school, so social studies teachers had to have their classes in roughly the same place at the end of the semester in January.
- Depending on holidays and the weather, each semester included approximately 88 lessons. The calendar had to include space for orientation, review lessons, tests, and projects.
- Although the U.S. Constitution, the structure of government, and the economic system needed to be introduced, they would be studied primarily in separate government and economics classes.
- Within the department, teachers preferred to emphasize different aspects of U.S. history. For example, some wanted to spend time examining the origins of U.S. society during the colonial era, whereas others emphasized the issues facing the new government and nation.
- We wanted to guarantee that there would be sufficient time at the end of the year for students to examine the post-World War II United States.

- We decided to identify lesson topics by suggesting possible AIM, or guiding, questions.
- Students had to be prepared for a statewide final examination. Some teachers wanted to reserve extra days for review; others wanted time allocated for student presentations and discussions of current events.

Each unit and lesson in this curriculum calendar involves numerous teacher choices. For example, in the first unit, a teacher must decide how much time to spend on native peoples and the colonial era and whether to introduce African civilizations in a U.S. history curriculum. We recommended one lesson on Virginia and one on Massachusetts, but some teachers wanted to spend more time. Even the title of a unit, which reflects a point of view about the topic, involves choices. When we wrote it in 1989, we called it "Discovery and Settlement," but I now refer to it as "Encounter and Settlement." Another teacher might call it "Encounter and Conquest."

By the end of the 1990s, the State of New York high school social studies curriculum had changed again. Study about Meso-American civilizations, the "Encounter" between the Eastern and Western Hemispheres following the Colombian exchange, the colonization of the New World, and the Atlantic Slave Trade was shifted to the global history curriculum. These changes were designed to allow social studies teachers time to cover events through the conclusion of World War I in the first semester of U.S. history and ensure a comprehensive examination of events in the 20th century. Many teachers use the extra time for intensive review for year-end standardized tests. I prefer to "open the curriculum up" and involve students in special research and classroom projects (student dialogues are discussed in the essay at the end of chap. 4; oral history reports and Web-based research projects are discussed in chap. 8). The sample 11th-Grade U.S. history calendar presented here reflects changes and state mandates and my own teaching preferences.

Example: 11th-Grade U.S. History Calendar First Semester Calendar of Lessons

1. Orientation: How can I do well in this class?
2. What are the "BIG" questions? (See essay 2, chap. 2)

Unit 1: British America: From Settlement to Revolution (12 lessons)

3. When does American history begin? (See essay 1, chap. 2)
4. Mercantilism and Empire: Why did Great Britain want new world colonies?
5. What was life like in the British colonies?
6. How did Enlightenment ideas change America?
7. Why did Great Britain redefine its relationship with its American colonies?
8. How did the colonists respond to changes in British colonial policy?
9. Why did Thomas Paine call independence "Common Sense"?
10. What is the "promise" of the Declaration of Independence?
11. Social conflict in the colonies: Were all people "created equal"?
12. Global War: How did the British colonies win independence?
13. Unit review: Was the revolutionary war "inevitable"?
14. Unit test: British America: From settlement to revolution

Unit 2: Creating a Government (10 lessons)

15. Why did national leaders write a new constitution?
16. Original Intent: Why is the U.S. Constitution a bundle of compromises?
17. How are checks and balances structured into the U.S. government?
18. How was the constitution ratified?
19. Why was a Bill of Rights added to the U.S. Constitution?
20. What problems did a new government have to solve?
21. How did the Supreme Court emerge as a constitutional "umpire"?
22/23. (2 days). Trial of the Founding Fathers: Did the U.S. Constitution violate principles established in the Declaration of Independence? (See essay 3, chap. 6)
24. Unit test: Creating a government

Unit 3: Building a New Nation (12 lessons)

25. How did the American people become a nation?
26. How did the U.S. role in world affairs change?
27. Why did Congress try to retain sectional balance?
28. How did the expansion of the right to vote change U.S. society?
29. Why did women demand rights?
30. How did sectional conflict threaten union?
31. Manifest Destiny: Why did the new nation expand westward?
32. How did U.S. expansion affect native peoples?
33. Texas: How should we remember the Alamo?
34. What were the consequences of war with Mexico?
35. Unit test: New Nation
36. Review previous unit tests

Unit 4: Sectionalism, Slavery, and War (12 lessons)

37. How did the industrial revolution change the United States?
38. How did changes in transportation connect the North and West?
39. Why did cotton production lead to the expansion of slavery in the South?
40. How did the South justify slavery?
41. What was life like for enslaved Africans?
42. How did enslaved Africans resist slavery?
43. Why did balance and compromise fail to settle sectional differences?
44. Why did abolitionists battle against slavery?
45. Why was the Supreme Court unable to resolve the controversy over slavery?
46. Why did the election of 1860 lead to the Civil War?
47. Unit review: What were the main causes of the Civil War?
48. Unit test: Sectionalism, Slavery, and War

Unit 5: Civil War and Reconstruction (9 lessons)

49. Why did the South try to leave the union?
50. How did the North win?
51. What role did women, immigrants, and African Americans play in the war effort?
52. What were the goals of conflicting Reconstruction plans?
53. Could the wounds of war be healed?
54. How did the Reconstruction Amendments rewrite the U.S. Constitution?
55. Was Reconstruction a "dawn without noon"?
56. What was the cost of the "failure" of Reconstruction?
57. Document-based essay unit test: Civil War and Reconstruction

Unit 6: Industrialization Reshapes the United States (17 lessons)

58. How did technology change the United States?
59. What was the impact of industrial growth on native peoples?
60. How did industry change the way Americans did business?
61. Why was government corrupted?
62. How did workers respond to industrialization?
63. Why did farmers demand reforms?
64. What was the Populist vision for the United States?
65. Why did a new wave of immigrants come to the United States?
66. What was life like in urban America?
67. Why did conflicts between workers and corporations sometimes lead to violence?
68. Why did muckrakers and progressives demand reform?
69. Why did women emerge as champions of reform?
70. How did Progressive reforms change the United States?
71. Why did some Americans demand radical change?
72. How did women achieve political rights?
73/74. Presentation of student projects on the impact of industrialization and reform
75. Unit test: Industrialization and Progressive reform

Unit 7: The United States Emerges as a World Power (13 lessons)

76. Why did the United States look overseas?
77. What was the ideology of imperialism?
78. Was U.S. policy in Asia imperialistic?
79. Why did the United States go to war with Spain?

80. Should the United States intervene in Latin America and the Caribbean?
81. Panama: Does the end justify the means?
82. What were the origins of the "Great War"?
83. Why did the United States enter the World War?
84. What were Woodrow Wilson's goals?
85. What was the U.S. role in the World War?
86. How did participation in the World War change life in the United States?
87. Should the United States have joined the League of Nations?
88. Unit (or mid-term) test: The United States emerges as a world power

Example: 11th-Grade U.S. History Calendar: Second Semester Calendar of Lessons

1. What are the "BIG" questions? (Review student defined essential questions.)
2. Organizing the 20th-Century America Oral History Project (See essay 1, chap. 8).
3. Researching and writing oral histories.

Unit 1: Prosperity and Depression (15 lessons)

4. Could America return to "normalcy" at the end of World War I?
5. Why were immigrants targeted by the Palmer Raids?
6. Who were Sacco and Vanzetti?
7. Why did the Scopes trial create so much controversy?
8. How did African Americans create culture and community in the northern cities?
9. What was happening to the U.S. economy and workforce during the 1920s?
10. Why did the economy collapse?
11. What was the Republican concept of the role of government?
12. What was the impact of the Great Depression on life in the United States?
13. What was the promise of the New Deal?
14. How did the Great Depression and New Deal affect life in New York (or any locality)?
15. How did the New Deal change U.S. government?
16. Unit review: Did the New Deal solve the Great Depression?
17. Unit test: Prosperity and Depression
18. Review unit test

Unit 2: World War II (13 lessons)

19. Organize student dialogue teams on the atomic bombing of Hiroshima and Nagasaki (see chap. 8).
20. What were the underlying causes of World War II?
21. Why did many Americans demand isolation during the 1930s?
22. What were the underlying causes of U.S. entry into the war?
23. What were the immediate causes of the U.S. entry into the war?
24. How did the allies win in Europe?
25. How did the allies win in the Pacific?
26. Was total war justified?
27. Rosie the Riveter and Civil Rights: How did the war change life in the United States?
28. The internment of the Japanese: How could it happen here?
29. Cold War or United Nations: What will the postwar world look like?
30. Unit review (Dialogue): Should the United States have dropped the atomic bomb on Japan?
31. Unit test: World War II

Unit 3: Post-War America—A Changing Society (15 lessons)

32. Student teams read and edit oral histories for presentation in class.
33. How did life in the United States change after World War II?
34. How did highways and suburbs transform life in the United States?
35. Was the United States becoming a consumer society?
36. How did science and technology change life in the United States?
37. Were internal communists a threat to the "American way of life"?
38. Should the New Deal grow or be reined in?
39. What was the promise of the Kennedy era?
40. Could the United States be a "Great Society"?
41. Was Watergate a threat to democracy in the United States?
42. How did conservative forces reshape government and society?
43. Presentation of oral histories on life in the 1940s, 1950s and 1960s
44. Presentation of oral histories on life in the 1940s, 1950s and 1960s
45. Document-based essay: Post-War America—A Changing Society
46. Introduce web-based research reports

Unit 4: The African American Struggle for Civil Rights (14 lessons)

47. Organize student dialogue on the Civil Rights movement.
48. What was life like for African Americans at the end of World War II?
49. How did African Americans respond to these conditions?
50. What were the responses of Southern whites and state and local governments?
51. How did the federal government respond to the Civil Rights movement?
52. What were the ideas of the Civil Rights movement?
53. What were strategies of the Civil Rights movement?
54. What was Martin Luther King Jr.'s vision for U.S. society?
55. Did the Civil Rights movement significantly change the laws of the United States?
56. Why did African American communities explode?
57. Why did a new generation of African American activists challenge the ideas and strategies of the Civil Rights movement?
58. Who was Malcolm X and what did he teach?
59. Unit review (Dialogue): Did the Civil Rights movement succeed?
60. Unit test: The African American struggle for Civil Rights

Unit 5: Vietnam and the Cold War (15 lessons)

61. Why did wartime allies fight a "cold war"?
62. Why did "hot spots" emerge in Berlin, Korea, and Cuba?
63. How did the nuclear and space races shape the world?
64. How did the United States respond to anticolonial movements in the Third World?
65. Did events in the Middle East threaten U.S. security?
66. Why did East Asia play a central role in U.S. foreign policy?
67. Why was the United States in Vietnam?
68. What happened to U.S. troops in Vietnam?
69. What was the impact of U.S. involvement in Vietnam on the American people?
70. Did U.S. policy in Vietnam "fail?"

71. How did Middle Eastern conflicts affect life in the United States?
72. What happened to the Russian "Evil Empire"?
73. Can the United States establish a "New World Order"?
74. Document-based essay: The Vietnam War
75. Unit test: Cold War and Vietnam

Unit 6: Life in the Contemporary United States (10 lessons)

76. How did the women's rights movement change the United States?
77. Why did Supreme Court decisions spark controversy?
78. What is life like for the newest immigrants to the United States?
79. How has computer technology changed the way we live?

80. Can the United States become a more equal society?
81. What is the responsibility of government in an economically developed society?
82. Can nuclear weapons be eliminated?
83. Should the United States be the police force for the world?
84. What are the "BIG" questions for the 21st century?
85. Unit test: Document-based essay on life in the contemporary United States

Standardized Test Preparation (3 lessons)

86. Regents review: Examine essay format/practice essays
87. Regents review: Discuss short answer strategies/review prior exams
88. Regents review: Student study teams complete prior exams

Teaching Activity: Examining a Curriculum Calendar

Think it over:

1. The unit "British America: From Settlement to Revolution" includes 10 regular lessons, a review lesson, and a unit test. Write a paragraph describing what you think each of the first 10 lessons might include.
2. What primary source documents could you use as resources in the unit "Creating a Government"?
3. Slavery is the focus in 9 of the 12 lessons in the unit "Sectionalism, Slavery, and War." Do you agree or disagree with this emphasis? Why?
4. In the first semester, Lesson 51 directs attention toward the role of women, immigrants, and African Americans in the Civil War. Lesson 69 asks Why did women emerge as champions of reform? In the second semester, Lesson 8 explores how African Americans created "culture and community" in the northern cities, and Lesson 27 examines changes in the lives of women and African Americans as a result of World War II. What do you think about focusing lessons on particular groups of people? Why?
5. The units "Prosperity and Depression" and "World War II" include lessons on the Palmer Raids, Sacco and Vanzetti, the Scopes trial, and the bombing of Hiroshima, as well as discussions of wartime discrimination against Japanese and African Americans. In your opinion, does this focus present the United States in an unnecessarily negative light? Explain.
6. This calendar includes a 14: lesson thematic unit on the African American struggle for Civil Rights in the 1950s and 1960s (outlined in greater detail in chap. 4). Do you agree or disagree with this emphasis? Why?
7. How would you answer the question, What are the "BIG" Questions for the 21st Century?
8. What is your general opinion of this lesson calendar? Why?

It's your classroom:

1. What would you include that is missing in this calendar? Why?
2. Would you leave only three days for review for a standardized final exam? Why?

"Some Educators Say Recent Events Are Not Yet the Stuff of History Class"
The *Boston Globe* (Greenberger, 2001) reports the following debate in Massachusetts:
"The Clinton administration is over, but is it history? It is, according to a draft of the state's new American history curriculum. High school students would have to study NAFTA and Clinton's welfare reform law, and 'explain the causes and consequences' of his impeachment. Studying recent events energizes teenagers, supporters of the new guidelines say. But Abigail Thernstrom, a member of the State Board of Education and a political scientist, argues that it is much too soon to put Monica Lewinsky, let alone Bush vs. Gore, in their proper historical context. Those characters and events are still 'too politically and emotionally charged' to be taught well, Thernstrom said. 'I wouldn't trust myself to teach the last 20 years.' "

Add your voice to the discussion:
1. Which recent events do you consider "history"? Why?
2. Where would you end the curriculum calendar? Why?

Classroom Activity: Mock Trial in a U.S. Government Course

New York State offers options in its 12th-grade "Participation in Government" curriculum. They include a political science class that focuses on the U.S. government and legal system; classes which explore local, state, and national public policy issues, the rights and responsibilities of citizens, or the political process; and a program that emphasizes community service activities. Working within the framework of the U.S. government and legal system model, Michael Butler (NTN) organized a two-week criminal mock trial with students in his high school class.

At the start of the project, students selected a "case" after viewing videotaped coverage from the local evening news and reading articles in the newspaper. The case they selected involved the high-speed police chase of a truck transporting suspected illegal migrants from Mexico. Two police officers were accused of beating up passengers from the truck. In the mock trial, the officers were charged with attempted murder, first-degree assault, and criminal negligence.

Lesson Schedule
Day 1: Students examine different cases and select the case for their mock trial.
Day 2: The class discusses the case and the participants in a trial, and divides up the roles.
Days 3 and 4: Students learn about the responsibilities of different participants in a trial.
Days 5 and 6: Student teams representing the prosecution, the defense, and witnesses write opening statements, prepare questions, and outline testimony.
Day 7: Trial participants practice their parts in a dress rehearsal.
Day 8: The trial. Michael Butler, the teacher, plays the judge.
Day 9: The jury deliberates, reaches a decision, and announces its verdict.
Day 10: The class views segments from a video of the trial and evaluates the entire project.

Add your voice to the discussion:
1. In your opinion, would students learn more by studying the transcripts of an actual court case or by creating and role-playing a case such as this one? Why?
2. How do you respond to suggestions that this type of activity reinforces student antipathies toward the police?

Think it over:
1. Would you have allowed students to select the case? Why or why not?
2. How much leeway do you think students should be permitted during the trial and the deliberations? Why?
3. What do you think of Michael Butler's decision to be the judge? Why?

It's your classroom:
Would you schedule so much class time for one project? Why or why not?

*Essay 1: Teaching Global History**

Curricula are written on paper, not etched in stone, and they are often the product of sharply contested political battles.

Soon after the first edition of *Social Studies for Secondary Schools* (Singer, 1997) was published, the State of New York changed its high school global studies curriculum. The original curriculum was an area studies approach integrating geography, culture, and history. Students studied the non-Western world (Africa, Asia, the Islamic world, and Latin America) in 9th grade and the history of Western civilization in 10th grade. The new curriculum was intended as a two-year chronological study of global history; however, it generally followed the perimeters of developments in European society. It concluded the 9th grade with the era of the European Enlightenment and began 10th grade social studies with the French Revolution and impact of industrialization.

TWO-YEAR CHRONOLOGICAL GLOBAL HISTORY CURRICULUM

9th Grade Topics:

Ancient World: Civilizations and Religions (4000 B.C.E.–A.D. 500)
Expanding Zones of Exchange and Encounter (500–1200)
Global Interactions (1200–1650)
The First Global Age (1450–1770)

10th Grade Topics:

An Age of Revolutions (1750–1914)
A Half Century of Crisis and Achievement (1900–1945)
The 20th Century Since 1945

The old curriculum was a victim of battles over multicultural inclusion and whether students should be studying social studies or history. In *The Great Speckled Bird* (1995), Catherine Cornbleth and Dexter Waugh argued that campaigns to rewrite social studies curricula were part of a conservative nationwide drive for fact-based direct instruction and a celebration of the Western core of American civilization.

In an unlikely coalition, conservatives were joined by progressive historians who saw an opportunity to extend the influence of the history profession in precollegiate education and a chance to root out what they describe as "the old mishmash known as 'social studies.'" The heart of their position was a belief that teachers must present the "pastness of the past," not turn the study of history into a "mere prologue of the present." In an essay published in *The New York Times*, Sean Wilentz (1997: 4: 15) of Princeton University argued that "the past is not a 'process'" and that social studies topics should not be selected based on their current "relevance to our own world."

The change in the curriculum presented social studies teachers the difficult task of integrating essential questions and themes, conceptual understandings, social and academic skills, hands-on activities and student projects, *the things many of us consider most important*, into a chronologically organized curriculum while stimulating and maintaining student interest.

It also raises a number of important questions teachers must consider as they develop units and lessons.

• Will students be able to acquire a cultural understanding of, and appreciation for, the regions of the world as they continent-hop through history? Does it make sense to combine

---

*An earlier version of this essay appeared in A. Singer, A. Libresco, and J. Balantic, "SSR Forum: Teaching Social Studies with the New Global History Curriculum," *Social Science Record* 35, no. 1 (1988), 6–8. Used with permission.

independent developments occurring in different parts of the world in the same chronologically organized unit?

- In a chronological curriculum will there be room to integrate art projects, cultural investigations and comparisons, and world literature?
- Will students be able to understand the role of geography in the development of a region if they do not study an area as a cohesive unit?
- Will comparative study of different regions during the same epoch (e.g., 20th century nationalist movements) be organized so that students learn that the historical narrative is complex and composed of many voices? Will the focus on chronology lead to an abandonment of historical actors and movements that were defeated and reinforce a sense that the world today was somehow predetermined?
- Will a predominance of information about the western world, greater teacher knowledge about this region, the availability of European primary source documents, and Europe's role in the development of the United States transform global history into a two-year European history class with occasional side trips to examine other parts of the world?

In theory, the new curriculum allows teachers to teach a concept and give multiple examples of its application within the same chronological period. For example, the European motivations for imperialism will be followed directly by a study of the effects of imperialism in Africa and Asia. However, a danger is that non-Western societies will be completely defined by their interactions with European imperialist powers.

Another strong argument for a chronological approach is that students can learn the historical context of major principles and discover how they play out over time. For example, students will study the industrial revolution as a background to Marxism and the ideas of Marx before examining Lenin, Stalin, Mao, and Pol Pot. This change may help students better understand the interconnectedness of the regions of the world. On the other hand, its emphasis on linear progression may rob these movements and countries of their individual national dynamics and feed into a Cold War–like notion of a ideological communist monolith.

State curriculum guidelines also include basic concepts that are intended to be woven throughout the curriculum. This does provide a mandate to incorporate many of the social science understandings developed in the area studies approach. In alphabetical order, the concepts are belief systems, change, culture and intellectual life, diversity, economic systems, environment, geography, imperialism, interdependence, justice and human rights, movement of people and goods, nationalism, political systems, science and technology, and urbanization.

One way to ensure that these concepts are covered in the new curriculum is to make thematic stops along the journey through time. Origami is the Japanese art of paper folding. In Japanese, *oru* means "to fold" and *kami* means "paper." Paperfolding originally developed in China, probably soon after the invention of paper in the first century A.D. In an example of cultural diffusion, paper and paperfolding were brought to Japan in the sixth century A.D. by Buddhist monks. In Japan, paper and paperfolding became important aspects of architecture and the Shinto religion. *Kami* (paper) is a homonym for spirit or god.

During the Edo period in Japanese history (approximately 1600–1868), with the increased availability of inexpensive paper, origami developed as a more elaborate art form. The creation of symbolic objects, such as cranes and boats, replaced simpler designs. The first written work about origami was published in 1797. The beginning of modern origami was developed by Akira Yoshizawa in the 1930s. He is responsible for the creation of thousands of modern-day techniques and patterns.

In an example of parallel cultural development, paperfolding (papiroflexia) also developed independently in Spain after Islamic merchants imported paper in the eighth century A.D. Papiroflexia is still popular in Spain and Argentina.

To learn more about origami, start with http://library.thinkquest.org/27458/nf/origami/history.html. To get help making origami, try Joseph Wu's Origami Page at http://www.origami.vancouver.bc.cal/.

I use origami workshops in global history classes to reinforce the concepts of cultural diffusion and parallel development, to illustrate Buddhist philosophy and to introduce the Japanese concept of Shibui, beauty through simplicity. One aspect of Zen Buddhism is coming to terms with life's contradictions. Both Zen Buddhist meditation and origami teach relaxation through concentration and focusing on the process rather than the result.

"Cranes for Peace" Christmas Tree at the American Museum of Natural History in New York City

I usually teach a few simple origami designs to student volunteers during a free period and they serve as an expert team that assists in teaching the designs in class. Once they get the hang of it, most of the students are better at paperfolding than I am. Origami can also be part of a broader class project (discussed in chap. 8), especially if you are teaching sixth grade.

While leading the class in paperfolding, I stress three basic rules:

1. Symmetry (what you do to one side you must do to the others).
2. Concentration (the open side must always be down).
3. Precision (folds must be done carefully and firmly).

Teaching Activity: Origami Paper Crane

The crane is usually not for beginners, but I think it is worth a try. Everyone is not going to be able to create one the first time. It is easier if you work in pairs with one person reading the directions aloud. For help visit http://www.unr.nevada.edu/~jsanweb/english/Features/origami-crane/2.htm.

Start with a square of paper. Usually it is brightly colored or patterned on one side. While you can use any size, I prefer a 6-inch square. A larger piece can be awkward to work with and a smaller one is just plain difficult for inexperienced or clumsy fingers.

"Top" means the corner or side pointing away from you.

"Bottom" means the corner or side pointing toward you.

1. Place a square of paper on a flat surface with the colorful side underneath. Turn it so that it is a diamond shape.
2. Fold top corner to the bottom corner creating a triangle. Note the bottom side (the side pointing toward you) is always open.
3. Press carefully and firmly along the fold at least three times. You must do this after each fold.
4. Create a smaller triangle by folding the right corner over to the left corner. Press.
5. The next step is tricky. Lift up the flap you just created so your paper forms a right angle. Insert your index finger into the opening of the vertical flap, carefully pushing to the back.

Gradually open the flap. As you do this, the top point of the flap will start to come down, creating a new diamond. Press the new folds.

6. Remember the principle of symmetry. Turn the paper over with the open side remaining down. Create a new vertical flap. Again, insert your index finger into the opening of the vertical flap. Gradually open the flap. As you do this, the top point of the flap will start to come down, creating a new diamond. Press the new folds.

7. With the open side down, fold the bottom right side so it touches the middle axis of the diamond. Fold the bottom left side the same way. Flip your figure over and repeat on the other side. The new figure will look like a kite. Press the new folds.

8. Fold the top section of the kite over and press.

9. Another tricky step. You are going to open the "kite" and let the figure form a new shape. If you do it correctly, it will want to do this on its own. You just have to help it. Pull back the top flap. The place where it bends is a key fold. Open the two side flaps. You have returned to the diamond shape. The bottom of the diamond is open. Lift the upper sheet of paper from the bottom of the diamond. Placing a finger from your other hand on the key fold, push the upper sheet all the way back away from you. As you do this, the new sides will start to fold in. Help them. You will now have an elongated diamond shape with an opening in the front.

10. Flip the diamond and repeat the transformation on the other side. Press the new folds. If you have done everything correctly, the bottom of this new figure will have two "legs." To make sure everything is okay, let them walk a little.

11. There are openings on both sides of the diamond. Place one index finger in each opening and bring the upper sheets together. Bring the lower sheets together as well. Lay the figure flat on your surface. It should look a little like a wolf. Press the new folds.

12. We will now repeat step 7. With the open side down, fold the bottom right side so it touches the middle axis. Fold the bottom left side the same way. Flip your figure over and repeat on the other side. The new figure will look like a wolf with a narrower face. Press the new folds. Do not despair. You are almost finished.

13. You should have two pointy flaps at the bottom of the figure and two "ears" at the top. Lift one of the pointy flaps up as far as it will go and fold. Fold the top inch of the tip down. Press the new folds. Turn the figure over and lift the other pointy flap up as far as it will go and fold. You are finished folding. Firmly and carefully press the entire figure.

14. We now must open the crane. Let the last two folds spring out. This should leave two folds of paper standing upright. These are your wings. Place one index finger in each opening of the wings and gently pull out and up. A box or body will form in the middle. Keep tugging gently until the body is unfolded. Straighten the head, tail, and wings. Tuck the tail up against the box. Your origami paper crane is now complete.

Add your voice to the discussion:
How do you view the debate over areas studies versus a chronological global history? Explain.

Try it yourself:
Experiment with creating a paper crane and other origami figures.

It's your classroom:
Would you use an activity such as origami? Explain.

Essay 2: Multicultural Social Studies*

One of the difficulties in discussing multicultural social studies is that there is not general agreement about what *multiculturalism* means, let alone what a multicultural social studies curriculum should look like. In her book *Empowerment through Multicultural Education*, Christine Sleeter

*Based on A. Singer (1994). Used with permission.

(1991), identified five different approaches to multiculturalism: (1) a human relations approach intended to increase student sensitivity toward others, (2) curriculum designed to enhance the self-esteem of minority youth, (3) single group studies programs, (4) culturally inclusive classrooms with pluralistic curricula, and (5) a transformative approach that combines pluralism with critiques of social injustice. Sleeter did not mention more modest infusion approaches that try to incorporate the heroes and holidays of different groups into more traditional social studies curricula.

Despite a two-decade–long debate (or perhaps because of it), multiculturalism remains a perspective in the making and is beset with conflicts about implementation that will probably never be completely resolved. Some of the ideas suggested as organizing principles for a social studies curriculum are broadly held by people who identify themselves as multiculturalists whereas others are sharply debated.

Most teachers who identify themselves as multiculturalists are committed to the idea that the study of history must respect the integrity of the past. No matter how comforting or convenient, educators should not present myth as history. However, we also need to remember that historical interpretations continually change and that the ideologies of historians and societies shape these interpretations.

Shaped by this perspective, multicultural social studies becomes a way of looking at the world that is rooted in scientific exploration, a challenge to cultural limitations distorting our vision, and a call for more inclusive and reflective teaching. Multiculturalism has the most relevance for subjects such as social studies, art, music, and literature,

but it is not limited to these areas. Multicultural social studies is an effort to present a fuller picture of the world's history, people, and cultures. Since the 1960s, social history, the study of ordinary people, has played an expanding role in the history profession's understanding of the past. However, most public school social studies curricula continue to be based on political, economic, intellectual, and institutional history.

Social history is multicultural history. Its exploration of the United States is based on the notion that all people—not just presidents, generals, inventors, and business leaders—contribute to making a nation. For social historians, the history of the United States is the history of people: Africans, Latinos, Native Americans, the Irish, Poles, Slavs, Italians, Germans, Asians, Jews, the English, and others, their relationships to one another and to our society as a whole.

Multicultural social studies is based on the idea of "multiple perspectives": there is more than one way to view and understand an event, idea, or era. As an example, consider this question: Did industrialization unleash waves of progress and prosperity? For some people, the answer is yes, but the answer is no if you were a shepherd or small farmer in Europe, the Sahel region of Africa, or Southeast Asia, driven off your traditional lands by large-scale commercial agriculture; a hand-loom operator in England or India displaced by water-powered machinery; an African, kidnapped and sold into slavery to produce cash crops for capitalist factories and markets; or a member of any one of thousands of ethnic groups that were drawn into crowded, polluted, and disease-ridden cities out of fear of starvation and the desperate need for work.

Learning Activity: Impact of Capitalist Development

A curriculum that explores multiple perspectives tries to help students understand how different groups of people experienced the same historical forces. Capitalist development and industrialization in Great Britain and Europe were financed by the African slave trade and the wealth expropriated from the Americas. It affected people all over the world.

General Ludd's triumph

The following song was sung by British weavers (Thompson, 1963: 534, 547) called "Luddites" as they destroyed new textile machinery at the end of the 18th and the beginning of the 19th centuries. They rose in scattered rebellion against industrial progress that had undermined their skills and standard of living.

> The guilty may fear but no vengeance he aims
> At the honest man's life or Estate,
> His wrath is entirely confined to wide frames

And to those that old prices abate.
These Engines of mischief were sentenced to die
By unanimous vote of the Trade
And Ludd who can all opposition defy
Was the Grand Executioner made.

Then the Trade when this arduous contest is o'er
Shall raise in full splendor its head,
And colting and cutting and squaring no more
Shall deprive honest workmen of bread.
Chants no more your old rhymes about bold Robin Hood,
His feats I but little admire.
I will sing the Achievements of General Ludd,
Now the Hero of Nottinghamshire.

Oloudah Equiano describes being kidnapped into slavery

Oloudah Equiano was born in Benin on the west coast of equatorial Africa in 1745 and was kidnapped and sold into slavery when he was 11. While enslaved, he worked on a Virginia plantation as the servant for a British naval officer and for a Philadelphia merchant. After purchasing his freedom, he wrote his memoirs (Katz, 1971: 32–33) and became active in the antislavery movement. A selection from his memoir follows. The full text of *The Interesting Narrative of the Life of Oloudah Equiano, or Gustavus Vasa, Written by Himself* (London, 1789) is available on the web at http://docsouth.unc.edu.

The first object which assaulted my eyes when I arrived on the coast was the sea, and a slaveship, which was riding at anchor, and waiting for its cargo. These filled me with astonishment, which was soon converted into terror, which I am yet at a loss to describe. . . . When I was carried on board I was immediately handled, and tossed up, to see if I were sound, by some of the crew; and I was now persuaded that I had got into a world of bad spirits, and that they were going to kill me. . . .

I was soon put down under the decks, and there I received such a salutation in my nostrils as I had never experienced in my life; so that with the loathsomeness of the stench, and the crying together, I became so sick and low that I was not able to eat, nor had I the least desire to taste anything. . . . but soon, to my grief, two of the white men offered me eatables; and on my refusing to eat, one of them held me fast by the hands . . . and tied my feet, while the other flogged me severely. . . .

Amongst the poor chained men, I found some of my own nation, which in a small degree gave ease to my mind. I inquired of them what was to be done with us? They gave me to understand we were to be carried to these white people's country to work for them. . . .

The closeness of the place, and the heat of the climate, added to the number in the ship, which was so crowded that each had scarcely room to turn himself, almost suffocated us. . . . The shrieks of the women, and the groans of the dying, rendered the whole scene of horror almost inconceivable. . . . I was soon reduced so low here that it was thought necessary to keep me almost always on deck. . . .

One day, when we had a smooth sea, . . . two of my wearied countrymen, who were chained together, preferring death to such a life of misery, somehow made it through the nettings, and jumped into the sea; immediately another quite dejected fellow . . . also followed their example; and I believe many more would very soon have done the same, if they had not been prevented by the ship's crew, who were instantly alarmed. . . . Two of the wretches were drowned, but they got the other, and afterwards flogged him unmercifully, for thus attempting to prefer death to slavery. In this manner we continued to undergo more hardships than I can now relate; hardships which are inseparable from this accursed trade. . .

It's your classroom:

1. How could you use these documents in your classroom?
2. Would you edit these documents or use their original language? Why?
3. What questions would you ask to promote student understanding and discussion?
4. What other sources (documents, historical and contemporary literature, movies) from different parts of the world might you include in a unit on the impact of capitalist development?

Differences in perspective can also be more subtle. For example, most U.S. slave narratives were published by abolitionists, who used them to illustrate the horror, irrationality, and inhumanity of human bondage. Because morality plays are designed to outrage readers, historians cannot simply rely on them to shed light on the experience of enslaved African Americans or the motives and culture of southern white slave owners. Works of fiction can be particularly useful for understanding the way other people view the world. Three of my favorite authors are Rohinton Mistry (*A Fine Balance*, 1997), who writes about India; Chinua Achebe (*Things Fall Apart*, 1994), who writes about Nigeria; and Mongane Serote, who writes poems about apartheid in South Africa (available on the web at http://www.uct.ac.za/projects/poetry/serote.htm and http://www.club.it/culture/culture97/itala.vivan97).

Multicultural social studies is a call for "inclusion" in the curriculum. It says, "I should be visible in this classroom, but so should you, and so should all the people that inhabit this nation and world." It is important that students know where their ancestors fit into the historical picture. It generates a sense of pride. It engages them in the study of the past. But it is also important that students know how Irish canal builders, White Protestant New England women mill workers, Chinese railway construction crews, Jewish garment workers, and enslaved African agricultural workers made possible the industrial development of the United States. Multiculturalism allows students and teachers to explore the similarities and differences in human experience, and it shows the broad range of human contributions to historical development. I was touched by both the cartoon dialogues of *Maus* (Spiegelman, 1986) and the biographical narratives of *The Joy Luck Club* (Tan, 1989). One author was a male American Jew and the other a Chinese American woman. Both helped me reconsider my own experience trying to understand the choices and struggles of my parents' and grandparents' generations. Multiculturalism is not "feel-good" history or the watering down of literature; it is an expanded and more detailed picture of the social, cultural, and intellectual histories of our country and our world.

Although not all human differences are cultural, a multicultural approach supports respect for and inclusion of other kinds of differences as well. Feminist research has shown the importance of "positionality" in shaping human understanding (Code, 1991; Alcoff, 1988). Gender, racial, ethnic, class,

A statue at the entrance of the American Museum of Natural History in New York City shows Theodore Roosevelt "leading" a Native American and an African to civilization. An interpretation of world events that was considered acceptable in the early 20th century is viewed very differently today.

sexual orientation, physical ability, and religious differences, the collectivity of group social experience, and the individuality of personal experience all contribute to the way that people see the world and the insights that students bring to our classrooms.

Multicultural social studies insists that we see the world in all of its global complexity. Billions of actors are on the world stage, and a viewpoint that ignores most of them leaves us unable to understand the forces that are shaping our planet. For example, environmental problems such as the destruction of the rain forests and the threat of global warming cannot be solved in the United States alone or without taking into consideration the needs of people in other countries and other regions of the world.

Global complexity is not just pertinent, however, when we discuss the contemporary world. New histories emphasize that the Nile River Valley was a crossroads where diverse cultures met, interacted, and created new cultures. The Seeds of Change exhibit, organized by the National Museum of Natural History at the Smithsonian Institution, explored the cultural exchanges that followed the Colombian Encounter of 1492 and the ways they reshaped the lives of people in Africa, Europe, and the Americas. Before students can understand the U.S. war in Vietnam, they need to examine the Cold War between the United States and the Soviet Union; the competition between the United States, Japan, and European nations for economic influence in Southeast Asia; and the deep-seated nationalistic aspirations of the Vietnamese people.

Classroom Activity: Food Changes the Way We Live

As part of the 500th anniversary of 1492, the Smithsonian Institution, the National Council of Social Studies, and Addison-Wesley published *Seeds of Change, The Story of Cultural Exchange after 1492* (Hawke and Davis, 1992). It focuses on the impact of five major exchanges on world history: disease, maize (corn), the potato, the horse, and sugar cane. For example, "old world" diseases decimated Native American populations, sugar cane production led to the introduction of slavery in the Americas, and potato cultivation contributed to skyrocketing population growth in Europe.

Pasta with red sauce is one example of what happened when a European crop (wheat) was combined with an American product (the tomato). Students can discuss their assumptions about the origins of different foods, ways that the post-Colombian encounter modified cultures and led to the creation of new dishes, and the broader concepts of cultural diffusion and blending.

Foods from the Americas:

avocados, beans, Chile peppers, coca, maize (corn), peanuts, pineapples, potatoes, pumpkins, squashes, sweet potatoes, tomatoes, turkeys

Foods from Europe, Asia, and Africa:

bananas, barley, beets, cabbage, cattle, grapes, oats, olives, onions, pigs, rice, sheep, wheat

Try it yourself:

Name dishes made from these items that illustrate cultural diffusion and blending.

Viewed within this context, multicultural social studies requires dialogue between people with different points of view, acknowledgment of different experiences, and respect for diverse opinions. It creates space for alternative voices, not just on the periphery, but in the center. Multiculturalism values creating knowledge through research, analysis, and discussion. It rejects the idea that there is only one possible answer that everyone must accept and recognizes that what people believe to be "true" is constantly changing.

Proposed multicultural texts and curriculum often offer one event, work of art, or cultural manifestation to represent the sum total of a people's experiences. This type of sampling takes people's experience out of context and can marginalize their roles in world history. Students need to understand that (1) there are many different African cultures and that their histories did not begin with the Atlantic slave trade, (2) Jews existed between the times of Christ and Hitler, (3) Native American civilizations flourished before Europeans arrived, and (4) Egypt did not disappear when Cleopatra died.

Educators need to know where the lives of different groups of people intersect on the world stage, but unless we also understand how different groups of people developed, how they perceived themselves, and how they lived before and after the points of intersection, we cannot understand their roles and contributions to human history and culture.

A key precept for a multicultural education should be respect for the richness of difference. This is a crucial value for the survival of a diverse and democratic society and a fundamental component of how we learn. Learning in general and learning and developing a sense of self-identity in particular are parts of a process of comparing similarities and differences. I become conscious of who I am and what I am as I compare me with you. Without difference, identity has no meaning.

Some educators are concerned that valuing cultural difference contributes to moral relativism and leads to the acceptance of oppressive practices simply because they are part of another group's culture. They have raised the issue of the continuing subjugation of women in many societies, including genital mutilation, female infanticide, the absence of reproductive freedom, and the denial of political and economic equality. The issue of how to address the treatment of women around the world in our classrooms is clearly a complicated one. Students need to think about a number of factors as they discuss gender equity and explore different cultures.

Respecting the right of other people to do things differently and recognizing that a practice plays a role in a particular culture do not mean we must surrender our right to voice disagreement, accept every aspect of a culture, or encourage its extension or survival. Cultures are not stagnant, and cultural traditions based on racism and patriarchy often generate internal tension within national or ethnic cultures that can stimulate social change. This has been the case in most of the Western industrial societies.

When looking at cultures that continue to subjugate women, especially in Third World countries, we have to ask what actions on our part create the greatest possibility for change. When "outsiders" challenge a group's cultural practices, it can have the undesired consequence of reinforcing the practice by transforming it into a symbol of national opposition to imperialism. This is one of the factors that has contributed to the growth of religious fundamentalist movements in a number of countries.

In the United States, an expressed goal of education is the creation of an active citizenry committed to democratic values. Promoting democratic values means that social studies educators need to be involved in developing antiracist, nonsexist curricula that allow students to explore social contradictions. A major theme in U.S. history classes can be examining the conflict between the promise of America outlined in the Declaration of Independence and the reality of life in the United States. Through involvement in this type of historical exploration, students learn how societies change and how they can become agents of change.

Multicultural social studies also promotes democratic values as students come to recognize the dynamic nature of culture. Students are exposed to a broad range of possibilities that enhance the likelihood of conscious cultural choices. A focus on similarity and difference and multiple perspectives can ultimately make possible a more integrated national culture in the United States.

The notion of multicultural social studies described here points to a different way for organizing our classrooms. In most classes, the teacher is the expert, the conveyor of all knowledge, and the job of the student is to absorb passively what the teacher presents. Too frequently, social studies teachers present history as a collection of isolated and seemingly random facts to be memorized. Students see little logic in this approach and are unclear why some facts but not others are included. Teachers need to abandon reliance on lectures, allowing students to discover patterns and create connections through their own thinking and research. Our goal should be for students to become active learners who see history as a way of examining the past so they can better understand the present and participate in shaping the future. Educators should help students learn to frame and evaluate hypotheses about why things happen and why people and nations act the way they do. We must be willing to take the risk that students will arrive at conclusions that might not make us happy.

I would like to share an example of how this kind of multicultural perspective has helped me learn in my social studies classroom. Over the years, a number of African American students have expressed in class that they resent only learning about slavery and how their people were oppressed. They were not really interested in learning about the glories of ancient African civilizations either.

Learning Activity: The Missing Passage

The following charges against the King of England were removed from the original draft of the Declaration of Independence before it was signed on July 4, 1776 (Franklin, 1974: 88):

> He has waged cruel war against human nature itself, violating its most sacred rights of life and liberty in the persons of a distant people who never offended him, captivating and carrying them into slavery in another hemisphere, or to incur miserable death in their transportation thither. . . . Determined to keep open a market where men should be bought and sold, he has suppressed every legislative attempt to prohibit or to restrain this execrable commerce.

Think it over:
1. Why do you think this passage was dropped from the original draft of the Declaration of Independence?
2. What does its removal suggest about the principles of the founders of the new nation?

The challenges by African American students have forced me to reconsider a number of my ideas about teaching social studies and to think about how I had felt as a teenager learning about the history of my own people. I remember growing up in the Bronx after World War II and the upset that I felt because Eastern European Jews, including my relatives, had walked to their deaths into the gas chambers of Nazi Germany. Knowledge of oppression did not satisfy me then. I felt humiliated and I wanted to scream out, Why didn't we fight back?

What finally helped me come to terms with the Holocaust was reading about Jewish resistance in Leon Uris' book (1961) about the Warsaw Ghetto, and—whatever my problems with it now—the creation and defense of the State of Israel (Uris, 1958). I realize that the key for me was the recognition of struggle, or, as Alice Walker identified it so powerfully in her book *Possessing the Secret of Joy* (1992), resistance.

In response to my students and the connections they have helped me to understand about my own life, I shifted the emphasis in our classroom from examining the burdens of oppression to exploring the history of people's struggles for justice.

Learning Activity: Songs of Resistance and Struggle

Singing has always been part of human resistance to tyranny and struggles for social change. Following are three songs sung by different peoples but expressing some of the same ideas.

"Zog Nit Keyn Mol"

This partisan hymn from the Vilna Ghetto of Lithuania was inspired by Jewish resistance to Nazi forces in the Warsaw, Poland, Ghetto uprising. "Zog Nit Keyn Mol" was sung in Yiddish, the language of Eastern European Jews. It was translated from Yiddish by Rhoda L. Epstein for this book. It is recorded in Yiddish on "Voices of the Ghetto, Warsawa 1943," CD 7 Productions, U.S. Holocaust Memorial.

> Never say that you are going your last way,
> When leaden skies hide the blue of day;
> Our designated time will also come,
> Our steps shall thunder—we are here!
> This song was written with blood and not with lead;
> It's not a song of birds flying free,
> But a people standing amid falling walls,
> Sang this song with pistols in their hands.

"Certainly, Lord"

Songs were an important part of the Civil Rights movement of the 1950s and 1960s in the United States. Many of these songs of resistance and struggle originated as spirituals in southern African American Protestant churches. "Certainly, Lord", a traditional song, was adapted by members of the Congress of Racial Equality. A version that includes music appears in *Sing for Freedom* (Carawan and Carawan, 1990: 69).

> Well, have you been to the jailhouse? Certainly Lord,
> Well, have you been to the jailhouse? Certainly Lord,
> Well, have you been to the jailhouse? Certainly Lord,
> Certainly, certainly, certainly, Lord.
>
> Well, did they give you thirty days? . . .
> Well, did you serve your time? . . . .
> Well, will you go back again? . . . .
> Well, will you fight for freedom? . . . .
> Well, will you tell it to the judge? . . . .
> Well, will you tell it to the world? . . . .

"Kevin Barry"

This song tells the story of an 18-year-old student who enlisted in the Irish Republican Army to fight for Irish independence from Great Britain. Kevin Barry was captured by British troops and executed in 1920. Ireland finally became an independent nation in 1921. A version that includes music appears in *Songs of Work and Protest* (Fowke and Glazer, 1973: 194–95).

> Early on a Monday morning,
> High upon a gallows tree,
> Kevin Barry gave his young life
> For the cause of liberty.
> Another martyr for old Ireland,
> Another murder for the crown!
> Brutal laws to crush the Irish
> Could not keep their spirit down.
> Lads like Barry are no cowards—
> From their foes they do not fly,
> For their bravery always has been
> Ireland's cause to live or die.

Think it over:

Are injustices like racism and imperialism central features of Western civilization or incidental and peripheral developments? Explain your answer and provide specific examples to support your views.

Add your voice to the discussion:

1. Everything cannot fit in the curriculum. In your opinion, do teachers distort history by including the contributions of women and minorities? Explain your answer and provide specific examples to support your views.
2. In your opinion, are we in danger of minimizing the history of oppression if we focus on resistance movements? Explain your answer and provide specific examples to support your views.

It's your classroom:

1. Would you use songs such as these in your social studies classes? How?
2. Can connections be drawn among these songs? What are they?

When I explain these ideas about multiculturalism to groups of teachers, they generally respond that it seems so reasonable, and they do not understand why it has generated such intense controversy. I think the reason for the controversy is that most of the debate about multiculturalism has little to do with the nature of history, the relative merits of different types of art and literature, or the most effective ways to teach about them. They are political debates about who will hold power and shape educational policies in U.S. society.

There is nothing wrong with educators being political activists. Given the nature of our democratic society, educators must always be political. Political ideology informs the topics we choose to teach, the ways we organize our classrooms and relate to young people, our relationships with colleagues, and the battles we wage with Boards of Education and various local and state funding agencies. But we need to be conscious of our political preferences because they shape and are shaped by our professional judgments. We have to insist that educators reflect on their assumptions and goals, and evaluate standards for knowing.

I do not pretend that the kind of multicultural education I have described in this chapter will solve all of America's educational and social problems. But by embracing a multicultural perspective, social studies educators can make a statement that we take the divisions in American society seriously and we are committed to bridging them.

Teaching Activity: Join the Multicultural Debate

Consider the issues raised in this chapter, and read the following statements by different authors who discuss multicultural social studies.

- **James A. Banks** (1993: 22–28): "One misconception about multicultural education is that it is an entitlement program and curriculum movement for African Americans, Hispanics, the poor, women and other victimized groups. . . . Multicultural education . . . is not an ethnic- or gender-specific movement. It is a movement designed to empower all students to become knowledgeable, caring, and active citizens in a deeply troubled and ethnically polarized nation and world."

- **Maxine Greene** (1993: 17): "Learning to look through multiple perspectives, young people may be helped to build bridges among themselves; attending to a range of human stories, they may be provoked to heal and to transform. Of course there will be difficulties in affirming plurality and difference and, at once, working to create community. Since the days of De Tocqueville, Americans have wondered how to deal with the conflicts between individualism and the drive to conform."

- **Octavio Paz** (1993: 57–58): "You are already a hybrid culture, which to me is a positive thing. I believe all cultures are richer when they assimilate others, and change. I don't believe in a pure culture. Here we are sitting and talking in New York, a city populated by the minorities that are the world's majority. It is marvelous, no?"

- **Diane Ravitch** (1990c: 3): "Almost any idea, carried to its extreme, can be made pernicious, and this is what is happening now to multiculturalism. . . . Advocates of particularism propose an ethnocentric curriculum to raise the self-esteem and academic achievement of children from racial and ethnic minority backgrounds. Without any evidence, they claim that children from minority backgrounds will do well in school only if they are immersed in a positive, prideful version of their ancestral culture."

- **Arthur Schlesinger Jr.** (1992: 29): "The use of history as therapy means the corruption of history as history. . . . Let us by all means teach black history, African history, women's history, Hispanic history, Asian history. But let us teach them as history, not as filiopietistic commemoration."

- **Albert Shanker** (1995): "As practiced by some, 'multiculturalism' takes the shape of something approximating a new ideology of separatism. It challenges the idea of a common identity and rejects the possibility of a common set of values. . . . Often, the claims of multiculturalists and other separatists reflects [sic] the attitude that no one group may make a judgement on any other, since all 'depends on your point of view.' This extremely relativistic viewpoint conflicts with the need that all societies have of establishing some basic values, guidelines and beliefs."

- **Christine Sleeter** (1991: 12): "Education that is multicultural and social reconstructionist forges a coalition among various oppressed groups as well as members of dominant groups, teaching directly about political and economic oppression and discrimination, and preparing young people directly in social action skills."

Add your voice to the discussion:

1. Which statement(s) come(s) closest to your understanding of multiculturalism? Why?
2. Which statements do you disagree with? Why?
3. What are the implications of this chapter and the quotations for planning social studies curricula?

REFERENCES AND RECOMMENDATIONS FOR FURTHER READING

Achebe, C. *Things Fall Apart*. Garden City, N.Y.: Doubleday, 1994.

Adler, M. *The Paidea Proposal: An Educational Manifesto*. New York: Macmillan, 1982.

Alcoff, L. (1988, Spring). "Cultural Feminism versus Post-Structuralism: The Identity Crisis in Feminist Theory." *Signs: Journal of Women in Culture and Society* 13 (Spring 1988), 405–36.

Apple, M. *Ideology and Curriculum*. New York: Routledge & Kegan Paul, 1979.

Banks, J. "Multicultural Education, Development, Dimensions, and Challenges." *Phi Delta Kappan* 75, no. 1, (1993), 22–28.

Banks, J. and C. A. McGee Banks. *Multicultural Education: Issues and Perspectives*. Boston, MA: Allyn & Bacon, 1989.

Berenson, R. "The California History–Social Science Project: Developing History Education in the Schools." *American Historical Association Perspective*, December 1993, 21–24.

Berkin, C., and L. Wood. *National Treasures*. Glenview, Ill.: Scott, Foresman, 1987.

Carawan, G., and C. Carawan, eds. *Sing for Freedom*. Bethlehem, P.A.: Sing Out, 1990.

Cheney, C. *American Memory: A Report on the Humanities in the Nation's Public Schools*. Washington, D.C.: Government Printing Office, 1987.

Code, L. *What Can She Know? Feminist Theory and the Construction of Knowledge*. Ithaca, N.Y.: Cornell University Press, 1991.

Cornbleth, C., and D. Waugh. *The Great Speckled Bird*. Mahwah, N.J.: Lawrence Erlbaum, 1995.

Derman-Sparks, L., and The A.B.C. Task Force. *Anti-Bias Curriculum: Tools for Empowering Young Children*. Washington, DC: NAEYC, 1989.

Dow, P. "Past as Prologue: The Legacy of Sputnik." *Social Studies* 83, no. 4 (1992), 164–71.

Evans, R. "Diane Ravitch and the Revival of History: A Critique." *The Social Studies*, May/June 1989, 85–88.

Foner, E. "Slavery's Fellow Travelers." *The New York Times*, July 13, 2000.

Fowke, E., and J. Glazer, eds. *Songs of Work and Protest*. New York: Dover Publications, 1973.

Frank, A. *The Diary of a Young Girl*. New York: Bantam Books, 1995.

Franklin, J. *From Slavery to Freedom*. 4th ed. New York: Knopf, 1974.

Greenberger, S. "Thinking in the Present Some Educators Say Recent Events Are Not Yet The Stuff Of History Class," *Boston Globe*, December 28, 2001, B1.

Greene, M. "The Passions of Pluralism: Multiculturalism and the Expanding Community." *Educational Researcher* 22, no. 1, 1993.

Hawke, S., and J. Davis. *Seeds of Change: The Story of Cultural Exchange after 1492*. Menlo Park, Calif.: Addison-Wesley, 1992.

Hirch, E. "Teach Knowlege, Not 'Mental Skills.' " *The New York Times*, September 4, 1993.

Horne, C., ed. *Source Record of the Great War, Vol. 1*. Indianapolis, Ind.: American Legion, 1931.

Jordan, W., M. Greenblatt, and J. Bowes. *The Americans: A History*. Evanston, IL: McDougal, Littell & Co, 1992.

Katz, W. *Eyewitness: The Negro in American History*. New York: Pittman, 1971.

McKenzie, R., with L. Hellerman. "Civic Learning through Deliberation." *Social Science Docket* 2, no. 2 2002.

Mistry, R. *A Fine Balance*. New York: Vintage, 1997.

Nash, G. "Creating History Standards in United States and World History." *Organization of American Historians Magazine of History* 9, no. 3, 1995.

Natale, J. "Bone of Contention." *The American School Board Journal*, January 1995, 18–23.

National Center for History in the Schools. *National Standards for United States History, Grades 5–12*. Los Angeles: NCHS, 1996a.

National Center for History in the Schools. "Newly Revised Voluntary History Standards Released Today, Endorsed by Leadership of National Review Panels." Press release, April 3, 1996b.

National Commission on Social Studies in the Schools. *Charting a Course: Social Studies for the 21st Century.* Washington, D.C.: NCSSS, 1989.

National Council for the Social Studies. *Expectations of Excellence, Curriculum Standards for Social Studies,* NCSS Bulletin 89. Washington, D.C.: NCSS, 1994.

National History Standards Project. "Fact Sheet on National Standards for United States History." Press release, November 1, 1994.

National History Standards Project. Press release, November 16, 1994.

New York Historical Society. *Teaching Local History: New York City as a National Model: Teacher Resource Manual.* New York: NYHS, n.d.

The New York Times. "Mock Auction of Slaves: Education or Outrage?" October 8, 1994a.

The New York Times. "Tears and Protest at Mock Slave Sale," October 11, 1994b.

Noddings, N. "Social Studies and Feminism." *Theory and Research in Social Education* 20, no. 2 (1992).

Paz, O. "Talk of the Town." *New Yorker,* December 29, 1993.

Ravitch, D. *The American Reader: Words That Moved a Nation.* New York: HarperCollins, 1990a.

Ravitch, D. "Diversity and Democracy." *American Educator,* Spring 1990b.

Ravitch, D. "Multiculturalism: E Pluribus Plures." *The Key Reporter* 56, no. 1 (1990).

Ravitch, D., and A. Schlesinger Jr. "The New, Improved History Standards." *The Wall Street Journal,* April 3, 1996.

Reinhold, R. "Class Struggle." *The New York Times Magazine,* September 29, 1991.

Schlesinger, A. Jr. *The Disuniting of America: Reflections on a Multicultural Society.* New York: Norton, 1992.

Shanker, A. "Education and Democratic Citizenship: Where We Stand." http://www.civnet.org/civitas/shanker.htm, June 3, 1995.

Singer, A. "Multiculturalism and Democracy: The Promise of Multicultural Education." *Social Education* 5, no. 2 (1992), 83–85.

Singer, A. "Multiculturalism and Afrocentricity: How They Influence Teaching U.S. History." *Social Education* 57, no. 6 (1993), 283–86.

Singer, A. "Reflections on Multiculturalism." *Phi Delta Kappan* 76, no. 4 (1994), 284–88.

Singer, A. *Social Studies for Secondary Schools.* 1 ed. Mahwah, N.J.: Lawrence Earlbaum, 1997.

Sleeter, C., ed. *Empowerment through Multicultural Education.* Albany, N.Y.: SUNY Press, 1991.

Spiegelman, A. *Maus: A Survivor's Tale.* New York: Pantheon, 1986.

Takaki, R. *A Different Mirror: A History of Mulicultural America.* Boston: Little, Brown, 1993.

Tan, A. *The Joy Luck Club.* New York: Putnam, 1989.

Thomas, J. "Revised History Standards Defuse Explosive Issues." *The New York Times,* April 3, 1996, B8.

Thompson, E. *The Making of the English Working Class.* New York: Vintage, 1963.

U.S. Department of Education. *High Standards for All Students.* Washington, D.C.: Government Printing Office, June 1994.

Uris, L. *Exodus.* Garden City, N.Y.: Doubleday, 1958.

Uris, L. *Mila 18.* Garden City, N.Y.: Doubleday, 1961.

Walker, A. *Possessing the Secret of Joy.* New York: Harcourt Brace Jovanovich, 1992.

Weis, L., ed. *Beyond Silenced Voices: Class, Race, and Gender in United States Schools.* Albany, N.Y.: SUNY Press, 1993.

Wilentz, S. "The Past Is Not a 'Process.'" *The New York Times,* April 20, 1997.

II

Preparing to Teach Social Studies

4

How Do You Plan a Social Studies Unit?

Overview

Explore issues related to unit planning
Present a rationale for formal unit plans
Compare strategies for unit organization
Develop sample unit plans for different grade levels

Key Concepts

Planning, Structure, Flexibility, Choice, Middle Schools, Tracking, Inclusion

Questions

Why Plan Units?
What Should Be Included in a Unit Plan?
How Do Social Studies Teachers Plan Units?
How Do Teachers Use Plans Effectively in the Classroom?
How Can Social Studies Curricula Address Differences among Students?
What Does a Unit That Focuses on Content Look Like?
How Is a Document-Based Thematic Unit Organized?
What Is a Comparative Thematic Unit?

Essays

Teaching about Slavery in the Americas
Using Student Dialogues to Teach Social Studies and Promote Democracy

WHY PLAN UNITS?

For a number of years, the New York City union local of the American Federation of Teachers (AFT) challenged formal lesson and unit plan requirements as inappropriate restrictions on a teacher's professional judgment. They finally secured a contract provision that supervisors could not insist on a specific format for lesson and unit plans, nor could they require that the plans be reviewed unless a teacher's performance during classroom observations was considered unsatisfactory.

AFT President Albert Shanker explained the union's position on planning in a pamphlet entitled *The Making of a Profession* (1985). In the pamphlet, Shanker recounted the story of James Worley, an experienced and highly regarded teacher who was fired for insubordination.

According to Shanker, supervisors, parents, peers, and students all considered

James Worley an excellent teacher. However, when a new principal required teachers to prepare units in advance and submit them to their supervisors for review, Worley refused. He defended his position, arguing that the directive was based on a rigid notion of teaching that ignored the fundamental role of classroom interaction and student participation in lesson and unit development. He felt that compliance with a directive that was educationally unsound would injure his students and violate his professional integrity. Paul Goodman, author of the book *Growing Up Absurd*, was one of many educators who rallied in support of Worley's decision. In a letter to the State Commissioner of Education, cited by Shanker, Goodman wrote: "It has been my universal experience that formal preparation of a lesson plan beyond the next hour or two is not only unrealistic but can be positively harmful and rigidifying, for it interferes with the main thing, the contact between the teacher and his class. . . . A teacher who would seriously comply with the order would likely be a poor teacher" (3).

During my teaching career, I have also experienced unit and lesson plan requirements that I considered to be interfering and less than useful. I worked in schools where teachers submitted unit plans to supervisors, who held onto them for days and then returned them without comments. I knew teachers and supervisors who wrote elaborate plans but were not considered adequate educators by either their colleagues or their students. Despite these experiences, I strongly disagree with Goodman, Shanker, and Worley's position on planning. I am convinced that most teachers need to plan even more than they do, that extensive advanced planning is an essential feature of effective teaching, and that planning is where we, as teachers, get the chance to think and act as historians and social scientists. It is our opportunity to consider broader ideas, frame questions, suggest hypotheses, and research potential resources before we go into the classroom to teach about them.

Unit plans do not have to be rigid templates that stifle the imaginations of teachers and students. When a teacher is teaching a lesson and decides to leave something out, changes the order that materials are presented in class, or takes time to respond to student questions and listen to student views, a building is not going to collapse. Unit plans are only ideas about useful ways to subdivide and integrate concepts, skills, and content information. They are neither eternal documents nor etched in stone.

Sometimes I think of unit plans as guides to a mountain hike. They suggest supplies you will need, warn you about potential dangers and difficulties, alert you to alternative paths, provide strategies for using your energy most effectively, offer a time frame, and direct attention toward interesting views. The guides help you know where you are going and to predict how long it will take you to get there. They leave room for turn-offs, but when time is a factor, hikers know they can take only a limited number of side trips.

Unit plans are the primary conceptual and organizing frameworks in teaching social studies. A 180-day curriculum calendar is too long and contains too many things to think about and teach to be useful in planning lessons, activities, and projects. Although people need to be aware of the "big picture," the reality is that we live and plan our lives in much smaller parcels of time.

However, planning on a day-by-day, lesson-to-lesson basis means that a teacher is never really prepared. Without setting aside time to consider our own thoughts about a topic, it is difficult to give direction in class. Main ideas about history, society, and social studies and general academic skills that could have been integrated into a series of lessons if they were organized in advance are forgotten and end up never being included. Teachers feel squeezed for time, so they lecture instead of involving students in figuring things out. Concepts that take a number of days to develop while students examine a point from different perspectives are either rushed or dropped.

At the last minute, that wonderful video segment, photograph, or quote that provides evidence for a historical interpretation or illustrates an economic concept cannot be located, so it cannot be used. It is too late to reserve the VCR, camcorder, record player, or computer room.

Can you imagine a football team going into a big game without a game plan or having decided on only its first play from scrimmage? It is not the best strategy in football, and it is not the best strategy for teaching. The questions we need to consider here are not whether teachers should plan, but what to plan, how to plan, and how to effectively utilize our advanced plans in the classroom.

Teaching Activity: The Politics of Lesson Planning

Add your voice to the discussion:
1. What do you think about James Worley's refusal to submit unit plans to his supervisor for review? Why?
2. Do you agree or disagree with the union position that formal lesson and unit plan requirements are inappropriate restrictions on a teacher's professional judgment? Why?

WHAT SHOULD BE INCLUDED IN A UNIT PLAN?

At the preliminary stages, a unit plan is an outline of teaching ideas that are organized into a schedule for presenting them in class. The outline has integrated conceptual components (e.g., chronological, causal, or thematic relationships), which makes it more than just a list of possible lessons. Eventually the ideas get reworked into a series of detailed individual lesson plans that retain the unit's conceptual connections. A complete unit plan contains completed lesson plans.

What gets included in a preliminary unit plan varies, depending on what a teacher finds most useful for planning actual lessons. This changes as a teacher gains experience. It can also differ from unit to unit. The following are some items to consider when starting a unit plan:

1. **Scope and time** include the range of topics or questions that will be examined during the unit and the number of lessons available to explore them (e.g., 10 lessons covering the United States from 1920 to 1941).
2. **Concepts** are broad, overarching social studies terms or statements that

are continually reexamined throughout a curriculum, such as democracy, environment, nationalism, or scarcity, or the thematic strands developed by the National Council for the Social Studies.

3. **Main ideas/understandings** include the relationships among people, places, ideas, and events, and the conclusions about history and society that inform the way a teacher, textbook, or curriculum presents a topic.

4. **Goals** are general projections about the main ideas, content, academic, and social skills that teachers want students to learn during the unit.

5. **Objectives** are specific results you expect students to achieve.

6. **Content** refers to the factual information about a topic that will be considered during the unit.

7. **Skills** include the general academic (e.g., thinking, writing, speaking, mastery of technology), social studies (e.g., gathering information, document analysis, decision making), and social skills (e.g., group participation and leadership) that will be focused on during the unit.

8. **Materials** include the software (e.g., documents, videos, songs) and hardware (e.g., overhead, VCR, cassette recorder) that will be needed on specific days.

9. **Lesson design** refers to the different ways that lessons can be organized (e.g., cooperative learning projects, group work, full class activities, student presentations).

Most new teachers and many experienced teachers start their planning from a textbook, following its organization of the subject and emphasizing its concept, main idea, content, and skill choices. In history classes, this generally leads to content-based chronological lessons. In economics, political science, and sociology classes, it generally means focusing on the major institutions in a society. Starting from the textbook is helpful when teachers do not feel comfortable with their own knowledge of the subject or the scope of the curriculum. It can also make it easier for students to follow the sequence of lessons. There are potential problems with this approach, however: Students become inundated with facts, main ideas are lost in a swirl of details, lessons are dry, and students become bored. In addition, when teachers depend on packaged textbook-based units, they sacrifice much of their own creative energy. They become part of an information conveyor belt instead of being historians and social scientists.

Alternative ways of organizing units include a document-based thematic approach (discussed again in chap. 7) and a comparative approach. Both formats place greater demands on teachers and students to locate materials and draw their own connections. Document-based thematic units are organized to answer questions and actively involve students as researchers. In these units, fewer events, ideas, people, or practices are examined, but they are examined in greater depth. Comparative units pull events, ideas, people, and practices out of their local context and place them in a broader global perspective that allows students to discover unexpected relationships.

Teachers can choose to organize units using different formats for the same class at different points during the year, or they can use one format in one subject and another format for another. Samples of three unit formats will be examined in greater depth later in this chapter.

Teaching Activity: Defining a Unit; U.S. History and Economics

Try it yourself:

1. You are teaching 7th-grade students about how the American colonists became independent of Great Britain.
   a. Where would you start the unit? Where would you finish it?
   b. How much time would you spend on the entire unit?
   c. What are your concept, content, and skill goals?
   d. What are the main ideas you want students to learn about this period? Why?
2. You are teaching a 12th-grade economics class about the role of a central government in a complex modern "mixed" economy.
   a. How would you start the unit? How would you finish it?
   b. How much time would you spend on the entire unit?
   c. What are your concept, content, and skill goals?
   d. What are the main ideas you want students to learn about this topic? Why?

HOW DO SOCIAL STUDIES TEACHERS PLAN UNITS?

The length of time a unit takes to teach varies depending on the topic, the importance a teacher, department, or district assigns to it, decisions about how lessons will be organized, student interest, and time pressures (e.g., approaching the end of a semester or a scheduled departmental exam). I generally find that 2 to 3 weeks, or between 8 and 15 lessons, is a manageable amount of time for a unit. It allows a class to explore a topic with some depth and to reach intellectual closure on an issue. With every unit, I try to provide students with a lesson schedule and a homework assignment sheet, design some form of unit project, and include a unit test.

In most high schools and middle schools, social studies teachers are assigned to teach two different subjects or grades. When I teach secondary school social studies, I try to flip-flop planning; every other week I plan a two-week long unit (with daily lesson plans) for each subject area.

Often the most difficult point in planning for beginning teachers is simply starting. Part of the problem is that there is not just one way to begin, and there is no easy formula to apply. I suggest using a chart like the one on page 149 and brainstorming by yourself or with colleagues. List the things you want to include in the unit, group them, and then start to break the groupings up into lessons. Once a unit plan is outlined this way, it becomes easier to create individual lessons.

It is also very difficult to decide in advance how much planning is enough. Certainly unit planning is more an art than a science, and decisions become easier as a teacher gains experience. As you plan, it is useful to ask yourself some questions.

Does this unit build on previous work and understanding?
Does this unit lay the basis for future explorations?
Do I understand the period, the broader issues, or the topic? Will students understand them based on these lessons?

Continued

Is there sufficient material for students to analyze in class? Do the lessons include enough active things for students to do?

Does the unit cover the same scope and/or information as the textbook assignments? How closely do I want them to parallel each other?

Are my lesson designs varied and interesting?

If planning seems daunting, remember that there is no reason that supervisors, experienced teachers, and beginners should not work together to develop a curriculum. Lesson and unit planning does not have to be a private, individual experience or a competitive sport. When teachers work together, old-timers benefit from new insights and perspectives, and rookies do not have to discover every document for themselves and reinvent every teaching strategy. At a minimum, new teachers should not be afraid to borrow. That is why they invented the copy machine.

Teaching Activity: Outlining Units on India and Sub-Saharan Africa

Try it yourself:

1. Make a list of the major historical, social, cultural, and geographical points you would include in a unit on the river valley civilizations and empires of ancient India. Divide the list into potential lessons.
2. Make a list of the principal questions a class should consider in a unit on the history of sub-Saharan Africa prior to the European Age of Exploration. Divide the list of questions into potential lessons.

HOW DO TEACHERS USE PLANS EFFECTIVELY IN THE CLASSROOM?

In the controversy over lesson planning, there is a very important area where I agree with James Worley. The interaction within the classroom between students and between teachers and students is crucial to effective learning and teaching. I often advise student teachers: "Put your lesson plan away when the class begins."

Carefully constructed unit plans provide structure for our teaching, but they also make it possible for creative flexibility in the classroom. Advanced planning means that, when students raise unexpected questions or introduce valuable new ideas, lessons can change and important material that gets skipped over can be inserted into other lessons. It also means

that, when necessary, we can say to a student, "That's a good idea, but I want to hold it for a couple of days until more of the class is with us."

Sometimes the most difficult thing to decide when unit and lesson planning is what *not* to include. At the planning stage, I recommend overplanning. It avoids potentially long and embarrassing silences when something takes less time or invokes less student interest than anticipated. While teaching, I try to remain aware that all of the material I have available and all of the goals I would like to achieve will not necessarily fit in a particular lesson or unit; that I need to make choices about what to introduce based on student involvement. I do most of my editing, shifting things around, sliding them into other lessons, or dropping them altogether while teaching or after a class, when I can reflect on how students responded to what we are learning. Even when you have to drop something that took time to prepare, it is good to know you had it available if you needed to use it to answer student questions or to illustrate an important point.

Teaching Activity: Brainstorming a Unit

Subject _____ Topic _____ Grade _____

Lesson	Time/ Scope	Concepts	Main Ideas	Goals	Objectives	Content	Skills	Materials	Lesson Design
1									
2									
3									
4									
5									
6									
7									
8									
9									
10									

Try it yourself:
1. Working by yourself or with a group of colleagues, use these categories to brainstorm a preliminary unit for a social studies subject area and topic of your choice.
2. Reorganize your ideas into possible lessons.

HOW CAN SOCIAL STUDIES CURRICULA ADDRESS DIFFERENCES AMONG STUDENTS?

Chapter 2 argued that a curriculum based on structured experiential learning is the most effective way to teach social studies on every grade and academic level. In my experience, this approach provides social studies educators with the flexibility necessary to meet the individual and group needs of diverse student populations. Teachers have to find ways to engage students who have different intellectual interests, academic strengths, social and cultural experiences, and levels of emotional maturity. If social studies curricula are student centered, they will differ in middle schools and high schools, in cities and suburbs, and in different neighborhoods and sections of the country. Units and lessons will even vary for classes taught at different times of the day as teachers adjust to the ebb and flow of teenage emotions, anxieties, and predilections. The key to curriculum design is connecting to students. At the conclusion to Chapter 5, this is discussed in greater depth in the essay "Text and Context."

Middle School Social Studies

In general, middle school social studies programs are more attuned to the developmental profile of adolescents than are junior and senior high schools. In middle schools, learning is frequently interdisciplinary; students and teachers are encouraged to work in teams, and teachers try to consciously connect historical events and social studies concepts with their students' experiences.

According to a National Council for the Social Studies Task Force report "Social Studies in the Middle School" (1991), middle school social studies curricula should emphasize concern with student personal growth and identity, the development of ethics and knowledge of right and wrong, the fostering of citizenship and community, and an understanding of global connections. Experiential and cooperative learning (see chap. 6), performance-based assessment (see chap. 9), and heterogeneous grouping are encouraged. In addition, the report suggests that teachers begin instruction with ideas that students are familiar with, help students develop their historical perspectives,

emphasize clear communication in the classroom, provide opportunities for student participation in decision making, and create a sense of classroom community. I wholeheartedly support this view of teaching, but I do not agree that it should be restricted to middle schools (see chap. 8 for a discussion of a project approach to social studies in middle school and high school).

Academic Level and Inclusion

Recent decades have produced continuing debate on the academic organization of middle, junior, and senior high schools, especially the placement of students who are considered either "gifted" or "challenged." Most of my secondary school teaching experience was in academically "tracked" programs where efforts were made to mainstream special education students into "appropriate" classes.

Philosophically, I oppose academic tracking because it stigmatizes students in the lower tracks, encourages competition for grades rather than learning, and teaches students to value hierarchy and individual benefit instead of democracy and community. However, I recognize that social studies teachers must be prepared to work in both tracked and nontracked settings. In both types of programs, I encourage students to work in teams, drawing off each other's strengths. In nontracked classrooms, students with more developed academic skills have an opportunity to polish their understanding as they work with other students to master complex skills and concepts. I also prefer heterogeneous grouping and the inclusion of special education students because they maximize student diversity, bring multiple perspectives into the classroom, and enrich everyone's experience.

A problem in planning social studies units and lessons for a heterogeneous class is that there may be a wide disparity in student reading and writing levels. I use a number of approaches to address this problem.

- In class, I vary the difficulty of assigned readings, recognizing that certain material will be too difficult for some of the students to understand.
- When documents are particularly difficult to interpret, I make excerpts brief and provide vocabulary clues.
- Sometimes, I provide students with *differentiated text*, activity sheets with a series of documents as originally written or as edited so that they offer a range of academic difficulty.
- Before the class discusses documents, I either have students go over the material in small groups or I review it in some detail as a full class.
- For group projects, I assign students to teams so that each team has members with a range of academic skills.
- On individual projects, I provide a variety of choices and encourage students with greater academic skills to pursue more challenging assignments.

Teaching Activity: Editing a Primary Source Document

When Cheryl Smith (NTN) works with heterogeneous cooperative learning teams in her middle school classes, she assigns individual students different reading passages or versions of an edited document, depending on their reading skills. This enables all the students on the team to participate in research and discussion. Examine the primary source documents that follow.

Magna Carta (Greaves Cannistrataro, Zaller, and Murphy, 1990: 277):
In 1215, nobles forced King John of England to accept a "Magna Carta" that placed limits on the power of the monarch. The Magna Carta, considered one of the seminal documents in the development of democratic institutions in Western society, is usually discussed in high school social studies classes.

> 1. In the first place, we have granted to God, and by this our present charter confirmed for us and our heirs forever, that the English church shall be free, and shall hold its rights entire and its liberties uninjured. . . .
>
> 12. No scutage or aid shall be imposed in our kingdom save by the common council of our kingdom, except for the ransoming of our body, for the making of our oldest son a knight, and for once marrying our eldest daughter; and for these purposes it shall be only a reasonable aid. . . .
>
> 39. No free man shall be taken, or imprisoned, or dispossessed, or outlawed, or banished, or in any way injured . . . except by the legal judgement of his peers, or by the law of the land.

Starving Time (Meyers Cawleti, and Kern, 1967: 16–17):
Captain John Smith's *General Historie of Virginia* (1624) recounted the "starving time" in Jamestown, Virginia, during the winter of 1609–1610. It is a graphic story that illustrates the precariousness of early settlements. Its gruesome qualities can capture the imagination of middle school students.

> Now we all found the loss of Captain Smith, yea, his greatest maligners could now curse his loss: as for corn provision and contribution from savages, we had nothing but mortal wounds with clubs and arrows; as for our hogs, hens, goats, sheep, horse, or what lived, our commanders, officers, and savages daily consumed them, some small proportions sometimes we tasted till all was devoured; then swords, arms pieces, or anything, we traded with the savages, whose cruel fingers were so oft imbrewed in our bloods that what by their cruelty, our Governor's indiscretion, and the loss of our ships, of five hundred within six months after Captain Smith's departure, there remained not past sixty men,

women, and children, most miserable and poor creatures; and those were preserved, for the most part, by roots, herbs, acorns, walnuts, berries, now and then a little fish.

Nay, so great was our famine that a savage we slew and buried, the poorer sort took him up again and eat him; and so did divers one another boiled and stewed with roots and herbs. And one amongst the rest did kill his wife, powdered her, and had eaten part of her before it was known, for which he was executed, as he well deserved. Now whether she was better roasted, boiled or carbonadoed, I know not, but of such a dish as powdered wife I never heard of.

Add your voice to the discussion:
Would you provide students with different versions of a reading based on their reading skills? Why or why not?

It's your classroom:
How would you edit these documents to make them accessible to students in your classes?

The inclusion of special education students can enhance learning for all students when districts provide necessary support services. At Edward R. Murrow High School, teaching assistants were assigned to work in mainstream classes to help students with disabilities. Some of these students felt that this added a stigma to what was already a difficult situation for them. After meeting with the students and teaching assistants, we developed a strategy that addressed this problem and benefited all of the students in class. Instead of teaching assistants working solely with an individual student partner, they worked with whichever group of students the student with disabilities was assigned to. Because students with disabilities changed groups during the year, all of the students in class eventually had an opportunity to work with one of the teaching assistants. As a result of experiences in inclusive classrooms, students with disabilities and the general student population can learn that all people have the ability to make contributions to society and should be included in our definition of *community*.

Cultural Diversity and Gender

In the essay concluding the introductory chapter of this book, I argued that culture is dynamic and that, in the United States, individual and group identity are constantly changing. The dynamic nature of culture and identity, as well as the challenge of developing social cohesiveness in a diverse and democratic society, are important reasons for encouraging diversity in schools. In racially, ethnically, religiously, or gender-segregated classes, students experience separation as the norm and difference as strange and undesirable. In culturally diverse and gender-mixed classrooms, there is at least the possibility that student experiences will encourage respect for difference.

Classroom diversity places a heavy responsibility on teachers. There is often tension between students from different racial, ethnic, religious, or class backgrounds. Students feel pressure to conform, take sides, or be silent. Young women may withdraw from active involvement in class and play roles they think will make them more attractive to young men. Even when tension remains below the surface, students who feel marginalized can suffer academically and socially. The challenge for teachers is to build classroom communities where students feel welcomed and have confidence that conflicts will be openly and sensitively examined and resolved.

The social studies play a crucial role in this process. In social studies classrooms, social conflict is part of our field of study. Students can study the historical roles of different people; the meaning of concepts such as equity, justice, and citizenship; and ways to creatively reduce tension so that people who are different are able to work together effectively. In social studies classrooms, conflict can provide learning opportunities that help students better understand each other, and the present and past.

During the recent national standards debate (discussed in chap. 3), some proponents of a national curriculum expressed concern that allowing social studies curricula to diverge contributes to the polarization of our society. A student-centered social studies curriculum does not mean that students study only about themselves and their own racial, ethnic, or religious groups. Rather, in student-centered classrooms, social studies teachers use what students are familiar with, the *contexts* of their lives, as the starting point for examining the world in all of its complexity and diversity.

Teaching Activity: Dealing with Diversity

Laurence Klein (NTN) teaches in an ethnically diverse middle school in Queens, New York. The school is tracked, and the lowest track classes tend to have a mixture of students who are either recent immigrants or American-born students, largely African Americans, with a history of failure in school. Often there is tension between these two groups.

In a lesson designed to help his eighth-grade class understand conditions in the United States at the end of the U.S. Civil War, Lawrence asked students who had immigrated from countries with civil strife to discuss the impact of these conflicts on their families. Among the students who reported to the class were young women born in El Salvador, Yugoslavia, Israel, and Afghanistan. Although it was sometimes difficult to follow them because of their accents, the other students were mesmerized by their presentations. The discussion that followed allowed students to bridge many of their cultural gaps and helped them perceive each other as fellow human beings for the first time.

As a follow-up homework assignment, students wrote statements explaining their views on contemporary conflicts in the United States and whether they have the potential to lead to another civil war. This activity and follow-up discussion gave the American students an opportunity to explain their frustrations with the conditions of their lives. The tension between students in this class was not resolved by two discussions. However, Laurence Klein believes that possibilities were expanded for creating a cohesive classroom community.

Add your voice to the discussion:
Do you agree with the inclusion of students from diverse backgrounds with a range of abilities and interests in heterogeneous social studies classrooms? Why or why not?

It's your classroom:
1. How would you design lessons to accommodate differences among students?
2. Would you have your class discuss racial, religious, ethnic, or gender conflicts between students? Why or why not? How would you introduce it? How would you follow up?

HIGH SCHOOL UNIT PLANS

The next three sections examine sample high school unit plan outlines that illustrate three approaches to unit planning. It includes a content-based unit from a Western civilization curriculum, a document-based thematic unit on the post-World

War II struggle for civil rights for African Americans, and an outline for a comparative unit from a course on the history of the non-Western world. In addition, a thematic middle school unit on the history of women in the United States is presented in Chapter 7.

WHAT DOES A UNIT THAT FOCUSES ON CONTENT LOOK LIKE?

High school history unit plans are generally organized chronologically. They focus on content while weaving in broader social studies themes and concepts. Traditionally, the content emphasizes political events and intellectual and economic trends. Units such as these frequently follow the outline of the textbook.

John McNamara, who was my department chair when I taught at Edward R. Murrow High School, designed this unit.

John begins planning units by dividing a broad time period into smaller periods of time or topics and by listing the content he wants to include in each lesson. He recommends units and individual lessons that are sequentially structured and carefully organized. After John decides on the social studies content of each lesson, he works on how he will teach them. He formulates broad introductory aim questions that have more than one possible answer. He uses these questions to promote discussion and disagreement and to encourage students to examine, organize, and understand the content materials. At some point in each lesson, John introduces a primary source document, cartoon, or reading passage for student evaluation. He prefers that his students work in groups. He also schedules writing activities whenever possible. Each unit is accompanied by a homework assignment sheet and concludes with an exam.

Revolutionary France—a High School Content-Based Unit

1. Was France under the Old Regime ripe for revolution?
   a. *Identify/define*: First, Second, and Third Estates, tithe, taille, gabelle, Old Regime, peasantry, aristocracy, clergy, established church.
   b. *Describe/analyze*: Political, economic, and social conditions in France under the Old Regime.
   c. *Explain/analyze*: powers and privileges of First and Second estates.
   d. *Discuss*: whether the Old Regime was ripe for revolution.
2. Did the writers of the Enlightenment prepare people's minds for revolution?
   a. *Identify/define*: natural law, natural rights, checks and balances, separation of powers, Social Contract, "philosophes," civil liberties, laissez-faire, tyranny, Enlightenment, Age of Reason, physiocrats.
   b. *Explain*: criticisms of the Old Regime made by the philosophers and writers of the Enlightenment including Locke, Montesquieu, Rousseau, Voltaire, Adam Smith, Diderot, Thomas Jefferson.
   c. *Explain/analyze*: views of the Enlightenment held by philosophers and writers of the era.
   d. *Assess*: whether the writers of the Enlightenment prepared people's minds for revolution.
3. Should the French have been satisfied with the changes enacted by the National Assembly after the fall of the Bastille?
   a. *Identify/define*: feudalism, assignats, abolition, emigres, limited monarchy, legislative assembly.
   b. *Explain*: how reforms enacted by the National Assembly changed the conditions existing under the Old Regime: (1) abolition of feudalism and special privileges, (2) Declaration of the Rights of Man, (3) seizure of Church lands, (4) Civil Constitution of the Clergy, (5) reform of local government, (6) Constitution of 1791.

   c. *Evaluate*: whether the French should have been satisfied with the changes enacted by the National Assembly after the fall of the Bastille.

4. Did the Reign of Terror go too far to preserve the French Revolution?
   a. *Identify/define*: Danton; Marat; Robespierre; Committee of Public Safety; Jacobins; Girondists; Liberty; Equality; Fraternity; National Convention; Directory.
   b. *Explain*: How different groups responded to the Revolution of 1791: (1) emigres, (2) churchmen, (3) radicals, (4) monarchs of Europe, (5) peasants, (6) bourgeoisie.
   c. *Explain*: how the National Convention protected and promoted the French Revolution.
   d. *Describe*: the causes and results of the Reign of Terror in France.
   e. *Assess*: whether the French Revolution significantly improved the lives of the French people and changed French government for the better.

5. Was Napoleon the right man to rule France?
   a. *Identify/define*: Directory, coup d'etat, plebiscite, the Consulate, sister republics.
   b. *Describe*: the conditions in France that helped make Napoleon's coup d'etat possible.
   c. *Describe/analyze*: traits of character and personal achievements that helped Napoleon rise to power in France.
   d. *Critically evaluate*: the advantages and disadvantages of one-man rule.

6. Did Napoleonic rule preserve or destroy the gains made by the French Revolution?
   a. *Identify/define*: Confederation of the Rhine, Grand Duchy of Warsaw, universal manhood suffrage, concordat, Code Napoleon, Continental System, exile, the Consulate, Legion of Honor, Bank of France.
   b. *Locate on a map of Europe*: areas conquered and/or controlled by Napoleonic France.
   c. *List, describe, and analyze*: Napoleon's reforms in each area: law, education, taxation, money and banking, relations with the Catholic Church.
   d. *Explain and analyze*: Napoleonic measures that turned France into a dictatorship.
   e. *Explain*: the reason's for Napoleon's downfall.
   f. *Evaluate*: whether Napoleonic rule preserved or destroyed the gains made by the French Revolution.

7. Was the Metternich System effective in stopping the spread of European nationalism?
   a. *Identify/define*: conservative, reactionary, liberalism, balance of power, legitimacy, compensation, Concert of Europe, Congress of Vienna, Holy Alliance, Quadruple Alliance, nationalism.
   b. *Show*: how territorial changes made at the Congress of Vienna violated the principle of nationalism.
   c. *List and explain*: the methods Metternich and his allies used to suppress nationalist and democratic ideas: (1) military power, (2) alliances, (3) censorship and spies.

8. Did the French Revolution have global impact?
   a. *Describe*: the spread of nationalism to other nations and parts of the world: (1) Revolutions of 1820–1821 in Italy and Spain, (2) Latin American revolutions from 1810 to 1832; (3) Greek revolution from 1821 to 1829, (4) revolutions of 1830–1832 in France, Belgium, Italy, and Poland, (5) revolutions of 1848 in France, the Austrian Empire, Italy, and Germany.
   b. *Evaluate*: the impact of the French Revolution on other revolutionary movements.
   c. *Evaluate*: Metternich's statement, "When France sneezes, all Europe catches cold." Discuss this statement in the light of events from 1830 to 1848.

Teaching Activity: Design a Content-Based Unit

Try it yourself:
Using a high school social studies textbook and a collection of primary source documents, design a content-based unit plan (containing between 8 and 10 lessons) for a specific historical era or on a specific topic.

Add your voice to the discussion:
How do you view this approach to social studies unit planning? Why?

HOW IS A DOCUMENT-BASED THEMATIC UNIT ORGANIZED?

This social studies unit about the African American civil rights movement in the United States after World War II is based on an inquiry approach to social studies curricula. It is organized so that students use historical documents to answer questions about the period and theme. Documents can be pictures, cartoons, songs, newspaper articles, quotes, artifacts, charts, or graphs (i.e., any materials that an historian might find useful).

Content information remains important in this unit, but it is not the central element in planning or student learning. The educational principle underlying this type of unit is that, as students examine the documents, they become historians who understand broader concepts, draw connections between events, and formulate explanations (hypotheses). Academic and social skills and social studies content are learned while students examine documents and answer questions. A document-based unit allows a teacher to focus class time on questioning and guiding students rather than on presenting information. Written homework assignments and textbook readings along with class discussions are used to provide narrative continuity.

Initially, document-based units require more research and preparation time than the traditional content-based chronological unit. However, as a document file grows over time, it becomes easier to construct units and individual lessons. Some publishers provide document packages geared to their texts, either in the form of a collection of handouts or as a document book. I recommend the two-volume *The American Spirit*, 9th ed. (Bailey and Kennedy, 1998), which is published by Houghton Mifflin as a companion volume for its advanced placement text, *The American Pageant*, 11th ed. (Bailey, Kennedy, and Cohen, 1998); *Voices of Freedom: Sources in American History* (Prentice Hall, 1987); and the sourcebook that accompanies the middle school series, *A History of Us* (Oxford University Press, 1999). New York City publishes an excellent collection of edited and adapted multicultural documents designed for 7th- and 8th-grade classes. They can also be adapted for high school. Well-designed commercial document packages are available from *Jackdaws* (http://www.jackdaw.com). The federal National Archives and Records Administration (http://www.nara.gov/education/publications/publicat.html) publishes an excellent two-volume set of documents (1988; 1998). Document resources available on the web are discussed in Chapter 10.

STEPS IN PLANNING A DOCUMENT-BASED THEMATIC UNIT

Start the unit planning with a broad historical unit question. It can come from the teacher, classroom discussion with students, a textbook, or a work of history.

Break the broad historical unit question into smaller pieces, statements, topics, or questions that need to be explored so the class can start to answer the broader question.

Continued

Assemble a list of available historical resources (primary source documents, secondary source interpretations, and audio- and videotapes) that allow students to discuss the smaller pieces, statements, topics, or questions.

Divide the questions, historical resources, social studies concepts, and research, communication, and social skills needed to utilize resources and answer questions into segments for organization into individual lessons. Because they are being used to answer specific questions, the documents may or may not be used chronologically.

Make decisions about the amount of time available for the unit and the number of topics, documents, questions, and so on that can be included. These decisions need to be reconsidered continuously while teaching the unit. Depending on student involvement in class discussion, questions, and insights into historical issues, some of the documents may never be used.

Edit documents to an appropriate length for use in class, adapted if necessary, and individual lessons that use different formats and different types of sources are developed.

Unit Topic: The Post-World War II African American Struggle for Civil Rights and Equality in the United States

The sample unit that follows provides more document choices than can possibly be integrated into the lessons. A teacher can decide that one document best illustrates a historical point and introduce only that document in class. Another option is to edit a series of documents so that each is a single paragraph long. Sometimes student teams work with different documents and bring insights based on their research into full class discussions.

Unit Question: Can the "promise" of the Declaration of Independence ("We hold these truths to be self-evident that all men are created equal") be achieved in the post-World War II United States?

Historical resources available for this unit include the following.

Video Documents:
- *Eyes on the Prize*, parts 1 and 2 (Prize 1/Prize 2).
- *Martin Luther King, From Montgomery to Memphis* (King).
- *The Video Encyclopedia of the United States* (encyclopedia).

Documents and Collections:
- Bailey, Thomas, and David Kennedy. *The American Spirit: United States History As Seen by Contemporaries*, volume II, 9th ed. Boston: Houghton Mifflin, 1998 (Bailey).
- Berkin, Carol, and Leonard Wood. *National Treasures*, 2nd ed. Glenview, Ill.: Scott, Foreman, 1987 (National Treasures).
- Bracey, John H. Jr., August Meier, and Elliot Rudwick. *Black Nationalism in America*. Indianapolis, Ind.: Bobbs-Merrill, 1970 (Black Nationalism).
- Carawan, Guy, and Candie Carawan. eds. *Sing for Freedom, The Story of the Civil Rights Movement through its Songs*. Bethlehem, Pa.: Sing Out, 1990.
- Feder, Bernard. *Viewpoints: USA*. Woodstock, Ga.: American Book Company, 1967 (Viewpoints).
- Katz, William L. *Eyewitness: A Living Documentary of the African American Contribution to American History*. Englewood, N.J.: Jerome Ozer Publishers, 1995 (Katz).
- New York City, Grade 8. *United States & New York State History*, 1995 (NYC).
- Washington, James, ed. *A Last Testament of Hope: The Essential Writings and Speeches of Martin Luther King Jr*. San Francisco: New York: Harper, 1991.

- Williams, Juan. *Eyes on the Prize: America's Civil Rights Years, 1954–1965*. New York: Penguin Books, 1988. (Prize).
- Malcolm X and Alex Haley. *The Autobiography of Malcolm X*. Ballantine, 1992.

Historical Questions and Documents

1. What was life like for African Americans at the end of World War II?

Documents:

- Fourteenth Amendment to the Constitution of the United States (Viewpoints, 331).
- The majority opinion from *Plessy v. Ferguson* (1896) (Viewpoints, 332).
- Justice Harlan dissent from *Plessy v. Ferguson* (1896) (Viewpoints, 332–33).
- Myrdal, Gunnar. *An American Dilemma*. New York: Harper, 1944, 1009–21 (Viewpoints, 350–51).
- Garland, Phyl. "A. Philip Randolph: Labor's Grand Old Man." *Ebony*, May 1969 (National Treasures, 190–91).
- Carl Rowan. *South of Freedom* (1952) (NYC, 64).
- Kenneth Clark. The Doll Test (Prize, 23).
- Anne Moody writes about the Emmett Till murder in *Coming of Age in Mississippi* (Prize, 56).

Video:

- Emmett Till (Prize 1)

2. How did African Americans respond to these conditions?

Documents:

- Philip Randolph. Testimony on desegregating the armed forces, *Congressional Record*, 80th Cong. 2nd sess., 19pt IV, 4313–17 (Katz 1995: 471–72).
- The Highlander Folk School (Prize, 64–65).
- Jo Ann Robinson. Organizing before the Boycott (Prize, 70–71).
- Rosa Parks. From Howard Raines. *My Soul Is Rested*. New York: G.P. Putnam's Sons, 1977 (National Treasures, 199–200).

Video:

- Montgomery bus boycott (King).

3. What were the responses of southern Whites and state and local governments?

Documents:

- One Hundred Southern Congressmen Dissent, *Congressional Record*, 84th Cong., 2d sess., 1956, 4515–16, (Bailey, 847–48).
- Governor Faubus defies desegregation, 1957 (Viewpoints, 335).
- Karr Shannon. *Arkansas Democrat*, March 10, 1958 (Bailey, 851–52).
- James Jackson Kilpatrick. The Southern Case for School Segregation (Prize, 28–30).
- A Dixie White's View (Prize, 54–55).
- *The Klan-Ledger*, Special Neshoba County Fair Edition, 1964 (Katz, 501–2).
- "White Backlash in Mississippi." *Memphis Press-Scimitar*, September 12, 1966, 1, 3 (Katz, 532).

Video:

- Governor Wallace blocks the door at the University of Mississippi (Encyclopedia).

4. How did the federal government respond to the Civil Rights movement?

Documents:

- The majority opinion from *Brown v. Board of Education of Topeka* (1954) (Bailey, 846–47).
- President Eisenhower responds to southern defiance at Little Rock, Arkansas (1957) (Bailey, 848–49).
- Elizabeth Eckford. First-hand account of Little Rock school desegregation effort. From Daisy Bates. *The Long Shadow of Little Rock*. New York: David McKay, 1962, 73–76 (Katz, 492–94).
- The Civil Rights Act of 1957 (Viewpoints, 336).
- President Kennedy Calls for Equal Rights, June 1963 (Katz, 499–501).

Video:
- Black students enter Little Rock High School (Prize 1).

5 & 6. What were the ideas and strategies of the Civil Rights movement?

Documents:
- Guy and Candie Carawan, eds. *Sing for Freedom, The Story of the Civil Rights Movement through its songs.* Sing Out, Bethlehem, Pa., 1990.
- *Sit-Downs*: An Interview with Diane Nash (Prize, 130–31).
- *Freedom Riders*: James Peck. *Freedom Ride.* New York: Grove Press, 1962, 98–99 (Katz, 495–96).
- *Desegregating Universities*: James Meredith. "I'll Know Victory or Defeat." *The Saturday Evening Post*, November 10, 1962, 17 (Katz, 497).
- *Birmingham, Alabama*: Mary Hamilton. "Freedom Now." Pacifica Radio (Katz, 498).
- *Mississippi Summer*: Excerpts from Dave Dennis' Eulogy for James Chaney (Prize, 239–40).
- *Voting Rights*: Fannie Lou Hamer. Hearing before a Select Panel on Mississippi and Civil Rights at the National Theater. Washington, D.C. June 8, 1964. *Congressional Record*, Cong. June 16, 1964 (Katz 1995, 503–4).
- Fannie Lou Hamer. *To Praise Our Bridges* (Prize, 245–47).
- *Selma, Alabama*: Sheyann Webb and Rachel West Nelson. *Selma, Lord, Selma.* Tuscaloosa, Ala.: University of Alabama Press, 1980.

Video:
- Freedom Rides (Prize 1); Birmingham, 1963 (King); Selma, Alabama (Prize 2).

7. What was Martin Luther King Jr.'s vision for U.S. society?

Documents:
- King, Martin Luther Jr. *Stride Towards Freedom.* New York: Harper, 1958, 212–17.
- King, Martin Luther Jr. *Why We Can't Wait.* New York: Harper and Row, 1963, 74–100.
- King, Coretta. *The Words of Martin Luther King.*
- Washington, James, ed. *A Last Testament of Hope: The Essential Writings and Speeches of Martin Luther King Jr.* San Francisco: New York: Harper, 1991, 7–8, 50, 447, 647. Specifically, excerpts from. A Letter from Birmingham Jail (1963); March on Washington (1963); Nobel Prize Address (1964).

Video:
- Birmingham, 1963 (King); Washington, 1963 (King); Norway, 1964 (King)

8. Did the Civil Rights movement significantly change the laws of the U.S.?

Documents:
- Lyndon Johnson, speech, March 15, 1965 (Bailey 868–74).
- Civil Rights Act of 1964.
- Voting Rights Act of 1965.

9. Why did African American communities explode?

Documents:
- Bayard Rustin. "The Watts Manifesto' and the McCone Report." *Commentary*, March 1966 (Viewpoints, 341).
- Langston Hughes. "Harlem III." *New York Post*, July 23, 1964, 29 (Katz 1995, 535–36).
- Ernie Chambers. Official Transcript of Proceedings before the National Advisory Commission on Civil Disorders. Washington, D.C., September 21, 1967, 1533–96 (Katz, 538–41).
- Eliot Asinof. "Dick Gregory Is Not So Funny Now." *The New York Times Magazine*, March 17, 1968, 38–42 (NYC, 76).
- Excerpts from the Report of the National Advisory Commission on Civil Disorders. Washington, D.C.: US Government Printing Office, 1968 (National Treasures, 211–12).

Video:
- Riots (Prize 2, Encyclopedia).

10. **Why did a new generation of African American activists challenge the ideas and strategies of the Civil Rights movement?**

Documents:
- Stokely Carmichael. "Black Power." Notes and Comments. SNCC, 1966 (Black Nationalism, 470–76).
- Alvin Poussaint. "A Negro Psychiatrist Explains the Negro Psyche." *The New York Times Magazine*, August 20, 1967, 53 (Katz, 533–34).
- Stokley Carmichael and Charles Hamilton. *Black Power*. New York: Random House, 1967, 44–49 (Katz, 537–38).
- The Black Panther Party Program. *The Black Panther*, March 16, 1968, 4 (Black Nationalism, 531–34).

Video:
- Black Panthers (Prize 2, Encyclopedia).

11. **Who was Malcolm X and what did he teach?**

Documents:
- Malcolm X and Alex Haley. *The Autobiography of Malcolm X*. Westminster, Md.: Ballantine, 1992, 35–36, 108–10, 149–52, 197, 315, 375–76.
- "Minister Malcolm X Enunciates the Muslim Program." *Muhammed Speaks*, September 1960, 2, 20–22. (Black Nationalism, 413–20).
- Malcolm X press conference, March 12, 1964 (Katz, 536).
- Malcolm X. An Address to Mississippi Youth, December 31, 1964. George Breitman, ed., *Malcolm X Speaks*. New York: Pathfinder Press, 1965 (National Treasures, 212–13).

Video:
- Malcolm X (Prize 2, Encyclopedia).

12. **Did the Civil Rights movement succeed?**

Documents:
- Bayard Rustin. "From Protest to Politics." *Commentary*, February 1965, 25–26 (Viewpoints, 342–43).
- Editorial. *The New York Times*. October 2, 1966, IV, I (Viewpoints, 341–42).
- *Life Magazine*. December 24, 1965, 106–20 (Viewpoints, 343).
- Kenneth Clark in Peter Kihss. "Clark Scores 'Separation' at Antioch." *The New York Times*, May 23, 1969 (Katz, 544–45).
- Eldridge Cleaver. *Soul on Ice* New York: McGraw-Hill, 123–25 (Katz, 545–46).

13. Why does racial discrimination continue to be an issue in the United States?

Documents:
- Robert Coles. "The White Northerner: Pride and Prejudice." *Atlantic Monthly*, June 1966, 53–57 (Bailey, 996–1000).
- Black Enterprise Champions Affirmative Action, August 1978, 7 (Bailey, 991–92).
- George Will. "Reverse Discrimination." *Newsweek*, July 10, 1978, 84 (Bailey, 993–96).

Teaching Activity: Design a Theme-Based Unit

Try it yourself:
Using a high school social studies textbook and a collection of primary source documents, design a theme-based unit plan (containing between 8 and 12 lessons) for a specific historical era or on a specific topic.

Add your voice to the discussion:
How do you view this approach to social studies unit planning? Why?

Classroom Activity: Post-World War II African American Experience

Examine Tables 4.1–4.5, which illustrate different aspects of the African American experience in the post-World War II United States. One of the side benefits of document based lessons is that the same documents appear again on student assessments. I often provide students with a chart and have them "translate" it into a graph or provide a graph that they must "translate" into a chart. Most of this data is from United States Census Bureau or Bureau of Labor Statistics reports. Table 4.5 is adapted from *The New York Times*, August 28, 2002, A14. For more information see Loury, G., *The Anatomy of Racial Inequality*. Cambridge, Mass: Harvard University Press, 2002.

Try it yourself:
Using the graph provided for Fig. 4.1 as a model, select one of the other charts and create a graph.

It's your classroom:
Using the questions provided for Table 4.1 as a model, what questions would you ask students to guide their analysis of the information in the other tables?

TABLE 4.1
School Segregation and Voting Rights in the U.S. South

State	African American Children in Interracial Schools, 1964	Eligible African Americans Registered to Vote, 1960	Eligible African Americans Registered to Vote, 1964
West Virginia	58.2%	NA	NA
Delaware	56.5	NA	NA
Kentucky	54.4	NA	NA
Missouri	42.0	NA	NA
Oklahoma	28.0	NA	NA
Texas	5.5	32%	46%
Tennessee	2.7	59	64
Virginia	1.6	19	25
Florida	1.5	26	45
Arkansas	Less than 1	30	41
Alabama	Less than 1	14	19
Louisiana	Less than 1	22	31
Georgia	Less than 1	22	36
South Carolina	Less than 1	11	30
North Carolina	Less than 1	25	42
Mississippi	None	4	6

1. What percentage of African American children attended interracial schools in Missouri?
2. What percentage of African American children attended interracial schools in Florida?
3. In which of these states did the smallest percentage of African American children attend interracial schools?
4. What percentage of eligible African Americans where registered to vote in Texas in 1960?
5. Which of these states had the largest percentage of eligible African Americans registered to vote in 1964?
6. Which state(s) had the greatest percentage increase from 1960 to 1964?
7. What conclusions do you draw from this table?

TABLE 4.2
Standard of Living by Race, 1950–1970

Category	Year	All People	Whites	African Americans
Unemployment	1950	5.3%	4.9%	9.0%
	1960	5.5%	4.9%	10.2%
	1970	4.9%	4.5%	8.2%
Median Income	1950	$3,319	$3,334	$1,369
	1960	$5,620	$5,835	$3,233
	1970	$9,867	$10,236	$6,516
Life expectancy	1950		69 years	61 years
	1960		71 years	64 years
	1970		72 years	64 years

TABLE 4.3
Education of Head of Household of African
American Families in Poverty

Education	1978	1987
At least one year of college	12.6%	11.2%
High school graduate	18.7	27.8
High school dropout	34.2	39.4

TABLE 4.4
Income Distribution by Race, 1990

Income	White Families	African American Families
Over $50,000	32.5%	14.5%
$35,000–$49,999	20.8	15.0
$25,000–$34,999	16.5	14.0
$15,000–$24,999	16.0	19.5
$15,000 or less	14.2	37.0

TABLE 4.5
African American Males, Incarcerated or in College, 1980 and 2000

Status	1980	2000	Percent Increase
Incarcerated	143,000	791,600	450%
College	463,000	603,032	30

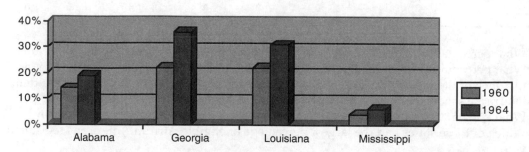

FIG. 4.1   Eligible African Americans Registered to Vote, 1960 and 1964

Teaching Activity: Design a Theme-Based Unit

Try it yourself:
Using a high school social studies textbook and a collection of primary source documents, design a theme-based unit plan (containing between 8 and 12 lessons) for a specific historical era or on a specific topic.

Add your voice to the discussion:
How do you view this approach to social studies unit planning? Why?

WHAT IS A COMPARATIVE THEMATIC UNIT?

In the chronological global history curriculum, teachers tend to focus on different groups, nations, or regions during each historical epoch. A problem with this approach is that it can give students the impression that all peoples and nations were undergoing similar experiences at the same time.

In an area studies curriculum, students briefly and separately examine the histories, geography, and cultures of each region (e.g., Latin America and the Caribbean, Sub-Saharan Africa, North Africa and the Middle East, Southeast Asia, China, Japan, and the Indian subcontinent). A problem with this approach is that students do not learn to draw connections between events taking place in different parts of the world.

A comparative/thematic unit is one way to address the limitations in both of these approaches. It makes it possible for students to examine the similarities and differences in the ways that peoples, nations, and civilizations interact and confront historical forces. For example, a class can examine the problems related to industrialization and modernization as well as solutions developed by people in different places during different historical periods. Another possibility is to study nationalist movements in various countries as people respond to colonialism and imperialism. A comparative/thematic approach can be used throughout the entire curriculum or as a way to organize occasional integrative units.

Comparative / Thematic Unit Outline: Nationalism vs. Colonialism and Imperialism

1. India Challenges the British Empire
   Focus: Gandhi and the idea and practice of nonviolent civil disobedience
   Question: Is it possible to build a unified nation in an ethnically, religiously, and linguistically diverse society?
2. Communist Revolution in China
   Focus: Mao Zedong and violent revolution as a vehicle to gain power and change society
   Question: Is Communism a viable alternative for oppressed people?
3. Irish Nationalism
   Focus: Opposition to forced cultural and political assimilation
   Question: Are members of the Irish Republican Army soldiers or terrorists?

4. Kenya and Algeria
   Focus: Independence struggles in settler colonies (colonies where large numbers of people from the imperialist power have established permanent homes)
   Question: Are attacks on civilian supporters of colonial regimes justified?
5. Vietnam
   Focus: Cultural and historical roots of resistance
   Question: How did a small traditional nation resist world superpowers?
6. Nigeria
   Focus: Creating one nation out of different peoples
   Question: Do nations have the right to suppress internal nationalist movements?
7. Conclusions
   Focus: Compare nationalist revolutions in different countries
   Questions: How do we decide whether nationalist movements are justified? How do we decide when nationalist movements are successful?

Teaching Activity: Design a Comparative Unit

Try it yourself:
Using a high school social studies textbook and a collection of primary source documents, design a comparative unit plan (containing between 8 and 10 lessons) for a specific historical era or on a specific topic.

Add your voice to the discussion:
How do you view this approach to social studies unit planning? Why?

It's your classroom:
Which approach to unit planning do you prefer? Why?

Learning Activity: Drawing Connections between Events

Frequently students learn historical events in isolation from each other or from only one perspective. The following questions are intended to encourage people to draw connections between peoples and events.

1. The Jewish holiday of Hanukah is the celebration of ancient Hebrew resistance to conquest and assimilation. Whom were they battling?
2. In 732 A.D., the victory of an army headed by Charles Martel at the Battle of Tours and Poiters (in contemporary France) prevented the integration of medieval European societies into a vibrant international civilization that already extended from the Pyrennes to China. Which army was defeated in this battle?
3. In 1325 A.D., a voyager from the Mediterranean region began his travels across the Eastern Hemisphere, probably reaching India in 1333 and China in 1345. Later he visited western Africa. As a result of his journals, dictated upon his return home, the known world became much more integrated. Who was this voyager?
4. Study of the Age of Exploration usually starts around 1450 A.D. with Portuguese voyages along the west coast of Africa. However, a half century earlier, this empire sponsored a series of major voyages to expand trade and find a water route connecting the east and west. One trip involved more than 300 ships and nearly 28,000 people. The voyages stopped in 1433 A.D., when the empire decided it had little to learn about or acquire from the rest of the world. Which empire sponsored these voyages?
5. What is the oldest permanently established community in what is now the continental United States?
6. In 1608 a separatist group of Calvinists left England to stay with coreligionists in the Netherlands. Unhappy over the assimilation of their children into Dutch society, the

"Pilgrims" returned to England a year later. In 1620, they left England again, this time to settle in the new world. Later in the 17th century, some of their former Dutch hosts followed their example and went into exile in the wilderness to establish a religious community. Who were they, and where did they go?

7. The American colonies and the United States were involved in the French and Indian War from 1754–1763 and the War of 1812 from 1812 to 1815. Both wars were actually the North American fronts of broader European conflicts. Which wars were they? Who were the primary European combatants?

8. In 1831, he led a slave rebellion that shook the entire slave system and directly led to emancipation in a number of new world territories. Who was he, and where was the rebellion?

9. Where did Mohandas Gandhi begin his involvement in opposition to British colonialism?

10. In the early 20th century, this future world leader sought a position in the French bureaucracy so that he could help the French develop his homeland. He was refused. In 1919, he tried to represent his homeland at the peace conference at Versailles, but he was denied admission. As a revolutionary leader, he later helped his people defeat the Japanese, the French, and the United States. Who was he, and what was his homeland?

Try it yourself:
How did you do on these questions? Answers are on the last page of this chapter.

Essay 1: Teaching about Slavery in the Americas*

In October 1994 in an effort to fulfill its responsibilities as a major public historical resource and provide a more accurate portrait of the American past, Colonial Williamsburg conducted a "mock" slave auction. It was intended "to educate visitors about a brutal yet important part of black American history" (*The New York Times*, 1994a; 1994b).

According to park spokesperson Christy Coleman, who directed the project and participated in the reenactment as a pregnant slave sold to pay her "master's" debts, "This is a very, very sensitive and emotional issue. But it is also very real history." Ms. Coleman felt that "only by open display and discussion could people understand the degradation and humiliation that blacks felt as chattel" (1994a: A7).

Critics, mobilized by the Virginia chapters of the National Association for the Advancement of Colored People and the Southern Christian Leadership Conference, protested that the auction trivialized slavery by depicting scenes "too painful to revive in any form" (1994a: A7)." A small group of demonstrators stood witness at the reenactment. Later, one of the demonstrators, who had initially charged Colonial Williamsburg with turning Black history into a "sideshow," changed his mind. He explained that as a result of witnessing the "mock" auction, he felt "(p)ain had a face. Indignity had a body. Suffering had tears" (1994b: A16).

I believe the controversy surrounding the "mock" auction at Colonial Williamsburg is a reflection of a larger debate taking place in classrooms across the United States where social studies teachers consider ways to help students understand the impact of slavery and the slave trade on U.S. society and the human beings who were its victims. Both historical issues and pedagogical questions are involved in these debates. Historians continue to argue over the nature of chattel slavery itself (for a recent synthesis published by the American Historical Association, see Foner, *Slavery, the Civil War & Reconstruction*), the treatment of enslaved people, and the long-term impact of slavery on U.S. society. There are disputes over the reliability of sources such as slave narratives, which were often ghostwritten and usually published by abolitionist organizations.

---

*An earlier version of this essay appeared in A. Singer, "Teaching about Slavery in the Americas," *Social Science Docket* 1, no. 2 (2001). Used with permission.

Secondary school teachers have to decide whether to assign literature such as Harriet Beecher Stowe's *Uncle Tom's Cabin* or show films such as *Amistad* to provide students with historical background. There are also disagreements about the accuracy, sensitivity, and efficacy of teaching approaches such as role-playing and historical reenactments, especially given continuing racial segregation and ethnic tension in classrooms, schools, and communities.

Teaching Activity: Main Ideas about Slavery in the Americas

1. West Africans were experienced agricultural workers whose labor was used to exploit the resources of the American continents. Profits generated by African slavery and the African slave trade made possible the commercial and industrial revolutions in Europe and the United States.

2. European societies accepted hierarchy, injustice, and exploitation as a normal condition of human life. Color and religious differences made it easier to enslave Africans. Europeans justified this slavery by denying the humanity of the African.

3. Africans had slaves and participated in the slave trade. Although slavery existed in many times and cultures throughout human history, slavery in the Americas, including the United States, was a fundamentally different institution. There was no reciprocal obligation by the elite to the enslaved. Enslavement was a permanent hereditary status; there was an impassable racial barrier.

4. Democracy and community among White, male, Christian property holders in the early American republic rested on the exploitation of other groups, especially the enslavement of the African. The founders of the United States were aware of the hypocrisy of owning slaves. Slavery was intentionally not addressed in the Declaration of Independence and the U.S. Constitution.

5. Africans in the Americas resisted slavery in many different ways. They built families, communities, and religious institutions that asserted their humanity. In the United States, enslaved Africans developed an emancipatory Christianity based on the story of Exodus and laced it with African symbols. In Haiti and Brazil, there were major successful slave rebellions. With 180,000 African Americans in the Union army, the American Civil War can be seen as an African American Liberation struggle.

6. White and African American abolitionists struggled for decades against slavery. Most White abolitionists based their beliefs on their Protestant religion. *Uncle Tom's Cabin* was the "Common Sense" of the antislavery crusade because it presented the humanity of the enslaved African.

7. While Christian religious beliefs were used to challenge slavery, they were also used to justify it. Defenders of slavery, particularly in the South, used Biblical citations to defend the "peculiar institution."

8. Slavery was a national, rather than a southern, institution. There was limited slavery in the North until 1840 and prosperity in the North rested on the slave trade and the processing of slave-produced raw materials.

9. The Civil War was not fought by the North to free Africans; it was fought to save the union. It ended legal bondage, but not the racist ideas that supported the system.

Add your voice to the discussion:
These are the main ideas about slavery in the Americas that informed my teaching as a high school social studies teacher. Which of these main ideas and understandings do you consider important to include in a high school curriculum? Which ones would you leave out? What ideas would you add?

It's your classroom:
Select one of the main ideas for teaching about slavery. Make a list of documents you could use in your classroom to illustrate this idea.

Some of my most successful lessons but also one of my greatest disasters have dealt with slavery. At the start of my teaching career, while working with African American middle school students, I presented a class with material on the Biblical defense of slavery that I had learned about in graduate school. The students believed these were my ideas, and they were furious with me; it took weeks to reestablish a relationship of trust with them. Today I know effective, well-intentioned teachers who reenact the middle passage and slave auctions in their social studies classes. However, based on my experience, I think this is a mistake. While students may tolerate these reenactments and participate in them, I do not believe they can be done with either sensitivity or authenticity. I suspect most White students think they have experienced and learned more about slavery than they have any right to believe while Black students are left embarrassed or alienated by the attempted reenactments.

For a number of years after my middle school debacle, I shied away from a serious discussion of slavery in my classes. Later, however, as a high school teacher, I developed what I consider to be effective lessons. I used traditional African American folk songs to explore the meaning of slavery, the longing for freedom and resistance to oppression. These included "All the Pretty Little Horses," "Go Down Moses" (available on the web at http://www.acronet.net/~robokopp/usa/gomoses.htm), and "Follow the Drinking Gourd" (available on the web at http://quest.arc.nasa. gov/ltc/special/mlk/gourd2.html).

I also have students read passages from Solomon Northup's autobiographical narrative, *Twelve Years a Slave* (Eakin and Logsdon, 1968; Eakin, 1990, available on the web at http://docsouth.unc.edu), and we viewed segments from the PBS version of his life, "Solomon Northup's Odyssey". I even revived my lesson on the Biblical defense of slavery, although I was very careful to introduce the lesson with an abolitionist's attack on slavery and a challenge to students that they respond to the quotations based on their own religious and moral beliefs.

Classroom Activity: Songs about Slavery—
All the Pretty Little Horses (Traditional)

The key to understanding this lullaby is that there are two babies.

> Hush-a-bye, don't you cry, go to sleep my little baby,
> When you wake, you shall have, all the pretty little horses,
> Blacks and bays, dapples and grays, all the pretty little horses.
> Way down yonder, in the meadow, lies my poor little lambie,
> With bees and butterflies peckin' out its eyes,
> The poor little things crying Mammy.

Try it yourself:
1. Who are the two babies in this lullaby? Which baby is the woman singing to?
2. Why do you think the woman was assigned to care for this baby?
3. What does this song tell us about the experience of enslaved Africans?

Learning Activity: Solomon Northup: Twelve Years a Slave

Solomon Northup was a free African American, a skilled carpenter, and an accomplished musician living in northern New York State with his family when he was kidnapped and sold into slavery in Louisiana. Northup brings the insights of a free man, a literate man, and a skilled worker to his discussion of slavery, slave community, and work on the plantation. In these passages, Northup describes cotton production in Louisiana.

> When a new hand, one unaccustomed to the business, is sent for the first time into the field, he is whipped up smartly, and made for that day to pick as fast as he can possibly. At night it is weighed, so that his capability in cotton picking is known. He must bring in the same weight each night following. If it falls short, it is considered evidence that he has been laggard, and a greater or less number of lashes is the penalty. An ordinary day's

work is considered two hundred pounds. A slave who is accustomed to picking, is punished, if he or she brings in a less quantity than that. . . .

The hands are required to be in the cotton fields as soon as it is light in the morning, and with the exception of ten or fifteen minutes, which is given them at noon to swallow their allowance of cold bacon, they are not permitted to be a moment idle until it is too dark to see, and when the moon is full, then often times labor till the middle of the night. They do not dare to stop even at dinner time, nor return to the quarters however late it be, until the order to halt is given by the driver.

The day's work over in the field, the baskets are "toted," or in other words, carried to the gin-house, where the cotton is weighed. No matter how fatigued and weary he may be . . . a slave never approaches the gin-house with his basket of cotton but with fear. If it falls short in weight: if he has not performed the full task appointed him, he knows what he must suffer.

It's your class:
Would you use this passage in your class? Explain your answer.

Try it yourself:
The year is 1841. You are a friend of Solomon Northup living in New York. You learn that he has been kidnapped and sold into slavery in Louisiana. Write a letter to your congressional representative protesting against slavery and demanding that Northup be released.

While I reject role-playing and reenactments about an issue as controversial and painful as slavery, I have participated in very effective dramatic presentations with students on different academic levels. I prefer dramas because a prepared script provides structure to the activity and content on the history of slavery. One summer at Camp Hurley, where I worked while a student, the teens performed scenes from Martin B. Duberman's documentary play about the Black struggle for freedom and civil rights, *In White America* (1964). Based on this experience, I later had my high school social studies students edit and present to other classes excerpts from the speeches and writings of African American and White abolitionists.

In an after-school program where I assisted, a multiracial group of fifth graders performed a version of Virginia Hamilton's story about slavery and the undying desire for freedom, "The People Could Fly" (discussed in chap. 2). The children were upset by a scene where a White overseer and a Black driver whip a young mother while she is holding her infant because she will not work harder. After discussing the meaning of the story, the children decided to perform it. However, they also decided not to cast the parts according to the race of the characters or of the actors. On another occasion, I worked with a middle school class that performed the same play. The students were African American, Caribbean, and Latino/a. Following a similar discussion, the students decided that none of them would play the oppressors.

Instead, they built giant puppets to represent the overseer and driver.

What each of these four productions had in common, what I believe is the key to successful learning about slavery in the United States, was not the production itself but student discussion of the meaning of the dramatization, how students wanted to cast it, what they believed about race and ethnicity in the United States, and what they had learned about slavery. In each case, the play was primarily the vehicle for promoting the discussion.

Another lesson that I learned is that a symbol can be more powerful than a reenactment. One of the most successful depictions of a human catastrophe similar to slavery in the Americas is the United States Holocaust Memorial in Washington, D.C. The two exhibits that had the most powerful effect on me were the pile of thousands of shoes standing in stark reminder of what happened to their owners and the gradual narrowing and darkening of the corridor as museum visitors prepared to enter a model of a cattle car that transported European Jews to death camps. Significantly, the memorial is able to evoke what happened during the Holocaust without reenacting what happened in a gas chamber, displaying a pile of human bodies, or having actors dressed in prison garb digging their own graves. Similarly, the best exhibit I have seen on slavery in the Americas was at the Schomberg Center for Research in Black Culture in New York City. It was a display of chains, metal collars, wooden yokes, metal rods, and other instruments for branding and imprisoning enslaved Africans.

As a teacher, I have also learned that no activity or exhibit by itself substitutes for the context created by a teacher and the relationship that exists in the classroom among students and between students and their teacher. Despite the outstanding qualities of the Holocaust Memorial, there were problems with it as an educational tool. Even as I was moved by what I saw and felt, it was disconcerting to watch a group of high school students from Middle America running through

the exhibits without reflection or even "seeing" the displays, as they raced to the next historical site on their itinerary. Clearly, the exhibit itself was insufficient to capture the imagination of students who were disengaged from the material. A lesson, a museum visit, or a classroom activity may seem like a good idea in the abstract, but this does not mean it will achieve its intended goals with a particular group of students. For a lesson to be meaningful, the teacher must consider who the students in the class are, what they already know, and how they will react.

Classroom Activity: Wall of Memory

Robert Kurtz, Stephanie Hunte, and Rachel Gaglione Thompson of the New Teachers Network brought their middle school classes together to create a Museum of Slavery. The center piece of the exhibit was a "Wall of Memory," an evocative display symbolizing the pain of slavery and the unending hope for escape and freedom. More than 100 white t-shirts were stained with coffee to make them appear old, ripped with scissors, speckled with reddish-brown paint, and hung on the wall.

Add your voice to the discussion:

1. What do you remember learning about slavery as a student in middle school and high school?
2. Do you agree or disagree with the issues raised in this essay? Explain.
3. How would you teach about a painful topic like slavery? Why?
4. Would you vary your approach, depending on the background of the students in your classes? Explain.

Essay 2: Using Student Dialogues to Teach Social Studies and Promote Democracy*

In the sample 11th grade U.S. curriculum calendar presented in Chapter 3, I listed but did not explain lessons using "student dialogues" to introduce and review units. Suggested questions for examination by classes were: Should the United States have dropped the atomic bomb on Japan? and Did the Civil Rights movement succeed?

The idea of using structured student dialogues to teach social studies content, concepts, and skills and as a vehicle for building classroom community and promoting democracy has been pioneered by Michael Pezone of the New Teachers Network. Michael's work with recent immigrants and mainstreamed special education students in a middle

school and hard-to-reach minority youth in a troubled high school has been described in *Social Education* (Pezone and Singer, 1997), the *American Educational Research Journal* (Singer and Pezone, 2001), a book on citizenship education (Miller and Singleton, 1997), and the *New York State Great Irish Famine Curriculum Guide* (Pezone and Palacio, 2001). It has been adopted and adapted by other members of the network, including Jennifer Palacio, Rachel Gaglione Thompson, Stephanie Hunte, and Lauren Rosenberg, who have made student dialogues an important part of their own teaching.

In his social studies classes, Michael Pezone employs many of the practices advocated by

---

*An earlier version of this essay appeared in M. Pezone and A. Singer (1997). Used with permission.

progressive and transformative educators (Apple and Beane, 1995; Banks, 1991; Bigelow, 1988; 1990). He believes that both the success of the dialogues and the experience in democracy depend on the gradual development of caring, cooperative communities over the course of a year (Noddings, 1992; Kohn, 1986). To encourage these communities, he works with students to create an atmosphere in which they feel free to expose their ideas, feelings, and academic proficiencies in public without risking embarrassment or attack and being pressed into silence. He stresses with students that the dialogues are not debates; but that as students learn about a topic, the entire class "wins or loses" together.

The student dialogues are highly structured. Michael believes that structure maximizes student freedom by ensuring that all students have an opportunity to participate. It also helps to ensure that classes carefully examine statements, attitudes, and practices that may reflect biases and demean community members.

Michael uses dialogues to conclude units; however, preparation for the dialogues takes place all the time. At the start of the semester, he and his students decide on the procedures for conducting dialogues so that everyone in class participates and on criteria for evaluating team and individual performance. Usually students want the criteria to include an evaluation of how well the team works together; the degree to which substantive questions are addressed; the use of supporting evidence; the response to statements made by the other team; whether ideas are presented effectively; and whether individual students demonstrate effort and growth. These criteria are codified in a scoring rubric that is reexamined before each dialogue and changed when necessary. Students also help to define the question being discussed. After the dialogue, students work in small groups to evaluate the overall dialogue, the performance by their team, and their individual participation.

During a unit, the class identifies a broad social studies issue that members want to research and examine in greater depth. For example, after studying the recent histories of India and China, they discussed whether violent revolution or nonviolent resistance is the most effective path to change. On other occasions they have discussed whether the achievements of the ancient world justified the exploitation of people and whether the United States and Europe should intervene in the internal affairs of other countries because of the way that women are treated in some cultures.

The goal of a dialogue is to examine all aspects of an issue, not to score points at the expense of someone else. Teams are subdivided into cooperative learning groups that collect and organize information supporting different views. The teams also assign members as either opening, rebuttal, or concluding speakers. During dialogues, teams "huddle-up" to share their ideas and reactions to what is being presented by the other side. After dialogues, students discuss what they learned from members of the other team and evaluate the performance of the entire class.

An important part of the dialogue process is the involvement of students in assessing what they have learned. In Michael's classes, students help develop the parameters for class projects and decide the criteria for assessing their performance in these activities. The benefit of this involvement for students includes a deeper understanding of historical and social science research methods, insight into the design and implementation of projects, a greater stake in the satisfactory completion of assignments, and a sense of empowerment because assessment decisions are based on rules that the classroom community has helped to shape.

Michael uses individual and group conferences to learn what students think about the dialogues and their impact on student thinking about democratic process and values. Students generally feel that the dialogues give them a personal stake in what happens in class and they feel responsible for supporting their teams. Students who customarily are silent in class because of fear of being ridiculed or because they are not easily understood by the other students become involved in speaking out. For many students, it is a rare opportunity to engage in both decision making and open public discussion "in front of other people."

From the dialogues, students start to learn that democratic society involves a combination of individual rights and initiatives with social responsibility, collective decision making, and shared community goals. They discover that democracy frequently entails tension between the will of the majority and the rights of minorities and that it cannot be taken for granted. It involves taking risks and is something that a community must continually work to maintain and expand. Another benefit of the dialogue process is that it affords students the opportunity to actively generate knowledge without relying on teacher-centered instructional methods.

Michael finds that the year-long process of defining, conducting, and evaluating dialogues involves students in constant reflection on social studies concepts, class goals, student interaction, and the importance of community. It makes possible individual academic and social growth, encourages students to view ideas critically and events from multiple perspectives, and supports the formation of a cooperative learning environment. He believes that when students are able to analyze educational issues, and create classroom policy, they gain a personal stake in classroom activities and a deeper understanding of democracy.

Students in Michael's 9th grade law elective and Jennifer Palacio's 12th grade participation in government classes participated dialogues while helping to field-test a document packet that is part of the New York State Great Irish Famine curriculum. They researched and examined the question, Was British policy in Ireland during the Great Irish Famine an example of genocide?

On Day 1, students read and discussed the definition of genocide by the United Nations which includes a number of different kinds of actions but requires proof of intent, and documents describing events that could be considered examples of genocide. The documents included the 1935 Nuremburg Racial Laws in Nazi Germany, an historian's account of Turkey's attack on Armenians during the era of World War I, an enslaved African's description of the middle passage, a newspaper photograph of an open burial site in Rwanda from 1994, a chart showing the decimation of native American population centers following the arrival of Europeans, and descriptions by contemporaries of famine-era Ireland. Students used the U.N. definition of genocide to evaluate the events described in the other documents. At the end of the first class period, students decided whether they wanted to be on the team that presented evidence that British policy was an example of genocide or on the opposing team.

On Days 2 and 3, student teams were subdivided into work groups that examined a series of primary source documents from the Great Irish Famine curriculum and prepared opening and closing statements. The documents included newspaper articles, editorials and political cartoons, government documents, speeches, and charts showing evictions, emigration, food availability, and population decline.

On Day 4 students held their dialogues. After opening round statements, teams caucused to prepare rebuttals. Following rebuttals, teams updated concluding statements. After the concluding statements, the class discussed what students learned from the dialogue and each other.

On the final day of the project, individual students used the documents and what they learned from the dialogue to write a document-based essay.

Teaching Activity: Rules for Student Dialogues in Ms. Rosenberg's Class

Choosing teams:
Students will select teams based on their opinions. Ms. Rosenberg may reassign some students so the teams are equally balanced.

Issues for the dialogues:
United States History: Should the United States be the police force for the world?
Global History: Do revolutions improve people's lives?

Preparation for the dialogues:
Student teams will be divided into study groups of three or four students. Each study group will research a topic. Using the research, individual students will prepare regents-style essays supporting their position. Study group members will edit each others essays before the dialogue.

Procedures for the dialogues:
There will be four rounds during the dialogues. Before Round 1, teams will meet together and plan their presentation. Students from each team will take turns speaking. In Round 1, five students from each team will introduce the team's views. After Round 1, teams will "huddle up" to think about what the other team said. In Round 2, students will take turns responding

to the ideas of the other team. Teams will huddle up again after Round 2 to plan how to conclude the dialogue. In Round 3, three students will summarize the main ideas of their team. After Round 3, teams will meet again to evaluate what students have learned. In Round 4, students will discuss what they learned from the other team.

During the dialogues:
Students should respect each other.
Students should not attack or interrupt each other.
One person speaks at a time.
Everyone must participate.
After your turn to speak, take notes and share them with your teammates.
The discussion should be as free and open as possible.
Students should speak loudly and clearly.
Team members should take turns. Don't speak too long.
Teammates must make sure that everyone speaks.
Some people who are comfortable speaking to the whole class should wait until the end.

Things to remember:
People must listen to each other.
People must give reasons for their opinions.
People must present facts.
People have to believe what they are speaking.
People need to talk about the things that other people say.
Express your ideas clearly.
Learn and understand the ideas of other people.
Share opinions.
Discussion is more important than winning. There are no right answers.

Add your voice to the discussion:
1. How do you evaluate student dialogues as an approach to teaching social studies?
2. Would you consider using them in your classroom? Explain.

It's your classroom:
1. Michael Pezone spends time every year having students in each class reinvent the dialogue process. Lauren Rosenberg prefers to provide students with guidelines for the dialogues. Which approach do you prefer? Why?
2. Dialogues in Jennifer Palacio's classes tend to be less structured than they are in Michael's classes. Would you prefer a tighter or looser structure? Explain.

Try it yourself:
1. Assemble a set of documents (between 5 and 10) that can be used as the basis for a student dialogue.
2. What question would you have students discuss?

REFERENCES AND RECOMMENDATIONS FOR FURTHER READING

Apple, M., and J. Beane. *Democratic Schools*. Alexandria, Virginia: ASCD, 1995.

Bailey, T., and D. Kennedy. *The American Spirit: United States History As Seen by Contemporaries*. 9th ed. Boston: Houghton Mifflin, 1998.

Bailey, T., D. Kennedy, and L. Cohen. *The American Pageant: A History of the Republic*. 11th ed. Boston: Houghton Mifflin, 1998.

Banks, J. "A Curriculum for Empowerment, Action and Change." In *Empowerment through Multicultural Education*, ed. C. Sleeter. Albany, N.Y.: SUNY Press, 1991.

Bigelow, W. "Critical Pedagogy at Jefferson High School." *Equity and Choice* 4, no. 2 (1988).

Bigelow, W. "Inside the Classroom: Social Vision and Critical Pedagogy." *Teachers College Record* 91, no. 3 (1990).

Butterfield, F. "Study Finds Big Increase in Black Men as Inmates Since 1980," *The New York Times*, August 28, 2002 A14.

Duberman, M. *In White America*. Boston: Houghton Mifflin, 1964.

Eakin, S., and J. Logdon, eds. *Solomon Northup: Twelve Years a Slave*. Baton Rouge, La.: Louisiana State University, 1968.

Eakin, S. *Solomon Northup's Twelve Years a Slave, 1841–1853*. Gretna, La.: Pelican Publishing, 1990.

Foner, E. *Slavery, the Civil War and Reconstruction*. Washington, D.C.: American Historical Association, 1997.

Greaves, R., P. Cannistrataro, R. Zaller, and R. Murphy. *Civilizations of the World: The Human Adventure*. New York: Harper and Row, 1990.

Hamilton, V. *The People Could Fly: American Black Folktales*. New York: Knopf, 1985.

Kohn, A. *No Contest: The Case against Competition*. Boston: Houghton Mifflin, 1986.

Loury, G. *The Anatomy of Racial Inequality*. Cambridge, Mass., Harvard University Press, 2002.

Meyers, M., J. Cawleti, and A. Kern, eds. *Sources of the American Republic*, vol. I. Glenview, Ill.: Scott, Foresman, 1967.

Miller, B., and L. Singleton. *Preparing Citizens, Linking Authentic Assessment and Instruction in Civic/Law-Related Education*. Boulder, Colo.: Social Science Education Consortium, 1997.

National Archives and Records Administration. *Teaching with Documents*, vol. 1, 1989.

National Archives and Records Administration. *Teaching with Documents*, vol. 2, 1998.

National Council for Social Studies. Task Force on Social Studies in the Middle School. "Social Studies in the Middle School." *Social Education* 55, no. 5 (1991) 287–93.

The New York Times (1994a, October 8). "Mock Auction of Slaves: Education or Outrage?," A7.

The New York Times (1994b, October 11). "Tears and Protest at Mock Slave Sale," A16.

Noddings, N. *The Challenge to Care in Schools*. New York: Teachers College Press, 1992.

Oxford University Press (1999). *A History of Us, Sourcebook and Index, Documents that Shaped the American Nation, Book 11*. New York: Oxford University Press.

Pezone, M., and A. Singer. "Empowering Immigrant Students through Democratic Dialogues." *Social Education*, February 1997, 75–79.

Pezone, M., and J. Palacio. "Democratic Dialogues about Genocide." In ed. M. Murphy and A. Singer. *New York State Great Irish Famine Curriculum Guide*, Albany, N.Y.: State Education Department, 2001.

Prentice-Hall. *Voices of Freedom: Sources in American History*. Englewood Cliffs, N.J.: Prentice Hall, 1987.

Shanker, A. *The Making of a Profession*. Washington, D.C.: American Federation of Teachers, 1985.

Singer, A., and M. Pezone. "High School Democratic Dialogues: A Response to Annette Hemmings." *American Educational Research Journal* 38, no. 3 (2001), 535–39.

Stowe, H. (1952). *Uncle Tom's Cabin*. New York: Dodd, Mead and Co, 1952.

Drawing Connections between Events

Answers to questions on page 164–165.

1. Between 334 B.C. and 326 B.C., the armies of Alexander the Great conquered Asia Minor and the lands between Egypt and India. The Hellenistic Age that followed was a period of cultural, social, and commercial integration in the Mediterranean world. The rebellion from

166 B.C. to 164 B.C. was in opposition to Greek administration and culture and its local Jewish supporters.

2. Charles Martel (Charles the Hammer) defeated an Islamic army and halted the advance of Islamic culture and religion into Western Europe.

3. During his lifetime, Abu Abdallah Ibn Battuta of Tunisia traveled widely, serving as an emissary for a number of Islamic rulers. In 1356, the ruler of Morocco had a young scholar record Ibn Battuta's experiences and observations about the Islamic world. After completing the book, Abu Abdallah Ibn Battuta became a judge in a small Moroccan town. As far as we know, he never traveled again.

4. In 1405, the Ming rulers of China sent Zheng He on the first of seven expeditions to India, Arabia, and the east coast of Africa.

5. The Hopi village of Orabi in Arizona.

6. The Dutch established a colony at the Cape of Good Hope in southern Africa in 1652. The Boers or Afrikaners soon declared Africans to be the descendants of the biblical "Ham,' justifying their enslavement and *apartheid*.

7. Both wars centered on Anglo-French competition for empire and efforts to build alliances. The French and Indian War was part of the Seven Years War in Europe. The War of 1812 was a battlefront in the Napoleonic Wars.

8. Sam Sharpe, a literate slave preacher, led an eight-day rebellion that spread across the entire island of Jamaica. He was captured and hung; however, his rebellion led to the abolition of slavery in the British Empire.

9. Mohandas Gandhi was a founding member of the African National Congress in South Africa in 1912.

10. Nguyen That Thanh of Vietnam was later known as Ho Chi Minh.

5

How Do You Plan
a Social Studies Lesson?

WHY HAVE WRITTEN LESSON PLANS?

Attitudes about formal lesson plans vary widely among social studies teachers, as do ideas about what needs to be included. In some school districts, lesson planning is treated as if it were a teacher's primary professional responsibility. Fre-quently, districts or departments insist that teachers use a standard lesson plan format and supervisors regularly examine teacher plan books to monitor the general quality of lessons. Supervisors also check whether curriculum goals are being met, ensure that departmental lesson calendars are being respected, and, some teachers suspect, guard against innovation and the introduction of controversial ideas into classroom discussions. Rationales for this approach to lesson planning include the ideas that quality lessons flow from quality lesson plans, that standardized lesson plan formats promote high-level and uniform instruction, and that the regular review of lesson plans is a way to ensure teacher accountability.

Many veteran classroom teachers are very critical of formal lesson planning. They argue that formal planning, especially standardized lesson plan formats, stifle creativity, create rigid teacher-centered classrooms, contribute to an authoritarian atmosphere in schools, deny students a say in their own learning, and undermine any notion that teachers are professional educators capable of deciding what should take place in their classrooms. This group of educators claims that elaborate lesson plans represent only teacher intentions. They insist that the only way supervisors can authentically evaluate how well teachers are teaching is by visiting classrooms where they can observe how their students are learning.

I tend to agree with most of the critics of formal lesson plans, but I draw a different conclusion from their criticisms. I am a strong advocate of lesson planning. I think the problems they identify are more related to the type of lessons they plan and the ways that plans are used than to the idea of planning itself. For me, planning is an essential part of what it means to be a professional educator and an historian/social scientist. Proficiency in lesson planning is a key to effective social studies teaching. It is what makes possible student and teacher creativity, flexible and interesting lessons, and the creation of student-centered, democratic classrooms.

WHAT DOES IT MEAN TO PLAN A LESSON?

Lesson planning should not be a technical task that requires social studies teachers to fill in slots on a prepared form. It involves much more than planning the sequence, content, and activities a teacher will include in a specific lesson. Lesson planning is part of the process of making pedagogical, intellectual, and ideological choices. It is where teachers get to think about and figure out historical and social science ideas. It is where we start making choices about what is important to know, how we want to explain it, and how we can make it possible for our students to figure it out also.

1. Lesson planning is the process of figuring out the intermediate steps necessary to achieve long-term goals. It is like putting together an intellectual puzzle.
2. Lesson planning includes researching different historical, economic, anthropological, sociological, political, and geographical ideas and information.
3. Lesson planning means integrating knowledge about historical epochs and social science fields and deciding what are the major ideas that students need to consider during a lesson.
4. Lesson planning involves breaking down complex ideas into manageable and understandable pieces.
5. Lesson planning involves translating abstract historical and social science concepts into concrete examples that teenagers can critically examine, struggle to understand, decide to accept or reject, and use to reshape their own conceptions of the world.
6. Lesson planning means figuring out the activity, document, or question

that promotes a student to say, "I got it!"

7. Lesson planning means making decisions about the most effective ways to organize classrooms and learning activities so students become involved as historians, social scientists, and citizens.

8. Lesson planning means finding, rewriting, or even creating appropriate text so that students in your class can read material with understanding.

9. Lesson planning means establishing a context for lessons and thinking of creative ways to motivate students to explore topics that might not initially attract their interest and thinking of questions that help them draw connections between ideas and events.

10. In inclusive classes, lesson planning means developing multiple strategies for presenting material so that all students learn to standards.

Teaching Activity: Outlining a Lesson

Try it yourself:

1. Select a social studies topic you would like to teach and formulate a question about the topic.
2. Divide a page into two columns. In the first column, list the important ideas and information a student would need to answer the question.
3. In the second column, list ways that the information could be made available to students.

WHY ARE THERE DISPUTES OVER LESSON PLANNING?

Lesson plans outline what students will actually be taught and how they will learn it. As a result, they are hotly contested terrain in many educational battles. Take, for example, the disputes over multiculturalism in social studies and the value of the transmission model of teaching (e.g., lectures).

As multiculturalism has become more acceptable, new topics have been included in social studies curricula. There appears to be a consensus that Native Americans, African Americans, women, working people, and immigrants should be included in the history of the United States, and that American students need to be familiar with the histories and cultures of other peoples. A typical high school social studies curriculum might expect students to compare and contrast the experiences of different groups, explain the values and cultures of different societies, and state opinions that are supported by evidence on the contributions of different civilizations or on the causes of events during different historical periods.

What exactly will students be comparing, contrasting, explaining, and supporting with evidence? This is the area where guidelines become murky and arguments increase in volume. There is no general agreement on a wide range of issues. Examples include the following:

1. The similarities and differences in the problems confronting eastern and southern European immigrants to the United States at the end of the

19th and beginning of the 20th centuries, the situation faced by African Americans during the Great Migration north, and the problems faced by immigrants to the United States or western European countries today.

2. The impact of different civilizations on world development (e.g., the contributions of West Africa to ancient Egyptian and Greek civilizations; the contributions of Native Americans to the United States).

3. The relationships between different events (e.g., European imperialism and World War I, the nuclear attack on Hiroshima and conflict between the United States and Soviet Union).

4. What constitutes sufficient evidence to support a controversial position (e.g., claims that communists infiltrated the U.S. government during the 1930s and 1940s, that the FBI and the CIA tried to discredit black leaders during the 1960s, or that U.S. soldiers are being held prisoner in Vietnam).

Teachers are continually required to make choices about what to teach about controversial topics as we create unit and lesson plans. For example, teachers must decide whether to include Malcolm X in lessons on the Civil Rights movement. If they decide to include him, what position should they take on his role? Was he a positive or negative force, an important advocate for his people, or a dangerous racist? If they want to leave it up to students to define Malcolm X's role, which contemporary and secondary sources do teachers bring into class for students to examine? The importance and difficulty of these decisions underscore the importance of lesson planning. They are among the reasons that I list the sources I plan to use and the main ideas about a subject that inform my thinking and shape the direction of my teaching when I plan lessons and units.

Historian Sean Wilentz of Princeton University and the National Council for History Education have defined another major war as "content" versus "process." In a widely distributed essay, Wilentz (1997: 4.15) divided the educational universe into two oppositional forces, "history-minded reformers" who are advocates of "more demanding history standards," and supporters of social studies who harbor "a fundamental disregard for history" characterized by a "one-dimensional" approach to the past and an unwillingness to make serious demands on students or teachers. Wilentz declared that "the past is not a 'process,' " and that social studies topics should not be selected based on their current "relevance to our own world."

Many historians, myself included (Singer, 1997), disagree, however, with Wilentz's conception of history and the role of the historian. For us, the practice of history involves a dialogue between past and present, and the process of understanding the past cannot be totally separated from the events themselves. E. H. Carr (1961), for example, argued that historians are engaged in a "continuous process of molding facts to interpretation and of interpretation to the facts. . . . The historian without facts is rootless and futile; the facts without their historian are dead and meaningless" (32–35). This process of rethinking the past based on contemporary concerns and understandings is fundamental to the work of the historian and should play a central role in social studies education.

Part of my problem with Wilentz and his supporters is their disregard for the validity of knowledge generated by other academic disciplines, especially by educational researchers and secondary school classroom teachers. They advocate an approach to the study and teaching of history based on their experience with graduate seminars at Princeton, Columbia, and UCLA, but these may not be the best strategies for engaging teenagers in Appalachia, South Central Los Angeles, rural Nebraska, or suburban Chicago, who often believe that what happened before they were born is irrelevant to their lives.

Secondary school social studies teachers, as opposed to university professors, must create a context that convinces students of the relevance of studying the past, introduces them to the "process" of historical and social change, encourages them to think critically about both assumptions and received "facts," and create classroom environments and projects that bring the past alive. While university professors assume student interest, knowledge, and academic skill, secondary school social studies teachers must have both educational and content goals, the ability to assess where students in their classes are starting from, and teaching strategies that make it possible for students to move from one place to another.

Learning Activity: Taking a Stand On Some Hot Issues

Think it over:

1. In the late 19th and early 20th centuries, U.S. industry was expanding. Today the country is deindustrializing. What is the significance of this change for immigrants?
2. In 1903, W. E. B. DuBois wrote that the major problem facing the United States in the 20th century was the "color line." In your opinion, how has race affected the opportunities available to different groups in the United States during the 20th century?

Add your voice to the discussion:

Where do you stand in the "content" versus "process" debate? Explain

It's your classroom:

The Smithsonian Museum's initial plan for an exhibit commemorating the 50th anniversary of the end of World War II became the subject of major political debate because it included questions about the decision to drop atomic bombs on Japanese cities. Would you involve historians in your high school class in critically examining this decision? Why or why not? If you would, how would you do it?

Learning Activity: Quotes From Malcolm X

Source: Wood, J., ed. *Malcolm X. In Our Own Image*. New York: St. Martin's Press, 1992.

- "You don't stick a knife in a man's back nine inches and then pull it out six inches and say you're making progress" (48).
- "No matter how much respect, no matter how much recognition, whites show towards me, as far as I'm concerned, as long as it is not shown to every one of our people in this country, it doesn't exist for me" (48).
- "One of the first things I think young people, especially nowadays, should learn is how to see for yourself and listen for yourself and think for yourself" (59).
- "There's new thinking coming in. There's new strategy coming in. It'll be Molotov cocktails this month, hand grenades next month, and something else next month. It'll be ballots, or it'll be bullets. It'll be liberty, or it will be death" (11).

- "There can be no black–white unity until there is first some black unity. There can be no worker's solidarity until there is first some racial solidarity. We cannot think of uniting with others, until after we have first united among ourselves" (73).
- "By any means necessary" (60).

Add your voice to the discussion:
Some of Malcolm X's ideas are considered very controversial. What do you think? Why?

It's your classroom:
Teachers are always making choices about what to include in a lesson. Your choices shape what your students learn. Which quote(s) would you give your students? Why? What would you want your students to understand about Malcolm X? Why?

HOW DO LESSON PLANS REFLECT IDEAS ABOUT LEARNING?

Lesson plans are also plans for how we will teach about a subject. Often students in my social studies methods classes write in their sample lesson plans that they will lecture about a topic. I always scribble in the margin of their plans, "Just because you say it, does that mean they learn it?" A report on what high school students think about during class supports my concern. Mihaly Csikszentmihalyi (Clinchy, 1995) found that "in a typical history class where the teacher was lecturing about Genghis Khan's invasion of China and conquest of Beijing in 1215, only two out of 27 students were thinking about China." That does not mean, however, that these two students were thinking about the lesson either. One of the students reported that, during the lecture, he "was remembering the meal he had when he last ate out with his family at a Chinese restaurant." The other student reported that he "was wondering why Chinese men wore their hair in a ponytail." This study certainly raises questions about the efficacy of lecturing.

Sometimes students in my social studies methods class write in their lesson plans that their secondary school students will "discuss" an issue. Making it possible for students to have a discussion takes a lot of planning. Over the years, I have had many "failed" discussions in my high school social studies classes. Sometimes no one had anything to say about what I thought would be a hot topic. Sometimes students had a lot to say but took the discussion in a direction I was unprepared for or had not even considered. I always ask prospective teachers who plan to "discuss" an issue: How will the discussion be organized? How do students know about the subject that they are supposed to discuss?

The best ways to actively involve students in learning social studies, avoid lecturing, and have discussions where students know things that they can share and evaluate together, are activity-based lessons that are part of long-term projects. On a day-to-day basis, activity-based lessons are the key to successful social studies teaching and student learning. Every lesson is organized around things that students are reading, examining, analyzing, and thinking, talking, and writing about a famous speech, a part of an essay, a newspaper article, an artifact, a song, a poem, a chart or graph, a picture, a political cartoon, or a hands-on activity. All students have the ability to contribute to the lesson because they have the material being studied in front of them.

Teaching Activity: What Did the Teacher Say?

Try it yourself:
Observe a secondary school social studies classroom where a teacher is lecturing. After the class is over, ask individual students what they remember about the lesson and what they were thinking about while the teacher spoke.

Promoting Student Discussion

It's your classroom:
Consider a topic you think middle school students would find interesting to discuss. What would you do to prepare students for this discussion? What would you do to promote student participation during the discussion? How would you bring discussion to a close?

WHAT DO BEGINNING TEACHERS WORRY ABOUT?

Students preparing to become teachers and beginning teachers always worry about lesson planning. I think their general sense of dread masks some particular issues that need to be examined.

Beginning teachers worry about "deadly silence": What will happen in the classroom if they have nothing to say and nothing for the students to do. I think every teacher remembers having nightmares about lessons petering out after 10 minutes and being forced to ad lib through the rest of a terrifying period. Sometimes in your nightmares you are performing before an audience of sharks or wolves, trying to distract them with a song and dance routine, and hoping they will not move in for the kill (see Fig. 5.1).

Another worry that new teachers have is that they will be unmasked by their students as frauds. Here you are, a social studies teacher who is supposed to have encyclopedic knowledge of everything, only you know how little you really know. Prospective teachers wonder if they are allowed to say, "That's a good question. I don't know the answer, but let's see if we can do some research and discuss it in another lesson."

Perhaps a beginning teacher's major in college was post-Renaissance European intellectual history, and now he or she is teaching about the development of Southeast Asian cultures, the relationship between employment and inflation rates, or contemporary American social movements. To cover for their insecurity, beginning teachers often want foolproof lesson plans that anticipate every possible student question and include every conceivable fact about the topic. Sometimes they produce plans that are so long and unwieldy that they have limited usefulness.

Because many new teachers are also beginning the first job in their career, they almost always live in fear of supervisor expectations. Will department chairs demand complex detailed lesson blueprints that allow no deviation? Will they be judged inadequate as teachers and human beings because of lesson plan design lapses? How should they handle important but unanticipated student questions that "threaten" to give a lesson a different slant, especially when a supervisor is in the room? Another one of my

FIG. 5.1   The teacher hoped he could maintain interest until the bell rang.
Used with permission of Pamela Booth.

recurring nightmares was that I arrived at school, began my first class, and simultaneously discovered that I had left my plan book at home and that my supervisor was paying an unannounced visit to my class (see Fig. 5.2).

Even when classroom observations go well and students seem to respond to a lesson, beginning teachers may fear that their ideas about history and social studies and about teaching methods will be challenged by supervisors, administrators, or parents who disagree with "the latest styles" coming out of college classrooms. There is often a sense among new teachers that they are always "walking on eggshells." During my first year of high school teaching, my department chair wanted to know how I justified asking my students if they thought "imperialist goals" might have influenced U.S. decisions during World War I. I knew my historical sources and the debate on this period, but I was still shaken. Finally, I managed to stammer, "It was just an opinion question." Since that time, I have learned that I need to carefully document my views, especially if they are out of the ordinary.

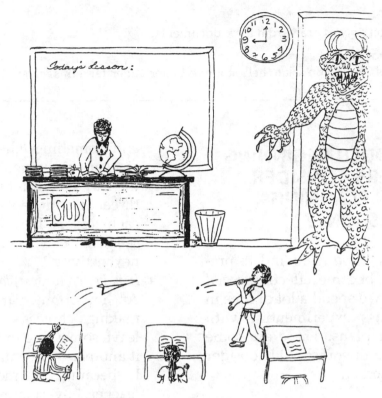

FIG. 5.2 "I have a lesson plan here somewhere."
Used with permission of Pamela Booth.

Classroom Activity: Was There an Economic Motive behind U.S. Entry into World War I?

A. Secretary of State William J. Bryan (1914):

"It is inconsistent with the spirit of neutrality for a neutral nation to make loans to belligerent nations, for money is the worst of all contrabands. . . . The government withdraws the protection of citizenship from those who do enlist under other flags—why should it give protection to money when it enters foreign military service?"

B. Secretary of State William J. Bryan (1915):

"It is not sufficient to say that according to international law, American citizens have a right to go anywhere. . . . If the authorities of a city are justified in warning people off the streets of the city in which they reside, surely a nation is justified in warning its citizens off the water highways which belong to no nation alone."

C. U.S. Trade with Belligerents, 1914–1916 (in millions of dollars):

Nation	1914	1915	1916	Percentage of Change
Great Britain	$594	$912	$1,527.00	+257%
France	160	369	629.00	+393
Italy	74	185	269.00	+364
Germany	345	29	0.29	−1,150

Source: Adapted from Bailey, T. and Kennedy D. (1983). *The American Pageant*, 7th edition, Lexington. MA: D.C. Heath. P. 653.

WHAT SHOULD BEGINNING TEACHERS CONSIDER WHEN PLANNING LESSONS?

To allay some of these fears and to pre-pare students to become effective social studies teachers, we spend a lot of time in our methods class experimenting with lesson ideas and plans. These are some general ideas I think you should consider in social studies lessons.

- *Lesson plans are necessary tools for teaching.* They are not works of art. They will never be perfect.
- *Lesson plan formats are suggestions based on other people's experiences.* They are not etched in stone. What works for one person may not work for someone else. There are a number of different ways to plan effec-tive lessons.
- *Successful teachers, even the most expe-rienced, always plan.* Some very good veteran teachers argue that they do not need *written* plans anymore be-cause everything is in their heads. It may be possible for them to teach this way, and it may be possible for you in the distant future, but it has never worked for me. I find social studies too complex a discipline and the effort to involve students in a les-son too demanding for me to just rely on my memory during a lesson.
- *Lesson plans are experiments.* Some-times they get the expected results

and sometimes they do not. Every teacher has lessons that did not work the way they wanted. I try to include three or four possible activities in each lesson. If something does not seem to be working, I go on to the next activity.
- *It is better to overplan than underplan.* An important part of teaching is making choices. You can always leave something out or decide to use it another day or in another way. As I became a more experienced teacher, I overplanned on purpose.
- *Lesson plans can (should) change.* If something does not work in one class, you can do it differently the next period, the next day, or the next year. At the end of a class or the day, I jot down comments on my lesson plans for future reference: what worked, what did not, and what to add, drop, or change.
- *Many goals require more than one pe-riod to achieve.* Just because time can be subdivided into discreet packets does not mean that human beings think in 40-minute blocks or that every (or any) idea can be grasped in one class period.
- *A structured plan makes it possible to be flexible in class.* You can choose from different built-in lesson alternatives based on student involvement in the lesson. Maybe you cannot change a horse in "midstream," but you can change a lesson.
- *Lesson plans must be adjusted to meet particular circumstances, and they need*

to be different for different students. A lesson that makes sense for a class of 15 may not work with a class of 34. A lesson planned for a class that meets in the morning probably has to be modified for a class that tears into the room at 2:30 P.M. Lessons planned for heterogeneous classes will differ from lessons planned for homogenous classes. Lessons must be planned with students in mind.

- *Lessons planned for middle school students differ from lessons planned for high school students.* Middle school teachers usually have fewer time constraints. This makes it possible for students to approach an idea from different directions and learn about it in different ways.

- *Sample lessons (including mine) may look great on paper, but teachers need to adapt them to their classes and their own personalities.*

- *The things a teacher includes in a lesson plan change as a teacher becomes more experienced.* Beginning teachers, knowing they will be nervous, should list possible questions in advance. Preparation makes it easier to think on

your feet. Later on, I found that I did not need to think up as many questions in advance because I was able to develop questions during the course of a lesson based on student questions and comments.

- *Whatever your individual preferences are for a lesson plan format, when you first start out, you will likely have to use the format recommended by your district or department.* Beginning teachers are generally monitored closely until they establish a reputation for competence. I think you will discover, however, that whatever format you are asked to use, you will be able to adapt it to what you believe should be included in a lesson plan.

- *Personal computers were probably invented with social studies teachers in mind.* I design lessons, modify them as worksheets, rearrange them into homework assignments, and recycle homework and classroom questions when I make up tests. The next time I teach the subject, I start with a lesson plan database that I can easily reorganize.

Teaching Activity: What Would You Include in a Lesson Plan?

Think it over:
List the things you think you would want to include in a lesson plan. Why would you include these things? After you finish, compare your list with "Ingredients for an Activity-Based Social Studies Lesson" that follows.

WHAT ARE THE INGREDIENTS OF AN ACTIVITY-BASED LESSON PLAN?

One of my students compared a lesson plan to a recipe. She said that when she first started cooking, she needed to follow all of the steps carefully. Later, as she became more experienced, she felt more comfortable varying the ingredients and experimenting with her own ideas. Following are the ingredients of an activity-based social studies lesson. Experiment with the ingredients you find useful in a lesson plan. Sometimes my lessons include some of these ingredients, sometimes they include others, and on a rare occasion, they include all of them.

Ingredients of an Activity-Based Lesson

Unit:
Where this lesson fits in the overall conceptual sequence

Aim:
A question that a particular lesson is designed to answer or a statement or phrase introducing the topic of a lesson. Usually it is written on the board at the start of the lesson. Sometimes it is elicited from students during the early stages of a lesson.

Goals/objectives:
The skills, concepts, and content that students will learn about during the lesson. Can also include social/behavioral/classroom community goals. Goals are broad and achieved during a long period of time. Objectives are specific short-term goals that are achievable during a particular lesson.

Main ideas/understandings:
The underlying or most important ideas about a topic that inform a teacher's understanding and influence the way lessons and units are organized, the ideas that teachers want students to consider. This can be formulated as statements or as broad questions that become the basis for ongoing discussion.

Materials:
The maps, documents, records, and equipment needed by teachers and students during the lesson to create the learning activities.

Activities/lesson development:
This is the substance of the lesson: the ways that students will learn the goals and objectives. Includes discussions, document analysis, mapping, cartooning, singing, performing drama, researching, cooperative learning, teacher presentations, and so on.

Do now activity:
An introductory activity that immediately involves students as they enter the room.

Motivation(al) activity:
A question, statement, or activity that establishes a learning context and captures student interest in the topic that will be examined. Motivations connect the subject of the lesson to things that students are thinking about or are interested in.

Questions:
Prepared questions that attempt to anticipate classroom dialogue; designed to aid examination of materials, generate class discussions, and promote deeper probing. Medial summary questions make it possible for the class to integrate ideas at the end of an activity.

Transitions:
Key questions that make it possible for students to draw connections between the information, concepts, or understandings developed during a particular activity with other parts of the lesson and to a broader conceptual understanding.

Summary:
A concluding question or group of questions that make it possible for the class to integrate or utilize the learning from this lesson and prior lessons.

Application:
Extra optional question(s) or activity(ies) planned for this lesson that draws on and broadens what students are learning in the unit. These can be used to review prior lessons or as transitions to future lessons.

Homework assignment:
A reading, writing, research, or thinking assignment that students complete after the lesson. It can be a review of the lesson, an introduction to a future lesson, background material that enriches student understanding, an exercise that improves student skills, or part of a long-term project.

Teaching Activity: Outlining an Activity-Based Lesson

Try it yourself:
Select a social studies topic you would like to teach. Outline a lesson using the ingredients for an activity-based lesson plan.

HOW IS AN ACTIVITY-BASED LESSON ORGANIZED?

There are probably as many different lesson plan formats as there are teachers. This section compares three different types of lesson plan formats and discusses how to use them in class. I learned the developmental lesson plan approach as a college undergraduate, and I thought it was an accurate description of the lessons I remembered from middle school and high school. It assumes that students did the homework the night before and come into class prepared to learn.

I should have realized from my own experience as a high school student that my friends and I usually were not prepared. Instead, we developed strategies to fake it or to get by. We would answer an easy question at the start of the lesson and then disappear into the woodwork. We would spend a lot of time in the bathroom, or we would try to throw the teacher off track by asking awkward, sweeping, or tangential questions (e.g., Is it true that Thomas Jefferson and George Washington had children with women

who were their slaves? Is the Declaration of Independence the most important document in world history? Could the colonies still have gained independence if George Washington had been captured at the start of the war?). Usually, questions like these would launch a teacher into a lecture and we would be left alone.

Whatever I forgot about being a middle or high school student while I was sitting in my college methods classes, I quickly remembered when I started trying to teach sixth and seventh graders at Macombs Junior High School in the Bronx. Learning along with my students, I struggled to come up with a lesson plan design that made sense to me. It was an act of survival. After a number of years (and many headaches), I gradually developed an activity-based lesson plan that is based on six principles:

1. Students are not inherently interested in social studies just because the clock says it is time for my class. It is my job to interest and motivate them. I must create a learning context for every lesson.

2. A lesson needs a clear structure. If students cannot figure out what I want them to do, they cannot do it.

3. Related to this, every lesson must have a beginning and an end, even if we will be discussing the same topic the next day.

4. Everyone can participate and learn if I organize a lesson around materials that I bring to class. If students do the homework in advance, their experience will be enriched. Even if they did not do the homework, they will be able to use the materials to participate in classroom activities and discussions.

5. Students have a range of reading facility so that a lesson that involves everyone must include material written on different levels.

6. Broadly defined lesson goals and objectives give a class more freedom to explore ideas during a lesson than does a list of specific lesson outcomes.

Over the years, I have had to use required lesson plan formats in different schools, but I always adapted the required format to what I knew was necessary for a successful lesson for my students. I generally start each lesson with an **Aim Question** and **Homework Assignment** written on the board and a brief **Do Now Activity**. I think about social studies a lot, I like it, and it is important to me, but I know my students have many other things on their minds. If nothing else, they have six or seven other subjects. The likelihood is that they have not thought about our last lesson since they left the room. Copying the **Aim Question** and **Homework Assignment** and starting the **Do Now** settles them, reminds them why we are here, and reintroduces the particular topic. When they are all ready, I start with a **Motivation**—an activity based on student interests and questions but related to the issues we will be exploring. The rest of the lesson is organized around a series of related **Activities,** beginning with an examination of the **Do Now.** Some of the activities are done by individual students, some in groups, and some are designed for a full class. Every **Activity** provides students with a document, idea, or exercise, that they can examine and discuss. I try to end lessons with a **Summary Question** or activity, but the reality is that it is not easy to summarize each lesson in a neat little package. Often the **Summary Question** is the **Aim Question** that started the lesson. Sometimes a class will examine the same **Materials** and **Main Ideas** for a number of days. However, I try to have each lesson stand on its own.

I also try to build flexibility into my lessons. The same points can be made in different ways. If something does not capture the interest of my students, if they are unable to understand a passage or get the point from the materials that I provide them, I try using something else. I plan lessons in 10-minute increments, with extra activities available "just in case."

Teaching Activity: Principles for Planning

Add your voice to the discussion:
Which of these principles do you agree with? Which would you change? What would you add? Explain the reasons for your choices.

If something goes really well, I may decide to stay with it. If my students have good ideas, we explore them. If an activity bombs, we move on.

Teachers must constantly make choices while they teach. In New York City, many high school students take the subway to school and there are always "transportation delays" in the morning. Sometimes, during the first period, I begin in the middle, using an activity, document, or passage that is less crucial for understanding the main ideas of the lesson. I wait until all the students are present and physically and mentally ready before I begin key *motivation* and other activities.

During the last period of the day, it usually takes students a little longer to settle down. I take more time with the *do now* and review it immediately. Students are already excited, although not about social studies, so I may use the lesson motivation at the end of the period as an application. At the end of the day, a class may be a little bumptious (maybe there will be a full moon that night, or the lunch served was particularly bad, and everyone is starving), so a teacher can decide to have students work as individuals rather than in groups. In all cases, teachers have to be prepared to make decisions about how to use their plans when it becomes time to actually teach.

In the lessons that follow, I try to give some sense of the differences between a middle and high school lesson. In the middle school, a teacher usually has fewer time restraints, the ability to personalize discussions, and more freedom to utilize long-term projects and themes. In high school, the curriculum tends to be tighter, and more time is spent searching for evidence that supports historical conclusions. Materials aimed at middle school social studies classes tend to be modified from the original, using simpler vocabulary and shorter, edited passages, but these differences are not absolutes, and teachers have to make judgments about which materials to use and how much time to spend on a topic based on their own classes. I include side comments to try to give some sense of how a lesson actually goes. I have also included more questions than I would usually write in a lesson plan.

There is one last problem. Preservice teachers frequently ask, Where do you start when constructing a lesson? This is a more complicated question than it seems because I do not start planning each lesson the same way. First, I try to conceptualize what the entire unit or theme will look like. Then I look at the number of days I have available, as well as the topics, major ideas, documents, and skills activities I want to include in this unit. At this point, I block out individual lessons. Some of the lessons are built around answering an historical question (the *aim*). Sometimes I start with a skill activity, like map reading, or a particularly juicy primary source document for students to interpret. Many times I start with main ideas and try to find ways to make them accessible to my students. To further complicate matters, some lessons are designed to take more than one day. Students act out an historical play on Day 1, analyze it in groups or as a full class on Day 2, and write about its implications on Day 3. I guess the answer is that I start constructing a lesson at the beginning.

Middle School Activity-Based Lesson on the Declaration of Independence

Unit:
Middle school (7th grade)—Revolutionary America

Aim:

Why did colonial Americans write a Declaration of Independence? [I try to keep aim questions simple.]

Goals/objectives:

- Read a primary source document with understanding
- Write explanations that demonstrate their understanding
- Work in teams
- Recognize an analogy
- Understand reasons for writing the Declaration of Independence
- Examine the meaning of the concepts of change, freedom, equality, responsibility, revolution, human rights, and government

Main ideas/understandings:

[These are from the main ideas/understandings for the entire unit. They will be developed and reinforced in other lessons as well.]

- People and societies are constantly *changing*. These changes affect their relationships with other people and societies.
- As people's lives *change*, they may demand greater *freedom* and want to take on new responsibilities.
- The authors of the Declaration of Independence felt a need to explain their *revolution*. They did not believe that *revolutions are always justified*.
- The meaning of concepts such as *equality* can *change* over time.
- The authors of the Declaration of Independence believed that *human rights* come from "the Creator," not from *government*.
- *Human rights* include the idea that "all men are created equal."
- The purpose of *government* is to protect *human rights*.
- When *governments* do not protect *human rights*, people have the right to *change* them.

Materials:

Activity Worksheet: The Declaration of Independence—In Your Own Words

Do now:

Read Passage 1 on your worksheet, The Declaration of Independence—In Your Own Words. Answer Questions 1–3 in your notebook. [Sometimes I have a class work in their notebooks and sometimes directly on the worksheets. The only rule is to give clear directions.]

Motivation:

Compare being a teenager in the United States today with the situation facing the maturing British colonies in the Americas after the French and Indian War. [Have students discuss the problems they are experiencing in their families now that they are in 7th grade and ready to become teenagers. Why are tensions between them and their parents escalating? How do they see the next few years? How have older sisters and brothers handled these problems? What will eventually happen between them and their families? Why do many families with teenagers seem to have similar conflicts?]

Activities/questions/transitions:

- [Transition] If you were going to write a letter of complaint to your parents about the problems in your relationship with them, what are some of the things you would include in your letter? Why? [List ideas on the board.]
- How would you organize the letter? (a) An introduction including main ideas. (b) A list of complaints or grievances. (c) A statement explaining your views about what would make things fairer. [Encourage multiple answers to questions and cross conversation.]
- [Transition] Let us say that a number of years went by and the tension between you and your parents became so great that you felt you had to move out of their house. If you wrote them a letter at that point, what could you title it? Why? Do you think it is fair to compare

the problems of teenagers in families today with the problems faced by the American colonies with Great Britain over 200 years ago? Why?

- [Transition] Have a student read the passage (from the *do now* assignment) aloud. According to this passage, why did colonial Americans write the Declaration of Independence?

- [Transition] The Declaration of Independence was written more than 200 years ago. Many of its passages are difficult to understand. Student teams will read the rest of the passages from the Declaration of Independence. In your notebooks, rewrite passages in language that is easier to understand today but still includes the main idea of the passage. [Depending on time, each team can complete either the entire sheet or only one passage. While students are working, the teacher can circulate around the room, helping students or checking homework assignments.]

- The second passage is one of the most often quoted statements in the United States. Have a student read the passage aloud. Have a student explain how she or he rewrote the passage in this way and why. Why do you think this quote is so famous? What does this quote tell us about the reasons that Americans wrote the Declaration of Independence? [Other passages will be reviewed at the start of the next lesson.]

Summary:

Based on our discussion today, why did colonial Americans decide to write a Declaration of Independence?

Application:

[These questions will be major parts of future lessons.] Do you agree with the reasons for independence explained in these two passages? What else do you think the Declaration of Independence needed to include? Do you think the statement that "all men are created equal" meant the same thing in 1776 as it does today? Why?

Homework assignment:

Reread pages_____. Using your textbook and based on our discussions in class, make a list of grievances (complaints) the colonies might have had against Great Britain. Explain why the colonists were upset by each of these actions by Great Britain. [The next night's homework will have students rewrite their translations of the Declaration of Independence based on class discussion.]

ACTIVITY SHEET: THE DECLARATION OF INDEPENDENCE—IN YOUR OWN WORDS

Do Now:

Read Passage 1 and answer Questions 1, 2, and 3 in your notebook.

1. "When in the course of human events, it becomes necessary for one people to dissolve the political bands which have connected them with another, and to assume, among the powers of the earth, the separate and equal station to which the laws of nature and of nature's God entitle them, a decent respect to the opinion of mankind requires that they should declare the causes which impel them to separation."

Questions:

1. What does "in the course of human events" mean?
2. What do the Americans want to do?
3. Why did Americans write the Declaration of Independence?

Continued

Activity:

In Your Own Words

1. "We hold these truths to be self-evident:—That all men are created equal; that they are endowed by their Creator with certain unalienable rights; that among these are life, liberty, and the pursuit of happiness."
2. "That, to secure these rights, governments are instituted among men, deriving their just powers from the consent of the governed."
3. "That, whenever any form of government becomes destructive of these ends, it is the right of the people to alter or to abolish it, and to institute new government, laying its foundation on such principles, and organizing its powers in such form, as to them shall seem most likely to effect their safety and happiness."
4. "Prudence, indeed, will dictate that governments long established should not be changed for light and transient causes, and, accordingly, all experience hath shown that mankind are more disposed to suffer, while evils are sufferable, than to right themselves by abolishing the forms to which they are accustomed."
5. "But when a long train of abuses and usurpation's . . . evinces a design to reduce them under absolute despotism, it is their right, it is their duty, to throw off such government, and to provide new guards for their future security."

Teaching Activity: Evaluating an Activity-Based Middle School Lesson Plan

Think it over:
What do you see as the strengths and weaknesses of this lesson plan? Why?

It's your classroom:
1. How would you change this lesson plan? Why?
2. Rewrite the lesson so that you feel comfortable with it.

High School Activity-Based Lesson on the Declaration of Independence

Unit:
High school (11th grade)—Revolutionary America

Aim:
What is the promise of the Declaration of Independence? [I try to keep aim questions simple.]

Goals/objectives:
- Read a primary source document with understanding
- Recognize the continuing importance of ideas and documents
- Place the Declaration of Independence within philosophical and political contexts
- Recognize connections between ideas in different historical eras
- Draw conclusions based on historical decisions and evidence
- Understand the benefits and problems of compromise and consensus
- Examine the meaning of concepts of change, human rights, government, revolution, equality, law, injustice, compromise, and consensus

Main ideas/understandings:
[These are from the main ideas/understandings for the entire unit. They will be developed and reinforced in other lessons as well.]

- The ideas about *human rights* and *government* expressed in the Declaration of Independence have roots in the scientific rationalism of European Enlightenment philosophy of the 17th- and 18th-centuries.
- The ideas about *human rights* and *government* expressed in the Declaration of Independence continue to have meaning in the contemporary United States. These ideas can be considered the promise of America.
- The meaning of concepts such as *equality* can *change* over time.
- The authors of the Declaration of Independence believed that *human rights* come from "the Creator," not from a monarch or *government*.
- Human rights include the idea that "all men are created equal."
- The purpose of *government* is to protect *human rights*.
- When *governments* do not protect *human rights*, people have the right to *change* them.
- The authors of the Declaration of Independence believed that *laws* of nature and society determined whether a *revolution* was legitimate. They wanted to ensure that there were limits on the right to *revolution*.
- Enslavement, class hierarchy, and what we would consider social *injustice* were accepted in the communities where many of the authors of the Declaration of Independence lived.
- The Declaration of Independence is intentionally vague about the level of public support needed to justify a *revolution*. It was partly an attempt to convince the colonists of the legitimacy of independence.
- The general nature of the philosophical statements about *human rights* and *government* represented an effort at *compromise* and *consensus* by people who disagreed about many specific points, especially the continuing existence of slavery.

Materials:
Videotape or record, Martin Luther King Jr.'s "I Have a Dream" speech at the August 1963 Civil Rights march on Washington, D.C., VCR/Monitor or record player.

Do now:
Read Passage 1 on your worksheet, Excerpts from the Declaration of Independence. According to this passage, why do the American colonies claim the right to "dissolve the political bands which have connected them with" Great Britain? [Sometimes I have students work in their notebooks and sometimes directly on the worksheets. The only rule is to give clear directions.]

Motivation:
Play excerpt from Martin Luther King Jr.'s "I Have A Dream" speech, where King quotes from the Declaration of Independence. Identify the source of the speech. (In your opinion) why is Martin Luther King Jr. quoting from the Declaration of Independence in a speech at a rally in Washington, D.C., over 187 years after it was written? Suffragists also quoted from the Declaration of Independence during their struggle to win women's right to vote. Why has the Declaration of Independence been quoted in this way throughout U.S. history? Why is the Declaration often called "the promise of America?" [Ask a number of students. Encourage cross conversation.]

Activities/questions/transitions:
- [Transition] On July 2, 1776, the second Continental Congress approved a resolution by Richard Henry Lee of Virginia to declare colonial independence from Great Britain. The Congress decided to wait two days until Thomas Jefferson and the committee could write a formal declaration before making its decision official. Why do you think they made this decision to wait?
- [Transition] Have a student read the passage (from the *do now* assignment) aloud. Does this passage give a clue to why Congress felt a formal Declaration of Independence was necessary? What is the clue? What do you think is the reason? [Ask other students if they agree or disagree, and why.]
- [Transition] Following the introduction, the Declaration of Independence contains the statement of principles quoted by Martin Luther King Jr. What does this passage mean?

[Encourage multiple answers to questions and cross conversation.] We studied the ideas of European Enlightenment thinkers including Newton, Locke, Montesquieu, and Rousseau. Where do you think Jefferson got these ideas? Why? Why do you think Congress decided to include this statement of principle in the Declaration of Independence? What do you think Congress meant by the statement that these were "unalienable rights" granted by their "Creator?" Do you think the statement, "All men are created equal," meant the same thing then as it does to us today? Why?

- [Transition] Let's read through the third passage from the Declaration together. What is the main issue being discussed in this passage? According to this passage, what is the source of government power? Why do you think Congress is concerned with the source of government power? According to this passage, when do people have the right to overthrow a government? Is this right limited or unlimited? How is it limited? What would you expect to be discussed in the next part of the Declaration of Independence? Why?

- [Transition] The third passage states that "it is the right of the people to alter or abolish it," meaning the government. Which people is this talking about? Does it require an election, a simple majority vote, a two-thirds vote, or a unanimous vote? In your opinion, why didn't the authors of the Declaration of Independence make this clear? What does this suggest about the reason for delaying a formal decree on independence until the Declaration was ready?

Summary:

Based on our examination of these passages and our discussion of American history, why do you think the members of the second Continental Congress decided to have Thomas Jefferson write the Declaration of Independence? Why has this document come to represent the "promise of American society"?

Application:

If you had the ability to rewrite these passages from the Declaration of Independence, would you change them? How? Why?

Homework assignment:

Read pages _____ – _____ [discussing the Declaration of Independence] and answer the following questions:

1. How is the Declaration of Independence organized?
2. Which section of the Declaration of Independence do you consider most important for people at that time? Why?
3. Which section of the Declaration of Independence do you consider most important for people today? Why?
4. Write a paragraph supporting your opinion on this question: Should people who signed a document stating that "all men are created equal" while owning slaves or profiting from the slave trade be treated as national heroes or criticized as hypocrites?

ACTIVITY SHEET: EXCERPTS FROM THE DECLARATION OF INDEPENDENCE

Do Now:

Read Passage 1 on your worksheet, Excerpts from the Declaration of Independence. According to this passage, why do the American colonies claim the right to "dissolve the political bands which have connected them with" Great Britain?

1. "When in the course of human events, it becomes necessary for one people to dissolve the political bands which have connected them with another, and to assume, among the powers

Continued

of the earth, the separate and equal station to which the laws of nature and of nature's God entitle them, a decent respect to the opinion of mankind requires that they should declare the causes which impel them to separation."

2. "We hold these truths to be self-evident:—That all men are created equal; that they are endowed by their Creator with certain unalienable rights; that among these are life, liberty and the pursuit of happiness."

3. "That, to secure these rights, governments are instituted among men, deriving their just powers from the consent of the governed; that, whenever any form of government becomes destructive of these ends, it is the right of the people to alter or to abolish it, and to institute new government, laying its foundation on such principles, and organizing its powers in such form, as to them shall seem most likely to effect their safety and happiness. Prudence, indeed, will dictate that governments long established should not be changed for light and transient causes, and, accordingly, all experience hath shown that mankind are more disposed to suffer, while evils are sufferable, than to right themselves by abolishing the forms to which they are accustomed. But when a long train of abuses and usurpations, pursuing invariably the same object, evinces a design to reduce them under absolute despotism, it is their right, it is their duty, to throw off such government, and to provide new guards for their future security."

Teaching Activity: Evaluating a High School Activity-Based Lesson Plan

Think it over:
What do you see as the strengths and weaknesses of this lesson plan? Why?

It's your classroom:
1. How would you change this lesson plan? Why?
2. Rewrite the lesson so you feel comfortable with it.

HOW IS A DEVELOPMENTAL LESSON ORGANIZED?

The developmental lesson (Dobkin et al., 1985) is designed to teach about a major concept, event, or relationship, and it is tailored to one lesson period. A lesson has an *aim*, either in the form of a question or a statement, that defines the topic for the day. Sometimes a social studies teacher will open the lesson with the aim already written on the board, and sometimes the aim question or statement will be elicited from students during a motivation. By the end of the lesson, students in the class should be able to answer the aim question or, if it is a statement, a question based on it. This developmental lesson includes performance objectives: specific short-term goals achieved during the lesson. Ideally, a lesson plan that contains performance objectives should also include some way of assessing whether students achieved these objectives.

The developmental lesson begins with a **Motivation** which introduces the topic or poses the problem that the class will examine during the period. The **Development** outlines the steps that the class follows as students master the content, skills, and concepts that allow them to answer the aim question. The class ends with a **Summary** question, which is frequently a restatement of the aim question.

If there is enough time at the end of a developmental lesson, a teacher can introduce an **Application**, which has the class apply the material learned during the lesson in a different context or to another topic. The application can also be a homework assignment that prepares the class for the next lesson.

The following sample developmental lesson plan is based on one developed by Barry Brody, a retired social studies chairperson at a New York City high school. Barry is a colleague, friend, and very good teacher. He supervised many teachers during his career and stresses that "all methods are only as good as the teacher who uses them. They are only tools." He wanted teachers in his department to use a variety of approaches to enhance student participation.

Barry and I observed each other teach on many occasions over the course of 10 years. We frequently taught lessons together, but we continually argued about how to plan the lessons. I am convinced that our disagreements about lesson planning really reflected differences in how we saw students learning social studies.

Barry often felt that my reliance on student analysis of documents and student-generated questions made my lessons unpredictable and that they ran the risk of remaining uncompleted at the end of the period. Although Barry agreed that the exploration of important ideas can take several days, he encouraged teachers to plan lessons that would be brought to closure at the end of each class period, with a concluding or summary question that makes it possible to measure student learning (performance objectives).

Developmental lesson plans rely on student desire to perform well in class. Homework assignments introduce students to material prior to a lesson. Teachers craft questions that are designed to elicit the factual content from students, provide the answer to the aim question, and move the class from one point to the next in the lesson.

This sample lesson plan includes prepared questions and board notes. During the lesson, board notes can be modified based on student responses to questions. The lesson is tied together at the end with a broad conceptual summary question that a number of students are involved in answering. Teachers who use this method try for maximum student involvement in answering questions and discussions. The assumption is that students who do not actively participate learn the material by listening to the teacher and other students, from the notes, and from the homework assignments.

High School Developmental Lesson with Performance Objective

Aim:
Does the Declaration of Independence justify revolution?

Performance objectives:
- Students will be able to define the basic rights described in the Declaration of Independence.
- Students will be able to list three colonial complaints against British rule.
- Students will be able to explain when the authors of the Declaration of Independence believe a revolution is justified.

Preparation:

Homework: Prior to this lesson, students read the Declaration of Independence for homework and answered the following questions:

- The Declaration of Independence is organized into three sections: A Brief Introduction, a Statement of Principles, and a List of Complaints. What is the reason for each of these sections?
- The Declaration includes a series of complaints against Great Britain. Which complaints do you consider the most serious? Why?
- According to the Declaration of Independence, what rights do all people have?

Classwork:

In the previous lesson, students learned about the basic rights described in the Declaration of Independence.

Motivation:

Throughout history, governments have been threatened by violent revolutions. Many revolutionaries today argue that the U.S. Declaration of Independence supports their right to overthrow existing governments. How would you respond to this claim? Why?

Development:

Questions	**Notes**

• Why was the Declaration of Independence written?
• What does most of the Declaration consist of? Why?
	I. Purpose of the Declaration
	  A. Declare independence from Great Britain.
	  B. List basic human rights.
	  C. Establish a theory of government.
	  D. Justify the American Revolution.

Medial summary:

In your opinion, which is the most important purpose of the Declaration of Independence?

Questions	**Notes**

• What are inalienable rights?
• What does the Declaration of Independence mean when it says that we are all created equal?
• According to the Declaration of Independence, why do governments exist?
	II. Theory of government
	  A. People have rights that governments cannot take away.
	  B. The power of governments comes from the people of the country.
	  C. The purpose of government is to protect the rights of the people.
	  D. U.S. government is based on the idea that all men are created equal.

Medial summary:

Why would the American colonists want these ideas included in a new government?

Questions	**Notes**

• According to the Declaration of Independence, when would I be justified in leading a revolution against our government?
• What, if any, limits are there on my right to rebel?
• In your opinion, which rights are so important that violation of these rights by government would justify rebellion?
	III. The Right to Rebel
	  A. When a government does not respect people's rights, citizens have a right to rebel against the government.
	  B. People should rebel against a government only when:
	    • It has a long history of abusing their rights.
	    • It is a dictatorship.
	    • Other methods of changing the government have failed.

Medial summary:
Why did the authors of the Declaration of Independence believe that the colonies had the right to rebel against Great Britain?

Final lesson summary questions:
According to the Declaration of Independence, when are revolutions justified? Why? When are revolutions not justified? Why? Does the Declaration of Independence justify revolution against our government today?

Application:
In your opinion, which aspects of the Declaration of Independence have the most meaning for people today? Why?

Teaching Activity: Evaluating a Developmental Lesson

Think it over:
What do you see as the strengths and weaknesses of this lesson plan? Why?

It's your classroom:
1. How would you change this lesson plan? Why?
2. Rewrite the lesson so you feel comfortable with it.

Although Barry Brody was a thoughtful and effective teacher who adjusted his lessons to student responses and interests, I have a number of problems with preparing new teachers to organize lessons using this format:

1. The format is based on a teacher-centered transmission model of teaching. It lends itself to content-driven curricula and student acquisition of discreet packets of factual information that can easily be measured (performance objectives). As an historian, I think this approach presents an oversimplified linear conception of historical development, and it masks important historical debates.

2. Although Barry disputes this, I think there is an assumption in this approach that individuals will master complex ideas and relationships during 40-minute learning bytes while sitting in classrooms of more than 30 people.

3. The format encourages beginning teachers to choreograph lessons (including questions and answers) in advance. As a result, teachers are not prepared to allow alternative directions based on student insights, questions, and contributions.

4. Questions ask students for their opinions about the meaning of Declaration of Independence and about reasons for revolutions. What if some of the students have sharp disagreements with what the Declaration of Independence says or how it has been interpreted? A discussion of their views could take up more than one lesson. It might require shifting the whole focus of the course. This type of lesson does not make time for student ideas. Insight becomes an interference with the progression of the lesson rather than

a goal. Eventually students get the message to keep quiet or give the answer that the teacher wants.

5. The answers to the questions that direct the lesson are based on prior student knowledge. Usually teachers rely on students having done the homework the night before, having understood it, and being able to remember and explain it. When students do not answer the questions or do not answer them in the anticipated way, teachers often end up passing out textbooks for them to read in class or lecturing about the material.

6. This format assumes academic interest and motivation on the part of students. I have observed many classrooms where teachers using this model end up talking to a small group of students sitting in the front of the room while everyone else is "lost in space."

Teaching Activity: Once You Were a Student in This Class

Think it over:

1. When you were a high school student, were you aware of structure in the way teachers planned social studies lessons?
2. During your secondary school student career, you probably participated in many lessons organized according to the developmental lesson format. Based on your experiences as a student, how do you evaluate this type of lesson and the criticisms raised here? Why?

WHAT IS THE "MADELINE HUNTER MODEL"?

A number of school districts across the country have adopted a seven-step lesson design that is part of the "Madeline Hunter Teacher Effectiveness Training Program" (Hunter, 1982). This design, which is intended to be applicable in all subject areas, tries to systematize lesson planning. In theory, it makes it easier for teachers to have clear learning objectives that students can master by the end of the instructional period.

Critics of the Hunter approach (Berg, and Clough 1990/1991), myself included, are unhappy with its claim to be useful in all subject areas and adaptable for all types of lessons. They find it inflexible and fear it will stifle teacher and student creativity. Because of its emphasis on measurable results, it tends to be even more heavily scripted than traditional developmental lessons, and it relies on extrinsic motivations and rewards (grades, praise, and special favors).

Critics also believe that evaluating teachers and lessons based on whether students master specific measurable learning objectives by the end of a given time period ensures lessons that focus on teaching facts and low-level skills rather than encouraging students to think about ideas and concepts and express opinions. In addition, many of the categories that I find most useful in lesson planning are missing in the Hunter model.

Hunter has defended herself against critics, claiming that, although her model "is deceptively simple in conceptualization," it is "incredibly complex in application."

ELEMENTS OF A HUNTER LESSON

Each section of the lesson plan may include questions that the teacher uses to measure student understanding up until that point.

Anticipatory set: A brief opening activity or statement that focuses students' attention on what they will be learning.

Objectives: A detailed list of what students will know or be able to do at the end of the instruction period. It includes information that a teacher provides to students about what they will be able to do at the end of the lesson and how the lesson is relevant to their learning.

Instructional input: Information that a teacher provides to students so they can perform a skill or complete a process. Questions that a teacher asks to ensure that students understand procedures.

Modeling the information: The teacher leads the class in an activity so students understand what they are supposed to do.

Checking for understanding: Teacher asks questions and examines student work to ensure that students possess the essential information and skills necessary to achieve the instructional objective.

Guided practice: Teacher assists students as they work on assignments to ensure that student efforts are accurate and successful.

Independent practice: Students have mastered the basic skills and understandings needed to complete activities without direct teacher intervention. This is the final measure of whether lesson objectives have been achieved.

Middle School Lesson on the Declaration of Independence Using the Hunter Model

[Please note that this is my adaptation of the Hunter model].

Anticipatory set:

Let's review yesterday's discussion of the human rights promised in the Declaration of Independence. Can anyone explain those rights to us? [If necessary, a teacher can ask students to reread the passage they examined the day before or to consult their notes or homework.]

Objectives:

- Students will be able to explain the meaning of a passage from the Declaration of Independence in their own words.
- Students will be able to define the words *citizen* and *government*.
- Students will be able to explain the relationship between government and citizens defined in the Declaration of Independence.
- Students will state three contemporary examples of the relationship between government and citizens in the United States.
- Students will be able to explain what the authors of the Declaration thought people should do when governments do not respect the rights of citizens.
- Students will be able to define the words *limits* and *revolution*.
- Students will be able to write a letter that expresses their opinions on this concept from the Declaration of Independence.
- Students will be able to use evidence to support their opinions.

Main ideas/understandings:

Today we will be working independently and in groups, examining the part of the Declaration of Independence that describes how governments must protect the rights of citizens. By the end of the lesson, each of you will be able to explain what the authors of the Declaration thought people should do when governments do not respect these rights. Before we begin,

I want to review some ideas from previous lessons and from your homework. [Encourage maximum class participation in discussion.]

- Can someone explain what a citizen is? According to the Declaration of Independence, what rights do citizens have?
- Can anyone tell us what a government is and what it does?
- In the United States today, what responsibilities do citizens have to the government? What responsibilities does government have to citizens?

Instructional input:

Each student will read the passage from the Declaration of Independence, rewrite it in his or her own words, and then answer the questions at the end of the worksheet. When everyone in your group is finished, group members should compare answers and see where they agree or disagree. Group members should try to resolve their differences. Does anyone have any questions?

Modeling the information:

Before you begin to read on your own, let's go over the first passage together. The first passage says, "That, to secure these rights, governments are instituted among men, deriving their just powers from the consent of the governed." Can someone put this passage into her or his own words for us? [Encourage maximum class participation.]

Checking for understanding:

While students work on their own, the teacher circulates around the room, asking questions and ensuring that students understand the assignment.

Guided practice:

The teacher helps individual students understand the reading passage and think about the questions. Students check their work with the other members of their group. The entire class discusses what the authors of the Declaration thought people should do when governments do not respect their rights. [Encourage maximum class participation in discussion.]

- Does the Declaration of Independence place limits on the power of government? What are these limits? Do you agree with them? Why?
- Does the Declaration of Independence place limits on the rights of citizens? What are these limits? Do you agree with them? Why?
- What do we call a decision by people to overthrow a government? Does the Declaration of Independence support all revolutions? Why?

Independent practice:

To demonstrate your understanding of this part of the Declaration of Independence, each student will write a letter to Thomas Jefferson, explaining whether you agree with his ideas about what people should do when governments do not respect their rights. In your letter, be sure to explain the reasons for your opinion. Give at least three reasons to support your opinions.

Homework:

Complete your letters to Thomas Jefferson. Continue collecting current events newspaper articles on revolutions in other parts of the world.

ACTIVITY SHEET: DECLARATION OF INDEPENDENCE—CITIZENS AND GOVERNMENTS

1. "That, to secure these rights, governments are instituted among men, deriving their just powers from the consent of the governed; . . ."

_____

_____

_____

Continued

2. "... that, whenever any form of government becomes destructive of these ends, it is the right of the people to alter or to abolish it, ..."

_____

_____

_____

3. "and to institute new government, laying its foundation on such principles, and organizing its powers in such form, as to them shall seem most likely to effect their safety and happiness."

_____

_____

_____

4. "Prudence, indeed, will dictate that governments long established should not be changed for light and transient causes, ..."

_____

_____

_____

5. "and, accordingly, all experience hath shown that mankind are more disposed to suffer, while evils are sufferable, than to right themselves by abolishing the forms to which they are accustomed."

_____

_____

_____

6. "But when a long train of abuses and usurpations, pursuing invariably the same object, evinces a design to reduce them under absolute despotism, it is their right, it is their duty, to throw off such government, and to provide new guards for their future security."

_____

_____

_____

Questions:

1. Does the Declaration of Independence place limits on the power of government? What are these limits? Do you agree with them? Why?

_____

_____

2. Does the Declaration of Independence place limits on the rights of citizens? What are these limits? Do you agree with them? Why?

_____

_____

3. What do we call a decision by people to overthrow a government? Does the Declaration of Independence always support this decision? Why?

_____

_____

_____

Teaching Activity: Evaluating a Hunter Lesson

Think it over:
What do you see as the strengths and weaknesses of this lesson plan? Why?

It's your classroom:
1. How would you change this lesson plan? Why?
2. Rewrite the lesson so that you feel comfortable with it.

Essay 1: Using "Text" and "Context" to Promote Student Literacies

Many veteran social studies teachers, especially in the high schools, insist that their job is to teach content material to students who already possess the required academic skills. However, no matter what social studies content you are teaching, your students likely also need to learn how to learn, find and evaluate information available in different formats, think systematically, support arguments with evidence, present ideas clearly, and evaluate their own work and the work of others so they can participate in conversations within the subject discipline. Whatever your position is on this issue, social studies teachers are increasingly being required to be full partners in promoting student literacy in its multiple forms: critical literacy, which involves thinking, understanding and acting on the world and technical literacy, which include finding, processing, and using information from different media and fields of study.

Maureen Murphy and I (MacCurtain et al., 2001) recently completed a multi-year project developing interdisciplinary activities, lessons, and units for teaching about the Great Irish Famine in Grades 4–12. Our initial plan was to prepare separate high school (9–12) and upper elementary/middle-level (4–8) packages. High school material would be minimally *edited*, while the middle-level package would include documents that were *adapted* for classroom use.

Through field-testing the lessons in classrooms, participating in and observing group work, and following up discussions with students, we discovered that our distinction between the two levels did not take into account the full range of student academic performance. Many high school students were more comfortable with the *adapted* documents, and some middle-level students were capable of reading with understanding the minimally *edited* text. In addition, in both middle and high school classes, some students with a record of poor academic performance could not read either set of material. Teachers working with these students recommended that documents be completely *rewritten*. As a result of their input, the final curriculum guide offers teachers the option of using differentiated edited, adapted, and rewritten text with major language revisions, either with an entire class on any grade level or with selected students.

Teaching Activity: Irish Immigrants in New Orleans, Louisiana

Source: Powers, T. (1836). *Impressions of America During the Years 1833, 1834, and 1835* (Binder and Reimers, 1988).

Edited version:
One of the greatest works now in progress here is the canal planned to connect Lac Pontchartrain with the city of New Orleans. I only wish that the wise men at home who coolly charge the present condition of Ireland upon the inherent laziness of her population, could be transported to this spot. Here they subsist on the coarsest fare; excluded from all the advantages of civilization; often at the mercy of a hard contractor, who wrings his profits from their blood; and all this for a pittance that merely enables them to exist, with little power to save, or a hope beyond the continuance of the like exertion.

Adapted text:

One of the greatest works now in progress here is a canal. I only wish that the men in England who blame the condition of Ireland on the laziness of her people could be brought to New Orleans. Here the Irish survive on poor food and are at the mercy of hard employers who profit from their blood; and all this for a low wage that only allows them to exist, with little power to save or hope.

Rewritten text with major language revisions:

A great canal is being built in Louisiana. I wish people in England who think the Irish are lazy could see how hard they are working here. Irish immigrants in New Orleans are treated badly by their employers. Their wages are low. Their food is poor quality. They have little hope.

Add your voice to the discussion:

How would you respond to the charge that teachers "water down" the curriculum and lower standards when they modify text? Explain.

While field-testing the curriculum, we also learned that the way material was presented to students was fundamental for capturing their interest and promoting learning. When teachers engaged students in activities, used references that had meaning to a particular group of students, reviewed vocabulary and provided a context for language, provided readings that were accessible, and encouraged freewheeling discussions, every group of students responded enthusiastically to the curriculum. Inner-city and suburban students, immigrants and native-born students, and students from different ethnic backgrounds were all fascinated by events prior to, during, and after the Great Irish Famine.

Some of our most successful lessons about the Irish were taught in low-performing inner-city middle schools, with students who were largely African American, Caribbean, and Latino/a. The keys to these lessons were our ability to create a context for literacy and learning as well as to provide students with appropriate text. Students sang traditional songs such as "Paddy on the Railway" and "No Irish Need Apply," examined political cartoons and newspaper illustrations downloaded from the Internet, and compared the experience of the Irish with their own experiences with discrimination and inequality. In a few classes, volunteers transformed the songs into contemporary "raps." During opening discussions, a number of students testified about their personal experiences as immigrants or discussed problems faced by their families and relatives when they arrived from other countries. In concluding discussions, students drew connections between the treatment of immigrants in the past and present as they tried to understand the Irish experience. Our experience in these classes was consistent with Maxine Greene's (1995) idea that learning is a search for situated understanding that places ideas and events in their social, historical, and cultural contexts.

Teachers who field-tested the curriculum modified lessons to make them more appropriate for their classes and used different teaching strategies successfully. Adeola Tella and Nichole Williams worked with students who had academic difficulties. They each spent a significant amount of class time having students read, sing, discuss, and rewrite the traditional Irish songs. Lynda Costello-Herrara and Rachel Gaglione Thompson focused on team projects in their classes. Their students participated in creating exhibits for a "museum" about the Great Irish Famine (see chap. 8).

Cheryl Smith worked primarily with inclusion classes and emphasized differentiated group-based instruction (Tomlinson, 1999). Cheryl prefers mixed-level student teams and assigned edited, adapted, or rewritten versions of documents to individual students in each group based on their reading performance. When possible, each team member examined a different aspect of the topic by using a different source. In one lesson, each team member studied conditions faced by Irish immigrants in a different North American location: New Orleans, New York, New Brunswick, Canada, and Philadelphia. Students who examined New Orleans read *edited* text. Students who studied about New York and New Brunswick, Canada, read *adapted* text. Students assigned Philadelphia read *rewritten* material.

Cheryl's approach makes it possible for all students to understand the material they are working with and requires that they provide information for their group's final report to the class. Smith is a strong proponent of teacher-prepared organizers that help student teams arrange information and necessitate contributions from every team member. The organizer for this assignment required the team to report evidence of anti-Irish stereotypes, violence against immigrants, unsafe working and living conditions, and positive experiences in each locality.

I sometimes compare learning to read with weight lifting. If your goal is to bench press 200 pounds, you start with a lower weight and build up your skill and muscle over time. If you were given a bar with 200 pounds on the first day and told to lift, you would probably just give up. Using differentiated texts offers social studies teachers a strategy to maintain student interest while helping them gradually develop literacy skills and reach higher academic standards.

Learning Activity: Text And Context

1. Sample Lesson Organizer: Ms. Smith's Team Reports on Irish Immigration

Evidence of . . .	In New Orleans	In New York	In Philadelphia	In Canada
Anti-Irish stereotypes Violence against the Irish Unsafe working conditions Poor living conditions Fair treatment of Irish immigrants Success by Irish immigrants				

Add your voice to the discussion:
In your view, will the use of differentiated text and lesson organizers facilitate inclusive instruction?

2. The song "Paddy Works on the Railway" contains a nonsense phrase, "Filly-me-oori-oori-ay," that is repeated over and over again. Many students with weaker reading skills were stymied when they tried to decipher it and gave up reading the song. When we explained that it was a nonsense phrase before asking students to read the song, we eliminated the problem.

Think it over:
1. Can you remember a situation as a student when you were stymied trying to do an assignment? What kind of help would have made it possible for you to be successful?
2. In your opinion, are teachers lowering standards when they provide this kind of help? Explain.
3. In a number of classes, students compared their own experiences as members of immigrant families with what they had learned about the Irish. Many students argued that immigrants in the United States are subject to discrimination today. Some spoke about personal experiences being harassed by police or store owners. Would you have permitted or even have encouraged these discussions in an effort to create "context"? Explain.

REFERENCES AND RECOMMENDATIONS FOR FURTHER READING

Berg, C., and M. Clough. "Hunter Lesson Design: The Wrong One for Science Teaching." *Educational Leadership*, December 1990/January 1991.

Binder, F., and D. Reimers. *The Way We Lived: Essays and Documents in American Social History*, vol. I. Lexington, Mass.: D. C. Heath, 1988.

Carr, E. H. *What is history?* New York: Vintage, 1961.

Clinchy, B. "Goals 2000: The Students as Object." *Phi Delta Kappan*, January 1995, 384–85.

Dobkin, W., J. Fischer, B. Ludwig, and R. Koblinger. *A Handbook for the Teaching of Social Studies*. Boston: Allyn and Bacon, 1985.

Greene, M. *Releasing the Imagination: Essays on Education, the Arts, and Social Change*. San Francisco: Jossey-Bass, 1995.

Hunter, M. *Mastery Teaching*. El Segundo, Calif.: TIP Publications, 1982.

MacCurtain, M., M. Murphy, A. Singer, L. Costello, R. Gaglione, M. Miller, D. Smith, A. Tella, and N. Williams. "Text and Context: Field-Testing the NYS Great Irish Famine Curriculum." *Theory and Research in Social Education* 29, no. 2 (2001), 238–60.

Singer, A. "Forum on Teaching: Divisions Real and Imagined," *OAH Newsletter*, 25(3), August 1997, 3.

Tomlinson, C. *The Differentiated Classroom*. Alexandria, Va.: ASCD, 1999.

Wilentz, S. (1997, April 20). "The Past Is Not a 'Process'," *The New York Times* (4.15).

6

What Are the Building Blocks of an Activity-Based Lesson?

HOW CAN LESSONS ACTIVELY INVOLVE STUDENTS IN LEARNING?

People in our society adopt a wide range of styles in the ways that they dress, work, and live their lives. Their styles suit their personalities, talents, preferences, and experiences. Teachers are no different. Some prefer and consider themselves more effective using one style or method of teaching, some prefer others, and some experiment with different approaches. Early in my teaching career, my lessons tended to be teacher-centered largely because I was unsure of myself and afraid of what would happen if students experienced freedom in the classroom. Whether I was struggling with students to get them to complete a particular assignment or was entertaining them in an attempt to draw them into lessons, I tried to hold the classroom reins tightly in my hands. It was not until I became more confident of

207

my own knowledge of social studies and in my ability as a teacher that I was comfortable organizing a classroom where students actively participated as historians and social scientists and were allowed to make choices about what and how they would learn.

Although I am an advocate of student-centered activity-based lessons, I do not believe there is only one way to teach a social studies lesson or that it is desirable to always teach the same way. A strength of the activity-based approach is that the types of activities are very different. They include analyzing primary source documents, discussions, graphing and mapping, singing and dancing, performing drama, or creating cartoons, posters, and poems. What the activities have in common is that they all involve students in learning by doing. Variety in instructional methods helps keep students interested, and flexibility in lesson design allows teachers to take into account the dynamic of a particular class.

Classroom Activity: Dancing Social Studies

As part of global history, I involve students in learning international folk dances. Although I know the steps, I am not much of a dancer or dance teacher. The activity has been most successful when we jigsaw. I teach the dances to a small group of volunteers (between 3 to 5 students) during free periods, and then they teach the dances to the rest of the class. I have a small repertoire of dances from different cultures and time periods that I use to teach different social studies concepts. While dancing, the class discusses the dances, their similarities and differences, and the roles that dance and the arts play in different cultures.

1. *Pata Pata* is a dance from South Africa that was part of the antiapartheid movement. It blends traditional African dance steps with contemporary music. It is an example of art as a form of social protest.
2. *Tanko Bushi* is a 19th-century Japanese pantomime dance with precise stylized movements. In this dance, the dancers reenact the work of pre-industrial women coal miners.
3. *Alunelul* is a Romanian harvest celebration dance. It is a vigorous dance with a lot of stomping because the dancers are symbolically breaking open the shells of hazelnuts.
4. *Tininkling* is a dance from the Philippines in which dancers step between sticks and act out efforts to capture a bird. It is an example of the blended Asian and European culture of the archipelago.
5. *Mayeem* is an Israeli dance that originates on collective farms called *kibbutzim* and represents a hopeful call for rain. It is an example of efforts to create new cultural symbols after Israel became an independent nation in the 1940s.

It's your classroom:
How could you use dance or other art forms to teach social studies concepts about culture?

Add your voice to the discussion:
Is it worth the investment of time to involve secondary school students in this kind of activity in social studies classes? Why?

Acknowledging that competent teachers can have different teaching styles does not mean, however, that all teaching is equally effective for every grade level and for achieving every classroom goal. Advocates of direct instruction (e.g., lecturing, "chalk and talk"—the teacher says something and then writes it on the board) claim that students in their classrooms learn because the classrooms are well structured and students remain focused. Students are told what they need to know, drilled to impress it on their memories, required to copy from the board, tested, and either punished or rewarded based on their scores.

I am suspicious about what students actually learn in this kind of classroom. If John Dewey is correct and experience is the most significant teacher, whatever the content presented in these classes, the primary lessons students learn are related to values and behavior. Students learn to be passive, to submit to authority without questioning, to blend in, to remain silent and hidden, to memorize enough data so they can pass a test, and to avoid the consequences of a poor grade. They also learn that people should compete rather than work together. They learn that some people's ideas are not valued and that, although teachers have the right to choose a teaching style that suits them, there is no room for individual difference in student learning styles.

Direct instruction classrooms run counter to the type of classrooms and effective teaching described by Dewey, Paulo Freire, Maxine Greene, and James Banks (discussed in chap. 2). I think this is the case in any secondary school subject but especially for social studies, where our expressed goals include developing active citizens and critical thinkers prepared to offer leadership in a democratic society.

Sometimes preservice teachers ask, Is it ever okay to lecture? They are talking about lessons dominated by extended presentations of information or long, detailed answers to student questions. For middle school social studies classes, my answer is always no. When teachers do this, they only lose the students.

In high school, I think that this kind of "teacher talk" should be avoided. At best, it is a last resort when a teacher is unable to find a way to involve students in examining materials and questions. I do not mean that a teacher is not allowed to express any ideas or answer a question. Rather, I am suggesting that, instead of launching into long extemporaneous monologues, we need to find materials that make it possible for students to participate in our lessons.

Formal lectures—the kind we associate with college classes, where a teacher thinks out loud about an idea while students are jotting down their reactions and questions—can be consistent with an activity-based approach. High school students need to be able to gather, organize, and evaluate information that is presented in a number of forms. When a teacher has a clear skills goal for students, an engaging manner, an interesting topic, and uses the technique judiciously, formal lecturing can be an effective approach.

This chapter focuses on the building blocks of activity-based lessons, lessons that involve students as historians and social scientists who learn social studies content and skills as they examine documents and are engaged in activities. It looks at ideas and strategies for stimulating students' interest, expanding their ability to understand the world, encouraging them to think and ask questions, and making it possible for them to draw connections between different disciplines, the past and present, and the academic world and their own experiences. This chapter also includes strategies for dealing with heterogeneous ability groups.

WHAT IS DOCUMENT-BASED INSTRUCTION?

The most common activity in a social studies classroom is probably document analysis. Recently there has been a big push in a number of states for document-based assessment (see chap. 9), but I prefer to talk about document-based instruction. Document-based instruction gives students the opportunity to act as historians and social scientists and draw their own conclusions. It also helps enhance analytic and literacy skills. Many textbook companies and social studies organizations now publish original, edited, and modified versions of primary source material organized on ready-to-use activity sheets. Some of this material can be downloaded directly from the web (see chap. 10).

I define the word *'document'* very broadly to include both written sources and nonwritten artifacts, pictures, and photographs that can be used to understand or tell a story. In the Pacific Northwest, preliterate societies created totem poles whose symbols described the history of their tribes and clans. In the American Southwest, the Navaho people use sand paintings to explain their religious beliefs. In medieval Europe, stained glass windows performed a similar function. The totem poles, sand paintings, and stained glass are all "documents" that students can "read" to learn about these people.

Ideally, our goal as social studies teachers is to prepare students to "read" historical documents in their original or unedited form. This is a goal, however, and students need to develop their skills working with material that takes into account their level or interest and performance. I would also like students to be able to pick up a document and analyze it on their own, but until they develop this ability, I provide questions that guide them and help them discover key information and patterns.

Teaching Activity: Reading Photographs

Try it yourself:
Both of these photographs are from a 1999 trip to the Irish countryside. Read the photographs. Describe what you see. What stories do they tell about life in rural Ireland today?

It's your classroom:
What questions could you ask students about these photographs?

Teaching Activity: Constructing a Document-Based Activity Sheet

1. Define a broad question that the lesson examines. The documents provided in the lesson should make it possible for students to answer the question.
2. Select a photograph, graph, political cartoon, chart, song, quote, or series or mixture of photographs, graphs, political cartoons, charts, songs, and quotes that are appropriate to the reading and interest level of your students. Analysis of the documents should make it possible for students to draw broader conclusions about a person, event, or era.
3. Provide students with directions so they know what you want them to do.
4. Provide either three or four guiding questions to assist in analysis of the document. One or two questions should be on the content of the document (WHAT, WHERE, WHO, DESCRIBE, or IDENTIFY). This directs student attention to key information. These are followed by a conclusion (WHY or HOW) and an opinion question. The conclusion question asks students to draw a connection (Why is something happening?) between different information provided in the document or between information in the document and what they already know about the person, events, or era. The opinion question asks students to evaluate the importance of what they have learned for understanding the broader historical context.

SAMPLE GRADE/SUBJECT: High school–level U.S. history
AIM QUESTION: What was the impact of the transportation revolution on the new nation?
DIRECTIONS: Work in pairs. Examine the chart and answer questions 1–4.

Impact of the Erie Canal on Central New York Cities, Population and National Rank, 1810–1840

City	1810 (Rank)	1820 (Rank)	1830 (Rank)	1840 (Rank)
Albany	10,762 (10)	12,630 (11)	24,209 (9)	33,721 (9)
Buffalo	—	—	8,668 (28)	18,213 (22)
Rochester	—	—	9,207 (25)	20,191 (19)
Troy	—	5,264 (35)	11,556 (19)	19,334 (21)
Utica	—	—	8,323 (29)	12,782 (29)

Source: Campbell Gibson. *Population of the 100 Largest Cities and Other Urban Places in the United States: 1790 to 1990.* U.S. Bureau of the Census, Washington, D.C.: 1998.

Questions:

1. **What** is the population of Buffalo in 1830?
2. **What** is the national ranking of Rochester in 1840?
3. **How** does the Erie Canal affect this region of New York state?
4. In your opinion, **what** other changes would you expect to find in this part of the country? **Why?**

HOW DO TEACHERS ORGANIZE SOCIAL STUDIES ACTIVITIES?

Activities:

The ways that students will learn the goals and objectives of a lesson. Activities include document analysis, mapping, cartooning, singing, writing, reading, presenting dramas, researching, and creating projects. Instructional methods include class discussion, group work, cooperative learning, teacher and student presentations/demonstrations, and coaching work teams.

This is the part of planning I like the most: finding the quote, picture, chart, or cartoon that opens everything up for the students. It can also be frustrating when you cannot find what you want or when none of the students understand or are interested in your "perfect" illustration. To protect myself from illfounded assumptions about what will work in class, I usually plan three or four activities for a 40-minute period. If all goes well, the class may look at only one or two of them, but just in case, I always have other materials and activities available.

For example, analyzing the song "Talking Union" (Seeger and Reiser, 1986) is a way to promote class discussion of why workers organized unions in the past and the role of unions in today's U.S. economy. The song gives students some information about why workers organize labor unions. In the discussion, students can supplement this with information they learned from other readings, charts and graphs, current events articles, or discussions with union members or employers. When using a song in class, I usually give students a copy of the lyrics to read and play it for them (this song is available on the cassette "Carry It On" from Flying Fish Records, Inc., 1304 W. Schubert, Chicago, Ill. 60614). When I really feel adventurous, I try to get them to sing along.

The questions at the end of the song help focus student attention on the subject of the lesson and give them a chance to think about their own ideas before full class discussion begins. The questions can be on the song sheet or the board, or the teacher can just read them aloud. Students can work on answering them individually, in pairs, or in groups. If combined with current events headlines or articles about recent labor union–employer conflicts, assuming that students get involved in discussion, this activity will span an entire class period.

AIM: SHOULD WORKERS JOIN UNIONS?

Instructions: Read the lyrics to the song "Talking Union" and write the answers to the questions in your notebook.

Talking Union:

TALKING UNION by Lee Hays, Millard Lampell, and Pete Seeger, Copyright © 1947 by Stormking Music, Inc. All rights reserved. Used by permission.

According to Pete Seeger, this song almost wrote itself while he and the other songwriters were helping to organize labor unions for the Congress of Industrial Organizations in 1941. The song has eight stanzas. Parts of four are included here.

1. If you want higher wages,
Let me tell you what to do:
You got to talk to the workers
In the shop with you;
You got to build you a union,
Got to make it strong,
But if you all stick together,
Now, 'twont be long.
You get shorter hours,
Better working conditions.
Vacations with pay,
Take the kids to the seashore.

2. It ain't quite this simple,
So I better explain
Just why you got to ride
On the union train;
'Cause if you wait for the boss
To raise your pay,
We'll all be waiting
Till Judgment Day;
We'll all be buried—
Gone to Heaven—
Saint Peter'll be
The straw boss then, folks.

Continued

3. Now, you know you're underpaid,
But the boss says you ain't;
He speeds up the work
Till you're about to faint.
You may be down and out,
But you ain't beaten,
You can pass out a leaflet
And call a meetin'—
Talk it over—
Speak your mind—
Decide to do something
About it.

4. Suppose they're working you so hard
It's just outrageous,
And they're paying you all
Starvation wages:
You go to the boss,
And the boss would yell,
"Before I raise your pay
I'd see you all in hell."
Well, he's puffing a big cigar
And feeling mighty slick,
He thinks he's got your
Union licked.

Questions:

- According to this song, what are three benefits of belonging to a labor union?
- How does this song view the relationship between employers and employees?
- In your opinion, why were songs used in campaigns to organize labor unions?
- Labor unions might have been necessary for working people in 1941 when this song was written. Do you think they are still necessary today? Why?

Teaching Activity: Analyzing a Song

It's your classroom:
What questions would you ask students about this topic or about this song?

Try it yourself:
Design a lesson that uses the words to a song to provide students with information about a topic and helps generate discussion.

HOW DO TEACHERS OPEN AN ACTIVITY-BASED LESSON?

Much of the time, the hardest part of a lesson is getting started. You planned a brilliant lesson. You thought about it for days and gathered engaging and appropriate learning materials. Your students have not thought about social studies since they left your classroom the last time, however, or if you are lucky, since they did their homework. They have been too busy with the important things in their lives: friends, family, food, jobs, sports, music, and movies. In addition, they are squirming in their seats because it is hot or cold in the room; half asleep because its 8 A.M. or falling asleep because it's 2 P.M.; starving because they have not had lunch yet, or all charged up because of the fight in the hall, the basketball game in gym, or the fire drill. Their last class was boring. Hormones are kicking in. Four students walk in late without a pass. Maybe your students are just a rambunctious group. In any event, it is not a perfect setting for social studies. Clearly, a lesson needs some kind of activity designed to get the class started.

Do Now Activity:

A brief introductory activity that immediately involves students as they enter the room.

Motivation(al) Activity:

A question, statement, or activity that captures student interest in the topic to be examined. Motivations connect the subject of the lesson to things that students are thinking about or that interest them.

Transitions:

Key questions that make it possible for students to draw connections between the information, concepts, or understandings developed during a particular activity, with other parts of the lesson, and to broader conceptual understanding.

Step 1

A **Do Now** is a quick way to establish that class has begun, to introduce a topic to students, or to remind them of what they are going to be studying. The do now activity does not have to be a big deal. Have a regular spot on the board where students can find the do now assignment as they enter the room. Students can copy some notes or a definition, think about answers to a question, read a quote from the board or a passage from a handout, and answer a couple of questions.

While they are working—individually, in pairs, or in small groups—you have the chance to move among them as a calming presence. You can chat with individual students, give instructions to the class or to groups, check homework, collect excuses, and get feedback from students on what they do and do not understand about the topic or their assignments. I usually carry a memo pad as I travel around the room so I can jot down student responses to the do now assignment. This helps me draw students into the discussion as the lesson progresses.

SAMPLE DO NOW ACTIVITIES

Subject: U.S. History:

Lesson topic: 19th-century immigrants to the United States.
Objective: To examine attitudes toward 19th-century immigrants to the United States.
Do Now: Examine the political cartoon on the next page and use it to answer questions 1–3.
1. What is happening in the political cartoon?
2. In your opinion, what is the main idea of the political cartoon?
3. What is a good title for this political cartoon?

Subject: Economics:

Lesson topic: The changing nature of the U.S. economy.
Objective: To show the relative importance of the agricultural, manufacturing, and service components of the economy.
Do Now: Use the information from the chart on the next page to complete 1–3.
1. Construct a line graph comparing income in the three subcategories.
2. Describe the trend for each subcategory.
3. What conclusion can you draw about changes in the U.S. economy during this period?

Continued

Source: *Harper's Weekly*, 1888 Reprinted by permission of Documentary Photo AIDS, Box 956, Mount Doria, FL 32757.

National Income by Industry, 1930–1970 (in billions of dollars)

Year	Total Income	Agriculture, Forestry, Fishing	Manufacturing	Services
1930	75.4	6.4	18.3	8.4
1940	81.1	6.1	22.5	8.0
1950	241.1	17.6	76.2	21.8
1960	414.5	16.9	125.8	44.5
1970	800.5	25.6	217.5	102.9

Source: U.S. Department of Commerce (1975). *Historical Statistics of the United States.* vol. 1. Washington D.C.: Government Printing Office, 1975.

Subject: Government:

Lesson topic: Federal responsibility for health programs
Objective: To examine the debate over the responsibility of the federal government to provide health programs for the poor, aged, and uninsured.
Do Now: Examine these headlines from *The New York Times* from September 22–24, 1995:

"House G.O.P. Plan Doubles Premiums of Medicare Users," September 22, 1995
"Democrats Say Republicans Are Pushing Medicare Plan Too Fast," September 22, 1995
"Gingrich Threatens U.S. Default If Clinton Won't Bend on Budget," September 22, 1995
"Republican Blitz Shakes Congress/Democrats Aghast as Pillars of U.S. Health Care Crack," September 23, 1995
"Redesign of 2 Vast Systems Advances," September 23, 1995
"Medicare Prognosis for New York Is Grim/Cuts to Teaching Hospitals in G.O.P. Plan Could Mean Less Care," September 23, 1995
"State Lawmakers Prepare to Wield Vast New Powers/Republicans Plan to Transfer
Authority over Welfare and Safety to Legislatures," September 24, 1995

Based on the information in these headlines:
  What issue(s) are being debated in the federal government?
  What positions are being taken in this debate?

Subject: Sociology:

Lesson topic: Comparing class and caste
Objective: To examine different systems of social stratification.
Do Now: Copy vocabulary words:
- *Stratification.* The formal or informal division of society into groups that receive different levels of power, prestige, and economic rewards.
- *Class.* A social group whose members have similar occupations or income levels. Status is not hereditary. People can change their class position.
- *Caste.* A social group whose members are born into the group. People cannot change their caste status. Caste status is passed to descendants.

Subject: Global History:

Lesson topic: Golden Age for India.
Objective: To examine the factors leading up to the creation of a powerful civilization during the early history of India.
Do Now: Copy the chronology of events.

Golden Age for India

Year(s) B.C.	Events
500	Persia controls the Indus Valley and the Punjab.
400	Kingdom of Magadha rules plain of the Ganges and northern India.
323	Alexander and the Greek army defeat Persian and Indian forces.
300	Under Maurya, Magadhan Empire expands north and west.
261–232	Asoka rules Mauryan Empire. Era of growth, stability, and peace.

Teaching Activity: Using Activities in a Lesson

It's your classroom:
How could you use these activities as parts of lessons?

Step 2

Once students are settled and the subject of the lesson is established, you need to establish a context for what students will be learning, grab their attention, and hold onto it. A motivation can flow from the do now activity, or the do now can be set aside for later discussion. The key to motivation is capturing the imagination of students by creating a metaphoric image or analogy that connects who and where they are with the topic under discussion. The motivation does not have to be directly related to the main idea of the lesson, but it is more effective if it is. The motivation should also provide a transition from the activity to the social studies concepts that are going to be explored during the lesson.

SAMPLE MOTIVATIONAL ACTIVITIES

Opening a Lesson with a Demonstration:

U.S. History: Understanding the Constitution
Checks and balances. A balance scale and loose change (or blocks, rocks, etc.) are on a desk in front of the room. Students take turns using the change to balance the scale. If we have enough scales, students can work in groups. Why is it difficult to balance the scales? Why is it difficult to keep things in balance? Why would the authors of the U.S. Constitution want to make certain that the powers of the different branches of the government were balanced?
Unconstitutional. In *Marbury v. Madison* (1803), the U.S. Supreme Court concluded that, in the Judiciary Act of 1789, Congress had violated the guidelines established by the U.S. Constitution. Therefore, the law was null and void. I hang a piece of oak tag on the front board with a strangely shaped piece cut out. The oak tag is labeled CONSTITUTION. While the class reviews the process of how a law is made, I cut a series of shapes out of cardboard to represent laws. At the last step, we hold the cardboard pieces up to the cutout in our oak tag Constitution. What happens to the "laws" that do not fit? What happens to the laws that do?
Stretching the Constitution. Article 1, Section 8, Part 18, the Elastic Clause, empowers Congress "to make all laws which shall be necessary and proper for carrying into execution the foregoing powers and all other powers vested by this Constitution in the government of the United States, or in any department or office thereof." The extent that these powers can legitimately be stretched has been debated for 200 years. While students discuss the meaning of the clause, I have two students pull on a large piece of elastic. Beware when they pull too far; the elastic snaps back.

Opening a Lesson with Questions and a Discussion:

Global History: Impact of Technology on History
Think of a small thing or event that has had a major impact on world history.
What thing or event did you choose? Why did you choose it?
How do you think changes in technology have influenced world history?

Continued

Government: The Changing Powers of the Presidency

In your opinion, what are the major problems facing the United States today?

Would you support expanding the power of the President of the United States if you believed it was the only way to solve the problems of the country? Why?

Would you allow the President to become a dictator? Why?

U.S. History: The Importance of National Symbols to the New Nation

What are some important symbols to different groups of teenagers today?

Why do think teenagers from different communities and groups have their own symbols?

Why are symbols important to teenagers?

What are the symbols of the United States? Why are symbols important?

Why do you think symbols were important to the creation of a new nation?

Opening a Lesson with a Dramatic Guest:

Most of this material is available on the Internet.

In the press conference, the teacher acts out a speech by an historical figure. The students listen to the speech and make up questions they would ask if it were a press conference. Some interesting speeches include President William McKinley's explanation of how he decided that the United States should annex the Philippines (1898), Senator Margaret Chase Smith's 1950 statement against the excesses of McCarthyism, Richard Nixon's resignation as President in 1974, and President Ronald Reagan's 1985 State of the Union Address, in which he explained his "Second American Revolution." In addition, many recent public figures can "visit" your classroom on videotape. Students can design questions to ask Martin Luther King Jr., John F. Kennedy, or Malcolm X.

Sometimes I wrap a toga (sheet) around my clothes and pretend I am Socrates. I illustrate the Socratic method by asking students to define an inanimate object (What is a chair?) and then a concept (What does good mean?).

Student volunteers can do a dramatic reading of a brief statement. Examples include the conclusion of Patrick Henry's 1775 "Give me liberty or give me death" speech, Anne Hutchinson's 1637 statement to the Massachusetts General Court, William Lloyd Garrison's January 1, 1831 editorial in *The Liberator* in which he warned his opponents that he would not be silenced on the issue of slavery, Susan B. Anthony's statement to the 1860 National Women's Rights Convention on the "one-sided" nature of marriage, excerpts from Frederick Douglass' 1883 speech at the National Convention of Colored Men in which he demanded that the nation abide by the promises of the Constitution, and Bartolomeo Vanzetti's statement to the court during his politically charged trial for murder during the 1920s.

Teaching Activity: Motivational Activities

It's your classroom:

1. What other demonstrations can you think of to illustrate constitutional principles?
2. How would you use them?
3. How would you connect the interests of teenagers to the subject of the lesson?
4. What historical guests would you invite to your class? Why?
5. Which of these motivational activities would you use in middle school? Which would you use in high school?

Step 3

The next step is to move the class from the do now or motivational activity to the content, concepts, and skills of the lesson. There needs to be some sort of transition: a question by the teacher that connects the introduction with the lesson, a question by a student, or even a "eureka" statement that students give to explain what they discovered about the topic.

Three samples follow that illustrate the progression from do now to motivation to transition.

MOTIVATIONS WITH TRANSITIONS

U.S. History:

AIM: Why did the British colonists demand independence?
DO NOW: Examine the map of Boston harbor in 1775.

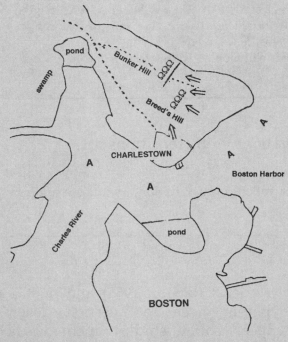

1. Locate Breed's Hill, Bunker Hill, Colonial forces, roads, and British troops and ships.
2. On what type of land formation are Bunker and Breed's Hills located?
3. If you wanted to capture the colonial forces, how would you attack? Why?
4. According to the map, how did the British launch their attack?

Ω   Colonial forces   **A**   British ships
......   roads   ⇐   British attack route

MOTIVATION: Review the do now assignment (for more information on the Battle of Bunker Hill, see http://www.wpi.edu/Academics/depts/milsci/BTSI/hill/bhill_obj.html). Did anyone see the 2002 Super Bowl (or any other sports event in which a highly rated team was upset by an underdog)? What makes it possible for an underdog to win these games? (Overconfidence) You've examined the map of Boston Harbor. Why do you think the British launched a frontal assault instead of cutting off the colonists at the neck of the peninsula?
TRANSITION: What would be the impact of the British defeat in this battle? Why?

Economics:

AIM: How did industrialization change the world?
DO NOW: Make a list of what you consider to be the 10 greatest inventions in human history.
MOTIVATION: Hold up a small can and rattle it. In this can is what I consider the greatest invention of the 19th century. Can anyone guess what it is? Open the can. In the can are 10 bolts. A washer and a nut are on each bolt. Pass the bolt-washer-nut assemblage to

Continued

10 students and have the students take them apart. Pass the bolts, washers, and nuts around the classroom until they are all mixed up. Now have each person with a bolt collect a washer and a nut and reassemble. Do they fit together? How can they if we mixed them up? What invention have we illustrated? Why is this an important invention?
TRANSITION: In your opinion, what makes an invention "great"?

Economics:

This lesson was developed with Brendalon Staton of the NTN.
AIM: What is money?
DO NOW: Answer these questions.
How much money do you spend in an average week?
What are your major purchases?
MOTIVATION: Offer inflated prices to purchase a student's backpack. When a student agrees to sell, pull out a wad of enlarged photocopies of $20 bills (the teacher's picture can replace Andrew Jackson). When students ask what they are, tell them "big bills."
TRANSITION: When the student denies that it is real money, ask the class to define *real money*.

Teaching Activity: Motivations with Transitions

Try it yourself:
Design an aim question, a do now activity, a motivation, and a transition to stimulate student discussion of apartheid in South Africa.

ARE THERE PERFECT QUESTIONS?

My ideas about the types of questions to include in social studies lesson plans draw on traditional approaches, including Benjamin Bloom's system for classifying questions based on their ability to promote higher-order thinking by students (Bloom, 1985) and on the emphasis given to question design in most social studies methods books. However, questions have been considerably modified by my experience as a classroom teacher using an activity-based approach and because of the emphasis in my teaching on student-centered lessons.

Questions:

Prepare questions that attempt to anticipate classroom dialogue and that are designed to aid examination of materials, generate class discussions, and promote deeper thinking. Medial summary questions make it possible for the class to integrate ideas at the end of an activity.

Summary:

A concluding question or questions that make it possible for the class to integrate or utilize the learning from this and prior lessons.

In my college teacher education program and during my early years as a teacher, the emphasis in lesson planning was on designing predetermined "perfect questions" that would stimulate student interest, invoke higher-order thinking, and, in theory, unleash sustained student discussions. After 10 years of teaching high school social studies, I finally asked my first "perfect question" at the end of a unit on the emergence of the United States as a world power between 1870 and 1920. I asked the class, Do you think the United States acted as an imperialist power during World War I? In previous lessons, students had examined a package of quotes, cartoons, maps, and charts that included excerpts from essays by historians Arthur Link, Harry E. Barnes, and William Appleman Williams and statements by Secretaries of State William Jennings Bryan and Robert Lansing, Senators Robert La Follette and George Norris, and President Woodrow Wilson. Based on this document package, students could effectively support a number of different positions. There was no single right answer.

I still remember that a student started the discussion by citing William Jennings Bryan to support the idea that U.S. actions were imperialist. His comments unleashed a period-long argument among the students as they sorted through the documents to find references needed to make their points. My role for the rest of the period was trying to get them to listen to each other and occasionally asking questions like Why do you believe that? How do you respond to what so-and-so said? What evidence do you have to support your position?

I had been asking the question Do you think the United States acted as an imperialist power during World War I? for years without getting this kind of response. It was not the question that made the discussion possible. Rather, it was made possible by all of the work done by students during the unit and their sense of a classroom community where they could express their opinions without fear of being dismissed. My job during this discussion was to listen to students, hear what they had to say, and encourage them to think their ideas through more completely. If I had asked any of my other prepared questions, I am convinced that I would have stifled their discussion.

A Handbook for the Teaching of Social Studies (Dobkin et al., 1985: 37–65) published by The Association of Teachers of Social Studies (ATSS) recommends that teachers plan lessons around carefully crafted pivotal questions that focus on higher-order thinking skills. The chapter "The Art of Questioning" stresses that "the nature of the questions asked by the teacher" and "the sequence in which they are asked" (37) are keys to successful social studies teaching. Predetermined questions play such a crucial role in this version of lesson plan design that the book offers nine rules for designing questions, seven rules for wording them effectively, and 14 common pitfalls to avoid when asking questions, as well as directions on how to react to student responses. In addition, new teachers are provided 159 sample pivotal questions from different social studies disciplines that they can incorporate in their lesson plans or use as models.

This approach to lesson planning is frequently coupled with Benjamin Bloom's hierarchical question classification system (Manson and Clegg, 1970). Bloom classifies questions based on whether they encourage critical thinking by students. The lowest level of questions asks students to recall information; the highest level requires them to exercise judgment. Bloom's system is useful because it emphasizes that students should be learning to use information to formulate and support their ideas.

Benjamin Bloom's classification system organizes questions into six categories based on the "level of thought" required from students. They are ranked here from lower-level to higher-level thinking. I have to confess that I am not clear how *application* differs significantly from *synthesis* or why *evaluation* ranks higher than *analysis*. Consider the following categories:

Category	Definition	Example
Knowledge	Students are asked to recall or describe information that they have been provided in an assignment or by the teacher.	According to the document, what was the author's first job?
Comprehension	Students are asked to interpret or explain information.	Explain why the author decided to return to school.
Application	Students use information to explain other related events, solve a problem, or speculate about broader causes or issues.	What other reasons would a person have to give up a job and return to school?
Analysis	Students use information to draw conclusions.	Which of the author's statements are facts and which ones are opinions?
Synthesis	Students use information to arrive at a new understanding.	What would you do if you were faced with a similar situation?
Evaluation	Students use information and established criteria to make a judgment or support an opinion.	Which experience was most significant in shaping the author's ideas?

Teaching Activity: Designing Questions for a Lesson on the Scopes Trial

Examine the edited transcript of William Jennings Bryan's testimony at the 1925 Scopes ("monkey") trial in Dayton, Tennessee (from *The New York Times*, July 21, 1925). John Scopes was a high school biology teacher who was put on trial for violating a Tennessee law that prohibited teaching about evolution. The trial, including this dialogue between Bryan and defense attorney Clarence Darrow, was immortalized in the play, *Inherit the Wind*. Bryan, a member of the prosecution, was called to the stand by the defense as an expert witness on the Old and New Testaments. This document is useful in an elective course studying law, a government class examining religious freedom, or a high school U.S. history class.

Excerpts from the Transcript of the Scopes Trial:

Darrow: You have given considerable study to the Bible, haven't you Mr. Bryan?
Bryan: Yes, sir. I have tried to.

Darrow: Well, we all know you have; we are not going to dispute that at all. But you have written and published articles almost weekly, and sometimes have made interpretations of various things?
Bryan: I would not say interpretations, Mr. Darrow, but comments on the lessons. . . .

Darrow: Do you claim that everything in the Bible should be literally interpreted?
Bryan: I believe everything in the Bible should be accepted as it is given there; some of the Bible is given illustratively. For instance: "Ye are the salt of the earth." I would not insist that man is actually salt, or that he had the flesh of salt. . . .

Darrow: The Bible says Joshua commanded the sun to stand still for the purpose of lengthening the day, doesn't it, and you believe it?
Bryan: I do.

Darrow: Do you believe at that time that the entire sun went around the earth?
Bryan: No, I believe that the earth goes around the sun.

Darrow: Do you believe that the men who wrote it thought that the day could be lengthened or that the sun could be stopped?
Bryan: . . . I think they wrote the fact without expressing their own thoughts.

Darrow: Have you an opinion as to whether whoever wrote the book, . . . thought the sun went around the earth or not?
Bryan: I believe that he was inspired. . . . I believe that the Bible is inspired, and an inspired author, whether one who wrote as he was directed to write, understood the things he was writing about, I don't know.

Darrow: Whoever inspired it, do you think whoever inspired it believed that the sun went around the earth?
Bryan: I believe it was inspired by the Almighty, and he may have used language that could be understood at the time. . . . (to the court) His purpose is to cast ridicule on everybody who believes in the Bible, and I am perfectly willing that the world shall know that these gentlemen have no other purpose than ridiculing every person who believes in the Bible.

Darrow: We have the purpose of preventing bigots and ignoramuses from controlling the education of the United States, and you know it, and that is all.
Bryan: I am glad to bring out that statement. . . . I want to defend the Word of God against the greatest atheist or agnostic in the United States. I want the papers to show that I am not afraid to get on the stand in front of him and let him know that agnosticism is trying to force agnosticism on our colleges and on our schools, and the people of Tennessee will not permit it to be done. . . .

Darrow: I object to your statement. I am examining you on your fool ideas no intelligent Christian on earth believes.

Learning Activity: Evolution, Creation and Religion

Think it over:
Religious issues can be very controversial in the classroom. How would you prepare students for this lesson?

Add your voice to the discussion:
In your opinion, does the debate over evolution and creationism belong in the social studies classroom? Why?

Try it yourself:
Design a question for each of the categories in Bloom's taxonomy for use in a lesson based on excerpts from the transcript of the Scopes ("monkey") trial.

Although I support encouraging students to think critically and carefully planned lessons, a fixation on question design can be counterproductive. Predetermined questions are intended to get elicit preconceived responses that are directed back to the teacher, not to the class. Answers that deviate the least from teacher expectations are judged to be the best. Lessons tend to be teacher centered and scripted, with little space for students to think. Although the ATSS handbook recommends that "an effective teacher should not insist upon a particular phraseology or pattern of thinking unless accuracy or precision of thought is involved," it warns that "regardless of interest or absolute value, digressions are ill-advised" (122–24). I think that Bloom's system, because it encourages teachers to think of certain types of questions as inherently more worthwhile, also lends itself to rigid application.

An anecdote told to me by a high school student illustrates the problem with this approach. The student's biology teacher asked the class the difference between studying science and history: a higher-order question that requires comparison and synthesis. The student raised his hand and responded, "I don't think there is that much of a difference." Before he could elaborate or explain, the teacher shouted out: "Wrong!" Then the teacher called on the next volunteer.

Clearly, predetermined questions are useful for teachers. They help us to think about main ideas and goals and to plan logical lessons. They are good to have written down in reserve just in case we get stuck during a lesson. They are especially useful for directing students as they analyze a document. Once the information is on the table, once discussion has begun, however, predetermined questions can become a hindrance to examination and discussion in a student-centered classroom. If we want to promote higher-order thinking, teachers need to worry less about designing and asking perfect questions and more about listening to and responding to the ideas of our students.

Teaching Activity: Designing Questions for a Primary Source Document

Students might read excerpts from the United Nation's Universal Declaration of Human Rights (United Nations General Assembly, 1953) while studying U.S. or global history or U.S. government.

> Whereas recognition of the inherent dignity and of the equal and inalienable rights of all members of the human family is the foundation of freedom, justice and peace in the world,
>
> Whereas disregard and contempt for human rights have resulted in barbarous acts which have outraged the conscience of mankind, and the advent of a world in which human beings shall enjoy freedom of speech and belief and freedom from fear and want has been proclaimed as the highest aspiration of the common people,
>
> Whereas it is essential, if man is not to be compelled to have recourse, as a last resort, to rebellion against tyranny and oppression, that human rights should be protected by the rule of law, whereas it is essential to promote the development of friendly relations between nations, whereas the peoples of the United Nations have in the Charter reaffirmed their faith in fundamental human rights, in the dignity and worth of the human person and in the equal rights of men and women and have determined to promote social progress and better standards of life in larger freedom, ...
>
> Now, therefore, The General Assembly, Proclaims this Universal Declaration of Human Rights as a common standard of achievement for all peoples and all nations. . . .

Try it yourself:

1. What AIM question would you use for a lesson on the Universal Declaration of Human Rights?

2. Which sections of the preamble to the Declaration of Human Rights would you have students read in class? Why?

3. Design different types of questions (content, comparison, opinion, and analysis) to help students understand the meaning of the document, its historical context, and its implications for today's world.

4. Would you have students write the answers to these questions as a classroom activity or homework assignment, or would you ask the questions during class discussion? On what basis would you make your decision?

5. What SUMMARY question would you use for a lesson on the Universal Declaration of Human Rights?

HOW CAN TEACHERS REINFORCE STUDENT UNDERSTANDING?

Applications:

Extra questions or activities that draw on, broaden, or review what students learned in a lesson or unit. They can be part of a lesson, a follow-up homework assignment, or a new lesson. They can be used to review prior lessons, as transitions to future lessons, or to bring units to a close and prepare students for exams. At the end of a class period, many teachers have students write a summary of what they learned during the lesson in their social studies journal.

Applications allow teachers to assess student learning. They are also a way for a class to review for a test. Written applications can be completed in class as part of a lesson, during a separate period, or as a homework assignment. A simple application is to have students keep a social studies learning log. After each lesson, they informally write their thoughts about what they learned. Applications such as the cooperative learning team dramatic activity included later in this chapter can also be more complicated.

Sample Lesson Organizers

Jeannette Balantic, Laura Pearson, and Rozella Kirchgaessner (NTN) provide structured lesson organizers to guide discussions and writing to their classes. They find that the organizers provide students clear directions and visual representations that are particularly useful in classes where students have a wide range of writing skills. Organizers can be visual aids, such as diagrams, charts, and idea webs that allow students to see the relationships among people, places, ideas, and events, or a list of questions that help direct their writing.

Jeannette, Laura, Rozella, and I share a commitment to designing thought-provoking lessons that involve all students in our classes. Organizers are one of the tools that makes this possible. Jeannette's sample organizers are used to review broad content areas in global history classes. Students use the first organizer to write speeches supporting their candidate for "Best Leader in Indian History." After the speeches have been presented in class, students use the second organizer to evaluate the candidates before they cast their ballots.

ORGANIZER 1: ELECTION FOR BEST LEADER IN INDIAN HISTORY

Candidates: Asoka of Maurya, Akbar of Mughal, Chandragupta of Gupta, Jawaharlal Nehru, Indira Gandhi

Directions: You have been hired as speech writers for one of the candidates for "Best Leader in Indian History." You must write a speech for your candidate so he or she can persuade the people of India to support his or her candidacy. Use the following organizer to help you write the speech.

My name is _____.

I was the leader of India during _____.

I should be elected "Best Leader in Indian History" because (give at least three reasons)

_____

_____

_____.

My opponents will criticize me because _____

_____,

but my accomplishments outweigh my setbacks.

There are good reasons not to elect my opponents.

_____ should not be elected because (give at least three reasons):

_____

_____

_____.

ORGANIZER 2: EVALUATING THE CANDIDATES FOR BEST LEADER IN INDIAN HISTORY

Leader/Empire	Positive Achievements	Negative Actions
Asoka of the Maurya Empire		
Akbar of the Mughal Empire		
Chandragupta of the Gupta Empire		
Jawaharlal Nehru of modern India		
Indira Gandhi of modern India		

Cast your ballot wisely. Which candidate do you support for Best Leader in Indian history? Why?

_____

_____

_____.

Laura uses formal organizers to help middle school students working individually to evaluate supplemental primary source documents at the end of a lesson.

ORGANIZER 3: DOCUMENT REPORT

Document Title: _____

1. Who is speaking/writing/illustrating?

_____

2. What is the date? (Make an educated guess if necessary.)

_____

3. What is the *explicit* meaning of this document (what is in the lines)?

_____

_____

4. Does the document have a hidden or implicit meaning ("between the lines")?

_____

_____

5. What type of document is this (primary or secondary source)?

_____

_____

6. In your opinion, is this a reliable source? Explain.

_____

_____

ORGANIZER 4: MAKING DIFFICULT DECISIONS

Please answer these questions in your social studies log.
1. Have you ever had to make a difficult decision about who should get something? Explain.
2. When your friends are planning an activity, how does the group decide what to do?
3. If you had free tickets to a special event but were not able to attend, how would you decide to whom to give them?
4. If you had enough rare medicine for two people but six people were sick, how would you decide who would receive it?
5. What factors would you consider when making a difficult decision?
6. How would you weigh a person's need, ability, and past history when making decisions about the distribution of scarce resources?

As an application, Rozella has her law elective classes write in their social studies logs at some point during nearly every lesson. She always provides students with prepared questions, which helps connect their experiences and understandings with the main ideas of the lesson.

Teaching Activity: Constructing Lesson Organizers

Try it yourself:

Select a primary source document or a newspaper article. Design a series of questions, a chart, or a graphic organizer that will guide students as they read and analyze the material.

Essay 1: Which Document Do You Choose?

While document-based instruction gives social studies students the opportunity to act as historians and social scientists, draw their own conclusions, and enhances analytic and literacy skills, there are drawbacks. Depending on the primary source document, or even the way it is edited, students can learn a very different version of history. As you can see from these selections, document-based instruction requires that teachers have a broad and deep understanding of events.

WHICH DOCUMENT DO YOU CHOOSE?

It's your classroom:

Would you use the activity sheets that follow in your high school class in lessons on the "home front" during the Civil War? Explain?

Do you have questions about the news articles and headlines? What are they? Why?

In your opinion, are the questions effective for guiding students through the passage? Explain.

A. *The New York Times*, Saturday, November 7, 1863:

The Pennsylvania Coal Mines/An Irish, Welsh And German Row At Mauch Chunk
The Fruits Of Copperhead Teachings
The Buckshots And The Molly McGuires On The Rampage/Four Men Killed

Last night Mr. C. K. Smith, coal operator at Yorktown, Carbon County, was murdered in a most brutal manner in his house, in the presence of his family, by a gang of Irish outlaws, known as 'Buckshots.' Mr. Smith was a loyal and highly respected gentleman, and was suspected of giving certain information to the Deputy Provost-Marshal, by which the latter, with the military under Capt. Yates, was enabled to arrest the drafted men.

"No Union man's life is safe in . . . Beaver Meadows and other mines of the middle coal fields. Seven or eight murders were committed there within the last few weeks. . . .

"Last August, a peaceable law abiding citizen, residing in Beaver Meadows, was made the object of an attack from a riotous crowd of Irishmen, who, under the names of *buckshots* and *Molly McGuires*, have disciplined themselves into an organization. . . .

"The success of this insolent violation of law and order inaugurated the reign of terror which has settled down on the district. Mob orators from Mauch Chunk have told these deluded miners that 'they must not submit to the Lincoln tyranny, . . . that they must stand in the door and resist every officer connected with the draft who comes near them. . . .'

"The draft enrollment has been made from the books of the mine owners. No man alive dare serve the notice. . . . These men have openly boasted that "no draft dare ever be made amongst them, . . . that they would murder any soldier or body of soldiers that came near them."

Questions:

1. What is going on in the United States at the time of these events?
2. According to this news article, what is going on the coal towns of Pennsylvania?
3. According to the news article, who is responsible for these actions?
4. In your opinion, should the people involved in these actions be punished? Why? How?

This article seems to be a good illustration of anti-war and anti-draft sentiments among both Copperheads and immigrants in the North during the Civil War and raises questions about the need to punish violence and prevent treason. But the article only tells a small part of the story. Based on War Department correspondence in the National Archives, it seems that the military draft was being used by coal mine owners allied with local Republican Party officials to break strikes by impoverished miners who were seeking higher wages.

According to a report from General Rausch, the arrival of troops returned the mines to operation and the operators proposed to "discharge the bad characters" if they were assured government support. The military eventually arrested about 70 miners but found little to prove disloyalty or resisting conscription. Charges against most of the accused were dropped, yet despite the lack of evidence, a military tribunal convicted 13 defendants who spent the remainder of the war in a prison camp. This part of the story did not appear in *The New York Times* until December 2001 in an article discussing military tribunals proposed by President George W. Bush (Bulik, 2001).

B. *The New York Times*, Headlines, May 9, 1863:

Examine the following headlines from *The New York Times*.

The Conscription Law. Important Proclamation By The President. May 9, 1863, p. 1

The Draft Begins. July 11, 1863, p. 3

The Mob In New York. Resistance To The Draft—Rioting And Bloodshed. Conscription Offices Sacked And Burned. Private Dwellings Pillaged And Fired. An Armory And A Hotel Destroyed. Colored People Assaulted—An Unoffending Black Man Hung. The Tribune Office Attacked—The Colored Orphan Asylum Ransacked And Burned—Other Outrages And Incidents. A Day Of Infamy And Disgrace. July 14, 1863, p. 1

The Reign Of The Rabble. Large Numbers Killed. Streets Barricaded, Buildings Burned. July 15, 1863, p. 1

Another Day Of Rioting. Mobs Armed With Rifles. Negroes Hung. July 16, 1863, p. 1

The Riots Subsiding. Triumph Of The Military. July 17, 1863, p. 1

Quiet Restored. Continued Precautions Of Authorities. July 18, 1863, p. 1

The Draft Here And Elsewhere. The Laws And The Mob. Aid For The Injured. Justice To The Victims. July 18, 1863, p. 1

The Law Of The Draft. The Question Of Exemptions. July 19, 1863, 1

Questions:

1. What happened in New York City between July 13 and July 18, 1863?
2. In your opinion, why did it happen?

I confess that I used these headlines in a lesson for many years without carefully reading the articles. While they point out the injustice of the draft, they primarily paint a very unsympathetic picture of the draft rioters. They are mainly Irish immigrants who assault and kill free African Americans in New York City.

While working on the New York State Great Irish Famine curriculum, I examined the articles more carefully and was surprised by what I learned. I have used bold type in two articles from *The New York Times* on July 14, 1863, to draw attention to specific points. Note three things: the "mob" did not burn the orphanage until after the attack on the armory; at the armory, police opened fire on a crowd that consisted largely of boys; and the majority the "rioters" at the orphanage were women and children. While this information does not justify what happened, it offers a different explanation of events.

THE ATTACK ON THE ARMORY IN SECOND AVENUE

At about 4 o'clock the crowd proceeded from . . . Lexington Avenue and Forty-fourth street to the armory situated on the corner of Second Avenue and Twenty-first street. The building was a large four story one, and was occupied for the manufacture of rifles for the Government. In the early part of the day the police authorities had placed in the building a large number of Policemen. **Their instructions were to protect the building and the property inside**, and to resist with force any attempt of the invaders to enter the premises. . . . At the time the first attempt was made to force the doors of the building, **the mob amounted to from three to four thousand, the greater part of whom were boys**. . . . The doors were burst open by means of heavy sledges, and the crowd made a rush to enter the building. **Those in charge of the building, acting under instructions, fired upon those who were entering** and four or five were wounded. One man was shot through the heart and died immediately.

"By this time the Fire Department of the District arrived on the ground, and were preparing to work on the fire, but were prevented from doing so by the mob, who threatened them with instant death if their orders were disobeyed. The cars were stopped from running and the horses in several instances were killed. . . . The rioters meanwhile danced with fiendish delight before the burning building, while **small boys sent showers of stones against the office**, smashing its doors and windows. . . . The military soon appeared, but was immediately routed, they fled to the side streets."

BURNING OF THE ORPHANAGE FOR COLORED CHILDREN

"The Orphan Asylum for Colored Children was visited by the mob **after 4 o'clock**. . . . Hundreds, and perhaps thousands of the rioters, the **majority of whom were women and children**, entered the premises and in the most excited and violent manner they ransacked and plundered the building from cellar to garret. . . . It was a purely charitable institution. In it there are on an average 600 or 800 homeless colored orphans. . . . After an hour and a half of labor on the part of the mob, it was in flames in all parts."

In a lesson using both the headlines and the excerpts from the articles in the Great Irish Famine curriculum, we ask students to do the following:

1. Use the newspaper articles to construct a time line of events.
2. Consider the accuracy and biases of the reports. Whose voice is included in these excerpts? Whose voice is missing? Is there anything that makes you question the accounts? Explain.
3. Why would people protest during a time of war? Why did protests turn into riots? What actions, if any, should be taken against people who participated in the riots?
4. If you were sitting on a jury trying rioters for murder and other crimes, would you find them guilty based on the evidence provided here? Be prepared to explain your views to the class.

Important goals in document-based instruction are teaching students to construct a story from component pieces, having them to base opinions on evidence, helping them to understand why people often have multiple perspectives on an issue, and encouraging them to seek more information when possible. I say this cautiously, but I think these are more important goals than them getting the facts "just right." To "force" students to think and to promote debate in class, I try to find sources that disagree about events as often as possible.

For the lesson that follows, students are introduced to the documents and our task as historians by a *DO NOW* activity. They read the statement by John Hains and answer questions that focus attention on key points in his testimony. As a motivation, they discuss their own experiences with the police and the problems of historical objectivity and weighing evidence carefully. We may also discuss the responsibility of a jury at a trial. After reviewing the Hains testimony as a full class, students work in teams to complete the rest of the activity. At the end of the period, teams report back to class on their investigations and conclusions.

Teaching Activity: Did New York City Police Participate in Anti-Black Riots in 1900?

Do Now:

Read the statement by John Hains (Nelson, 2000: 62–64) and answer the following questions.

1. What happened to John Hains on the evening of August 15, 1900?
2. According to his account, how was Mr. Hains treated by the police?
3. In your opinion, why would Mr. Hains swear to his testimony before a "Notary Public"?

> John Hains, being duly sworn, desposes and says: I reside at No. 341 West 36th Street. I am a laborer, and am at present employed as a longshoreman at Pier 16, North River. On the evening of August 15, 1900, I went to bed as usual at 9:30 o'clock. About two o'clock in the morning I was awakened by somebody beating me on the back with a club. When I awoke, I found six policemen in the room; they had broken in the door. They asked me for the revolver with which they said I had been shooting out of the window. I told them I did not have a revolver. One of the officers said that he had seen me shoot out of the window. Three officers then began to club me, while the other three were searching the house. . . . They dragged me out of the house, and proceeded to take me to the station house. I was only in my undershirt, being asleep at the time they broke into the house, and begged them to allow me to put on my trousers and my shoes. They only sneered at this, and one of the officers said, "You'll be d—d lucky if you get their [sic] alive." Here another of the officers pulled out a revolver and said, "Let's shoot the d—d nigger," to which a third officer replied, "We can take the black son of a b—to the station house as he is." When I got to the station house, I was bleeding from my head and other parts of my body, as a result of these clubbings. Sworn before me this 28th day of August, 1900. GEORGE HAMMOND JR., Notary Public.

Team Activity: Acting as historians:

1. Summarize the events described in the newspaper articles.
2. Do you believe New York City participated in anti-Black riots in 1900?
3. What evidence supports your position?
4. Why do you reject alternative explanations?
5. What other evidence would you want to examine to better understand what took place?

A. The New York Times, "Race Riot On West Side," August 16, 1900

> For four hours last night Eighth Avenue, from Thirtieth to Forty-second Street, was a scene of the wildest disorder that this city has witnessed in years. The hard feeling between the white people and the Negroes in that district, which has been smoldering for many years and which received fresh fuel by the death of Policeman Thorpe, who was shot last Sunday by a Negro, burst forth last night into a race riot which was not subdued until the reserve force of four police precincts, numbering in all over 100 men, headed by Chief Devery himself, were called to the scene and succeeded in clearing the streets by a liberal use of their night sticks.

B. The New York Times, "Police In Control In Riotous District," August 17, 1900

> The race trouble which was first encountered by the New York police force Wednesday night is now practically at an end. The burial of Policeman Thorpe and the arrest of the Negro Harris, who, it is alleged, killed him, both had much to do with quieting the feeling in the neighborhood of Ninth Avenue and Thirty-seventh Street, where the rioting started. . . . That policemen were not too active in stopping the attacks on the Negroes, and even went so far as to use their clubs on colored men who had been arrested, was fully developed at the West Thirty-seventh Street Station yesterday. The policemen, according to their own statements, are feeling vindictive against the colored people generally.

C. New York Times editorial, "A Disgrace To The Police," August 17, 1900

> The record of the police in the riotous attacks on the Negroes in their quarter on Wednesday night may briefly be summed up. They stood idly by for the most part while the

Negroes were being beaten except when they joined savagely in the sport, until the rioting threatened to extend dangerously; then they gradually dispersed the crowds, arresting almost no whites and many blacks, most of the latter being clubbed most unmercifully. This record is fully established by the testimony of many eye-witnesses, and there is nothing in the official reports so far published to contradict it.

D. The New York Times, "Negro Aliens Complain," August 18, 1900

Dr. M. S. N. Pierre of 318 West Forty-first Street, a Negro from British Guiana, and 200 of his fellow-British subjects have prepared a petition to Percy Sanderson, British Consul, asking him to take the necessary steps for their protection. The petition alleges that the signers were brutally attacked by the mob in the recent riots, and that the police, instead of giving them protection, actually urged and incited the mob to greater fury.

E. The New York Times, "Race Riot Investigation," September 20, 1900

The investigation conducted by President York of the Police Board into the charges of brutality made against the police during the late race riots on the west side was continued yesterday afternoon in the courtroom at Police Headquarters. . . . President York said: "I am going to examine these witnesses, and don't care whose cases they insure."

F. The New York Times, "Police Are Exonerated," December 9, 1900

Bernard J. York, President of the Board of Police Commissioners, who conducted the investigation made by the Police Board into the charges made against policemen in connection with the Negro troubles on the west side last August, made public yesterday a report on his investigation. The report fails to fix the blame for the clubbings on any policeman. It goes into detail in several cases, and states in substance that the police did no more than their duty during the days of the race riots.

Essay 2: Cooperative Learning in Social Studies Classrooms*

Social studies classes have heavy responsibilities. Students must learn content and concepts while mastering the skills needed for analytical thinking and information processing. In addition, they are expected to become members of learning communities, where they develop the ability to work with people from diverse backgrounds and explore the values they need to be productive citizens in a multicultural, democratic society. Making the situation for teachers even more complicated, there is increasing pressure to detrack schools so that students are no longer grouped into classes based on past academic performance. Often this change includes the mainstreaming of students who had previously been assigned to special education classes because of difficulties learning in traditional settings.

There is no magic wand that will transform students into avid social studies fanatics and change them from passive recipients of "knowledge" to active participants in learning. However, teachers have discovered strategies that can increase student involvement and interest in learning social studies, and enhance the social skills they need to work together. One of the most effective strategies is "cooperative learning."

Cooperative learning is not completely new. Students taught and learned from each other in colonial and frontier America; fans of author Laura Ingalls Wilder know that cooperative learning was used in her one-room prairie school house. As a result of the ideas of educators like John Dewey and Francis Parker, cooperative learning was popular in the late 19th and early 20th centuries, and many social studies teachers continue to use elements of cooperative learning in group work, projects, and reports.

*Based on A. Singer "A Teacher's Guide to Cooperative Learning in Middle School Social Studies Classrooms." *In Transition, Journal of the New York State Middle School Association* 10, no. 2 (1993), 16–21.

As with any other educational "innovation," advocates of cooperative learning frequently disagree with each other about the best approaches and the most important goals. However, some common points do emerge in the educational literature and in teacher discussions:

> Cooperative learning enhances student interest in social studies and other subjects because it gives them a greater stake in what is happening in their class and in their education. In large classes, it provides students with more "individual attention" because they are involved in helping each other. Students at all academic levels, including students who need remediation and students who are academically advanced, seem to learn more, and to learn more effectively, in cooperative learning teams.
>
> Cooperative learning is an especially effective way to teach inclusive classes. While students work together and help each other, content and support teachers are free to circulate around the room and provide assistance where it is needed.
>
> Cooperative learning enhances the social skills and values that are so important for future academic and economic success, and that are essential for participation in a multicultural, democratic society.
>
> Teachers must be able to define their own classroom goals and to experiment with the approach or approaches that successfully involve their students in learning.

I used cooperative learning teams in large high school classes with over thirty students, and I consistently found three major benefits. First, there is significant improvement in the willingness of students to write and in the quality of their writing. Working in cooperative learning teams, students are able to stimulate and support each other and to edit each other's work. Second, participation in discussions in their cooperative learning teams gave students an opportunity to test their ideas before presenting them to the full class and in front of me. It enabled students who generally did not participate in class discussions to participate more freely, either presenting their own ideas or representing their teams. As a result, class discussions were enriched by the addition of diverse viewpoints. Third, class attendance and punctuality in handing in assignments improved because students were able to make demands on their team members and follow up on each other. People having difficulty were less likely to get lost in the shuffle.

Before you experiment with cooperative learning in your classroom, I recommend reading additional resource material, participating in workshops sponsored by school districts, union-sponsored teacher centers, or local colleges. You should also talk with your colleagues. Someone may already be using cooperative learning in your school. Someone might want to start with you. It is easier to experiment with something new when you have a support group.

Teaching Activity: Goals and Objectives for Cooperative Learning

In classrooms using cooperative learning teams, students will learn to:

1. Work cooperatively in small groups.
2. Work cooperatively with students from other racial, ethnic, and religious backgrounds, and across differences created by gender, class, interest, and academic achievement level.
3. Give leadership to and accept leadership from others.
4. Respect the abilities and contributions of others.
5. Understand the roles of cooperation, compromise, and consensus in democratic decision making.
6. Participate in group and class activities with greater confidence in their individual abilities.
7. Explain their ideas orally and in writing more effectively.
8. Score higher on class and standardized tests.

Think it over:
Based on your experience as a student and your knowledge about the way that you and other people learn, how do you evaluate cooperative learning as a teaching strategy for social studies?

It's your classroom:
Many claims are made about the importance of cooperative learning. Which of these objectives would you consider most important in your classrooms? Why?

How do you begin?

Once you are committed to using cooperative learning in your classroom, the first step is defining your goals. What do you want to achieve? Do you want to focus on content or skills learning? Do you want to concentrate on group process and the development of democratic values? Do you want to address intergroup tensions in your class?

I advise beginning teachers to set achievable goals and integrate cooperative learning into their regular classroom approach. It also makes sense to involve students in discussions about the goals and processes involved in cooperative learning from the start. Listening to their ideas can be helpful, and it gives them a sense of ownership and responsibility from the beginning.

How do you organize cooperative learning teams?

How you organize teams depends on your goals. In general, a teacher has to make two basic decisions: Will students be permitted to choose their groups or will they be assigned to groups? Will groups be homogenous (students are more alike) or heterogeneous (students are more different)? If students choose their own cooperative learning groups, the groups will most likely be based on friendships or shared interests.

Advantages of student choice are: (a) group members will more likely have prior experience working together; (b) group members will share more interests in common, (c) there may be fewer intragroup conflicts for the teacher, the group, and the class to deal with, and (d) students may have a greater sense of identification with the process if they feel that they selected their own groups. Disadvantages of student choice are: (a) groups will more likely be segregated by race, ethnicity, gender, class, or academic achievement levels; (b) friendship bonds can be socially constraining as students try to learn and experiment; (c) some students will feel left out because they do not have a group of friends in the class; (d) teams based on friendship groups may tend to compete with each other in destructive ways; and (e) students will not have the opportunity to work

with a new and diverse team of people where they all start out on an equal footing.

Sometimes teachers prefer to assign students to academically homogenous cooperative learning teams. Usually this happens when a class has a wide range of achievement or reading levels. Homogenous groupings allow cooperative learning teams to focus on particular skills. They allow teachers to help some students with remediation while others are allowed to accelerate.

The disadvantage of homogenous grouping is that it imitates academic and social tracking. Students are separated out and can be stigmatized. Frequently students feel trapped in "lower-level achievement" groups and so are unwilling to invest in learning. Meanwhile, other students, working in accelerated groups, can become arrogant about their placement and contemptuous of their classmates. Instead of teaching students how to live and work with people who are different from them, homogenous groupings can reinforce the divisions that already exist in our society. Heterogeneous cooperative learning teams require more work from teachers. Student differences can contribute to group conflict, so teams will need active teacher involvement. Despite this, I recommend heterogeneous cooperative learning teams because they can provide students with a unique learning experience that helps teachers achieve key social goals.

Heterogeneous teams: (a) provide settings where people from different racial, ethnic, class, gender, and achievement groupings learn to work together in a structured, supportive, and mutually respectful environment; (b) allow students to learn from each other's strengths; (c) allow students to share across their differences, thereby enriching everyone's experience; (d) allow students to learn about shared interests, concerns, and humanity; (e) help teachers create miniature multicultural democratic communities that prepare students for active citizenship roles; and (f) stimulate all team members as students grapple with new ideas, concepts, and skills, and try to explain them to each other.

Students should discuss the advantages and disadvantages of choosing their own cooperative learning teams, and of heterogeneous versus homogenous groupings. After discussion, a teacher has the option to allow the class to make a decision or to make the decision for the class. Often after a discussion of the goals of cooperative learning, a class will reach consensus that it wants teams to be heterogeneous, and that the fairest way is for the teacher to set them up.

Some parents and educators have questioned whether heterogeneous cooperative learning teams penalize "high-achieving" students. Studies conducted by cooperative learning specialists from the University of Minnesota show that high achievers working in heterogeneous cooperative learning teams do at least as well on standardized academic tests as high achievers who work in competitive individualized settings. "Low-level achievers" and "middle-level achievers" who are involved in heterogeneous cooperative learning teams almost always do better on these types of tests. Meanwhile, all groups of students benefit from the important social skills they develop by working in cooperative learning teams.

Teaching Activity: Organizing Cooperative Learning Teams

It's your classroom:
Considering the different goals in social studies classrooms, how would you organize cooperative learning teams? Why?

How do I insure that all students on a team are involved in the team's activities?

Cooperative learning teams are not just a group of students who are given an assignment and left alone to complete it. In our society, young people, as well as adults, need to learn how to work cooperatively. For cooperative learning teams to work successfully, teachers and students must have clear group process goals. There must be a clear structure for democratic group decision making, and there must be a sense of shared group responsibility for the team. In *Circles of Learning* (1984), David Johnson, Roger Johnson, Edythe Johnson Holubec, and Patricia Roy suggested that the following should be built into the cooperative learning process:

> Teams need to depend on all of their team members to achieve the team's goals; students have to work together.
>
> Team members must be held collectively and individually accountable for learning by group members; everyone is responsible for the group.
>
> Responsibilities are divided up so that all team members have the opportunity to play both leadership and supporting roles.
>
> Teams are concerned with learning, and with maintaining cooperative group relations.
>
> Team members need to learn how to run meetings, make decisions, organize projects, divide responsibilities, and evaluate progress. Teachers cannot assume that students already have social and organizational group work skills.
>
> Teams must evaluate themselves, and be evaluated by teachers as teams, on both group process and the completed team product.

How are team responsibilities divided up among students?

Responsibilities can be divided up among students and then rotated on a regular schedule or when a team finishes a project. Team members will need to learn how to perform all of these important assignments. Sometimes a student will assume more than one responsibility. When team responsibilities are divided up, possible tasks include:

> **Team Responsibilities**
>
> Chairperson/Facilitator: The person responsible for leading team meetings.
> Recorder: The person who keeps a record of what is said at meetings and of team decisions.

Continued

Reflector: A person assigned to listen carefully during discussions so they can summarize them at the end of meetings.

Reporter: A person who reports on team problems and progress when the class meets as a whole.

Liaison: A person who meets with representatives of other teams to share ideas.

Organizer: A person who makes sure that work is completed on schedule and is ready to be presented or submitted.

Mediator: A person who attempts to resolve internal conflicts between team members.

How big should the cooperative learning teams be?

There must be at least two students, but more than six is probably unmanageable. Every group does not have to be the same size. Generally, I recommend groups of four. That way, if one person in a group is absent, there are still three people in class who can work together. But it makes sense to experiment. See what works.

How long should groups be together?

If they are going to learn to work together, groups have to have some permanence. They should at least have an opportunity to finish a major project and a chance to evaluate what they have learned. However, some cooperative learning teams may never work well together. The class may need a new mix. It may make sense to reorganize teams every marking period or every semester. Why not see what your students think?

How frequently should teams meet?

It is impossible to answer in advance. You have to evaluate what makes sense in terms of the projects that the students are involved in, how well cooperative learning seems to be going in your classroom, and the other demands that you want to make on them.

What does the teacher do while students are in their cooperative learning teams?

The teacher is busy, very busy, being an ex officio member of each cooperative learning team: You may (a) stick your head in a team meeting, listen for a while, say and do nothing, and then move on to another team; (b) ask a team a question or give it direction, helping a team solve an especially difficult academic problem; or (c) ask questions about how a team is working together. Perhaps some people are being left out or are disruptive. You may decide to ask team members to stop what they are doing and examine how they are working together. They may need you to mediate. They may need the entire class to get involved in their problem. They may only need to reflect on what they are doing in order to figure it out by themselves.

Teaching Activity: Setting up a Classroom

The way you set up a social studies classroom depends on what makes sense to you and your class, what you are doing on any particular day, and what you have available. Do you have moveable desks, tables, and chairs? Is the room crowded, or is there space to breathe?

If I have a choice, I prefer moveable chairs with fixed arms. Even when I use cooperative learning with a class, I usually start every lesson with the room organized into rows. It makes it easier for me to perform clerical tasks (e.g., take attendance, check homework) and to get students started with the lesson. From there, we switch the room around depending on what we are going to do that day. Students can work individually, with a partner in the next row, or four chairs can be made into a pinwheel so that student cooperative learning teams can work together. If there is a student or teacher presentation, if we are watching a video, or if something needs to be copied off the board, we can keep the desks in rows. For a fullclass discussion, we can "circle up."

Think it over:

When you were in middle school and high school, how did you like the room set up? Why?

FURTHER READING ON COOPERATIVE LEARNING

"Cooperative Learning." *Educational Leadership*, 47, no. 4 (December 1989/January 1990). This is a theme issue focusing on cooperative learning. Articles present research on the effectiveness of cooperative learning, different cooperative learning approaches, and selected resources for using cooperative learning.

Johnson, D., R.T. Johnson, Ed. J. Holubec, and P. Roy. *Circles of Learning: Cooperation in the Classroom*. Alexandria, VA: ASCD, 1984. This book is a brief (89-page) presentation of how to use cooperative learning in a classroom. It explains the goals, procedures, and problems in a cooperative learning program.

Kohn, A. *No Contest: The Case against Competition*. Boston, MA: Houghton Mifflin, 1986. This book presents the case for cooperation in the classroom as part of a shift toward a more democratic, productive, and cooperative society.

Wigginton, E. "What Kind of Project Should We Do?". *Democracy and Education*, Fall 1988, 1. This article is a brief introduction to the Foxfire program developed by Wigginton. The Foxfire program utilizes a cooperative learning approach that places a class project at the center of the curriculum. The program is discussed in greater depth in a series of books, including E. Wigginton. *Sometimes a Shining Moment*. New York, Anchor Press, 1985.

Essay 3: Sample Cooperative Learning Activity: Founders Discuss the Reasons for a New Constitution

In middle school social studies classes, fewer topics are examined than in high school, and they are covered in less detail. As a result, more time can be set aside for cooperative learning projects, individual and group research, book reviews, and student presentations. I would explain the project to the class before we began studying the U.S. Constitution. Student cooperative learning teams could work on researching and writing parts for presentation as a culminating unit activity.

Introduction

The authors of the U.S. Constitution were mostly wealthy and conservative. They were lawyers, merchants, investors, bankers, landlords, and plantation and slave owners. The original government under the Articles of Confederation owed money to 40 of these men. Not one of the 55 delegates who met in Philadelphia during the summer of 1787 was a woman, an African American, a slave, an indentured servant, an urban craftsman, a Native American, or a poor White farmer.

Our final project goal is to produce a television roundtable discussion, to try to answer this question: Could these men write a constitution and create a new government that would be fair to all Americans?

This package contains primary source documents from the time of the writing of the U.S. Constitution. These documents discuss the rights of people and the job of government. Some of the people who speak here favor the U.S. Constitution, some of them oppose it, and some of them are not sure whether it is a good idea.

For this project, each student team will be assigned one of the speakers:

- Find out as much as you can about your person and prepare a one-page biography of his or her life.
- Work together to translate the speaker's statement into more modern English.
- Use the biography and the translation to prepare a statement your person might make about whether the new U.S. Constitution is a good idea.
- Select a team representative to portray your historical figure during the television roundtable discussion. Team representatives will explain their historical figure's ideas about the U.S. Constitution and join in a panel discussion discussing its merits and problems.
- After all of the roundtable participants speak, the studio audience asks them questions and joins in the discussion.

Roundtable participants

Abigail Adams, correspondent, wife of John Adams

John Adams, 1st vice-president, 2nd president of the United States

Benjamin Banneker, a free African American who lived in Maryland, a scientist and architect

Benjamin Franklin, member of the Continental Congress and the Constitutional Convention

Alexander Hamilton, 1st secretary of the treasury, an author of the Federalist Papers, member of the Constitutional Convention

Patrick Henry, governor of Virginia

Thomas Jefferson, principal author of the Declaration of Independence, 3rd president of the United States

James Madison, secretary of the Constitutional Convention, an author of the *Federalist Papers*, 4th president of the United States

George Mason, Virginia delegate to the Constitutional Convention

Amos Singletary, delegate to the Massachusetts Convention to Ratify the Constitution

George Washington, president of the Constitutional Convention, 1st president of the United States

Robert Yates and James Lansing, New York State delegates to the Constitutional Convention

Other participants can be a small farmer from New York, a skilled worker from New England, an indentured servant from Virginia, an enslaved African from South Carolina, and people living on the Appalachian frontier.

SOURCES FOR QUOTES

Aptheker, H., ed. *A Documentary History of the Negro People in the United States*, vol. 1. Secaucus, N.J.: Citadel, 1951.

Bailey, T., and D. Kennedy, eds. *The American Spirit*, vol. 1, 5th ed. Lexington, Mass.: D.C. Heath, 1984.

Farrand, M. *Records of the Federal Convention*, vol. 1. New Haven, Conn.: Yale University, 1911.

Feder, B. *Viewpoints: USA*. New York: American Book Company, 1967.

Fitzpatrick, J., ed. *The Writings of George Washington*, vol. 28. Washington, D.C.: Government Printing Office, 1939.

Madison, J. *Notes of Debates in the Federal Convention of 1787*. Athens, Ohio: Ohio University, 1966.

Rossiter, C., ed. *The Federalist Papers*. New York: New American Library, 1961.

Primary source statements

Thomas Jefferson wrote in the Declaration of Independence:

1776—"We hold these truths to be self-evident; that all men are created equal; that they are endowed with certain unalienable rights; that among these are life, liberty and the pursuit of happiness. That to secure these rights, governments are instituted among men, deriving their just powers from the consent of the governed."

Thomas Jefferson discussed Shays' Rebellion:

1787—"I hold it that a little rebellion now and then is a good thing, and as necessary in the political world as storms in the physical. . . . It is a medicine necessary for the sound health of government."

1787—"What country can preserve its liberties, if their rulers are not warned from time to time that this people preserve the spirit of resistance? Let them take arms! . . . What signify a few lives lost in a century or two? The tree of liberty must be refreshed from time to time with the blood of patriots and tyrants."

Thomas Jefferson commented on the new Constitution:

1787—"I will now add what I do not like. First the omission of a bill of rights providing clearly . . . for freedom of religion, freedom of the press, protection against standing armies, restriction against monopolies . . . , and trials by jury in all matters. . . . Let me add that a bill of rights is what the people are entitled to against every form of government on earth."

Alexander Hamilton explained why the country needs a new U.S. Constitution:

> 1787—"We may . . . be said to have reached the last stage of national humiliation. There is scarcely anything that can wound the pride or degrade the character of an independent nation which we do not experience. . . . Do we owe debts to foreigners and to our own citizens . . . ? These remain without any proper or satisfactory provision for their discharge. Have we valuable territories and important posts in the possession of a foreign power which, by express stipulations, ought long since to have been surrendered? These are still retained. . . . Are we in a condition to . . . repel the aggression? We have neither troops, nor treasury, nor government. . . . Are we entitled by nature and compact to a free participation in the navigation of the Mississippi? Spain excludes us from it. . . . Is commerce of importance to national wealth? Ours is at the lowest point. . . ."

Alexander Hamilton defended the new U.S. Constitution:

> 1787—"Inequality would exist as long as liberty existed . . . , it would unavoidably result from that very liberty itself. . . . Inequality of property constituted the great and fundamental distinction in Society."
>
> 1787—"All communities divide themselves into the few and the many. The first are the rich and the well-born, the other the mass of the people. . . . The people are turbulent and changing; they seldom judge or determine right."

Amos Singletary feared what would happen if the U.S. Constitution were approved by the states:

> 1788—"These lawyers, and men of learning, and moneyed men, that talk so finely and gloss over matters so smoothly, to make us poor illiterate people swallow down the pill, except to get into Congress themselves. They expect to be the managers of this Constitution, and get all the power and all the money into their own hands. And then they will swallow up all us little folks. . . . This is what I am afraid of."

George Washington was critical of the Articles of Confederation:

> 1785—"The confederation appears to me to be little more than a shadow without the substance. . . . Indeed, it is one of the most

extraordinary things . . . that we should confederate as a nation, and yet be afraid to give the rulers of that nation . . . sufficient powers to order and direct the affairs of the same. . . . From the high ground on which we stood, we are descending into the vale of confusion and darkness."

> 1786—"The better kind of people, being disgusted with these circumstances, will have their minds prepared for any revolution whatever. We are apt to run from one extreme to another. . . . Would to God that wise measures may be taken in time to avert the consequences we have but too much reason to apprehend."
>
> 1786—"We have probably had too good an opinion of human nature in forming our Confederation. Experience has taught us that men will not adopt, and carry into execution, measures the best calculated for their own good, without the intervention of coercive power. . . ."

George Washington discussed Shays' Rebellion:

> 1786—"Mankind, when left to themselves, are unfit for their own government. I am mortified beyond expression when I view the clouds that have spread over the brightest morn that ever dawned upon any Country."
>
> 1786—"Without an alteration in our political creed . . . we are fast verging to anarchy and confusion. . . . What stronger evidence can be given of the want of energy in our government, than these disorders? . . . Thirteen sovereignties pulling against each other, and all tugging at the federal head, will soon bring ruin on the whole. . . ."

George Washington defended the new U.S. Constitution:

> 1787—"The legality of this Constitution I do not mean to discuss, . . . that which takes the shortest course to obtain them, will, in my opinion, under the present circumstances, be found best. Otherwise, like a house on fire, whilst the most regular mode of extinguishing it is contended for, the building is reduced to ashes."

Benjamin Banneker wanted to extend rights to enslaved Africans:

> 1791—"I freely and cheerfully acknowledge, that I am of the African race, and in that color which is natural to them of the deepest dye. . . .

Suffer me to recall to your mind that time, in which the arms and tyranny of the British crown were exerted, with every powerful effort, in order to reduce you to a state of servitude.... This, Sir, was a time when you clearly saw into the injustice of a state of slavery.... But, Sir, how pitiable is it to reflect, that although you were so fully convinced of the benevolence of the Father of Mankind, ... that you should at the same time counteract his mercies, in detaining by fraud and violence so numerous a part of my brethren."

Abigail Adams discussed Shays' Rebellion:

1787—"With regard to the tumults in my native state which you inquire about, I wish I could say that the report had exaggerated them. It is too true Sir, that they have been carried to so alarming a height as to stop the courts of justice in several counties. Ignorant, restless desperadoes, without conscience or principles, have led a deluded multitude to follow their standard, under pretense of grievances which have no existence but in their imaginations. Some of them were crying out for a paper currency, some for an equal distribution of property. Some were for annihilating all debts, others complaining that the Senate was a useless branch of government, that the court of common pleas was unnecessary, and that the sitting of the General Court in Boston was a grievance. By this list you will see the materials which compose this rebellion, and the necessity there is of the wisest and most vigorous measures to quell and suppress it. Instead of that laudable spirit which you approve, which makes people watchful over their liberties and alert in the defense of them, these mobbish insurgents are for sapping the foundation, and destroying the whole fabric at once."

John Adams wanted a strong national government:

1787—"Property is surely a right of mankind as really as liberty. Perhaps, at first, prejudice, habit, shame or fear, principle or religion, would restrain the poor from attacking the rich, and the idle from usurping on the industrious; but the time would not be long before courage and enterprise would come, and pretexts be invented by degrees to countenance the majority into dividing all the property among them.... The moment the idea is admitted into society, that property is not as

sacred as the laws of God . . . anarchy and tyranny commence...."

Patrick Henry feared the new U.S. Constitution would create a new king:

1788—"This constitution is said to have beautiful features; but when I come to examine these features, sir, they appear to me horribly frightful: among other deformities, it has an awful squinting; it squints toward monarchy."

1788—"Our rights and privileges are endangered. . . . The rights of conscience, trial by jury, liberty of the press, all our immunities and franchises, all pretensions to human rights and privileges are rendered insecure, if not lost, by this change."

James Madison believed the U.S. Constitution solved many problems:

1787—"The diversity in the faculties of men from which the rights of property originate is . . . an . . . obstacle to a uniformity of interests. The protection of these faculties is the first object of government.... The possession of different degrees and kinds of property immediately results, and . . . ensues a division of society into different interests and parties."

1787—"The most common and durable source of factions has been the various and unequal distribution of property. Those who hold and those who are without property have ever formed distinct interests in society."

1787—"A pure democracy can admit no cure for the mischief of factions. A republic promises the cure for which we are seeking."

Robert Yates and John Lansing refused to sign the new U.S. Constitution:

1788—"A general government, however guarded by declarations of rights, . . . must unavoidably, in a short time, be productive of the destruction of the civil liberty of such citizens who could be effectively coerced by it."

George Mason condemned the new Constitution:

1787—"This government will set out a moderate aristocracy: it is at present impossible to foresee whether it will, . . . produce a monarchy or a corrupt, tyrannical aristocracy. It will most probably vibrate some years between the two, and then terminate in the one or the other."

Benjamin Franklin was not completely sure:

1787—"I confess that there are several parts of this constitution which I do not at present approve. . . . I agree to this Constitution with all its faults, . . . because I think a general Government necessary for us."

1787—"Few men in public affairs act from a mere view of the good of their country, whatever they may pretend; and though their activity may bring real good to their country, they do not act from a spirit of benevolence."

Teaching Activity: Dramatic Presentation of Constitutional Controversies

The historical background for this activity comes from Charles Beard, *An Economic Interpretation of the Constitution of the United States* (New York: Macmillan, 1913) and Howard Zinn, *A People's History of the United States* (New York: HarperCollins, 1995).

Add your voice to the discussion:
This activity is based on a particular interpretation of the Constitutional Convention. In your opinion, is it legitimate to introduce it into a middle school classroom? Why or why not?

It's your classroom:
As a middle school teacher, would you be willing to invest the time necessary for this type of project? Why or why not?

Teaching Activities: Sample Social Studies Cooperative Learning Activities

Project teams:
Cooperative learning teams can be organized to conceptualize, research, outline, write, and present group reports. Cooperative learning team projects can include craft activities such as Navaho sand paintings; dramatic presentations; preparation of international foods; class folk songs, spirituals, or a traditional folk dance. These types of activities allow students with skills that are not usually drawn on in social studies classes to play important leadership roles. A cooperative learning team project can involve producing a current events newspaper, a dramatic presentation in class, or radio/television news broadcast. Cooperative learning teams can design questionnaires and conduct interviews.

Class work teams:
Instead of students working individually on class assignments, teams can work together and help each other with problem-solving activities, reading comprehension questions, map assignments, or worksheets.

Study groups:
Students can meet regularly in cooperative learning study teams to prepare for tests and quizzes.

Writing pairs:
Students can be paired off within their cooperative learning teams to read each other's written work, respond to each other's ideas, edit written work, and suggest alternatives.

Add your voice to the discussion:
1. As a secondary school student, how did you respond to cooperative learning activities and projects?
2. How would you use your own experiences to better organize cooperative learning?

REFERENCES AND RECOMMENDATIONS FOR FURTHER READING

Bloom, B., ed. *Taxonomy of Educational Objectives, Handbook 1: Cognitive Domain*. New York: Longman, 1985.

Bulik, M. (Dec 30, 2001). "American Gothic: Terrorists' And Tribunals in the Civil War Era," *The New York Times*, 4.7.

Dobkin, W., J. Fischer, B. Ludwig, and R. Koblinger, eds. *A Handbook for the Teaching of Social Studies*. New York: The Association of Teachers of Social Studies, 1985.

Manson, G., and A. Clegg. "Classroom Questions: Keys to Children's Thinking." *Peabody Journal of Education* 47, no. 5 (1970), 302–7.

Nelson, J. ed. *Police Brutality, An Anthology*. New York: Norton, 2000.

Seeger P., and B. Reiser. *Carry It On!* New York: Simon and Schuster, 1986.

United Nations General Assembly. *The Universal Declaration of Human Rights: A Guide for Teachers*. Paris: UNESCO, 1953.

PART III

Implementing
Your Ideas

7

How Can Social Studies Teachers Plan Controversy-Centered, Thematic, and Interdisciplinary Units?

Overview

> Refine educational goals
> Discuss the role of controversial issues
> Explore thematic and interdisciplinary alternatives for unit planning
> Find ways to connect educational goals with unit planning

Key Concepts

> Themes, Controversy, Complexity, Interdisciplinary Teaching, Connections

Questions

> How Should Controversial Issues Be Addressed in Social Studies Curricula?
> Why Teach Thematic Units?
> Should Teachers Express Their Opinions in Class?
> How Do You Organize a Controversy-Centered, Thematic Curriculum?
> Should Thematic Units Focus on Particular Social Groups?
> How Can Different Subjects Be Connected in the Social Studies Classroom?

Essays

> Women's History Month Curriculum
> Responding to Crisis: What Can Teachers Do?

HOW SHOULD CONTROVERSIAL ISSUES BE ADDRESSED IN SOCIAL STUDIES CURRICULA?

In the spring of 1989, while my 11th-grade U.S. history classes were examining the U.S. Supreme Court's 1973 *Roe v. Wade* decision, five young women approached me after class and asked if I would take them to Washington, D.C., to participate in a "pro-choice" demonstration. I told them that I would be glad to accompany them if it were organized as an official school trip. I recommended that they speak with the school's student political action club (I was the faculty advisor) about sponsoring them. The students agreed; the club and the school's administration gave approval;

the trip was arranged; and we went to Washington with a contingent from a local public college.

Because reproductive rights, abortion, and anything else that relates to teenage sexuality are controversial subjects in nearly every American community, most teachers avoid them like the plague. I could have sidestepped the issue entirely ("I'm sorry but I'm not able to go") or simply referred the young women to the local college group. However, I made a decision that supporting these young women's interest in active political involvement created a potential "learning moment" for them and other students in our school. The next fall, these young activists spurred the political action club to organize a schoolwide dialogue on the reproductive rights of teenage women and to send an entire bus load of students to participate in another pro-choice rally in the nation's capital.

The excitement generated by these young women and amplified by the political action club, spilled over into my social studies classrooms. Because of their own uncertainties about and encounters with human sexuality, the controversy over reproductive rights was already on the minds of many students and emerged as a major theme in my "Participation in Government" classes. That semester, students considered moral, philosophical, and political attitudes about reproductive decisions. They became avid readers of the newspaper and engaged in meaningful writing activities that helped them achieve higher literacy standards. They wrote and circulated petitions supporting their individual positions and attended public meetings. They designed posters and flyers; wrote speeches and letters; and examined the division among national, state, and local authority under the federal system, the balance of power

within the federal government, how a bill becomes a law, the constitutional amendment process, Judicial Review, and the local social service budget. Students also debated the roles of citizens and government in a democratic society, the relationship between church and state in the United States, and their ideas about other first amendment principles. If I had avoided this controversial issue out of concern with becoming embroiled in community battles over abortion and teenage sexuality, it is likely that all of this would have been lost.

The official position of the National Council for the Social Studies (NCSS) is that social studies teachers should "face up to controversy and . . . assume the special responsibility to teach students how to think." In the forward to its 45th annual yearbook, which focused on teaching controversial issues, Council President Jean Tilford wrote (Muessig, 1975: viii): "With the Watergate debacle etched on every mind, with disputes over school textbooks providing many pages of copy for newspapers, and with nations continuing to tear at each other's boundaries, teachers of social studies have been living closely with controversy." She concluded that the secondary school social studies curriculum was the best place to prepare young people to become active citizens armed with the critical thinking and problem-solving skills needed to form opinions and address these controversies. However, Tilford also noted that, (viii) "[I]n spite of the dissent of the 1960s, Vietnam, and proliferating energy crises, some social studies classrooms have ignored all aspects of controversy. Perhaps in fear, or because of feelings of inadequacy about coping with volatile issues, they have ignored the critical examination of contemporary events. As one observer of the current social studies scene commented,

"Better the artifacts than the actualities of the present."

Although I agree with the NCSS's concern with educating a probing, critical citizenry, I believe that this requires social studies teachers to emphasize—not just introduce—controversial, contemporary, and historical issues in the curriculum. Recognizing and discussing controversies offers students a much more accurate picture of human societies and history. It also legitimizes student's perceptions of the existence of class, ethnic, racial, gender, ideological, and generational conflicts. It makes students uncomfortable with pat answers and their own preconceptions; it stimulates them to delve for deeper meaning, to reconsider their own ideas, and to buttress their conclusions with supporting evidence. Last, but not least, a thematic focus on a controversial issue makes social studies learning a whole lot more exciting.

Teaching Activity: Is History Too Straight?

Among the "blanks" in history is the recognition of achievements by gay men and lesbians. For example, evidence suggests that prominent historical figures, including Hadrian, Leonardo da Vinci, Michelangelo, Eleanor Roosevelt, and Walt Whitman, were homosexuals. Many gay and lesbian activists argue that ignoring their sexual identity contributes to the sense that homosexuals are somehow dangerous aliens and should be kept separate and denied rights by the rest of society.

Think it over:
In your opinion, should teachers identify the sexual preference of prominent historical figures where strong evidence exists that they were gay or lesbian? Why or why not?

It's your classroom:
During discussion in class, a student refers to a historical figure, someone in the news, or another student as a "faggot." What do you do? Why?

WHY TEACH THEMATIC UNITS?

Important and/or controversial social studies issues cannot be addressed effectively in a single class period. Issues are too complicated and lessons will be messy. When a class is excited by a topic, everyone wants to speak. Students often go off on extended tangents. When disagreements are real rather than fabricated, people can be short tempered and dismiss each other. Outspoken, forceful students who present controversial views may upset classmates. Many days are needed to clarify issues, gather supporting evidence for positions, develop and give a fair hearing to alternative voices, examine criteria for evaluating positions, and reach either consensus or respectful disagreement.

A controversy-centered approach to social studies requires long-term careful planning; it is best addressed in thematic units or with long-term themes that are woven throughout the curriculum. Possible social studies topics that allow students to explore multiple points of view on controversial issues through a series of lessons include the following:

1. Struggles for women's rights in the United States or around the world.

2. Racial and ethnic similarities and differences, and their cultural or biological roots.
3. The role of religion in history, in our society, and in world events.
4. The impact of scientific thinking on societies, including the debate over evolution and creationism.
5. The existence and origin of universal human rights.
6. The possibility of social justice in the United States or other countries.
7. Whether racism, imperialism, and exploitation are peripheral or fundamental elements of civilizations.
8. The possibility of a more equal distribution of economic resources in society without jeopardizing either its ability to satisfy human needs and wants or individual freedom.

With broad themes that extend an entire year, students can (1) compare the promise versus the reality of U.S. society throughout its history, (2) explore the thesis that democracy is a unique product of Western history with roots in the ancient Hellenistic world, or (3) examine theories about human nature while attempting to understand the institution of slavery or periodic genocides. As students study history, they can also become involved in exploring and critiquing historical explanations. Does history record gradual and inevitable human progress? Is multiculturalism an effort to combat forced assimilation or a divisive ideology that threatens the survival of the United States as a nation?

Thematic teaching does not necessarily have to focus on controversial issues. Long-term themes that explore relationships between geography and history, the causes of historical events, the impact of technological development on societies, or the importance of cultural diffusion and exchange can avoid classroom controversy. Isn't social studies more exciting for both students and teachers, however, when we examine whether environmental disasters are caused by acts of nature or people, whether individuals or groups can change the course of history, who benefits from technology and who suffers, and the impact of cultural, economic, and political imperialism on conquered peoples?

Classroom Activity: Behind the Headlines

At the start of the term or a unit, student teams examine recent newspapers to identify broad social, economic, and political issues and raise their own questions about current events. Lists of issues and questions are compared, consolidated, and developed into underlying themes for repeated exploration during the semester.

Try it yourself:
Using a recent edition of the newspaper, make a list of broad issues behind the headlines and questions about these issues.

Add your voice to the discussion:
In your opinion, can students identify useful themes for long-term study? Why or why not?

It's your classroom:
Would you use the same theme or themes for an entire unit, a semester, or a year? Why or why not?

SHOULD TEACHERS EXPRESS THEIR OPINIONS IN CLASS?

New teachers are often uncertain whether they should express their opinions during class discussions, especially when their views are politically controversial. In Chapter 1, two members of the New Teachers Network, Richard Stern and Bill Van Nostrand, debated this question.

As educators and employees, beginning teachers are concerned with the professional ethics of stating their views, the pedagogical implications of both expression and silence, and the impact their statements will have on the ideas of their students. In addition, they worry how their views and their willingness to express them publicly will be perceived by students, colleagues, supervisors, and parents. Many new teachers opt to take the "safe" way out of this conundrum and keep their views to themselves.

At this point, we need to put aside our political fears (at least temporarily) and examine the educational issues involved. Politically safe choices may not be the soundest educational policies. I do not have a set rule about when teachers should offer their opinion in class, but I have no question that a teacher's views can be vital contributions to discussion in a democratic and critical classroom. When teachers state their views and open them up for evaluation by the class, it is a judgment based on their short- and long-term goals for their students and on the dynamic of a particular lesson. Consider the following series of ideas as you think about whether you want to add your opinions to classroom discussion.

Chapter 2 examined Myles Horton's and Paulo Freire's belief that knowledge is never neutral. Horton and Freire argue that every curriculum decision made by a teacher (e.g., which documents to introduce, facts to emphasize, questions to ask, students to call on) reflects a point of view. If that is the case, and I think it is, the question is not whether we express our opinions in class, but whether we express them openly so that students can evaluate them and feel free to agree or disagree with them.

• As teachers, we have to consider our goals and how we will achieve them when we decide whether we want to add our views to the intellectual hopper. Will a statement of our views open up discussion, close it down, or send it off on a tangent? Will it make it possible for students to consider new ideas? Will it empower students, particularly those who feel silenced by the classroom majority, to express unpopular views?

• When teachers express personal views, it demonstrates their willingness to share in classroom dialogue and open their opinions up for evaluation. It says to students that it is okay to take intellectual risks.

• Dewey argues that people learn from what they experience in class rather than from what is said. If teachers are afraid to speak out because of intolerance or political pressure, how will students learn to function within and to defend a democratic society?

• Sometimes I withhold my opinion because I am concerned whether the class discussion is doing justice to a position with which I disagree. Rather than play devil's advocate, I search for material that presents that view. On occasion, I have invited another teacher, a parent, or someone from a local advocacy group to meet with the class. When these people express their views clearly, it gives me more freedom to respond.

• Some issues are emotionally charged, so sensitivity is required whenever teachers express their views, but that does not mean it is automatically wrong to upset students. Sometimes people need to get a little upset before they can reconsider their beliefs.

Whatever decision I make about expressing my views, I try to keep in mind that my goal is for students to think about ideas and consider their options, not to parrot my views. I want students to be critical thinkers, not disciples. If students accept something as true because I say it, that only means they will also accept what they hear from their next teacher.

Teaching Activity: Should Teachers Express Their Views?

Controversial issues continually emerge in social studies classrooms. Topics such as affirmative action, racial and ethnic tension, reproductive rights, freedom of speech and religion, and gender bias or harassment are almost always in the news, and they are frequently at issue in schools. Verdicts in highly publicized trials, the actions of celebrities, and government policy decisions (sending U.S. troops to other parts of the world or modifying social welfare programs) also stir widespread debate.

When I was a high school teacher, I made political buttons to respond to some of these events. Now, thanks to recent developments in technology, I make iron-on decals for t-shirts to wear in class. I have also purchased some really good "message" shirts from a company called Northern Sun (1/800-258-8579 or http://www.northernsun.com). I usually wear the t-shirts under my regular shirts and at the end of a lesson climb on a chair, take off my tie and shirt, and use the t-shirt to enter classroom debate. The students generally cannot decide whether I am being "cool" or ridiculous.

Add your voice to the discussion:

1. Should topics such as these be discussed if they arise in a social studies classroom? Why or why not?
2. Should topics such as these be included in social studies curriculum? Why or why not? How?
3. In your opinion, can teachers remain neutral in classroom discussions? Explain.
4. In your opinion, should teachers remain neutral? Why?
5. Under what circumstances would you give your opinion during classroom discussion? Why?

HOW DO YOU ORGANIZE A CONTROVERSY-CENTERED, THEMATIC CURRICULUM?

Conflicting ideas about the nature of human rights makes an exploration of human rights issues an excellent thematic focus for a high school social studies curriculum. It can be adapted for use in classes studying the history and government of the United States, the origins and development of Western civilization, or the history and cultures of the non-Western world. During the course of a semester or a year, students can examine the origin of ideas about human rights and human nature, different notions about what constitutes a human right, and the impact of ideas about human rights on different societies and social groups (Banks and Gregory, 1996; Singer, 1996).

A thematic focus on human rights issues provides a lens for examining social conflicts as well as social and individual choices. It involves students in understanding the complexity of ideas and issues, how the same events can be viewed from multiple perspectives, and the importance of making informed judgments based on evidence, thoughtful consideration of individual and social values, and respect for difference.

I have used songs and children's literature to open up class discussions on struggles for human rights. "Die Gedanken Sind Frei" ("Ideas Are Free," available on the web at http://www. ingeb.org/Lieder/diegedan.html) and "Moorsoldaten" ("Peat Bog Soldiers," available on the web at http://www.crixa.com/muse/ unionsong/u090.html) are songs of the Germany anti-Nazi resistance. I also use more recent popular songs, especially "Rebel Music" by Bob Marley and the Wailers (available on the web at http://www. bobmarley.com/albums/rebel) and the work of Public Enemy (available on the web at http://www.publicenemy.com) and Pink Floyd (available on the web at http://www.allfloyd.com/lyrics/Lyrics. html).

My wife, Judith Singer (2001) was a day care director and is now a elementary school social studies educator. She "turned me on" to using children's literature, especially the work of Eve Bunting, to introduce human rights issues in the classroom. Bunting has written extensively on the right of children to be protected from "terrible things." Judi recommends reading Bunting's books with preschoolers and their parents and with "children" of all ages between.

Exploring questions (e.g., Is there such a thing as an inalienable human right? Where do human rights come from? How are human rights defined and by whom? Do human rights include the right or obligation to resist injustice?) involves students in broad discussions of philosophy, religion, anthropology, political science, and history, and an examination of a number of controversial issues. For example, students can examine whether the idea of inalienable human rights is a uniquely Western invention or also has roots and relevance in other cultures.

Classroom Activity: United Nations Charter

"the peoples of the United Nations have in the Charter reaffirmed their faith in fundamental human rights, in the dignity and worth of the human person and in the equal rights of men and women and have determined to promote social progress and better standards of life in larger freedom" (Universal Declaration of Human Rights, United Nations General Assembly, December 10, 1948).

Think it over:
In your opinion, what are the origins of "fundamental human rights"? Why do you believe these are the origins?

Try it yourself:
Suppose you were on the United Nations committee drafting the Universal Declaration of Human Rights. Make a list of the specific rights you would want to include in this document. Write a brief explanation of why you would include each of these rights.

A human rights theme lends itself to the kind of animated classroom dialogue that engages secondary school students. Students can discuss whether belief in the idea of higher laws and human rights requires belief in a supreme being or whether these ideas can be based on human consensus and shared social values. A related question, premised on belief in divine law is this: Who interprets God's will? In the United States in the first half of the 19th century, both proslavery and abolitionist groups argued that the Christian Bible justified their position. More recently, feminists, including practicing Christians, have argued that the right to control one's body and freedom of reproductive choice are fundamental human rights. They are challenged by the Roman Catholic Church hierarchy, which continues to declare abortion a violation of God's commandments and of an inalienable human right to life.

Examining the question Do human rights include the right or obligation to resist injustice? involves students in the issue of whether it is ever right to break a civil law in the name of fundamental human rights. Most students would argue that complicity with the Nazi regime in Germany was immoral and that violating Nazi laws through armed resistance or efforts to help people targeted for extermination were morally justified. Choices are generally not so easy, however. For example, does a nation committed to a belief in human rights have an obligation to intervene in contemporary genocidal conflicts in the Balkans or Africa? Should citizens refuse to pay taxes that are used to build nuclear weapons or that support dictatorial regimes?

Because of its tolerance of slavery, William Lloyd Garrison denounced the U.S. Constitution as a "covenant with death" and an "agreement with hell" (Feder, 1967: 127). Henry David Thoreau declared that he could not "recognize that political organization as my government which is the slave's government also (Feder, 1967: 127)." He insisted that "if the law is of such a nature that it requires you to be an agent of injustice to another," people should "break the law." Was the United States guilty of massive human rights violations? Do descendants of enslaved Africans or Native Americans have a right to reparations? In U.S. history classes, students can discuss these questions and whether efforts to help enslaved people escape from bondage, including armed resistance to slavery, were justified as a defense of human rights.

Thomas Jefferson, who "owned" enslaved Africans, is perhaps the best known U.S. advocate of inalienable human rights, including the idea that resistance to oppression is a fundamental human right. In the Declaration of Independence, Jefferson asserted that "whenever any Form of Government becomes destructive of these ends [achieving inalienable rights], it is the Right of the People to alter or to abolish it . . ." (Bailey and Kennedy, 1984: 101).

During the debate over the ratification of the U.S. Constitution, Jefferson expanded on his position regarding the legitimacy of resistance to oppression. In a letter to James Madison, he declared, "I hold that a little rebellion now and then is a good thing . . . It is a medicine necessary for the sound health of government." In a letter to William S. Smith, he argued, "What country can preserve its liberties, if their rulers are not warned from time to time that this people preserve the spirit of resistance? . . . The tree of liberty must be refreshed from time to time with the blood of patriots and tyrants. It is its natural manure" (Feder, 1967: 45).

In the United States in the 20th century, the idea of resistance to oppression as a fundamental human right is central to the nonviolent civil disobedience championed by Martin Luther King Jr. In King's Easter 1963 letter to the clergy of Birmingham, Alabama, he referred to both traditional Christian beliefs and to the ideas of the founders of the United States in order to defend direct action and resistance to oppression as crucial components of human rights. In other statements, King even suggested that the right to resist oppression, if we are prepared to suffer the consequences of our actions, may be the only human right that cannot be taken away.

Classroom Activity: Declaration of Independence

"We hold these truths to be self-evident, that all men are created equal, that they are endowed by their Creator with certain unalienable Rights, that among these are Life, Liberty and the pursuit of happiness." United States, Declaration of Independence, July 4, 1776

Think it over:
In your opinion, did the United States inherit a commitment to human rights from the European Enlightenment? Explain.
Does this statement represent a sufficient commitment to human rights for today's world? Why?

Try it yourself:
If you could rewrite this statement, how would you change it?

Classroom Activity: Ideas of Martin Luther King, Jr.

"We have not made a single gain in civil rights without determined legal and non-violent pressure. Lamentably, it is an historical fact that privileged groups seldom give up their privileges voluntarily. . . . We know through painful experience that freedom is never voluntarily given by the oppressor; it must be demanded by the oppressed."
—Martin Luther King Jr., Letter from Birmingham Jail, April 16, 1963 (King, 1963).

Think it over:
What forms of resistance by oppressed people do you believe are justified when oppressors do not respect human rights? Why do you support these methods? Why do you reject other methods?

Try it yourself:
King argued that "freedom is never voluntarily given by the oppressor; it must be demanded by the oppressed." Can you cite some historical examples that support this position? Can you cite some historical examples that contradict this position?

It's your classroom:
How would you help your students consider the morality of violence?

The notion of resistance to oppression as a basic human right has also been advanced by groups and individuals representing more conservative and traditional ideas. For example, in March 1995, in an encyclical condemning abortion and euthanasia, Pope John Paul II (1995: 133–36) called on Roman Catholics and other people of good will "under grave obligation of conscience not to cooperate formally in practices which, even if permitted by civil legislation, are contrary to

God's law." He declared that resisting an injustice is "not only a moral duty—it is also a basic human right."

A thematic focus on resistance to oppression makes possible a comparative study of resistance movements in different societies around the world. Students can discuss similarities and differences in the philosophies and strategies of the Mau Mau rebellion against the British in Kenya, the African National Congress campaign against apartheid in South Africa, Gandhi and the Indian independence movement, Irish struggles against the British for home rule, and various anti-Nazi resistance movements in Europe during World War II. Frequently students will discover that people they are sympathetic with engage in activities that violate other human rights that they value.

Clearly, a human rights theme has the potential to introduce many complex issues into a social studies curriculum. One of its most important contributions is this: It encourages students to discuss individual responsibility, how they would respond to human rights claims and violations of civil law by people they agree with, and by people who hold ideas and embrace causes that they find unacceptable or even disturbing. It also helps them understand that explaining and justifying an event or social movement are not the same things.

Learning Activity: Anti-Slavery Resistance*

In 1850, the U.S. Congress passed the Fugitive Slave Law as part of the Compromise of 1850. Under the new law, anyone who helped enslaved Africans escape to freedom was subject to heavy fines and jail sentences. This law incited northern opposition to slavery. Especially hated was a clause requiring white northerners to join the slave-catching posses. Ralph Waldo Emerson, an abolitionist, declared, "The act of Congress . . . is a law which every one of you will break on the earliest occasion—a law which no man can obey . . . without loss of self-respect. . . ." (Singer, 1996).

William Parker was the head of a local African-American self-defense organization in Christiana, Pennsylvania. In September 1951, he received word that slavecatchers were in the area. Parker, two other African-American men, and two African-American women, decided to protect local escapees. A battle ensued, and one of the slavecatchers was killed. Following the skirmish, 36 local African Americans and five local Whites, most of whom were bystanders during the battle, were charged with treason against the United States for resisting a U.S. Marshall, with violating the Fugitive Slave Law, and with rebellion against the government. Their trial, which drew national attention, involved the largest group ever charged with treason at one time in U.S. history. Among the defense lawyers was Congressman, Thaddeus Stevens, a prominent abolitionist.

Eventually, the people brought to trial were found "not guilty" of treason, and other charges were dropped. The trial helped convince southerners that their "property rights" would never be respected by a northern-dominated federal government. It left northerners increasingly angered by what they perceived as southern attempts to force them to participate in maintaining and defending slavery. As a result of the antislavery resistance at Christiana, the country moved another step closer to civil war and the abolition of slavery.

For high school students, the story of the Christiana antislavery resistance and the trial provides the opportunity to examine the meaning of human rights, especially the right to resist oppression. William Parker and his supporters clearly broke the law, and in the process of

---

*Adapted from A. Singer (1996) with the permission of *Social Science Record*.

breaking the law, a member of the U.S. Marshall's posse was killed. Students can discuss the following questions:
- Did a higher law give William Parker and the other Christiana defenders the right to break civil laws and resist returning the escapees to slavery?
- Did free African Americans and formerly enslaved Africans have an obligation to obey the laws of the United States, or did they have the human right to resist the injustice of enslavement, even if it meant killing a slave owner?
- What happens when rights are in conflict (e.g., the right to own property and the right to personal freedom)?
- What happens to a country if resistance to its laws is recognized as a human right?
- Was resistance to slavery in the name of human rights a cause of the Civil War?
- Could slavery have ended without civil war if the people who wanted to abolish slavery had been willing to compromise instead of insisting on the human rights of enslaved Africans?
- What would you have done if you were William Parker? Why?
- What would you have done if you were a local White person ordered by a marshal to join a slave-catching posse? Why?

Teaching Activity: Resistance at Christiana, Pennsylvania

As follow-up activities, teachers can try some of these ideas.
- Students can stage a trial of William Parker and the Christiana defenders for treason and/or murder, using primary source documents as evidence.
- Students can write editorials for an 1851 newspaper about the antislavery resistance and the trial for treason. They can either express their own views or the views held by different groups in the United States at the time.
- Students can create a portfolio of current events articles about contemporary resistance movements that resort to violence in the name of "higher laws" or human rights. They can compare their reactions to these movements with the resistance at Christiana.
- As a final project for a thematic curriculum based on an exploration of human rights issues, a class or school can sponsor a convention at which students discuss historical and contemporary issues relating to human rights and draft their own statement on human rights. At the convention, students can represent themselves or different nations and historical groups.

It's your classroom:
1. Would you use activities such as these in your classroom? Why or why not?
2. Would the race or ethnicity of your students influence your approach to these questions and activities? Why or why not?

SHOULD THEMATIC UNITS FOCUS ON PARTICULAR SOCIAL GROUPS?

Throughout human history, including most of U.S. history, women have been, at best, second-class citizens. Their continuing second-class status is reflected in many social studies classrooms in which the roles played by women in society and their achievements in the past and present continue to remain virtually invisible. Although the names and faces of women now appear more frequently in social studies textbooks, their inclusion is generally an addition to an already existing curriculum. Female heroes are discovered and fit into previous topics and categories. There is little exploration of the role of women in earlier societies: the ways they lived, the accommodations they were forced to make to patriarchal and oppressive social mores, the familial and community networks and institutions they built, or the struggles women engaged in to achieve legal, political, and economic rights. Nel Noddings (1992) argues that a completely reconceptualized social studies curriculum should focus on women's culture, the realm of the home and family, the idea of women's work, and the role of women as community and international peacemakers.

Over the years, Andrea Libresco became so frustrated with the gaps in textbooks that she encouraged her students to place post-it notes in their social studies books adding new information about women and other groups. Each new "generation" of students learns from the previous generations and provides its own insights.

In the first edition of *Social Studies for Secondary Schools* (1997), I examined how major middle school, high school, and advanced placement U.S. history textbooks reported on woman's suffrage. For this edition, I decided to see how some of the publishers had changed their coverage. One of the first things I noticed was that publishers had expanded the teams that write and edit textbooks and have included more women. Whether this is the reason or not, coverage of the struggle of women to win the right to vote seems to have improved. What do you think?

Middle School—1984

Ernest R. May, *A Proud Nation* (1984) mentioned campaigns for woman's suffrage six times. An insert containing the

Constitution, the Amendments, and comments informed students that "the right to vote was finally extended to women in 1920" (266). The unit on An Era of Improvement discussed movements for reform, including the women's rights movement. It included a photograph of Susan B. Anthony and a caption that recounts her arrest and conviction for voting in the 1872 presidential election (370–71). This unit also included a full-page focus on "Lucy Stone's Solitary Battle" for women's rights (374). Campaigns for women's rights were reintroduced in the section on post-Civil War corruption and reform. This section contained a map showing when women gained the right to vote in different states, two pictures representing the suffragist campaign of the World War I era (525–29), and a full-page focus on Abigail Scott Duniway's leadership in the battle for woman's suffrage in Oregon (536). The right of women to vote also received brief mention in the section on reforms during Woodrow Wilson's administration, but the book failed to mention that Wilson opposed woman's suffrage and agreed to it only as an emergency wartime measure (553).

Middle School—2002

Recently, McDougal, Littell replaced *A Proud Nation* as a middle school textbook with *Creating America, A History of the United States* by Jesus Garcia et al. (2002). This book has expanded coverage on the struggle for the right of women to vote. The 19th amendment is discussed in the section on the Constitution (273), which includes a photograph of women marching with the banner "I Wish Ma Could Vote" and a recent photograph of members of the Congressional caucus for Women's Issues. The unit on A New Spirit of Change, 1820–1860 includes a chapter on "Abolition and Women's Rights." It includes three pages (443–45) on women reformers, photographs of Lucretia Mott, Susan B. Anthony, and Elizabeth Cady Stanton with extended captions quoted from the Seneca Falls manifesto and Sojourner Truth and a political cartoon on family "discord" resulting from the women's rights campaign. Women are discussed again in a chapter on westward expansion, which describes the battle by the Wyoming territory legislature to ensure that woman could vote (569). In Unit 7, Modern America Emerges, the battle for suffrage takes center stage. A march by suffragists in Washington, D.C., in 1914 and a quote from Susan B. Anthony open the unit. The third section of Chapter 22, "Women Win New Rights," discusses women in the Progressive Movement and has two pages on the successful campaign for suffrage (652–53). This includes a map showing when women gained the right to vote in different states. The material on Abigail Scott Duniway's leadership in the battle for woman's suffrage in Oregon was dropped. The impact of suffrage on the ability of women to run for office is discussed in the section of the 1920s (714). The book still fails to mention that President Wilson opposed woman's suffrage and agreed to it only as an emergency wartime measure (653).

High School—1985

Winthrop D. Jordan, Miriam Greenblatt, and John S. Bowes, *The Americans: The History of a People and a Nation* (1985) mentioned campaigns for woman's suffrage in three places. The section on amendments to the Constitution included a drawing of women attempting to vote for Susan B. Anthony for President of the United States. The caption read: "Forty

years after the first introduction of a bill in Congress, women secured voting rights. Susan B. Anthony was arrested for voting in 1872" (191). The chapter "Populism, 1876–1910," contained a two- and one-half-page subchapter, "Women Continue Their Struggle for Suffrage." It included a picture of Susan B. Anthony and Elizabeth Cady Stanton and a discussion of feminist objections when the 15th Amendment failed to make provisions for women. It also mentioned the formation of the National American Woman Suffrage Association in 1890, local initiatives and legal efforts to secure the right to vote, attempts to pass a constitutional amendment, and antisuffrage opposition (478–80). The final discussion of woman's suffrage occurred in three paragraphs on social change in the 1920s. They mentioned suffragist protests in front of the White House during World War I, Woodrow Wilson's decision to support voting rights for women, and a quote by Carrie Chapman Catt describing the long campaign by women to secure the right to vote. This section included a picture of women picketing the White House. The caption read: "The 1920s saw many changes, and one of the first and most important was the 19th Amendment" (566).

High School—1998

The 1998 edition of *The Americans* (1998) was edited by a team including Gerald Danzer, J. Jorge Klor de Alva, Louis Wilson, and Nancy Woloch. Early in the text (118–19), a two-page "Tracing Themes" section discusses the struggle for women's rights from colonial America through the 1996 presidential and congressional election campaigns, and the chapters on colonial America examine the debate over the "proper" role of women in the new republic (127). It mentions that the original New Jersey state constitution allowed women who owned property to vote, but this right was rescinded in 1807. The campaign for women's rights and the participation of women in reform movements (235–39) are covered in the unit on Jacksonian America, but the right to vote is not included. However, it is the focus of women's struggles during the Progressive Era and is discussed in several places (503–20). This section includes discussion of the major suffragettes and organizations, a special insert on Carrie Chapman Catt, an interesting addition on the strategies used to win the right to vote, and a detailed report on the final successful campaign.

Advanced Placement—1983

Thomas A. Bailey and David M. Kennedy, *The American Pageant: A History of the Republic*, 7th edition (1983) briefly mentioned woman's suffrage in four places. The chapter "The Ferment of Reform and Culture, 1790–1860," contained a two-page subsection, "Women in Revolt." It included a picture of Susan B. Anthony and a caption that identified her as "a foremost fighter in the women's rights movement, as well as in that for temperance and abolition." The caption mentioned her arrest in 1872 for voting. The section concluded, "The crusade for woman's rights was eclipsed by that against slavery in the decade before the Civil War. . . . Yet women were being gradually admitted to colleges, and some states . . . were even permitting wives to own property after marriage" (317–18). Two hundred pages later, four paragraphs discussed "Women's Rights and Wrongs." This section emphasized gains made by women after the Civil War, including securing the right to vote in some local elections and in western territories.

It concluded, "American females had long enjoyed a degree of freedom unknown in Europe" and that their "gradual emancipation" brought problems—an increasing divorce rate—as well as benefits (515–16). In the section on the Progressive movement, Bailey and Kennedy mentioned the revival of woman's suffrage and included an extended quote from a statement by President Theodore Roosevelt. Roosevelt offered lukewarm support for women's right to vote. He wrote, "Personally I believed in woman's suffrage, but I am not an enthusiastic advocate of it, because I do not regard it as a very important matter" (603). In the chapter "The War to End War, 1917–1918," a paragraph (accompanied by a picture of women picketing the White House) announced the passage of the 19th Amendment, crediting Woodrow Wilson's decision that woman's suffrage was "a vitally necessary war measure" (685).

Advanced Placement—2002

The American Pageant: A History of the Republic (2002), now edited by David M. Kennedy, Lizabeth Cohen, and Thomas A. Bailey and in its 12th edition, has undergone significant revision. The disenfranchisement of women is mentioned in an early section on the Massachusetts Bay colony (47) and the rights or lack of rights of women in colonial society in America receives extended coverage (73–83) in the chapter, "American Life in the Seventeenth Century, 1607–1692." The temporary New Jersey experiment with woman's suffrage is also mentioned (167–68) in a section that discusses the incomplete pursuit of equality in the new nation. The chapter "The Ferment of Reform and Culture, 1790–1860" still contains a subsection, "Women in Revolt," that is largely unchanged. However the picture of

Susan B. Anthony has been replaced by a picture of Anthony with Elizabeth Cady Stanton. The caption now discusses their commitment to suffrage but not Anthony's arrest (330–32). The new text contains a section on the outrage of Anthony and Stanton when the 14th and 15th Amendments granted African American males the vote but not women (490–91). Sections on the urbanization of the United States, immigration, the labor movement, and the Progressive era now highlight the role of women with new pictures and text. The voting break-throughs in the west (601) and the revitalization of the suffrage movement in the Progressive era (668–69) are included; the quote by Theodore Roosevelt has been dropped. The chapter "The War to End War, 1917–1918," now contains a two-page section, "Suffering until Suffrage" (711–13), with pictures that documents the final successful campaign for the vote. Woodrow Wilson's decision to support woman's suffrage as "a vitally necessary war measure" (712) is mentioned, but he no longer receives credit. *The American Pageant* (755) also describes how in the 1920s the Supreme Court used the 19th Amendment as a justification for removing minimum wage and workplace rules that had protected women workers.

Learning Activity: Evaluating Textbooks

Add your voice to the discussion:
1. What do you think of this textbook coverage? Is it sufficient? Is it good? Why?
2. Would textbook coverage be more effective if the sections on women were consolidated into one overall unit? Why or why not?

Try it yourself:
1. Become a textbook detective. Compare the way that different U.S. history textbooks discuss the struggle for woman's suffrage or another issue related to women in U.S. history. Do you feel coverage is adequate? Why or why not?
2. Language influences the way we think about ourselves and others. Examine a social studies textbook for possible sexist language. How would you address this use of language in your class?

It's your classroom:
1. Would you involve middle school (or high school) students as textbook detectives? Why or why not?
2. What would you do if classroom discussion showed that reactions to the textbook coverage differed for male students and female students? Why?

In his book, *The Disuniting of America: Reflections on a Multicultural Society* (1991), Arthur Schlesinger Jr. argued that the attention given to difference by multiculturalists and ethnocentrists threatens to reinforce "the fragmentation, resegregation, and tribalization of American life" (73–99). He was particularly concerned that school curricula that focus on specific ethnic or aggrieved social groups are celebratory rather than academic and critical. For most of my secondary school teaching career, I resisted efforts to have separate units on African Americans, immigrants, or women because I wanted their histories integrated into more comprehensive social studies curricula. However, what I have been forced to accept and what Schlesinger evidently refused to consider is that in most secondary school social studies curricula, the experiences of racial and ethnic minorities and the roles and contributions of women in our society are rarely considered unless separate units or classes are organized.

A Women's History Month unit can be included in social studies curricula on every grade level and in every subject area. In middle and high school U.S. history classes, a unit can focus on the participation of women in the development of the country. It can include the struggles waged to change the condition of, attitudes toward, and opportunities for women in the past and present. In a global history class, units can focus on women in a particular country, region, or century and examine findings from the United Nations Bejing Conference on the Status of Women (available on the web at http://www.un.org/Conferences/Women/PubInfo/Status/Home.htm). An economics unit could examine the changing role of women in the economy as producers and consumers. Units in U.S. government could focus on the struggle for women's rights, ideas about gender equity, and a comparison of the voting patterns of men and women. Contemporary issues of particular importance in a U.S. government curriculum include an Equal Rights Amendment, equal pay for equal work, reproductive freedom, women in government, and women in the military.

Teaching Activity: Women's History Month

Add your voice to the discussion:
Would you prefer a separate Women's History Month unit in the U.S. history curriculum, an independent women's history elective, or the integration of lessons about women into the regular curriculum? Why?

HOW CAN DIFFERENT SUBJECTS BE CONNECTED IN THE SOCIAL STUDIES CLASSROOM?

In the movie version of the *Wizard of Oz*, the Cowardly Lion sings, "If I Were King of the Forest." In the song, the lion explains what he would do if he were in charge of everything. If I were in charge of secondary education, students would define the questions they want to explore, all learning would be integrated, and social studies themes and projects would be at the center of our inquiry-based curriculum. Although I am not in charge, however, social studies can still be the focal point for interdisciplinary learning in our classrooms.

An interdisciplinary approach to teaching has a number of advantages. Subject classes explore similar ideas and reinforce similar academic and intellectual skills. Metaphors from one subject help students create meaning in other areas. Because knowledge is connected instead of atomized in unrelated pieces, it is easier for students to understand and remember information. Many middle schools now have a team approach that requires all subject area teachers to meet regularly and encourages integrated instruction.

In Chapter 1, I called social studies teachers the intellectual imperialists of secondary education. Because all knowledge is part of human experience and the creative arts and literature are central to human culture, social studies—especially when taught thematically—is interdisciplinary by its very nature. One reason for stressing the same social studies concepts over the course of years is that social studies understanding requires a tremendous breadth of knowledge, experience, and familiarity with a number of different academic disciplines.

In high schools that use block programming, thematic houses, or teaching teams, social studies is generally paired with language arts. For a number of years while I was teaching U.S. history at Franklin K. Lane High School, I shared students with Kevin McQuade, an English teacher. Working together informally, we drew up a list of historical novels for students to read during summer vacation, coordinated written assignments so that our classes emphasized similar skills, consulted on individual student performance, introduced common historical and literary references in our classes, and scheduled units so that Kevin could cover novels, stories, and poetry from the time periods students were studying in history class.

Social studies is easily integrated with other subjects as well. In my high school U.S. history classes, I used the 1925 *Tennessee v. John Scopes* ("Monkey") trial to explore scientific concepts such as fact and theory and to examine how scientists test their understanding of our world. In both U.S. history and global studies, the study of slavery and race prejudice provide opportunities to examine genetics, human origins, and human similarities and differences. Topics such as the development of river valley civilizations highlight the impact of the environment on human history. The Bronze Age, repeated agricultural revolutions, the era of industrialization in Europe, the study of modern wars, and the Space Age all illustrate the impact of technology on society. Students can study how technological development, especially during the U.S. Civil War, led to the defeat of native peoples living on the Great Plains and the transformation of the plains from semiarid pasture land to the "breadbasket" of the United States.

At Mepham High School in Bellmore, New York, Henry Dircks (NTN) uses geography to integrate biology, physics, chemistry, earth science, and mathematics into the global history curriculum. He works with teams of students to create demonstrations illustrating scientific principles behind seasonal monsoons in southern Asia, global warming, the depletion of the ozone layer, and the Pacific basin volcanic ring of fire. At St. Agnes High School in New York City, Daniel Bachman (NTN) organized a small band and chorus in his social studies classes so students could use music to study U.S. history. At Edward R. Murrow High School in Brooklyn, Sheila Hanley taught a 10th-grade Western Civilization course using works of art to illustrate changes in European society.

Interdisciplinary Ideas for Social Studies Classrooms

Science and social studies:
Henry Dircks (2002) uses the following activity in his global studies class to illustrate the impact of air currents and energy transformation on climate.

Adapted from Dircks (2002). Used with permission.

Why do seasonal rains return to India?

1. Place a large map of India on the floor. Cover the map with a sheet of oak tag. Blow up four balloons, tie 10-inch-long strings to each balloon, and place the balloons roughly where the Bay of Bengal and the Arabian Sea are located. Tape the ends of the strings to the floor.
2. Have students quickly lift the oak tag. This represents the upward movement of heated summer air rising over the northern mountains. As the hot air rises, clouds (balloons) are drawn off the water onto the land. The monsoons arrive in India.

Poetry and social studies:

The poetry of Walt Whitman, especially poems such as "O Captain! My Captain!" "I Hear America Singing," and "Thou Mother with Thy Equal Brood" provide vivid images of the United States in the era before and after the Civil War. In "Thou Mother with Thy Equal Brood," Whitman ascribes a special mission to the United States as a ship of democracy that carries the past and future of the entire world. The Harlem Renaissance poets, especially Claude McKay and Langston Hughes, are primary source commentators on conditions facing African Americans in the interwar years. I have had students read Hughes' work and write their own "I, Too Sing America" poems. Many poems, including those by Whitman, McKay, and Hughes, are available on the web at http://www.poets.org/poems.

Students can compare Robert Frost's poem prepared for the 1960 Kennedy inauguration with the poem by Maya Angelou delivered at the 1992 Clinton Inauguration. They both define what it means to be an American, but they do it very differently. These poems are available on the web at http://www.lib.virginia.edu/exhibits/frost/english/images/dedicat1.jpg and http://www.eserver.org/poetry/angelou.html.

In "To A Mouse," the 18th-century Scottish poet Robert Burns (available on the web at http://www.electricscotland.com/burns/mouse.html) explains that, despite human pretensions, human life and aspirations are just as fragile as the hopes of a humble field mouse. After reading this poem, students can discuss the role of individual action and will in shaping historical events and the contingent nature of history.

William Butler Yeats' 1922 poem, "The Second Coming," is an important historical document describing conditions in Europe and a sense of impending doom at the end of World War I. It is available on the web at http://www.cwrl.utexas.edu/~benjamin/316kfall/316ktexts/yeatssecond.html.

Literature and social studies:

Chinua Achebe. *Things Fall Apart*. Garden City, N.Y.: Doubleday, 1994. Jeannette Balantic has students in her global history classes read *Things Fall Apart* while they study 19th century European imperialism in Africa. In this novel, Achebe examines the culture of the Ibo people of Nigeria as they struggle to preserve their way of life in the face of European intrusion into their world. As students read the novel, Jeannette provides them with "organizers" that point them toward specific events and issues, help them gather information, and encourage them to think and draw conclusions about the experience of the Ibo people. For example, one organizer has students compile a list of "Aspects of Traditional Ibo Life" on the left-hand side of the page and "The Impact of Europeans" on these traditions on the right-hand side. They are asked to specifically consider family life, religious beliefs and rituals, village customs, community values, diet, government, and the division of labor. Another "organizer" has students draw a picture of the Ibo village of Umuofia as it is portrayed in the story.

Margaret Goff Clark. *Freedom Crossing*. New York: Scholastic, 1991. *Freedom Crossing* is the story of a young white girl named Laura who returns to her family's farm in western New York State after living with an aunt and uncle in Virginia. She discovers that her brother and a childhood friend are now conductors on the Underground Railroad and the farm is a station on the route to Canada. She must decide whether she is willing to violate fugitive slave laws and help a 12-year-old boy named Martin Paige escape to freedom. Rachel Gaglione Thompson of the NTN strongly recommends this book.

Music and social studies:

The song "Paddy on the Railway" dates to the 1840s. In the first edition of this book I identified it as the story of Irish immigrants to the United States during the potato famine in Ireland. I was wrong. Paddy leaves Ireland in 1842, but the potato blight does not begin until 1845. Large-scale Irish emigration to the United States, industrial England, and Australia actually started in the 1820s. Although their labor was crucial for the construction of the canals and railroads that bound the American north and west, they were generally not welcomed in this country. A traditional version that includes music appears in E. Fowke and J. Glazer, *Songs of Work and Protest* (New York: Dover, 1973), 84–85.

In eighteen hundred and forty-one I put my corduroy breeches on, I put my corduroy breeches on, To work upon the railway. *Chorus:* Filly-me-oori-oori-ay (3×) To work upon the railway.	In eighteen hundred and forty-five I found myself more dead than alive, I found myself more dead than alive, While working on the railway. *Chorus:* Filly-me-oori-oori-ay (3×) To work upon the railway.
In eighteen hundred and forty-two I left the old world for the new, Bad cess to the luck that brought me through, To work upon the railway. *Chorus:* Filly-me-oori-oori-ay (3×) To work upon the railway.	Oh in eighteen hundred and forty-six They pelted me with stones and bricks And I was in one hell of a fix, From working on the railway. *Chorus:* Filly-me-oori-oori-ay (3×) To work upon the railway.

"Asikatali" was sung by members of the African National Congress on picket lines as they protested against apartheid in South Africa. It is based on a traditional Zulu folk song. A version that includes music appears in E. Weiss et al., *Children's Songs for a Friendly Planet* (New York: Educators for Social Responsibility, 1986), 19.

Unzima lomtwalo, ufuna madoda,	A heavy load, a heavy, heavy load, it takes a man to carry it,
Unzima lomtwalo, ufuna madoda.	A heavy load, a heavy, heavy load, it takes a man to carry it.
Asikatali, nomasiya bozh, sizimiselu nkululeko,	We don't care if we go to jail, it's for freedom that we gladly go,
Asikatali, nomasiya bozh, sizimiselu nkululeko.	We don't care if we go to jail, it's for freedom that we gladly go.
Tina bantwan baseh Afrika, sizimiseli nkululeko,	We are the children of Africa, we struggle til our freedom's won,
Tina bantwan baseh Afrika, sizimiseli nkululeko.	We are the children of Africa, we struggle til our freedom's won.

Art and social studies—Comparing Madonnas:

In Christian European societies, the Madonna (the mother of Jesus) and her baby have been continuous subjects of paintings since the Middle Ages. A classroom can be set up as an art gallery and students can view pictures from different periods and countries. The portraits give insight into the way that people viewed both religion and the natural world. For example, in early paintings, the baby Jesus is drawn as a little man. Over the centuries, he is gradually transformed into an infant. Thousands of samples of the Madonna and child can be downloaded from the Web at http://images.google.com. You can also do special subsearches using the name of a painter.

Math and social studies:

Usually math and social studies cross paths when students need to read maps to calculate size and distance or to gather and use information from charts and graphs. The following activities use geometry to answer puzzling social studies questions. Sharon Whitton at Hofstra helped me design these examples.

1. How did people in the ancient Mediterranean world know the size of the earth? If we know the length of a section on the circumference of a circle (arc) and the angle created by lines

drawn from either end of the arc to the center of the circle, we can calculate the size of the entire circle. In the third century B.C., Eratosthenes, a Greek mathematician living in Egypt, used geometry to calculate the circumference of the earth.

At Syene, a city on the Nile River (now known as Aswan), the sun was directly overhead at noon on the day of the summer solstice (the first day of summer). The sun's reflection could be seen at the bottom of a deep well, but a vertical pole cast no shadow. However, at noon on the same day in Alexandria, about 500 miles north, the sun cast a shadow. Eratosthenes used a vertical pole and its shadow to create a right triangle and then measured the other angles. He then used a geometric principle (alternate interior angles created by a line crossing two parallel lines are equal) to figure out the angle created by imaginary lines drawn from Alexandria and Syene to the center of the earth. This angle represented approximately 1/50 of a circle (7°12). When Eratosthenes multiplied the distance from Alexandria to Syene by 50, he got the approximate circumference of the earth.

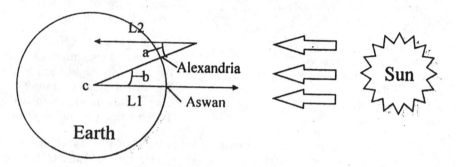

Used with permission of Sharon Whiton.

2. Did the Mayans learn how to build pyramids from Africans? Some Afrocentric scholars have argued that pyramids built by the Mayan people on the Yucatan Peninsula (in current-day Mexico) are evidence that African (or Egyptian) civilization spread to the Americas before the European arrival. Geometry suggests another explanation for the architectural similarities. Triangles are the most stable geometric shapes, and pyramids are the most stable large-scale structures. Attempts to build large temples and funeral monuments would lead both civilizations to these structures independently. Students can demonstrate the use of the triangle in construction with the following activity. Five student teams glue, masking tape, scissors, and an equal number of plastic straws. The goal is to build the largest stable structure using these materials. One team is required to build its structure using triangles as the basic building unit. The other teams can try anything but triangles.

Essay 1: Women's History Month Curriculum

This thematic middle school unit on the history of women in the United States is based on the work of Jeannette Balantic and Andrea Libresco and was part of their celebration of the 75th Anniversary of the 19th Amendment to the Constitution. They received support from a National Endowment for the Humanities teacher-scholar fellowship.

Jeannette and Andrea believe that their ideas on women's history can be taught as a unit in a U.S. history class as a U.S. women's history elective, although they prefer to integrate individual lessons throughout the regular social studies curriculum. This Middle School Women's History Month unit focuses on social history and includes 20 lessons (presented chronologically). The lessons mix attention to the achievements of individual women with an examination of women collectively. They include full-class, group, and individual activities.

1. Are women and men equally important in U.S. history?

Students discuss the significance of Women's History Month and establish criteria for evaluating the contributions of both men and women in U.S. history. Activities from this lesson can also be used as part of a final assessment of student learning at the end of the unit.

Activities: Students list either 5 or 10 women they believe made major contributions to the history of the United States (no entertainers, please). After completing their individual lists, students meet in small groups to consolidate lists and discuss evidence supporting their choices. After group ideas are written on the board, the class discusses criteria for deciding which individuals made major contributions to U.S. history. After establishing criteria, the class evaluates the initial list of famous women and discusses whether women and men are equally important in U.S. history.

2. What roles did women play among Native American peoples?

This lesson helps students understand that women have had different roles and rights in different societies.

Activity: Students read short passages about and discuss the position of women in different Native American societies.

3. What was life like for women in colonial America?

This lesson helps students imagine life on a colonial farm before the development of electricity and modern appliances.

Activities: Read and discuss excerpts from diaries of women from this era. Visit an historical restoration site and discuss ways that life then differed from that today. Recreate colonial or early American crafts.

4. How did women view the War for Independence and the founding of a new government?

Some activities are considered valuable contributions to society when performed by men, but are often minimized when performed by women. For example, Alexander Hamilton was an important advisor to George Washington during the Revolutionary War and the early years of the new government. Is his contribution to the revolutionary cause significantly different from that of Abigail Adams, whose correspondence with Thomas Jefferson and John Adams kept them aware of events affecting the nation and its people and advised them on the need for new laws and the Constitution?

Activity: Read and discuss excerpts from letters from Abigail Adams to John Adams and Thomas Jefferson.

5. What role did women play in the industrialization of the United States?

Because of traditional limits on the roles of women and legal restrictions on their property rights, women in the United States during the first half of the 19th century had little opportunity to acquire an education, enter a profession, or start a business. However, when workers were needed for the new factory system, New England farm women became the primary source of labor.

Activity: Student teams examine different primary source documents and report their findings about conditions for women in early mill towns and factories.

6. What role did women play in westward expansion?

A number of women documented the western expansion by the United States in their diaries and letters. Prudence Higuera, the daughter of a Spanish rancher, wrote about her impressions of the early U.S. settlers in California. Louise Clappe described the California gold rush in letters to her sister. A diary by Lydia Milner Waters reported on her family's experiences as they crossed the Great Plains and Rocky Mountains in 1855. Students can read and discuss excerpts from these sources. The *Little House on the Prairie* series by Laura Ingalls Wilder gives students insight into life on the frontier as the United States moved westward. Middle school students will also enjoy *My Antonia* by Willa Cather (Boston: Houghton Mifflin, 1918), a novel about the settlement of the prairie states during the 1870s.

Activities: Students read memoirs and books, write book reports that focus on the position of women, and present their reports in class as the basis for discussion.

7. Why did women rewrite the Declaration of Independence?

At the 1848 Women's Rights Convention at Seneca Falls, New York, Elizabeth Cady Stanton presented the Declaration of Sentiments that paraphrased the Declaration of Independence and declared "all men and women are created equal."

Activity: Students analyze the Declaration of Sentiments and compare it to the Declaration of Independence. The class discusses which grievances were most serious and whether the grievances outlined at Seneca Falls have been redressed in the United States in the last century and a half. As follow-up assignments, students compose a new Declaration of Sentiments that represents the views of other groups in American society in either the past or present (e.g., students, Native Americans, immigrants, or gay men and lesbians).

8. **How did women help end slavery in the United States?**

Women authors played a major role in the struggle to end slavery in the United States. Poetry and novels were used to express the hardship of slavery, protest against injustice, and celebrate resistance.

Activity: Students read and discuss excerpts from the work of Harriet Beecher Stowe, Phillis Wheatly, and Ellen Watkins Harper. Students write poems expressing their views on slavery.

9. **How did women help save the union during the Civil War?**

In the Civil War, women secretly passed as men in order to fight for their country and their families. Military action in the Persian Gulf in 1991 was the first time that large numbers of American women openly served as military personnel in a combat zone, but it was not the first time that American women went to war. Thousands of women served as nurses in World War II, Korea, and Vietnam.

Activity: Students read and discuss accounts of women who served in the Union Army during the U.S. Civil War (1861–1865). These accounts become the starting point to discuss whether women should participate in combat in the U.S. armed forces today.

10. **How were women stereotyped in 19th-century society?**

During the 19th century, middle-class women were taught to see themselves as fragile and ineffective. Despite these stereotypes,

housekeeping and "women's work" changed as increasing numbers of people moved from farms to cities. Changes also reflected the growing number of educated women.

Activities: Students examine 19th-century advice columns and children's books for examples of stereotypes about girls and women and compare them with attitudes today. The class compares life in contemporary families with 19th-century families. Students write to advice columns as 19th-century women. They exchange letters and answer each other's questions.

11. **Why did women emerge as leaders of reform campaigns?**

During the 19th and early 20th centuries, women were at the forefront of many U.S. reform movements. Women reform leaders included women's rights advocates Sojourner Truth, Lucy Stone, and Lucretia Mott; labor organizers Mary Harris "Mother" Jones and Elizabeth Gurley Flynn; populist orator Mary Lease; antilynching campaigner Ida B. Wells-Barnett; muckraking journalist Ida M. Tarbell; temperance leaders Frances E. Willard and Carrie Nation; Jane Addams, a founder of the settlement house movement; Clara Barton, who established the American Red Cross; Charlotte Perkins Gilman, a radical feminist; Florence Kelley, an advocate of protective wage and labor laws for women and an end to child labor; and Emma Goldman, an anarchist.

Activity: Student teams research female reform leaders. They present 3- to 5-minute "persuasive speeches" that explain a reform leader's view of U.S. society, the changes she advocated, and the tactics she used to achieve her goals. The class discusses issues that students are willing to support and how they would support them.

12. **What did women experience as immigrants and workers?**

From the 1880s to the 1920s, millions of women immigrated to the United States where they became workers, wives, mothers, and, eventually, citizens. These women and their families frequently suffered great hardships as they struggled to preserve families and build communities in a new country. Many women went to work in factories, especially in the garment industries, and became active labor union organizers.

Activities: Students read stories about women immigrants and workers and write "diaries" describing their lives.

13. Why did working women demand "bread and roses"?

In a spontaneous protest against a cut in their weekly pay, 20,000 workers walked out of the mills in Lawrence, Massachusetts, in 1912. During one of the many parades conducted by strikers, young girls carried a banner with the slogan, "We want bread and roses too."

Activity: Students read and discuss the poem, "Bread and Roses," and design and paint a wall mural depicting the struggle of women during the Lawrence strike.

14. How did women win the right to vote?

It took 133 years of struggle from the Constitutional Convention of 1787 until the ratification of the 19th Amendment to the U.S. Constitution for American women to secure the right to vote. The campaign for woman's suffrage produced outstanding women leaders, including Elizabeth Cady Stanton and Lucretia Mott, who organized the first women's rights convention in the United States at Seneca Falls, New York; Susan B. Anthony, a founding member of the National Woman's Suffrage Association in 1869; and Carrie Chapman Catt and Alice Paul, who led ultimately successful campaigns for the right to vote during World War I.

Activity: Lois Ayre (NTN) has her middle school students create half-hour news broadcasts of different historical topics, including the campaign for woman's suffrage. Student teams research an event; write a script that includes props, scenery, and costumes; and prepare a full-length video or act out a live broadcast in class. Every production includes an anchorperson, news reporters, and historical actors with different views of the event.

15. How did women reformers shape the 20th century?

During the 20th century, suffragists and feminists were frequently involved in other reform issues.

Activities: Student teams research the lives of 20th-century women reformers, including Ella Baker, Myra Bradwell, Rachel Carson, Marian Wright Edelman, Fannie Lou Hammer, Frances Perkins, Jeannette Rankin, Eleanor Roosevelt, Margaret Sanger, Mary Church Terrell, and Lillian Wald. After their research is completed, students organize their information into biopoems.

Biopoem Format

First name of person: _____

Title or role: _____

Descriptive words: _____

Lover of . . . _____

Who believed . . . _____

Who wanted . . . _____

Who used . . . _____

Who gave . . . _____

Who said . . . _____

Last name of person: _____

---

16. Why did African American women sing the blues?

Between 1900–1945, African American women experienced and described the "Great Migration" north, World War I, the "Roaring 20s," the Great Depression, and World War II. This interdisciplinary lesson draws heavily on art, music, and literature.

Activity: Students examine and discuss work by women writers Zora Neale Hurston, Jesse Redmond Fauset, Nella Larsen, Anne Spencer, Georgia Douglas

Johnson, Gwendolyn Brooks, and Margaret Walker; painter and illustrator Laura Wheeler Waring; sculptor Meta Warrick Fuller; and musical performers Marian Anderson, Ann Brown, Sippie Wallace, Camilla Williams, Gertrude "Ma" Rainey, and Bessie Smith. They also examine work by men who described conditions faced by women, including poetry by Langston Hughes ("Mother to Son") and Fenton Johnson ("The Scarlet Woman" and "The Lonely Mother"), and the mural art about the "Great Migration" by Jacob Lawrence.

17. Why did women lead opposition to war?
Throughout U.S. history, women have played leading roles in antiwar movements, even when this meant they risked being labeled as *traitors*. Examples include Jane Addams, president of the Women's Peace Party; Emily Greene Bach, 1946 Nobel Peace Prize winner; Congresswoman Jeannette Rankin; Coretta Scott King, Civil Rights and anti-Vietnam War activist; and Dr. Helen Caldicott, a leader in the campaign to eliminate nuclear weapons.

Activities: Students research the life of a woman in U.S. history who was an activist for peace. Students design a quilt square that presents the ideas, struggles, and achievements of the woman they researched. When all of the pieces are completed, squares are assembled into a giant "peace quilt."

Materials Needed for a Peace Quilt

Felt or paper (a large piece or pieces for the background; the number of square feet equals the number of students in the class)
12" × 12" pieces of felt or construction paper for the individual quilt pieces
Assorted colors of felt or construction paper
Markers
Glue sticks and glue guns
Scissors
Curtain rod for hanging

18. What role did U.S. women play in World War II?
Women's adaptation to the new roles created during World War II produced mixed feelings for women, men, and society in general and forced many people to reevaluate their perceptions of a woman's capabilities. Women proved they could build planes, tanks, and ships. Although thankful for the end of the war, many women were reluctant to give up their new jobs.

Activity: Diane Tully (NTN) has students examine articles in local newspapers about women during World War II.

19. How have women's lives changed since World War II?
Activity: Students interview their mothers, grandmothers, and other female relatives about changing attitudes toward women and new opportunities for women during their lifetimes. Topics include work, education, family roles, women's health issues, and access to political power. Women can be invited to come to class and discuss their experiences.

RECOMMENDED SOURCES ON UNITED STATES WOMEN'S HISTORY

American Social History Project. *Who Built America?* New York: Pantheon, 1989.

Eisler, Benita, ed. *The Lowell Offering: Writings by New England Mill Women (1840–1845).* Philadelphia: Lippincott, 1977.

Millstein, B., and J. Bodin. *We, The American Women: A Documentary History*. Chicago: Science Research Associates, 1977.

National Council for the Social Studies. "Homefront to Homelines." *Social Education*. Washington, D.C.: NCSS, 1994.

National Council for the Social Studies. "75th Anniversary of Woman's Suffrage." *Social Education*. Washington, D.C.: NCSS, 1995.

Schissel, L. *Women's Diaries of the Westward Journey*. New York: Schocken, 1992.

Schneiderman, R., and L. Goldthwaite. *All for One*. New York: Paul S. Eriksson, 1967.

Seller, M., ed. *Immigrant Women*. Philadelphia: Temple University Press, 1981.

Tanner, L. *Voices from Women's Liberation*. New York: New American Library, 1970.

Wenner, H., and E. Freilicher. *Here's to the Women*. New York: The Feminist Press at CUNY, 1987.

Wertheimer, B. We Were There: The Story of Working Women in America. New York: Pantheon, 1977.

Essay 2: Responding to Crisis: What Can Teachers Do?*

On the morning of September 11, 2001, I was visiting a student teacher and two members of the New Teachers Network at a junior high school in Queens, New York. We first learned of events at the World Trade Center when one of the teachers received a cell phone call from his sister. She was sobbing because her husband worked on a top floor in one of the towers and she feared he was dead.

Within minutes, school administrative personnel circulated around the building briefing teachers and telling us the school was in "lock down": no one was permitted to enter or leave. Administrators and teachers were calm and professional, but clearly there was no broader plan in place to address what was happening and how to respond to students who suspected something was going on, heard rumors about catastrophe and war, or simply wanted to know why they could not leave. Within an hour a crowd of concerned parents were outside the building and visible from classroom windows. Many were crying.

That afternoon teachers in the New Teachers Network began to exchange e-mail messages. They described their experiences and fears with each other in an effort to come to terms with what had happened and to figure out how to help their students understand events. Mentors, teachers from a number of schools in the area, and teachers educators

also met with more than 30 new teachers for three hours on Saturday morning, September 15.

What emerged from our conversations was a picture of what had taken place in the area's secondary schools on the day of the attack and the days that followed. In a number of schools in the city and the suburbs, students and teachers, alerted by cell phone calls or late arrivals to school, witnessed the second plane crash and the collapse of both towers from school windows. In some of these schools, teachers and students discussed what they saw and turned on news broadcasts to try to learn what was happening, but in others, teachers were ordered to remain silent and carry on with business in their classes as usual.

Unlike the well-coordinated emergency services response, each school and district seemed to go in a different direction. On the following days, some tried to return to normalcy and pretended that nothing had happened; others provided counseling for upset students but little else. A number of schools held memorial assemblies and then told students and teachers to get back to work. Some schools designated specific subject classes in which events would be discussed; other schools left it up to the discretion of individual teachers. Many New York City districts provided teachers with lesson plans. Some of these

---

*Maureen Murphy, S. Maxwell Hines, and Sandra Stacki, faculty advisors to the Hofstra New Teachers Network, helped with this essay. Other versions have appeared in Singer, et al, *Teaching to Learn/Learning to Teach*, and the newsletter of the New York State Council for the Social Studies.

encouraged teachers to involve students in open discussion and to challenge ethnic stereotyping. However, other plans limited teachers to responding to student questions with scripted answers.

Not one teacher in our network reported that districts either involved them in discussion of the events or asked how they thought they should respond to students. All they received were directives.

In a time of national and local crisis, when they were in the best position to help adolescents make meaning of events, the professionals most directly connected with young people were disempowered by our school systems. A number of teachers involved in the network reported to the group that as adults who know and are trusted by their students, they felt they had to act. They decided to "shut their doors," ignore the directives, and proceed on their own, no matter what the later administrative consequences. Many stressed that they believe their decisions helped to establish their classrooms as a communities where students felt able to speak out, could depend on each other, and were safe.

Maureen Murphy, the English educator working with the New Teachers Network put together a package of poetry to help students understand their feelings and suggested writing exercises that allow them to express their thoughts and emotions. Many classes wrote letters of condolence to victims of the attack. Michael Pezone's social studies classes published an entire magazine of student essays, drawings, and poems.

As the social studies educator working with the network, I distributed a simple lesson that a number of the teachers used in their classes. We divided the front board into four columns with these headings. What We Know, What We Need to Know, How We Feel about What Happened.

What We Think Should Happen Next. Working individually, in groups or as a full class, students filled in the columns and then discussed what they had written. Our goals were to help students distinguish between fact and opinion, substantiated information and rumor, and emotion and reason. We challenged stereotypes and stressed the difference between Islam, a religion with more than a billion believers, many of whom live in the United States, and the actions of one organized group or a few individuals. We also wanted to lay the basis for a long-term investigation of why the attack took place so students could analyze underlying and immediate causes, understand why many people in other countries believe they have been injured by the United States and its allies, and participate in debate over U.S. policy decisions. Many of the teachers followed up by having students use the Internet to collect newspaper articles from around the world on the attack and the U.S. response. Comparing reports helped students see multiple perspectives that were overlooked in the local media.

At the Saturday network meeting following the attacks, a biology teacher asked how she could be involved since events did not easily fit into her subject area. The group recommended that every teacher press schools and districts as part of professional development to involve teachers in discussion of these events and in designing a response strategy that includes lessons for different subjects. The teachers also believed that whatever their individual areas of expertise, in their classrooms, in extracurricular clubs, in the hallways, on teams, and in individual meetings, they needed to be there for their students as emotional supports and as role models to promote tolerance and to champion reason at a time when all of us may get swept up in a wave of irrationality.

Teaching Activity: Is It Acceptable to Question Government Policies in a Time of National Emergency?

It can be very difficult and politically risky to challenge government policies during a time of national emergency. The following elected representatives spoke out against war at different times in U.S. history. Examine each statement carefully and use your textbook or other sources to learn more about the situation the United States was facing at the time.

Questions:
1. What is the main point raised by the speaker?
2. In your opinion, was the speaker wrong to dissent in this way? Explain.
3. If you were a constituent, would you have voted for the speaker for reelection? Explain.

Resolution introduced by congressman Abraham Lincoln (1847)

Whereas the President of the United States has declared that "the Mexican Government . . . has at last invaded our territory and shed the blood of our fellow-citizens on our own soil." And whereas, This House is desirous to obtain a full knowledge of all the facts which go to establish whether the particular spot on which the blood of our citizens was so shed was or was not at that time our own soil; there, Resolved by the House of Representatives, that the President of the United States, be respectfully requested to inform the House . . . (w)hether the people of that settlement, or a majority of them, or any of them, has ever, previous to the bloodshed mentioned in his message, submitted themselves to the government or laws of Texas, or of the United States, by consent, or by compulsion, either by accepting office, or voting at elections, or paying taxes, or serving on juries, or having process served upon them, or in any way.

Representative Jeannette Rankin opposes U.S. entry into World War I (1917)

I knew that we were asked to vote for a commercial war, that one of the idealistic hopes would be carried out, and I was aware of the falseness of much of the propaganda. It was easy to stand against the pressure of the militarists, but very difficult to go against the friends and dear ones who felt that I was making a needless sacrifice by voting against the war, since my vote would not be a decisive one. . . . I said I would listen to those who wanted war and would not vote until the last opportunity and if I could see any reason for going to war I would change it.

Senator Wayne Morse votes "NO!" on the Gulf of Tonkin resolution (1965)

I believe that history will record that we have made a grave mistake in subverting and circumventing the Constitution of the United States. . . . I believe that within the next century, future generations will look with dismay and great disappointment upon a Congress which is now about to make such a historic mistake.

Statement by representative Barbara Lee (September 14, 2001)

I rise today with a heavy heart, one that is filled with sorrow for the families and loved ones who were killed and injured in New York, Virginia, and Pennsylvania. Only the most foolish or the most callous would not understand the grief that has gripped the American people and millions across the world. This unspeakable attack on the United States has forced me to rely on my moral compass, my conscience, and my God for direction. . . .

There must be some of us who say, let's step back for a moment and think through the implications of our actions today—let us more fully understand its consequences. We are not dealing with a conventional war. We cannot respond in a conventional manner. I do not want to see this spiral out of control. This crisis involves issues of national security, foreign policy, public safety, intelligence gathering, economics, and murder. Our response must be equally multifaceted.

We must not rush to judgment. Far too many innocent people have already died. Our country is in mourning. If we rush to launch a counter-attack, we run too great a risk that women, children, and other non-combatants will be caught in the crossfire. Nor can we let our justified anger over these outrageous acts by vicious murderers inflame prejudice against all Arab Americans, Muslims, Southeast Asians, or any other people because of their race, religion, or ethnicity.

It's your classroom:

Would you discuss these issues in class with students during a time of national emergency? Explain.

REFERENCES AND RECOMMENDATIONS FOR FURTHER READING

American Textbook Council. *History Textbooks: A Standard and Guide: 1994–95 Edition*. New York: Center for Education Studies/American Texbook Council, 1994.

Bailey, T., and D. Kennedy. *The American Pageant: A History of the Republic*. 7th ed. Lexington, Mass.: D. C. Heath, 1983.

Bailey, T., and D. Kennedy. *The American Spirit*. Vol. 1, 5th ed. Lexington, Mass: D.C. Heath, 1984.

Banks, D., and G. Gregory. "Introduction to the Special Issue on Human Rights." *Social Science Record* 33, no. 1 (1966), 4–5.

Feder, B., ed. *Viewpoints: USA*. New York: American Book Company, 1967.

Garcia, J., D. Ogle, C. F. Risinger, J. Stevos, and W. Jordan. *Creating America: A History of the United States*. Evanston, Ill.: McDougal, Littell & Company, 2002.

Jordan, W., M. Greenblatt, and J. Bowes. *The Americans: The History of a People and a Nation*. Evanston, Ill.: McDougal, Littell & Company, 1985.

Kennedy, D., L. Cohen, and T. Bailey. *The American Pageant: A History of the Republic, 12 ed*. Boston: Houghton Mifflin, 2002.

King, M. Jr. *Why We Can't Wait*. New York: Harper and Row, 1963.

May, E. *A Proud Nation*. Evanston, Ill.: McDougal, Littell & Company, 1984.

Muessig, R., ed. *Controversial Issues in the Social Studies: A Contemporary Perspective*. Washington, D.C.: National Council for the Social Studies, 1975.

Noddings, N. "Social Studies and Feminism." *Theory and Research in Social Education* 20, no. 3 (1992), 230–41.

Pope John Paul II. *The Gospel of Life*. New York: Times Books, 1995.

Schlesinger, A. Jr. The Disuniting of America: *Reflections on a Multicultural Society*. New York: Norton, 1991.

Singer, A. "Exploring Human Rights in a Thematic Social Studies Curriculum: With Lesson Ideas on the Christiana, Pennsylvania, Anti-Slavery Resistance of 1851." *Social Science Record* 33, no. 1 (1996), 16–23.

Singer, J. "Teaching Children about Human Rights Using the Work of Eve Bunting." *Social Science Docket* 1, no. 1 (2001), 61–62.

8

What Is a Project Approach to Social Studies?

Overview

    Introduce a project approach to social studies
    Examine current and past ideas for implementing a project approach
    Experiment with different project ideas

Key Concepts

    Project Approach, Interdisciplinary Learning, Integrated Curriculum

Questions

    How Do You Include Projects in Social Studies Curricula?
    What Are the Advantages of a Project Approach to Social Studies?

Essays

    Oral Histories—A Project Approach to Social Studies
    Technology-Based Projects Ideas

I think he made history in his own little way. I enjoyed this report because I got to know someone very special to me. Now I understand him better and I love him more. This report taught me that history can be made in many different special ways.—An 11th-grade high school student comments on her oral history of the life of an Haitian immigrant to the United States

My grandfather passed away on his 74th birthday, April 7, 1989. This was only two days after our second interview for this report. I am grateful that I had to do this oral report. It gave me precious time to spend with my grandfather. It let me see a side of him not too many people knew. He told me many stories. My favorite ones were of his childhood. He was a good man who I loved and will miss.—A note attached to an oral history report by a high school junior

HOW DO YOU INCLUDE PROJECTS IN SOCIAL STUDIES CURRICULA?

Over the years, many of my students have concluded oral history projects with personal statements about how important the class project was to them and their family. I believe that the most successful social studies projects achieve their goals because they connect the subject matter of the class with the lives of students. These projects engage students as historians or social scientists and stimulate them to want to know more about the events and people they investigate. They also encourage students to read and write, playing an important role in the development of student literacy.

During the late 1990s, a project approach to social studies education came under sharp attack from advocates of

273

content-based instruction, stricter standards, and a greater concentration on assessment. Critics including E. D. Hirsch (2000) charged that projects waste valuable instructional time that would be better spent in teacher-directed lessons where students learn concrete information. Gilbert Sewall (2000: 42–43) of the American Textbook Council suggested that "time-consuming, trivializing activities" were "displacing the cultivation of active minds." What I hope to show in this chapter is that a project approach is actually a more effective way to achieve higher social studies academic standards.

Project approaches to social studies can be used in secondary school classrooms in different ways, depending on the particular subject or grade level and on the teacher's or school's curriculum goals. Students can work as individuals or in learning teams. Projects can originate from student discussions, or teachers can present previously developed ideas to their classes. The focus of a particular social studies project can be on skill development, the research and development process, the product created by individuals or groups, or on student presentations in class. It can also be a combination of all of these. Projects can be at the center of the curriculum, or they can be used to supplement what students are learning.

Long-term projects are especially valuable because they help provide continuity from lesson to lesson. In a government class, an entire curriculum might be organized around citizenship participation projects. An oral history project can be integrated into a history curriculum so that the biographies researched and written by students become the primary sources that are used to introduce topics and events.

Project-based learning has its origins in the work of John Dewey (1938/1972),

William Heard Kilpatrick (1934), and the movement for progressive education in the early decades of the 20th century. Progressive educators argued for project-based learning as a way to promote democratic citizenship. Their projects encouraged critical thinking and allowed students to construct their own knowledge about the world around them. In addition, student decision making during the projects and the group nature of the activities provided students with democratic experiences.

Charles Howlett (1999), a cooperating teacher in the Hofstra program, avidly defends the project approach. He has students in his U.S. history classes research and write about the local history of their town; they have also published a local history journal. As part of the project, students conduct interviews with long-time town residents and examine diaries, autobiographies, letters, census data, official community documents, and local newspapers. Chuck finds that this project not only helps students understand the story of their town and its place in regional and U.S. history but also gives them an irreplaceable experience as practicing historians. I strongly agree with him. A project approach to teaching social studies supports calls for developing curriculum and activities that involve students in the work of historians and social scientists. These activities include developing hypotheses, organizing and conducting research, gathering data, answering questions, discovering trends, drawing conclusions, preparing and making presentations of findings, and conducting discussions with colleagues (teachers and fellow students).

A project approach to learning is a major component of the educational practice proposed by the Coalition of Essential Schools (CES); it is implemented at the Central Park East Secondary School (Meier, 1995; Meier and Schwartz, 1995) and in Foxfire programs. According to Ted Sizer (Sizer, 1984), the director of CES, student learning is best promoted through a program emphasizing that "less is more." The in-depth exploration that is part of a long-term project makes possible greater personalization of learning, more active involvement by students in shaping their education, and more authentic assessment of what students have actually mastered.

Foxfire programs (Wigginton, 1972, 1988), which began with efforts to motivate students and preserve southern Appalachian culture through the creation of a series of student-written publications, have formalized project-centered learning during the last three decades. In the Foxfire approach, students choose and design their projects, and they are involved in monitoring their own learning. The process tries to ensure that a project belongs to the students from start to finish.

In classrooms using the Foxfire approach, teachers act as mentors, not classroom bosses. Mistakes are expected and considered part of the learning process. Because reflection is crucial to learning, time is structured into the day so that students can think about and discuss their projects. Because learning is a social activity, projects are presented in the class, school, and the broader community.

In another approach, Dean Bacigalupo (NTN) provides his middle school students with a "project menu" at the start of the year. Each project is assigned a different point value based on complexity and the amount of work involved. Students select both the type of individual and group projects they want to complete and the topics they wish to explore so that the total point value of all their projects equals 100.

Teaching Activity: The Foxfire Approach—Perspectives and Core Practices

a. All the work that teachers and students do together must flow from student desire and student concerns.
b. The role of the teacher must be that of collaborator, team leader, and guide.
c. The academic integrity of the work must be absolutely clear.
d. The work is characterized by student action.
e. Emphasis is on peer teaching, small-group work, and teamwork.
f. Connections between the classroom work, surrounding communities, and the real world outside the classroom are clear.
g. There must be an audience beyond the teacher for student work.
h. New activities should spiral gracefully out of earlier activities.
i. We must acknowledge the worth of aesthetic experience.
j. Reflection—some conscious, thoughtful time to stand apart from the work itself—evokes insights and numerous revisions in our plans.
k. The work must include unstintingly honest, ongoing evaluation for skills and content and changes in student attitude.

It's your classroom:
The basic tenet of the Foxfire approach is that the interests and actions of students are central to a project and to learning. The teacher is seen as a "collaborator and team leader and guide." Do you think this is a feasible way to organize a social studies curriculum? Explain your reasons.

Source: Adapted from an article in *Hands On, A Journal for Teachers*, Spring/Summer 1990.

WHAT ARE THE ADVANTAGES OF A PROJECT APPROACH TO SOCIAL STUDIES?

In discussions of student portfolios and the authentic assessment of student learning, many teachers offer formal and informal methods for evaluating the learning that goes on during student projects. George Wood (1991) of the Institute for Democracy and Education recommends that teachers consider several points when they evaluate student projects. First, the criteria for evaluation should be clear, public, reflect student-generated goals, and include student ideas on what is important and well done. Wood believes that an evaluation should include discussion of how students have worked together as researchers as well as an examination of the final results of the project. He encourages the use of multiple evaluation points so that evaluations become part of reflection and learning.

Other useful organizing principles for a project approach to social studies include these:

1. Learning should be challenging as well as fun. Keep the projects interesting.
2. Students need to take responsibility for their learning. Do not be afraid to ease up on the controls. Student work will not be as polished without constant teacher involvement, but the projects will be theirs.
3. Invest time in student projects. Cover content by having students do things. Projects by their nature are hands on.
4. Encourage students to become historians and social scientists. What questions would they like to think about and answer? Have students consider hypotheses, design research, collect data, and discuss explanations.
5. The best projects tend to be interdisciplinary. Human understanding is not compartmentalized. Encourage students to use their talents from other areas. Include art, literature, music, and drama in social studies projects and presentations. Let students build on concepts they learn in science or math.
6. Projects should involve students in intellectual interaction with their colleagues. Learning is social. Knowledge spreads through exchange. Classrooms may get a little noisy.
7. Let students become teachers and present their findings to each other in classroom conferences and student publications. Let them use their imaginations to figure out creative ways to present their work to the class.
8. Projects should be long-term learning activities. This makes continuity possible in learning. Students think about what they are studying between classes and look forward to coming to school the next day.
9. Group projects provide students with experiences in democratic living and group decision making.

**Interdisciplinary Middle School Project Ideas—
Historical Restoration Site Guidebook and DBQ**

Laura Pearson (NTN) takes her seventh grade class to Old Bethpage, a local historical restoration site. Students prepare for the trip by reading about life in colonial America and the new nation. They travel around the site in teams and must answer questions about homes and buildings, food and farming, occupations and trades, education, clothing, recreation, and religion in the village. Teams take photographs that document their discoveries and prepare a guidebook based on their visit. As a concluding activity, students examine each others' photographs and must refer to them as "documents" in a document-based essay in which they describe life in the United States in the pre-Civil War era.

Museum Displays

Stephanie Hunte, Rachel Gaglione Thompson, and Robert Kurtz (2002) of the New Teachers Network developed this project jointly. They work at different middle schools, but brought their students together at Hofstra University to create a Museum of Slavery. The centerpiece of the exhibit was a Wall of Memory: Memorializing the Pain of Slavery and the Hope for Freedom. It consisted of more than 50 white t-shirts that had been torn, stained, and dabbed with brown and red paint. They represented both the pain of the slaver's lash and continuous resistance to bondage. Other exhibits included dioramas of slave life and the slave trade, symbolic representations of the artifacts of slavery, and replicas of slavery documents. Students from Stephanie's school also presented an African dance and a short play based on Virginia Hamilton's *The People Could Fly*.

At the museum, exhibits were displayed on tables or hung up with a card that explained what it depicted. After everyone had a chance to browse, each student or student team presented its exhibit to the entire group. At the end, students discussed with the group what they had learned from participation in the Museum of Slavery project. Many expressed surprise that students from other communities and ethnic groups had welcomed their involvement.

Each of the teachers approached preparation for the Museum of Slavery differently. While the class studied slavery, Rachel's students worked outside of class, independently, or in small groups to create a series of 3-dimensional displays. Students in Robert Kurtz's classes worked both individually and as a full class to create their exhibit. Stephanie organized the entire unit on slavery as a package for student teams, and the final team projects were made in class and used to assess student learning.

The Museum of Slavery   Escape on the Underground Railroad
Museum Displays section adapted from Hunte, Thompson, and Kurtz (2002). Used with permission.

The Great Depression and the New Deal

Henry Dircks (NTN) (Singer, Dircks, and Turner, 1996) developed these projects with eighth-grade classes. Students worked in cooperative learning teams. Sometimes all of the groups in a class did the same project and sometimes different teams worked on different things. Many of the projects can be adapted for other subjects and grade levels.

A. Front-page news:

Student teams create the front page of a newspaper. The date is January 1, 1930. This special issue of the newspaper explains the causes and impact of the Great Depression. In preparation for the project, students examine the structure and parts of newspaper articles. They can also read articles from local newspapers dating from the late 1920s and early 1930s. The following parts should be included in each story:

- A headline that discusses a specific cause of the Great Depression
- An introductory paragraph that explains this cause and its role in creating the depression
- The source on which the article is based: quote(s) from one or more imaginary or real local people who discuss the impact of the depression on your community
- An explanation of the impact of this cause of the Great Depression on the entire country

All of the stories should be typed and laid out as the front page of the local newspaper, either through cut and paste or using a desktop publishing program. The page should include a masthead and appropriate pictures and editorial cartoons. Students in a team can work on individual articles independently or as a group. The team is evaluated on the quality of its overall product.

Other front-page topics from U.S. history can include responses to the Declaration of Independence; reports on the completion of the Erie Canal or Transcontinental Railroad; coverage of Yorktown, Gettysburg, Pearl Harbor, Normandy, or Hiroshima; a Native American perspective on the arrival of Columbus or the Trail of Tears; Woman's Suffrage or the Civil Rights movement; or a union struggle such as the Homestead Strike, the 1937 GM sit-down strike, or Mother Jones and the coal miners' union. This project can also be used in global studies classes. They can focus on broad topics such as the French, Russian, or Chinese Revolutions; people such as Winston Churchill, Mahatma Gandhi, Nelson Mandela, or Corazon Aquino; or individual events such as Cinco de Mayo in Mexico; battles (Dunkirk, Dien Bien Phu, and Stalingrad); uprisings (the Warsaw Ghetto and Soweto); and historic elections or peace conferences.

B. Great Depression dramas:

This project involves English, art, and social studies classes. Students study history, literature, drama, and set and costume design. Teams should be organized at the start of the unit and work on their production while the class is studying the time period. The goal for students is to demonstrate their understanding of the impact of the Great Depression on the American people. Sample dramatic settings can include these:

1. Members of a family and their lives in a "Hooverville"
2. A public meeting where local government officials and citizens discuss New Deal relief proposals
3. Workers organizing a union or farmers responding to evictions
4. Life on the road or in a Civilian Conservation Corps camp

Questions for dramatizing a historical event:

- In what setting will your play take place?
- What events will provide the drama for your production?
- Who are the people in your production?
- What ideas from class and your research will you include in the play?
- How have events and social position affected the people in your play?
- How will your dialogue show the feelings of participants in your play?
- What message do you want viewers to learn from your play?
- What props and costumes will you need?
- What will be the background for your stage?
- How long will the play last?

C. Fireside chats:

Franklin D. Roosevelt (FDR) became President of the United States during a time of bank failures, high unemployment, and suffering by many people. At his inauguration, he promised a "New Deal" for Americans. In order to secure public confidence in the economy, FDR promoted recovery, relief, and reform. Periodically, FDR addressed the nation by radio to discuss his proposals. These talks are known as "fireside chats." They explained new legislation or programs, calmed public fears, and enlisted political support.

In this project, students write, perform, and audio tape a "fireside chat" designed to explain and sell a New Deal reform proposal to the American public. Students submit both a transcript and the audiotape for evaluation. Topics include the Emergency Banking Relief Act, the Federal Deposit Insurance Corporation, the National Recovery Administration, the Wagner Act, Social Security, the Security and Exchange Commission, Home Relief proposals, public housing projects, the Works Progress Administration, the Civilian Conservation Corps, or proposed Supreme Court reform. Each "fireside chat" should include the following:
- Explain the purpose of the proposed reform. Tell how the proposal will benefit individual Americans and the nation as a whole.
- Ask for the American people's support to make the new proposal work.

D. Alphabet agency posters:

The New Deal introduced the idea that active government was the solution to the problems created by the Great Depression. A number of government agencies were created to address these problems. Many of the agencies were best known to the public by their initials: the TVA, NRA, CCC, AAA, and WPA. For this project, students investigate the purpose of an agency and design and create a poster or mural that explains its role to the American people. This project works best when done in conjunction with an art teacher. As students design their posters, they should consider the following:
- Does the poster show the work being done by the agency?
- How is the work being portrayed?
- Does the poster illustrate the way the agency benefits the public?
- Will this poster win public support for the program?
- How does this poster present the New Deal's broader idea of active government as a solution to the problems created by the Great Depression?

E. The WPA guide to your community:

In the 1930s, the Works Progress Administration (WPA) sponsored Federal Writers' Project Guides to communities all over the United States. In addition, the Farm Security Administration funded professional photographers to document life in the United States. In this full-class project, students can examine sample guides and photos and use them as a model to create a WPA-style guide to their own community. Student teams can subdivide the project. Teams can investigate and write about the community's geography, history, architecture, local businesses, community resources, and important individuals.

Bridges and the City

Judith Singer and I (Singer et al., 1999/2000) developed this middle level U.S. history project as part of a summer school program. Part of its strength is that it is an interdisciplinary project that combines history, science, math, art, literature, and writing. As the final activity of the summer, students created a Museum of the City of New York that focused on the bridges that help unify its five boroughs and three major islands.

At the center of the museum was an 8-foot long, 7-foot tall replica of the Brooklyn Bridge that students could walk across. The actual bridge, completed in 1883, is a suspension bridge that spans the East River separating Manhattan Island and Long Island in New York harbor.

Since the original New York City was located on Manhattan Island and Brooklyn is located on Long Island, the bridge played a major role in creating one city of two.

Building the replica of the Brooklyn Bridge was a multistep process. Students began by reading *The Brooklyn Bridge* by Elizabeth Mann (1996) and preparing short reports about the history of the city and its bridges. The Brooklyn and Manhattan Bridge (McCullough, 1972), as the Brooklyn Bridge was originally known, was opened on May 24, 1883. At the time, the span between its towers was the longest in the world. The bridge dwarfed surrounding structures. It was the inspiration of an engineer named John Roebling, the inventor of a process for manufacturing wire cable. He first proposed building the bridge in 1867.

The project continued with a trip to the promenade overlooking New York harbor and a walk across the Brooklyn Bridge. On the promenade, students saw and discussed the bridge, the Statue of Liberty, Ellis Island, and the Manhattan skyline. They also sketched the bridge and read the poem, "The New Colossus," by Emma Lazarus. In the poem, written in 1883, Lazarus describes how the Statue of Liberty commanded the harbor shared by the twin cities of New York and Brooklyn.

As they walked across the bridge, students and teachers discussed what made it a suspension bridge. They examined the set of four woven steel cables that drape across the giant granite towers that stand near the opposing shores and the network of wires hanging from the cables that hold up the roadway. They could also see the Williamsburg Bridge (opened in 1903) and the Manhattan Bridge (opened in 1905) slightly upriver. These bridges were built decades after the Brooklyn Bridge when steel production had expanded and new technology was available. They have steel towers and can carry greater weight. As a result, subway lines connecting Brooklyn and Manhattan still run across these bridges.

When they returned to school, students discussed what they had learned and mapped out the activities for the next few days. They touched up and painted their sketches, wrote stories and poems about the history of New York City, and worked in teams to design and build model suspension bridges. The sketches, paintings, and models were all exhibited at the end-of-summer museum. When their models were complete, 10 students met with a community volunteer who is an amateur carpenter. He helped them design a wood-and-polyethylene rope suspension bridge that they could walk across. Students helped calculate the quantity of material that was needed to build the suspension bridge, measured and helped cut the wood, and assembled and painted it.

Even if they do not have the Brooklyn Bridge in their neighborhood, teachers can use interdisciplinary projects to help students discover the relationship between technology, history, and geography. Since ancient times bridges have been constructed using different designs because of the variety of geographical conditions and the availability of technology and materials. There are bridges made of rope, wood, rock, bricks, and concrete and steel. Modern suspension bridges such as the Verrazzano-Narrows in New York harbor and Golden Gate in San Francisco Bay span large open spaces. Arch bridges generally span shorter distances. Often an arch bridge consists of a series of connected arches that stand on a row of natural or humanmade islands. Very long bridges such as the Cheasapeake Bay Bridge in Maryland are actually parts of a series of different types of bridges attached to each other. Students can study ancient Roman arches and learn how this technological discovery made possible the construction of aqueducts, buildings, and bridges. Students can search for examples in their communities and build miniature keystone arches.

Just as bridges allow roads to cross rivers, canals make it possible for rivers to cross dry land. The construction of canals in the 19th century created a vast transportation network across the eastern United States. The remnants of famous canal systems have been turned into parks in New York, New Jersey, Pennsylvania, and along the Potomic River in Washington, D.C. and Maryland. Classes can visit the canals, study how they transformed society, and construct models of locks used to raise and lower boats along the canals. Similar interdisciplinary units can focus on the idea of crossroads or the way towns grew up along railroad lines.

Coming of Age Ceremony Mask Project

Many cultures have coming of age ceremonies that celebrate a young man or a young woman's entry into adulthood and the assumption of expanded responsibility within the community. Frequently they include special gifts from family and community elders that acknowledge puberty and the possibility of reproduction. Gifts can also be related to the acquisition of knowledge and expertise. Sometimes a coming of age ceremony includes taking a new name that symbolizes changed social status and spiritual transformation. In the contemporary United States, birthday parties and school commencements mark transformations in the lives of young people. Other coming of age ceremonies are religious in nature. They include the Roman Catholic confirmation, adult (or teenage) baptism among certain Protestant church groups, and the Jewish bar mitzvah.

Mask making can also have religious or spiritual significance. In West African cultures, wood carvers envision the spirit hidden within a piece of wood and hand carve a mask that liberates it. They do not start with an image and then construct it out of plaster, plastic, or paper mâché. In many traditional cultures, creating and wearing masks are part of the way people tell stories and pass along knowledge of tribal customs. Masks can represent spirits that protect or threaten a tribe and are often integral to dances and dramatic performances. The Barong dance of the island of Bali in Indonesia and similar dances in India and Sri Lanka use masks to tell the story of the struggle between good and evil. In an example of cultural diffusion, mask dances became an integral part of Buddhist religious ceremonies and spread with Buddhism into Myanmar (Burma), Cambodia, Thailand, and Tibet. In Tibetan Buddhism, masks are used in sacred mystery plays aimed at exorcizing malignant demons; the masks are believed to possess the qualities of the characters they depict. These masks are generally made of paper mâché and brightly painted.

In China and Japan, mask dances celebrate national history; in Korea, they tend to have a more local focus. More than 1,000 different masks were used in traditional Japanese No dramas to represent Gods, demons, animals, and human beings. The earliest known Japanese masks are made of clay and shell and are more than 2,000 years old. In Korea mask dances have political overtones. In the past, dancers used masks to hide their identities as they ridiculed the local elite. In Africa, masks often honor ancestors and are used in ceremonies that evoke their support for difficult personal or community decisions. Among the Ibo and Yoruba people of contemporary Nigeria and the Bambara of Mali, masks play an important role in initiation ceremonies for adolescents. In an example of parallel cultural development, they play a similar role in initiation rites among the people of Papua New Guinea in Oceania. In the ancient Mediteranean world, Egyptian, Greek, and Roman civilizations all had mask-making traditions. Until a 13th century papal order forbidding the practice, Roman Catholic clergy in Europe wore masks during some ceremonies and while dramatizing Bible stories.

Today, mask making remains important throughout Africa, among Native American people, and in the Pacific rim areas of Asia. Masks are also part of carnival celebrations in many European, Latin, and Caribbean societies.

This interdisciplinary activity developed with Stephanie Hunte (Singer et al., 1998) combines a coming of age ceremony with mask making. Instead of creating inauthentic versions of traditional masks, students create their own spirit masks using modern materials. The masks represent their hopes for their teenage years and adulthood.

Materials:

Clean plastic gallon jugs, any color (milk, water, paint, cooking oil, laundry soap, etc.); hammer, nails, and small wood block; retractable knife; latex acrylic paint (black, brown, white, blue, red, yellow, and green); brushes; markers; glue; scissors; construction paper; stapler; wool; straw; feathers; corn husks; needle and thread; buttons, cloth strips, index cards (*Note*: Tempera paint cracks and peels off the plastic jugs).

The section Coming of Age Ceremony Mask Project by Singer, A., L. Gurton, A. Horowitz, S. Hunte, P. Broomfield, and J. Thomas. "Coming of Age Ceremonies: A Mask Project." *Social Education Middle Level Learning* 3 (1998) with permission.

Procedure:

1. Close your eyes. Imagine a face that represents your inner spirit as it is transformed at a crucial point in your life. Is the spirit angry or happy, supportive or threatening? Are you an adolescent preparing for religious commitment or entering a new school or new grade, a teenager entering adulthood, an adult entering a new career, a person preparing for marriage or parenthood? Think of symbols and colors that describe the image in your mind.

2. Open your eyes. Draw a sketch of the face from your inner vision. Why do you make the choices that you make? Explain them to your neighbor.

3. Think of ways to transform your drawing into a 3-dimensional mask.

    a. Select a plastic jug. Holding it so the handle faces you (it will become part of the mask face), and cut up from the mouth of the jug until it is divided in half (discard the back piece).

    b. Use markers to sketch the face on the jug. Use the retractable knife to cut out the eyes and mouth. (*Note*: With younger students, teachers should do this part, or the eyes and mouth can be painted on later.) Use the hammer, nails, and wood block to punch small holes for attaching wool hair, feathers or buttons.

    c. Paint the entire mask with a base coat of paint. Allow to dry over night.

    d. Paint face and symbols on the mask. Allow to dry.

    e. Add wool, straw, cloth strips, buttons, corn husks, feathers, and paper designs. With thinner plastic water or milk jugs, it is easy to staple or sew on items. If the plastic is too thick, use paste.

4. On the index card, describe the transformation in life depicted by the spirit in the mask. Describe the spirit and the role it plays in your life. Describe the special symbols used in your mask.

RESOURCES ON MASK MAKING

Print (Reference books and pictures):

Brooklyn Museum of Art. *Ancestors and Art, African Gallery Guides.* Brooklyn, NY, Brooklyn Museum of Art, 1998.

Lechuga, R., and C. Sayer. *Mask Arts of Mexico.* San Francisco: Chronicle Books, 1994.

Mack, J., ed. *Masks and the Art of Expression.* New York: Harry N. Abrams, 1994.

Segy, L. *Masks of Black Africa.* New York: Dover Publications, 1976.

Singer, A., L. Gurton, A. Horowitz, S. Hunte, P. Broomfield, and J. Thomas. "Coming of Age Ceremonies: A Mask Project." *Social Education Middle Level Learning* 3 (1998), M14–M16.

Print (For students):

"Masks." *Faces* 3, no. 2 (1987).

Price, C. *The Mystery of Masks.* New York: Charles Scribner's Sons, 1978.

Hunt, K., and B. Carlson. *Masks and Mask Makers.* New York: Abingdon Press, 1961.

Web Sites:

http://www.Asiasociety.org/; www.Korea.com/; www.Japan-guide.com/

http://www.indo.com/culture/barong/; www.AskAsia.org/; www.AsiaCT.org/

Global History Projects for 9th and 10th Grade Classes—
Cultural Festivals

A number of network members have experimented with international festivals and culture days as part of the global studies curriculum. In some communities, they find parents or community residents who will come to school and share foods, clothes, stories, music, and family treasures. Stavros Kilimitzoglou, who lived in Greece for many years, uses a jigsaw approach to teach Greek culture to his class. Student volunteers learn Greek dances, perform them in class, and teach the dances to the other students. Lois Ayre and her students organize classroom stations where students can sample ethnic foods, listen to music, and examine cultural artifacts. Christina Agosti-Dircks, who teaches both regular and special education social studies classes, takes her students on trips to visit international restaurants. After sampling a national cuisine, they buy ingredients and prepare international foods as part of her global studies class.

Craft Ideas for Global History Classes

For the Great Irish Famine curriculum, Maureen Murphy and I included a series of traditional craft projects. We involved students in wool dyeing, Crios (belt) weaving, making a drum called the *Bodhrán*, dip candlemaking, and weaving children's toys and religious emblems out of straw.

This project is recommended by Christina Agosti-Dircks. Among the Jalisco and Nayarit people of Mexico, "Ojo de Dios" (God's Eye) is a sacred decoration that promises good luck, prosperity, health, and a long life. A father presents one to an infant at birth and on each birthday until the child is five years old.

Materials:
2-foot long pieces of yarn (multiple colors), 2 ice cream sticks per student

Instructions:
- Cross pairs of sticks. Staple or tie them together with yarn. Tie a piece of yarn to the center.
- Weave the yarn around a stick and then around the next stick, circling the cross. When a piece of yarn is almost finished, tie on a different colored piece of yarn and continue to weave.
- When the eye is complete, put a knot at the end so it does not unravel.

Cultural Museum Exhibits

Classes or student teams collect or re-create the material culture of a society or group of people. Artifacts and cultures are described on museum cards and displayed for the entire school. Students can give tours of the exhibit at scheduled times.

Hallway Maps for the Social Studies Corridor

Cover an entire wall with sections of white paper. Use an overhead projector and a transparency to project a map on the wall. Trace the map on the paper. Add political subdivisions, geographic features, or pictures illustrating local cultures or attractions. Paint and display.

Puppet Folk Theater

Middle and high school students can rewrite traditional, historical, or contemporary social studies stories written for elementary school age students as plays or puppet shows. They can create puppets and scenery and then present the shows in local elementary school classrooms. With this project, students in remedial classes can work with social studies ideas and materials, improve their reading and writing skills, and become positive role models for younger students.

Stories and books that can be dramatized include *Hiroshima No Pika* by Toshi Maruki (New York: Lothrop, Lee, and Shepard, 1990), a book about the effects of the dropping of the atomic bomb on Hiroshima; *The People Could Fly* by Virginia Hamilton (New York: Knopf, 1985), a collection of African American folk tales; *The Banza*, a Haitian story by Diane Wolkstein (New York: Dial Books, 1981); and traditional European and U.S. folk tales.

Archeological Grab Bag

The premise of this project is that you learn to be a social scientist by being a social scientist. Brendalon Staton (NTN) begins the project by giving each student team a mystery bag containing artifacts from a "lost society." Bags can contain dried bones and seeds, shaped rocks, plant fibers, plastic and metal items, coins, children's toys, cans, written items, and so on. Teams examine the artifacts, reconstruct the society, and report to the class about their findings. During the reports, fellow archeologists ask questions about interpretations and possible inconsistencies. Erin Hayden (NTN) has the artifacts buried in a sandbox and students have to carefully grid the archeological site. William McDonaugh (NTN) likes to begin by modeling the activity. The entire class gathers around him as he sits at a table in the center of the room and tries to reconstruct an animal from pieces of bone. As he works, he explains to students what he is doing and carefully writes down a description of each bone or fragment. In another variation, one team analyzes a web site with artifacts from an ancient society. For example, the Herakleion Archaeological Museum in Crete has a web site with artifacts from the ancient Minoian world at http://www. culture.gr/2/21/211/21123m/ e211wm01.html.

Depending on the amount of time you want to invest in the project, student teams can assemble their own artifacts and construct new societies. When they present these societies in class, they include the "history" of their society, a description of how people have adapted to their environment, and an anthropological discussion of its beliefs and values. Reports can include "maps" and dioramas. Once again, fellow archeologists ask questions about interpretations and possible inconsistencies.

Ancient World Alphabet Book

Tammy Manor (NTN) has students create an illustrated alphabet book (with topics ranging from A–Z) using history and myth from the ancient world. Students can focus on one society or include material from many groups. Each letter introduces a topic, person or event and contains a written description and an illustration (Xerxes of Persia invades Greece in 480 B.C.). Some of the illustrations are their own, others are downloaded from the web or pasted in from magazines and tourist fliers.

High School U.S. History Projects

Music videos:

Folk music from the 19th and the first half of the 20th centuries was rooted in the culture of ordinary people. We can study lyrics to learn about popular social, religious, and political concerns. If this music were written today, it would be very different. Vocabulary would change, and it would reflect different musical genres. An exciting project is to have students take the ideas expressed in a traditional song and present them in a contemporary musical context. An ambitious team could perform their work in class or produce a music video. The following example, based on the song "Union Maid," was written and produced as a video by students in one of my high school classes. The original version of "Union Maid" is available on the web at http://www.geocities.com/Nashville/3448/unionm.html.

> **Union Maid Re-mix**
> A long time ago, way back in the dayz
> There once was a group called the union maids
> A bunch of brave souls who were never afraid
> Of goons and ginks and company finks
> or deputy sheriffs who made a raid!
> As often as possible meetings were called
> At a place by the name of the union hall.
> But the meetings weren't always so pleasant and kind

The cops would come around next to no time
And try to chase everyone outta town
But the union maids would stand their ground and say . . .
We're sticking to the union (3×)
(you can't scare us) till the day we die.
These union maids were very wise
Wise to the tricks of the company spies
They'd never be fooled by the company stools
And made sure they'd always organize the guys
And always, always got their way
And made sure they struck for higher pay
They'd show their cards to the company guards
And this is what they'd say.
We're sticking to the union (3×)
(you can't scare us) till the day we die.
When the union boys had finally seen
the mad pretty, pretty, pretty union queens
They stood up and sang in the deputies' faces
They laughed and yelled in all of the places
And don't you know what the deputies done?
When they heard this song, they tucked their tails and began to run.
We're sticking to the union (3×)
(you can't scare us) till the day we die.
All you women that wanna be free
I got a little to you from me
When all of the workers come and unite
We'll be able to fight every fight
And instead of many we'll all be one—sticking to the union!
We're sticking to the union (3×)
(you can't scare us) till the day we die.

Political Cartoon History of the United States:

One year I found myself challenging my classes at the end of each period to design political cartoons illustrating an idea from the lesson. Students would shout out their ideas, and I would sketch them on the board. I shared the room with another teacher who liked the idea and started doing it also. Soon classes were competing with each other to come up with the best cartoons, and students with artistic ability replaced the teachers at the blackboard.

An interesting long-term project is to have student teams create a "Political Cartoon History of the United States." This is a good way of recognizing and encouraging students with artistic talents who might otherwise be lost in social studies classrooms. These cartoons were created by students in an 11th-grade class when we studied Industrialization and the Progressive Era.

Economics, Government, and Citizenship Projects

Consumer watchdogs: Investigative reporters: Students research local and state consumer laws and visit local supermarkets and restaurants to find out if they are in compliance with them. Stores that violate consumer laws can be reported to appropriate authorities. Stores that are in compliance can get commendations.

Product tests: Students decide on product standards, evaluate products, examine advertising, interview consumers, and compare prices. They can compare their results with studies by *Consumer Reports* and publish their own newsletter.

Public advocates: Students analyze local budgets, zoning codes, and laws and make presentations at public meetings.

News reports: Television news broadcasts aim for short sound bytes and older audiences. Students videotape and edit broadcasts into more in-depth thematic presentations. They can include their own research presented by student broadcasters and interviews with students, staff, and community residents.

Psychology and Sociology Projects

What is Normal Human Behavior?

Answering the question What is normal human behavior? provides an overall theme for a high school psychology course developed by Jeannette Balantic (NTN). This activity is designed to help students understand that *normal human behavior* is defined differently in different cultures, and that the definition of *normal* can be very broad. Students can work individually or in groups. As they read about actual individuals, they discuss and answer these questions:

- What types of behavior are considered normal behavior in this society?
- How does this individual behave?
- Is this behavior within the culturally defined boundaries of normal? Why or why not?

Who stops at stop signs?

This project, designed by Andrea Libresco (NTN), gives students experience using a structured scientific method. Working individually or in groups, students develop hypotheses about the types of people who stop at or drive through traffic stop signs. Variables can include vehicle type, location, characteristics of the driver (age, gender, race), and number and types of passengers in the vehicles. Stopping categories can include full stop, rolling stop, and no stop. After completing observations and sharing information with classmates, students write reports describing their results and conclusions. Reports include the following elements:

Identification of hypotheses being tested

Identification of variables

Discussion of how observations were conducted

Description of results

Analysis of results

Discussion of problems with the experiment (e.g., impact of stereotypes on hypotheses and assignment of categories)

Conclusion: assessing the validity of the initial hypotheses and suggestions for further experiments

Writing Projects

Global pen pals:

Over the years, I have obtained the addresses of schools in other countries through UNICEF, UNESCO, and government missions in the United States. However, the vagaries of international mail have always made a global pen pal project difficult. Teachers cannot count on getting responses in a timely fashion that would make them useful in class. The most successful pen pal project involved a ninth-grade remedial social studies class in Brooklyn, New York, and Native American students at a Santa Fe, New Mexico, boarding school. Both groups of students wrote about their own lives and asked questions of the other group. We mailed all the letters in one package and created a class magazine so that everyone could share the responses. The Internet offers an entirely new set of possibilities for global pen pals. Responses to e-mail are virtually instantaneous. Students get answers to their questions while they are still interested in them.

Messages to world leaders:

In the spring of 1995, the United Nations invited youth worldwide to use the Internet to send statements on international development, poverty, unemployment, and social conflict to world leaders attending the World Summit for Social Development in Copenhagen, Denmark. Lynda Costello-Herrara (NTN) had her ninth-grade global studies students send in their ideas.

Zen Buddhist Haiku by a 9th-grade global history class:

Michael Pezone (NTN) (Singer and Pezone, 1996) and his ninth-grade students study traditional Japanese culture with a focus on Zen Buddhism. Students are particularly intrigued by the Zen spirit of humor and irreverence. They are fascinated as well by the Zen emphasis on "immediate," as opposed to conceptual, knowledge. This emphasis is clearly evident in the Zen tradition of haiku writing. Haiku are short, three-line poems that employ "imagistic snapshots" to evoke profound perceptions. Students are encouraged to depart from a rigid syllable rule. After all, the duration or spoken tempo of Japanese is much more rapid than that of English. Students thoroughly enjoy writing haiku and reading each other's creations. Frequently their works focus on unexpected comparisons and metaphors.

Poems about life in the United States:

Students can write poetry that shows their understanding of social movements or major historical developments in U.S. history. In the poem that follows, an 11th-grade student discusses the impact of mechanization on working people and their families (Singer, 1994).

> **Newspaper Men**
> by Nicole Paciello
> The busy hustle of the city streets,
> The noise, the excitement, keys to the big city.
> The trains make my insides rattle—
> People run to catch it,
> Or stop at the stand for the morning paper.
> So easy in their strides, people hardly notice
> Newspapers are dwindling in number.
> Newspaper men on the sidelines,
> Machines have their jobs now.
> They watch the game,
> Waiting to be called in,
> They sit in their cardboard shelters
> Watching the world run by.
> The noise, the excitement,
> The strange faces hurrying by are noticed easily—
> Your eyes fix on their attaché cases, their hard-hats,
> And the morning paper under their arms.

Zen Buddhist Haiku section adapted from Singer and Pezone (1996) with permission.

The others are overlooked,
Others who don't read the morning paper,
They wear it.
I never noticed these people before,
When they were out in the cold clutching their cardboard homes,
Or inside their concrete houses, yet still cold.
One day, I stop and take a long hard look
As I hear the train above me.
The train drowns out all else
As I pass by the newsstand and head home.
My father's waiting for me,
Way before the 5:15 train.
There's a carpet mark behind the corner,
Where his attaché used to be.
I ask him what he's done today.
He looks at me,
With his glassy eyes,
And his five o'clock shadow.
He tells the youngest of his three daughters,
"I pressed the clothes in the dryer."
I reassure him—again,
A machine can do many jobs,
But it can't replace him as my father.
Newspapers are dwindling in number.
Newspaper men on the sidelines,
Machines have their jobs now.
They watch the game,
Waiting to be called in,
They sit in their cardboard shelters
Watching the world run by.

Editorials and speeches:

The Forum Club was an extracurricular political action student group organized by students in participation in government classes as part of a student civics program. Club activities included encouraging people to complete census surveys, voter registration, lobbying for a health clinic for the school, sponsoring a school forum and debate on abortion rights, and testifying on a condom availability proposal. Students in the club worked together in groups to help each other write political advocacy speeches and editorials.

The following are excerpts from a speech presented by a member of the Forum Club at a public hearing organized by the New York Pro-Choice Coalition and from an essay printed in *New York Newsday* on January 14, 1990.

Political advocacy speech:

I think it is a good idea to talk to your parents about a pregnancy and an abortion. But I also understand that you may not be able to do this. Some teenagers are afraid to tell their parents. Some teenagers have good reasons why they cannot tell them. . . . A law cannot take a distant relationship and make it a close one. That's why there are hotlines to call and all sorts of counselors, so that a pregnant teenager does not end up boxed into a corner unable to get out. . . . My mom has said to me, "If you make mistakes in your life, you are the one who has to live with them. But always remember that I am here for you." I think all teenagers should be able to talk with their parents. I wish all parents were like my mom, but I know that it's not that way. That's why I am fighting against parental consent and parental notification laws.

Editorial:

The members of the Forum Club strongly disagree with the behavior of some of the prochoice demonstrators at Saint Patrick's Cathedral. We believe that it was uncalled for and inexcusable to disrupt the mass and interfere with communion. We believe that the demonstrators who entered the church were wrong and hurt the ability of the prochoice movement to win people over to our ideas on human freedom and the rights of Americans.

However, we also believe that the newspaper coverage of events on that day misrepresented the prochoice movement. Of 5,000 people who demonstrated at Saint Patrick's Cathedral on that day, only 43 were arrested inside the church. Furthermore, only one person disrupted Holy Communion.

Meanwhile, the media buried reports about another demonstration that took place on the same day. In New Jersey, 125 members of Operation Rescue, an antiabortion group, were arrested at a health clinic. They had blocked the entrance to the clinic to prevent women from choosing to have safe and legal abortions. Six of these demonstrators had chained themselves together.

We believe that on this Sunday, both the prochoice and antiabortion groups did things that violated the rights of other Americans. What we don't understand is why the prochoice group was singled out for the harsher criticism.

Teaching Activity: Evaluating Interdisciplinary Project Ideas

Think it over:
1. How could you modify these projects to make them appropriate for students on different grade levels and in different subjects areas?
2. How would you ensure that the projects include social studies content and concepts?
3. How would you incorporate the projects into your overall curriculum?
4. How would you assess student learning?
5. How much voice and choice would you allow students in defining the projects, especially when they touch on controversial issues?
6. How would you respond to critics who charge that the students are not really learning social studies?

Try it yourself:
Select and complete three of the projects described in this section.

Teaching Activity: Respecting Cultural Integrity

Some educators (Bigelow, Miner, and Peterson, 1992) are concerned that social studies art and craft projects, by removing traditional activities out of their cultural and technological contexts, trivialize religious rituals and mislead students about the high level of skill these crafts require. The following are examples:

West African wood carvers envision the spirit hidden within a piece of wood and hand carve a mask that liberates it; they do not start with an image and then construct it out of papier maché.

Navaho religious leaders scatter sand paintings in the wind at the end of communal healing ceremonies to show reverence to the spirit world and to protect the secrets of their people from outsiders. Traditional sand paintings, which portray Navaho religious beliefs, are never made permanent, displayed, or sold.

Critics of these types of projects argue that few teachers would consider involving students in reenacting Judeo-Christian rituals or making models of our religious symbols.

Add your voice to the discussion:
In your opinion, should students engage in art and craft projects that are modified versions of traditional crafts or religious activities? Why or why not?

Think it over:
How would you address this issue in your class?

Try it yourself:
Create an art or craft project to use in a global studies class. Teach the students in your class how to do it. How would you use the project to teach social studies concepts?

It's your classroom:
What do you do if you do not have artistic ability?

Essay 1: Oral Histories—A Project Approach to Social Studies*

Oral history is a way to actively involve students in thinking about and understanding history and the contemporary world. It allows teachers to bring the cultural and historical experiences of students and their families directly into the classroom and the learning process. In many schools, it creates possibilities to enhance the multicultural nature of social studies curricula. An oral history class project has the potential to become the centerpiece of class discussions on recent U.S. and global history.

Different methods introduce students to oral history projects, depending on the interest and academic level of the class. Students can bring in and discuss family heirlooms that allow the class to examine cultural similarities and differences. Classes can complete family histories that help students pinpoint where their family's story has intersected with broader historical events. Classes can also read oral histories to figure out what questions the interviewer asked the subject and to allow students to think of questions they would like to ask.

Students can participate in oral history projects as individuals or in cooperative learning teams. However, a heterogeneous cooperative learning format is strongly recommended. It helps students learn how to work supportively in groups, and it allows them to learn more about their teammates' families and cultures. Cooperative learning teams of three or four students can create their own interview questionnaires or use questions prepared by the class or the teacher.

Interview subjects can be neighbors, family friends, members of senior citizens centers, participants in church or veterans' programs, and the school's older staff members. An entire cooperative learning team can interview one person, the team can interview a member of each student's family, or students can interview their family members by themselves and then meet to write their reports together.

Open-ended interviews using prepared questions as starting points encourage people to tell stories about their past. Sometimes during an interview, students ask all of their prepared questions, sometimes only part of their questions, and sometimes they think of new follow-up questions in the middle of the interview.

Before teams do their interviews, it is useful to conduct a practice interview in class. One of the student teams can interview a staff member, a family member, or a community resident. The practice interview teaches students how to conduct open-ended interviews that stimulate interview subjects into telling their stories.

Students can take notes during an interview, or audio- or video tape them. When the interviews are completed, cooperative learning teams can work together to write up their findings as biographical sketches or in a question-answer form. Team members compose, write, and edit the reports together. Sometimes interviews are conducted in languages other than English, and students need to work together to translate what they have learned.

Interview subjects should be asked for permission to include their stories in student magazines. Magazines can be used as student-created texts to teach about the Great Depression, World War II, the Civil Rights movement, the problems of workers in modern America, and the hopes and problems confronting immigrants and ethnic minorities.

Follow-up activities can include trips to local museums such as the Ellis Island Immigration Museum in New York City or the creation of a school exhibit using family photographs and artifacts. Students can also become involved in checking personal testimonies against primary sources and history books. They can discuss the subjectivity of our knowledge of the past and the importance of examining multiple sources before arriving at conclusions. The oral histories that follow were included in an article published by the New York State Council for the Social Studies (Singer, 1994).

Sample Oral Histories Written by High School Students

Life in Sicily:

I was born on December 17, 1913, in agricultural Sicily. My birth took place in my great grandfather's house, a house which had been handed down from generation to generation. It was always inherited by the eldest son in the family. My family was one of the more fortunate families in our village. We were a small family in comparison

*Based on A. Singer and B. Brody, "On Teaching—Franklin K. Lane High School Oral History Project and History Magazine," *OAH Magazine of History* 4, no. 4 (1990); and A. Singer, "Oral History and Active Learning", *Social Science Record* 31, no. 2 (1994). Used with permission.

to the enormous families with an average of ten children per household. That number decreased with time; for it was almost inevitable. Disease and sickness struck most families from all walks of life. I frequently heard neighbors gossiping late at night discussing deaths. "Poverino era piccolo, simpatico." Poor child, so young, so beautiful. . . .

Though poverty seemed to be in every direction your eyes led you, people still found it in their hearts to share what little they possessed with the more needy. Frequently neighbors would gather collections of blankets, bread, cheese, whatever they could afford to give. The package was then placed on the doorsteps of a family that was having a hard time. The person offering one month never knew if she would be receiving the following month.

A Black family comes north:

When he was almost ten years old, Marcus and his brother and sister got word that they'd soon be moving to the North. His father had gotten a job in Chicago, Illinois. In October of 1924, Evelyn and Cyril and their children headed for the train station. When he and his family boarded the train, the children were all surprised to see how many other men and families were making the same move. The ride was the most memorable moment of Marcus' young life. The trip meant a complete and total change from the way things were and had always been, to something very foreign and far off. Once Marcus and his family left the train and he could see the new place, he grabbed his younger sister and held her by the back of her collar. He never took his eyes off of the signs in the station. He was amazed that any place could be so big and afraid that it would swallow him whole. In Chicago, they were driven to a large brick monstrous building that gobbled up entire families of people. There was an empty room in the beast's belly where Marcus and his family settled. The tiny rooms stacked on top of one another and squished together side by side were different from the homes Marcus had known. Many things in the North took a lot of adjusting to.

Holocaust survivor:

My grandpa is a Holocaust survivor. When he was younger he lived in a small town called Cozova in Poland. There were five children in his family—Seymore, Carl, Yossel, Aliva and his sister Hencha. It all started in the summer of 1941. The Jews of his town knew that when the Jewish policeman threw up his night stick it was a warning to hide because the Germans were coming. When Carl's family saw the Jewish police, they jumped into a small covered ditch by their horse stables. When the Germans found them they yelled at them to get out or they would shoot. They grabbed Carl's three brothers, Aliva, Yossel and Seymore and dragged them off. His mother, sister and Carl were shoved into a truck and were rushed to a train station a few miles away. They were being taken away to concentration camps. There were many people on the train with him— so many that you couldn't even sit. The trains the people were packed in were mainly used to transport the cows. They still had the odor. The Germans didn't give them any food or water; not even a pail to urinate in. Everybody on the train was screaming and crying because they knew where they were headed. A man in the car with my grandfather had a razor. My grandpa started to cut away at the door by the latch. He finally cut a hole big enough for his fingers to fit through to lift the latch. He shoved the door open and jumped out of a speeding train. The last memory of the train was that his mother was very sick.

Life in Puerto Rico and New York:

My grandfather was born on December 6th, 1930, on the southeastern part of a beautiful island called Puerto Rico. He lived in a small town called Patillas with his native Puerto Rican parents and two brothers and a sister. My grandfather's reasons for coming to the United States were simple. First, to see a new country, and second, to look for new origins. He was hearing all the talk about how wonderful the U.S. was, so he decided to find out by himself. He secretly went and sold a cow they had by the name of Manuela, and with the money bought a plane ticket to New York.

Discrimination was something he remembers too well. When looking for jobs or apartments, he tells how there were signs put up saying, "NO SPANISH PEOPLE WANTED," or "NO P.R.'S WANTED!" I found it amazing when he told me how he had to sign the name Mike Maccio in order to get a lease on an apartment. He had to try to pass as an Italian. Using his real last name, Rodriguez, wouldn't have helped the situation. Because of his looks, he got away with acting as an Italian.

A Greek war hero:

Vangeli was born in 1921. In 1938 he was drafted into the Greek military. While he was in the military, World War II broke out and Vangeli was sent to the Albanian side of Greece. He fought many great battles and received the rank of sergeant. In 1945, World War II ended. Vangeli led his soldiers back home, but to his amazement, the war was not over. A civil war had started in Greece. Vangeli was very tired of fighting and did not want to see any more bloodshed. But he had no choice in the matter. Vangeli's father, Georgo, was killed by a Communist party member. Vangeli then sent his younger brother Fotis to America with an old friend to look after him until he was finished fighting the civil war. Vangeli was in a town called Nea Smirna. He was stationed there for seven months. During that time he and his soldiers captured many Communist followers and killed them. Vangeli often killed them himself, letting some of his anger out for his father's death. . . . He was slightly going mad and insane from all of the bloodshed and killing he had seen his whole life. . . . Vangeli wrote to his wife about his feelings. Vangeli wanted to move to America with Maritsa and live with his brother Fotis. . . . That night as Vangeli was fast asleep there was a Communist attack on the town. Vangeli ordered his men to open fire on anyone not wearing their uniform. Vangeli's men were outnumbered seven to one. There was no hope for victory. The next morning Vangeli was shot by a firing squad just like his father had been. Vangeli lived his whole life fighting wars. He died at the age of twenty-eight. The war ended in 1949, just two months after his death.

Life in Haiti and the U.S.:

Antoine was born in Haiti on March 20, 1930. On January 2, 1950, at the age of twenty years old, Antoine was arrested for speaking out against the government. The President of Haiti was Francois Duvalier. Nobody had the right to speak out against him. Antoine had spoken against the President for ordering the killing of peasants in Port-au-Prince, the capital of Haiti. He refused to let them hurt innocent people who did not do anything wrong. The police officers arrested Antoine and put him in a jail for three months before he could go before a jury. The jury was appointed by Duvalier. When Antoine finally went to court, he was convicted before he even had a trial. The jury didn't even bother to listen to his reasons for going against the President's wishes. They sentenced him to a lifetime of imprisonment.

After five years of hell, little food and beatings by the officers at the jail, his mother found a way for him to escape to freedom in America. He had to use a fake passport and a fake name but he made it through the American immigration.

Life in China:

I was born in 1907 in a big city in the south of China whose name is Guangzhou. My family was not very rich, but it couldn't be considered a poor family. My father was a professor in a university. We lived in a big mansion even though we didn't have much money. I had five brothers and sisters and I am the second daughter. My father died suddenly when I was only nine years old and we were forced to leave the mansion because we didn't have the money to pay for the rent. My mother brought her six children to live in a 10-meter-square room. Seven people lived in a small place without a bathroom. When we had to go, we went to the public bathroom.

My mother was working eighteen hours per day. My sisters and brother felt hungry every single day, especially my brother. He got sick all the time. Unfortunately, we really didn't have money to send him to see a doctor. After thinking of it for several nights, my mother decided to sell my brother! She told us that instead of the whole family dying together, we should sell our brother to a wealthy family and let him have a good life. We could get the money to live on also. After she sold our brother, she cried all day. Instead of letting her son die of starvation, she wanted him to be alive even though she couldn't see him any more.

Learning Activity: Writing Oral Histories

Try it yourself:

Design a questionnaire and interview a senior citizen about life in the United States or in another part of the world. Using your notes and tapes, write a first- or third-person account of the person's life.

It's your classroom:

How would you help students verify information they learned during their interviews?

FOR FURTHER READING ON ORAL HISTORY

Brecher, J. *History from Below*. New Haven: Advocate Press, 1988.

Brody, B., and A. Singer. "Franklin K. Lane High School Oral History Project and History Magazine." *Organization of American Historians Magazine of History* 4, no. 4 (1990), 7–9.

Hickey, M. G. "And Then What Happened, Grandpa?" *Social Education* 55, no. 4 (1991), 216.

Singer, A. "Oral History and Active Learning." *Social Science Record* 31, no. 2 (1994), 14–20.

Terkel, S. *Hard Times*. New York: Pantheon, 1970.

Essay 2: Technology-Based Project Ideas

In this essay, members of the New Teachers Network explain ways that they integrate computers into social studies projects.

A. Jennifer Debler (2002) is a middle school social studies teacher who has grappled with a series of problems that emerge when students surf the web doing research. Many waste a lot of time, others get distracted, and some end up discovering and using questionable information. To alleviate these problems, she created her own web site. Jennifer previews web sites that she plans to have students visit and links them to her site. This allows students to go directly to her homepage when they are working on an assignment. A number of companies offer teachers free web space. These include bigchalk.com, scholastic.com, myschoolonline.com, inspiringteachers.com, and teacherweb.com.

On her site, Jennifer includes homework assignments, project directions, class guidelines, her e-mail address so students and parents can contact her, and links to the school and district web pages. Research connections are organized by units and projects. She also has "just for fun" links to interesting social studies related sites that are not necessarily tied into what students are studying in class. She finds that her students like to visit these sites, so she continually updates them, which encourages students to visit her web page on a regular basis.

Jennifer advises that before teachers begin computer projects, they need to consider some things. Teachers must be familiar with their school or district's Internet policies. Many require that students have written parental consent before they use the Internet. Some computer labs have filters that block certain web sites. Often these blocks appear to be irrational. When choosing sites

for a project, check to make sure they are not blocked by the school's filter.

Jennifer recommends the program Inspiration (http://www.inspiration.com) for creating graphic organizers. Teachers and students can use the organizers for planning, organizing, outlining, webbing, and concept mapping. Social studies teachers can use PowerPoint to create and present slide shows, overhead transparencies, instructions for lessons and projects, maps and charts, class notes, and quiz or test reviews. Students can use Microsoft® PowerPoint to create presentations on topics that they research. Using slide shows to support oral presentations helps even the most nervous student learn to speak more easily in the classroom.

Some districts have video conferencing technology available for classroom use. Video conferencing allows students to take field trips and "visit" remote locations using video, computer, and communications technology. Students can conference with other classrooms or visit real life locations such as the American Museum of Natural History, the Museum of Modern Art, the National Science Center, the Baseball Hall of Fame, and NASA.

African Colonial Experience Project:

For this project, students utilized Microsoft® Word and the Internet to create class "books" about the experiences of Africans during the colonial period. Working in pairs, students selected and researched specific topics and created a page for our class book. Students learned about and wrote pages on African kingdoms, trade within Africa, the Atlantic slave trade, the Middle Passage, the evolution of African American culture, and customs and Phillis Wheatley, Benjamin Banneker, Prince Whipple, and Olaudah Equiano.

Students used the Internet for their research. All sites were categorized and book marked in advance. Students wrote their own text but could include images pasted from the Internet. Each group presented its page to the full class. At the end of the project, every student received a printed copy of the entire project.

Recommended Web Sites:

Africans in America (http://www.pbs.org/wgbh/aia/home.html)

African American Odyssey (http://lcweb2.loc.gov/ammem/aao.html)

George Washington art project:

This assignment was designed as an enrichment activity for Grade 7 "modified" classes. Students evaluated works of art featuring George Washington. Each student chose three paintings or works of art and created a PowerPoint presentation to share with other students. Students cut and pasted the artwork from a web site and then formatted the work into their presentation. They had to use the art to explain the historical period of Washington's life (pre-Revolution, Revolution, presidency, final days), provide information about the artist and the time when the work was created, and evaluate how the painting portrayed Washington. A painting such as Washington Crossing the Delaware by Leutze gave students the opportunity to learn about historical accuracy, themes, and artist perspective.

Recommended Web Sites:

Picture Gallery of Washington (http://www.historyplace.com/unitedstates/revolution/wash-pix/gallery.htm)

The Life of George Washington (http://earlyamerica.com/lives/gwlife/index.html)

Federal agencies:

This project is another enrichment activity for a Grade 7 "modified" classes. Students compiled a class book explaining various federal agencies. Many government agencies offer student pages explaining their function. Students used Microsoft® Word to format their information.

Recommended Web Sites:

Justice Department (http://www.usdoj.gov/kidspage)

Central Intelligence Agency (http://www.odci.gov/cia/ciakids)

Social Security Administration (http://www.ssa.gov/kids/teens.htm)

Supreme Court cases:

This project requires student teams to research Supreme Court Cases involving the Bill of Rights and present individual cases to the class using Power Point. The Oyez Project at the Northwestern University web site provides students with both case abstracts and actual Supreme Court decisions. The abstracts provide information appropriate for the middle-level students.

Power Point presentations explain the issues in the case, the constitutional amendment under examination, and the decision made by the court. Students are required to integrate two quotations from the court decision into their reports.

For this project students utilized government web sites to copy and paste photos and graphics into their presentation. They also practiced using Power Point features such as animation and layouts. Presentations were made in the school library on a large screen television that was connected to the computer lab.

Cases included *N.J. v. TLO; Gideon v. Wainwright; U.S. v. Eichman; Abington Township v. Schempp; Lee v. Weisman; Miranda v. Arizona; Hazelwood, S.D. v. Kuhlmeier; Tinker v. Des Moines; BOE v. Pico; Texas v. Johnson; Bethel S.D. v. Frasier; Schenk v. U.S.; Goss v. Lopez; and Engel v. Vitale.*

Recommended Web Site:

Supreme Court Database (http://oyez.nwu.edu)

Letter to Congress:

In conjunction with English classes, students write business letters to their U.S. congressional representative regarding their views on a bill she or he has sponsored. One year, students researched the National Language Act, HR 280, a bill to declare English the official language of the U.S. government. As part of this project, students learned how a bill becomes a law and identified where HR 280 was in the law-making process. They discovered when it was introduced, its sponsors and committee assignments, interpreted its meaning, and debated its implications. Students found text of the bill through King's web page at the Congressional Web site (http://www.house.gov/king) and THOMAS, a legislative information site of the Library of Congress (http://www.thomas.loc.gov).

The Transportation Revolution:

For this project, students examine the movement of people and goods, human–environment interaction, technology, and interdependence during the 19th century transportation revolution. Using

Internet sites, students created brochures publicizing different types of transportation innovations including roads, steamboats, canals, and railroads. Students used Print Shop Deluxe or Microsoft® Publisher to format their brochures. Again, students copied and pasted photos and graphics from the Internet to use in their projects.

Recommended Web Sites:

Erie Canal (http://www.history.rochester.edu/canal)

Transportation in the New Nation (http://xroads.virginia.edu/~HYPER/DETOC/transport/rivers.html)

History of the National Road (http://www.nationalroad.org/stories.htm)

National Railroad Museum (http://www.nationalrrmuseum.org)

B. Rachel Gaglione Thompson is a major proponent of both a project approach to teaching social studies and the integration of technology into the middle school social studies classroom. Over the last few years she has reorganized many of her favorite projects to include a technological component.

Industrialization project:

Students examine the period of industrialization in the United States, roughly 1870–1915, and prepare a HyperStudio slide show with a series of 13 slides. Presentations must address major historical questions, including Did industrialization improve conditions for all or lead to social inequality? Did changing technology make life in the United States better or worse?

Travel brochure:

Students use AppleWorks and the web to create a trifold brochure that describes one of the American states. The goal is to encourage tourism to the state. Each brochure must include the following:

Front cover: Name of the state, a picture or graphic, and an advertising slogan

Inside folds: Introduction of the state including a bit about its history, interesting or unusual facts about the state, pictures, things to do and places to visit

Back cover: A map of the state and traveling instructions

Technology project to answer essential questions:

C. Ken Dwyer is a high school social studies teacher who is a strong advocate of examining essential questions in global history (see Chapter 2). This project uses technology to engage students as historians to answer essential questions. As students review ancient civilizations, they focus on three questions: Is geography destiny? To what degree does religion provide order in society? and To what degree does government provide order in society? Their assignment is to use the web to find at least five documents (quotes, artifacts, maps, artwork, etc.) from or about societies they are studying that address one of the class, essential questions. When students locate the documents, they import them into a word processing file. When students are satisfied with their selections, they develop a "scaffolding question" for each document that can be answered using information provided by the document.

ACTIVITY SHEET: CREATING A GLOBAL HISTORY

These essential questions guide our study of ancient civilizations and early empires:
Is geography destiny?
To what degree does religion provide order in society?
To what degree does government provide order in society?

Task:

Using the Internet, research information about the civilizations we have studied. Evaluate the information and select sources that provide evidence to support your views. Assemble a set of documents that provide evidence for one of the essential questions. Each student must assemble a minimum of five documents. The documents should be imported into a word processing file. A scaffolding question must be written for each document.

Continued

Types of Documents:

Each packet of documents must include at least three different types of sources. Possible sources include charts, graphs, illustrations, maps, pictures, written primary sources (at least one is required), and written secondary sources.

Civilizations Studied:

Each set of documents must include sources from at least three of these civilizations: Egypt, Mesopotamia, Indus River Valley, Chinese river valleys, early empires of India, early empires of China.

Format:

Topic _____

Essential question _____

Document 1.

Type of Document _____

Civilization represented _____

Is the document the appropriate length? _____

Is the document understandable? _____

Does the document provide evidence for the essential question? _____

Can the scaffolding question be answered from the document? _____

Suggestions for improvement _____

D. Kenneth W. Leman (2002) uses a package of web sites and a set of questions to help high school economics students participate in the debate over globalization. While many of these sites require a high level of academic skill to understand, Ken encourages students to use as many of them as possible. Students can use multiple sites to write extended research reports or be responsbile for reporting to class on a specific site.

ESSENTIAL QUESTIONS ON GLOBALIZATION

What is a global economic system? How do international capital systems work?

How does globalization affect local, national, regional, and international economies?

How does globalization affect wages and prices?

Does globalization promote the removal of production and jobs from developed to underdeveloped countries? What are the social costs to both groups?

Why has globalization promoted child labor, environmental degradation, and poor health in many underdeveloped countries?

How have the power of multinational corporations and trade agreements affected the balances of national, international, and regional power around the world?

What will be the impact of globalization on movements for democracy and human rights?

Why should citizens and consumers care about globalization?

Can globalization occur without disrupting traditional cultures, religions, and economies?

Continued

Can the current global systems more uniformly benefit all people?
What can businesses, labor, governments and citizens do to make globalization more just?
If globalization cannot be made more fair, can and should the world undo or modify the current global business systems? Can the clock be turned back?

Sites Pertinent to Globalization

Center for Economic Policy and Research (http://www.cepr.net). This private think tank site offers a balanced and critical view of economic globalization, discussing many of the relative advantages and disadvantages to countries around the world. *Globalization: A Primer* is an excellent overview of the interrelated factors affecting the world economy. Vocabulary may challenge students with lower reading abilities.

International Monetary Fund (http://www.imf.org). Posted by one of the two supranational organizations that controls international capital, this site offers its own primer on economic globalization. It makes good use of graphs and requires prior understanding of key economic terms. The bias of this site is clearly toward globalization as an evolving process of expanding the market economy to all countries. It freely acknowledges bad consequences of globalization, but it takes the approach that such consequences are the by-product of change rather than systemic inequality.

The World Bank Group (http://www.worldbank.org). An excellent site for the better reader. It contains a wealth of information on World Bank policies and practices and explains how money moves around the world and why.

Clearing House Interbank Payments System (http://www.chips.org) and ***Asian Development Bank*** (http://www.adb.org). The CHIPS site explains international monetary exchange. The ADB site shows how the ADB provides funding for local economic and infrastructure development in Asia. These two are very accessible for students of all reading abilities.

JusticeNet (http://www.justicenet.org). This site provides articles and links to sites that take a more critical view of globalization. Articles discuss the social and economic disruption that the IMF and World Bank practices cause.

Resource Center of the Americas (http://www.americas.org). This activist think tank site offers an easy-to-use alternate view of the global economy being driven by the needs of multinational corporations. It gives students a basic understanding of the new economic inequalities affecting people in underdeveloped countries. Reading level is moderate, vocabulary defined, and critical comparisons are thought provoking.

Youth for International Socialism (http://www.newyouth.com). This is a key site in the antiglobalization movement. It offers a fairly balanced but

Site information is based on Leman (2002). Used with permission.

critical view of global inequalities and explanations of protests at WTO, G-8, and IMF meetings.

Worldwatch Institute (http://www.worldwatch.org). This site provides a wide variety of alternative analyses of globalization's downside. Its focus is on environmental degradation.

Global Challenge Initiative (http://www.challengeglobalization.org). This organization's sole purpose is challenging the current global system. The site offers access to a wealth of information, training programs, advocacy support to oppose the status quo, and a collection of political cartoons.

Mother Jones (http://www.motherjones.com) and *AFL-CIO* (http://www.aflcio.org). Easy-to-read Mother Jones reports on globalization's ill effects. The AFL-CIO site provides organized labor's view of issues.

The Fair Trade Federation (http://www.fairtradefederation.com). This site focuses on the FTF's activities to promote fair wages for overseas workers engaged in global production. The FTF's eight Practices and Principles challenge students to think about fair wages and employment practices and whether these can be promoted within the global economy.

Public Broadcasting System (http://www.pbs.org). This is the companion site to a PBS special on Globalization and Human Rights. Easy to use and easy to read, this site explores the human side of globalization and allows students to access transcripts from the series' episodes.

Human Rights for Workers (http://www.senser.com). This site addresses globalization and human rights issues such as child labor.

United Nations University (http://www.unu.edu). This site focuses on U.N. activities. Material on Africa and the global economy compares current African problems with Asia's earlier experience and suggests possible local, national, and international initiatives.

REFERENCES AND RECOMMENDATIONS FOR FURTHER READING

Bigelow, W., B. Miner, and R. Peterson, eds. *Rethinking Columbus*. Milwaukee, Wis.: Rethinking School, 1992.

Debler, J. "Ideas for Using Computers in Your Seventh Grade Social Studies Class." *Social Science Docket* 2, no. 2 (2002).

Dewey, J. *Experience and Education*. New York: Macmillan, 1938/1972.

Doane, C. "Global Issues in 6th Grade? Yes!" *Educational Leadership* 7 (1993), 19.

Foxfire Fund. *Hands On, A Journal for Teachers*, Spring/Summer 1990.

Hirsch, E. " 'You Can Always Look It Up' . . . or Can You?" *American Educator* 24, no. 2 (2002), 4–9.

Howlett, C. "Teach History Students Can Touch." *Newsday*, October 4, 1999.

Hunte, S., R. Thompson, and R. Kurtz. "Middle School Museum of Slavery Project." *Social Science Docket* 2, no. 2 (2002).

Kilpatrick, W. "The Essentials of the Activity Movement." *Progressive Education* 11 (1934), 346–59.

Korbin, D., E. Abbot, J. Ellinwood, and D. Horton. "Learning History by Doing History." *Educational Leadership* 50 (1993), 39.

Leman, K. "Web Site Directory on Economic Globalization." *Social Science Docket* 2, no. 1 (2002), 40–42.

Mann, E. *The Brooklyn Bridge*. New York: Mikaya Press, 1996.

McCullough, D. *The Great Bridge*. New York: Simon & Schuster, 1972.

Meier, D. *The Power of Their Ideas: Lessons for America from a Small School in Harlem*. Boston: Beacon, 1995.

Meier, D., and P. Schwarz. "Central Park East Secondary School: The Hard Part Is Making It Happen." In *Democratic Schools*, ed. M. Apple and J. Beane. Alexandria, Va.: ASCD, 1995, 26–40.

Mossman, L. *The Activity Concept*. New York: Macmillan, 1940.

Seeger, P., and B. Reiser. *Carry It On*. New York: Simon and Schuster, 1985.

Sewall, G. "Lost In Action." *American Educator* 24, no. 2 (2002), 4–9, 42–43.

Singer, A. "The Impact of Industrialization on American Society: Alternative Assessments." *Social Education* 58, no. 3 (1994), 171–72.

Singer, A., H. Dircks, and V. Turner. "Exploring the Great Depression and the New Deal: An Interdisciplinary Project Approach for Middle School Students." *Social Education* 60, no. 5 (1996).

Singer, A., and M. Pezone. "Interdisciplinary Projects That Explore Traditional Japanese Culture." *In Transition, Journal of the New York State Middle School Association*, Spring 1996, 28–29.

Singer A., Gurton, L., Horowitz, A., Hunte, S., Broomfield, P., and Thomas, J., "Coming of Age Ceremonies: A Mask Project," *Middle Level Learning*, September 1998, Issue 3, Supplement to *Social Education*, September 1998, 62(5), pp. M14–M16.

Singer, J., C. Goodman, T. Ridley, and A. Singer. "Bridges and the City: An Interdisciplinary Project." *Childhood Education* 76, no. 2 (1999/2000), 100–3.

Sizer, T. *Horace's Compromise*. Boston, Houghton Mifflin, 1984.

Wiggins, G. "Assessment to Improve Performance, Not Just Monitor It: Assessment Reform in the Social Sciences." *Social Science Record* 30, no. 2 (1993), 5.

Wigginton, E., ed. *The Foxfire Book*. Garden City, N.Y.: Doubleday, 1972.

Wigginton, E. "What Kind of Project Should We Do?" *Democracy & Education* 3, no. 1 (1988), 1–9.

Wood, G. "Project-Centered Teaching: A Tool for the Democratic Classroom." *Democracy & Education* 6, no. 1 (1991), 3–6.

9

How Should Teachers Assess Student Learning and Our Own Practice?

Attitudes toward assessment reflect the way teachers think about their goals, their students, and teaching social studies. This chapter includes discussion and examples of both traditional and alternative methods of assessing student learning. I hope it provides teachers and preservice teachers an opportunity to assess their own thinking about the ideas and issues raised in this book.

Assessment:

The ways students demonstrate understanding of concepts, mastery of skills, and knowledge of and ability to utilize information. Assessment devices include, but are not limited to, teacher-designed and standardized tests. Assessments are used to evaluate student performance, teacher effectiveness, and the success of social studies curricula and programs.

DOES ASSESSMENT EQUAL TESTING?

On November 2, 1995, newspaper headlines across the country announced that U.S. students "Don't Know Much About History." The press was not promoting Sam Cooke's classic rock and roll ballad, "(What a) Wonderful World" (lyrics available on the web at http://www. geocities. com/martynb88/Wonderfulworld.html); it was reporting the latest "failure" of the U.S. education system. Fifty-seven percent of the country's high school seniors had been unable to achieve "basic competency" on a U.S. history examination administered by the National Assessment of Education Progress (NAEP), an independent agency that conducts tests for the U.S. government (Newsday, 1995: 3). According to Education Commissioner William T. Randall of Colorado and chair of the citizens' board that oversees the NAEP, "The strikingly poor performance . . . indicates a major problem in how history is taught and learned—or not learned—in American schools." Randall concluded that, unless students master this information, "Our system of democratic self-government, which depends on knowledgeable citizens, will be weakened" (Newsday, November 2, 1995, 1, 3).

Two days after this report was released, the education commissioner of the state of New York announced his plan to raise the state's educational standards by instituting a policy of more rigorous testing. Most high school students in New York State were already taking standardized Regents examinations in global studies at the end of 10th grade and in U.S. history after 11th grade. Students who failed these exams were denied high school diplomas unless they could pass alternative statewide subject area competency exams. The state commissioner wanted to discontinue the competency exams and require students to pass more difficult versions of the Regents to graduate (Newsday, November 4, 1995, 3).

Emphasis on expanding student social studies content knowledge is often coupled with the demand for more rigorous testing. For people who support this view of social studies education, testing serves multiple functions. Tests direct classroom curricula and measure student knowledge, the competence of teachers, and the performance of schools and districts. In addition, fact-based multiple-choice exams are considered cost-efficient objective measures of performance.

What does this type of testing actually tell us about student understanding in social studies? Is there any correlation between more rigorous testing of content knowledge and the expansion of either critical understanding or a commitment to active citizenship?

Walter Parker (1989), who has been a leader in defining citizenship education for the National Council for the Social Studies (NCSS), argues that "knowledge of government and history is necessary to but not sufficient for cultivating civic virtue." He stresses that "more so than knowledge, civic virtue is a disposition to think and act on behalf of the public good," and that social studies classrooms should be organized "to encourage that disposition rather than discourage it." For Parker, "open, free, authentic talk is the coin of participatory citizenship" (353–54).

Focusing on content and testing does not promote this kind of "free, authentic talk"; it encourages teachers to prep students for tests. Social studies teachers drill students in basic skills and present them with long lists of facts to memorize. At best, this approach reduces the time available for the kind of education Randall claims to value. At worst, it destroys any hope that students will enjoy or value learning about social studies.

An examination of one of the questions on the NAEP test illustrates some of the problems with this type of test and with social studies assessment in general. Of the 12th graders who took the NAEP test, 72 percent got the answer to this question wrong:

> President Carter played a major role in negotiating the Camp David Accords, which promoted peace between . . .
> A. The Soviet Union and China
> B. The Palestinians and the Jordanians
> C. Egypt and Israel
> D. North Korea and the United States

Personally, I wish more U.S. high school seniors knew about the peace conference between Egyptian President Anwar al-Sadat and Israeli Prime Minister Menachem Begin, but I am not shocked that such a large percentage got the answer wrong. I do not think many veteran social studies teachers were surprised either. The Camp David Accords were in 1979. In curricula that are littered with thousands of years of detail, how many U.S. or world history classes actually get to 1979? Think back for a minute; when you were a high school student, how close did your class get to recent decades?

In addition, between 1979 and 1995, other events in world affairs, especially in Southwest Asia and North Africa (the Middle East), grabbed the historical and media spotlight away from the Israeli–Egyptian settlement. These events included the hostage situation and the Islamic Revolution in Iran, the death of 260 U.S. marines in Lebanon, the *Intifada*, the assassinations of both Sadat and Yitzhak Rabin, the Persian Gulf War, and the continuing negotiations between the Palestine Liberation Organization (PLO) and the nation of Israel. The Camp David Accords, which held out so much initial promise, did not succeed in bringing lasting peace to the Middle East. Twenty-five years after the event, they are not a major focus in many social studies classrooms.

A third problem with this question is that it is poorly designed. The number of correct answers would have been substantially higher if the question provided a historical or geographical context. For example, the question could have been reworded to read:

> "President Carter played a major role in negotiating the Camp David Accords, which promoted peace *in the Middle East* between . . ."
> or,
> "President Carter played a major role in negotiating the Camp David Accords, which promoted peace between *Arabs and Jews* in. . . ."

A fourth problem raises an even more significant issue for assessment in the social studies. A factual recall question requires no broad understanding of world events. Even when students get the answer right, we learn nothing about their understanding of social studies or their ability to be knowledgeable, thinking citizens.

Although the NAEP test tells very little about what students actually know and understand, it does suggest much about the failure of testing and test-driven curricula to stimulate students to think about history and the social sciences. It also raises many questions about the significance and purpose of assessment in social studies classrooms.

WHY SHOULD EDUCATORS ASSESS STUDENT LEARNING?

According to the NCSS (1991: 284–86), "the overriding purpose of testing in social studies classrooms is to improve learning." Unfortunately, that is not always the case.

As an education student in college, I was taught techniques to design "fair" tests with "good" questions. At the end of the marking period, we were supposed to average up test scores; add or subtract a few points based on factors such as class participation, attendance, and handing in assignments punctually; and then assign a scientifically precise numerical grade that summarized a student's performance in class. In theory, teachers did not evaluate students; our job was to calculate and record the grade they had earned.

We were also advised to do the following:

- Encourage competition between students for higher grades. This would ensure that they studied.

- Make all of the choices on multiple-choice tests the same length. Unequal length would tip off students to the right answer.
- Avoid making "B" the right answer too often. It is the most popular "wild guess" answer.
- Be careful not to make "All of the above" a choice only when the answer we want is "All of the above."
- Use different types of questions (e.g., fill-ins, matching, multiple choice, short description, and longer essays) so students cannot anticipate the kinds of questions you will ask. If they do, they will not study as hard.
- Throw in a few questions about really obscure points. This rewards students who do all of the homework, encourages the others to work harder, and gives you a spread of grades. (One of my high school teachers once gave us a fill-in question: Who invented barbed wire?)

Although some of this advice is useful, something is seriously wrong with this approach to assessment. Testing and grading are only indirectly related to instruction and the assessment of learning. Additionally, the assumption here is that education is a series of contests between students and between students and teachers.

In these methods classes, we never discussed why we test in social studies, the relationship between assessment and learning, or even why we test like this. The principles of testing and grading and the forms of tests were presented as eternal truths. Teachers gave tests. Students took tests. Parents and supervisors expected tests and test scores. The school system judged and sorted students based on test results.

The purpose of testing was to assign grades. Tests and grades were weapons to control classes and make students do the work through extrinsic rewards and punishments. Students who tried but did not do very well were offered extra help, but ultimately put in "slower" classes where they could "experience success." Those who failed the tests because they did not seem to care were cajoled with threats, calls or letters home, low grades, or failure for the course. Students who did well on tests were rewarded with high grades, certificates, and recommendations for better high schools and colleges.

As a beginning teacher, I used tests pretty much the same way they had been used in my classes when I was a student (although, of course, I considered myself fairer than the teachers who had tormented me). Sometimes I gave short weekly tests. At the end of units, I gave more comprehensive full-period tests. I worked with colleagues to design standard departmental midterms and finals. My students were supposed to know the information that had been presented in class, especially what I wrote on the board, and what they had been assigned for homework in the textbook. Like most of my colleagues, I fell into the pattern of tailoring lessons to prepare students for these tests.

Over the years, my relationships with students and my commitment to finding ways to motivate them to want to learn history and social studies forced me to think about my goals in assessing student learning. One incident from early in my career still stands out. A middle school student who loved social studies, was a leader in class discussions, and always made interesting points, refused to do any of the homework assignments and failed each test miserably. I gave him chance after chance, but I could not get him to do the work. Finally, I pleaded with him to go home and study and retake the same test

the next day. He was a remarkably tolerant and patient kid. He complied with my requests, took the test, and failed again. In desperation, I decided to try an experiment. During lunch I read him the multiple-choice questions and choices, and he checked off his selections. This time he scored in the high 80s. He understood what we were studying in class, but he did not know how to read well enough to do the homework assignments or distinguish between the choices on the multiple-choice tests.

Unfortunately, in teaching, as in life, there are few fairy tale endings. At the time, I had no idea what to do, and there was no one in the school who was able to help us. The student passed my class but very few others. Because he was already overage for middle school, he was passed on to high school the next year. Although this example is an extreme case, it is not unusual to have students who work very hard and are excited by social studies topics still get many questions wrong on tests because of inadequate literacy skills. One strategy I tried was to make tests easier, but then the more literate students got high grades without doing any work at all. To paraphrase the King of Siam from the Broadway musical *The King and I*, "Testing policy is a paradox."

It seems to me that the only way out of this testing paradox is to make assessment part of learning and to use a variety of assessment tools to discover what individual students understand. There are good reasons for testing and evaluating students. Students have a right to know how they are doing compared with other people doing similar work. This makes it possible for them to assess their activities, make decisions about their priorities, and evaluate their goals. In addition, as teachers, we need to know certain things so we can do our jobs effectively. Assessing student learning helps us evaluate our teaching. Assessment helps us think about some important questions including these:

- Does the curriculum make sense to the students? Does it connect with who they are? Does it take into account their level of academic and social studies skills and help to improve them?
- Am I teaching effectively? Is the class as a whole learning? Are the books and materials appropriate? What do I need to change?
- Do individual students understand what they are studying?
- How can I respond to their specific needs and motivate them to try again or try harder? How do I help students assess their own learning so they can use this knowledge as a way to expand their understanding? What will make it possible for every individual to succeed in class?
- Are students doing the classroom and homework assignments? Are the assignments reasonable and interesting? Which assignments should be kept? Which ones should be modified? Which ones should be dropped?
- Are my assessment tools accurate measures of what I am trying to assess? Am I testing recall, the ability of students to read and write, or their understanding and ability to use ideas?

- Can I assign students composite grades at the end of marking periods and semesters that have meaning to them and will encourage them rather than just reward or punish them?

Assessment is not an easy task. It is the area of my teaching practice where I am frequently the least comfortable with my decisions and judgments. I find I am always sweating over grades and offering students other opportunities to demonstrate what they have learned and what I have taught. As a high school teacher, I was regularly called down to an assistant principal's office to explain why I had so many missing grades on my roster sheets. In the "old days," I passed it off as a clerical error. Later, I blamed those "damned computers." I did not know how to explain that I could not figure out a grade because people are too complicated and learning is always incomplete.

By the way, historians usually credit Joseph F. Glidden, who was issued a patent in 1874, with the invention of barbed wire. I looked up the answer after I found out about the question during lunch from a student who took the test in the morning. As lifetime residents of the Bronx, neither she nor I understood the importance of barbed wire in U.S. history. In our neighborhoods, it was used to keep kids off the roofs of buildings, but with her help, I got the answer right on the test.

Teaching Activity: Why Test?

The following points were raised in discussions about testing and grading by graduate and undergraduate students in social studies methods classes at Hofstra University:
- "I don't like tests. They push for regurgitation of information. Teachers use them to sort people out and define them."
- "Tests help me discipline myself. They force me to think and get my ideas together. They help me bring something together, to finish it."
- "I like tests because I like to compete."
- "If we lower standards, kids are just pushed ahead without learning anything."

- "I'd try to see if students understand the main points and follow the directions."
- "It's hard for me to mark papers. It feels very uncomfortable being judged or judging."
- "I try to give my students tests that require them to organize information."
- "Why are we having a final exam in this class? Tests are oppressive."

Add your voice to the discussion:
1. With which statement(s) do you agree? Why?
2. How would you respond to the people with whom you disagree?
3. What points would you add to this discussion?

WHAT DO TEACHERS WANT TO MEASURE?

What do teachers measure when they give their classes a surprise quiz?

1. Student's short-term memory
2. Student's resistance to what is taking place in class
3. Whether the morning class told the afternoon class about the quiz
4. How intimidated students are
5. Whether students copied the answers to the homework questions from the book
6. What students understand about social studies and history
7. All of the above choices except 6.

In the last few years, increasing numbers of teachers and politicians have argued for more accurate and authentic assessment of student learning. When I ran a Google search on "state social studies assessment," there were 900,000 hits. However, there is little general agreement about what constitutes more accurate assessment. Proposals for the social studies include intensive testing of student skills and content knowledge, broader testing to include student performance as historians and social scientists as they evaluate primary source documents, and deemphasis of testing and evaluation of students based on work assembled over the course of a year or a span of a number of years (portfolio assessment). An issue always raised in discussions of authentic assessment is the reliability and validity of standardized multiple-choice tests: whether they discriminate against particular groups or measure what they claim to measure. The problem of subjectivity is even more pronounced when it comes to designing and evaluating essay questions and student projects. In general, people who argue for authentic assessment do not repudiate the idea of assessing students to see what they learned during a semester or year, but they do want fairer evaluations (Wolf, LeMahieu, and Eresh, 1992; Meyer, 1992).

Standardized Assessment:

Standardized assessment devices, especially multiple-choice tests, measure narrow areas of competence. Advocates for this type of assessment argue that results on these tests accurately and objectively measure a student's general level of achievement.

> **Performance Assessment:**
>
> This is direct evaluation of student competence in a number of different areas using a variety of assessment devices, including standardized tests. Performance assessment attempts to directly measure a student's ability to think critically, write clearly, express ideas orally, and work cooperatively.
>
> **Authentic Assessment:**
>
> This is a form of performance assessment that minimizes the use of tests and encourages the direct assessment of student performance during learning activities and through the evaluation of student work.

A different approach to assessing student learning is closely related to what John Dewey called developing "habits of mind." In Dewey's view, assessing (comparing, analyzing, sorting, organizing, exploring, experimenting) is how human beings learn. What teachers need to assess is not the information that students know, but how effectively students are assessing and integrating the information into their worldview. The Coalition for Essential Schools has tried to incorporate this view of assessment into programs at its affiliated schools. In these schools, teachers and students both learn and assess learning by trying to answer five basic questions:

How do you know what you know? (Evidence)

From what viewpoint is this being presented? (Perspective)

How is this event or work connected to others? (Connections)

What if things were different? (Suppositions)

Why is this important? (Relevance)

A significant question is whether teachers can effectively measure Deweyan "habits of mind" by using standard social studies assessment devices: short answer tests, essays, written reports, and classroom presentations.

Teaching Activity: How Do We Know What We Know?

For centuries, philosophers have been puzzled over this question: How do we know what we know? Plato's "Euthyphro" (Tredennick, 1980) is the story of a young man who charges his father with manslaughter because he caused the death of a servant. In the dialogue, Socrates questions Euthyphro about the certainty of his knowledge of right and wrong:

> Socrates: Do you really believe that you understand the ruling of the divine law, . . . so accurately that in the circumstances that you describe you have no misgivings? Aren't you afraid that . . . you may turn out to be committing an act of impiety yourself?
>
> Euthyphro: No Socrates; I shouldn't be worth much, . . . if I didn't have accurate knowledge about all that sort of thing.

Socrates continues the dialogue with a series of questions that press Euthyphro to clearly define *piety*. Euthyphro tries to distinguish between pious and impious actions, but each definition he offers proves to be unsatisfactory because it includes categories of behavior or ways of knowing which Euthyphro cannot accept as pious. Eventually, Euthyphro tells Socrates that he has another engagement but promises to continue the discussion the next time they meet. I am not sure I would have done much better than Euthyphro if Socrates questioned me about a social studies concept such as justice, democracy, or human rights. How much would anyone's knowledge stand up to grilling by Socrates?

Uncertainty, however, is not necessarily bad. Twentieth-century French philosopher John-Paul Sartre's existentialist philosophy suggests that people can never be absolutely certain of anything. Human beings have to make the best choices that they can based on limited knowledge. Contemporary postmodernist thinkers go one step further than Sartre to argue that there is no such thing as absolute knowledge or certainty because all knowledge is shaped by the experiences and understanding of the knower. Perhaps what Socrates, Sartre, and the postmodernists are all suggesting is that the key to understanding is not what we know, but how we know: the Deweyian "habits of mind" that we use to understand our world.

Think it over:

Is Euthyphro's problem his lack of knowledge about the meaning of piety, the unfair nature of Socrates' questions (the assessment device), or some other factor(s)? Explain the reasons for your answer.

Add your voice to the discussion:

Should social studies teachers focus assessment on content knowledge, skills competence, and student ability to understand and use concepts or "habits of mind?" Explain the reasons for your answer.

It's your classroom:

If Euthyphro were a student in your class, how would you assess his "habits of mind"? Explain the reasons for your assessment.

Grant Wiggins, a major advocate of performance assessment, is critical of most social studies testing for measuring the least complex levels of human thought (Nickell, 1992). Wiggins challenges social studies educators to assess student performance on the higher-order thinking skills identified in Bloom's taxonomy. For example, a student's ability to synthesize information and create new understanding requires creativity and judgment. This kind of thinking stimulates diverse and unexpected responses that are not easily measured on a multiple-choice exam.

Wiggins (1992; 1993) argues that the key to employing Deweyan ideas about learning in social studies assessment is to view assessment as an ongoing part of a learning process through which people repeatedly test their knowledge and their skills and adjust what they do and how they do it based on what they discover.

This is very different from creating tests that measure a limited form of knowledge at a particular point in time. Wiggins suggests that teachers think of their students as workers (historians and social scientists) who are continually enhancing their skills as they create increasingly more complex products. The difficult task for teachers is establishing criteria for evaluating these products during the process of creation and after they are completed.

I believe that certain principles can guide social studies teachers as we work to discover more authentic ways of assessing student understanding. These principles include the following:

- We should assess student performance based on the full range of what is being taught in class. That includes content knowledge and academic skills. It also includes the acquisition of social skills; an understanding of historical and social science concepts; the ability to gather, organize, present, integrate, and utilize information; and the ability to explore values and ideas and use new understandings to reconsider the ways people think and live.

- Assessment should be part of the learning process. It should be continuous so that students have feedback on how they are doing. We should use tests to discover what students know, not what they do not know. A reasonable assumption is that when students are excited about what they are learning and do well on tests, they will want to learn more.

- If test scores are going to reflect what students are learning, they need to be designed for specific classes. Prepackaged and standardized tests are based on the assumption that the same things are happening in widely diverse settings.

- Although the criteria for assessment should be clear to students, they should also be flexible. Assessment is relative, not absolute. It involves judgments about which people can legitimately disagree.

- Assessment is most effective when it includes individual self-assessment.

- Authentic assessment of student learning requires examining a number of types of activities at a series of points in the learning process and using different criteria and assessment devices to evaluate student performance. We do not measure temperature with a speedometer. How can a matching quiz measure a student's understanding of democratic values?

- The goal of assessment is to encourage and assist learning. Tests and projects should not be used to punish or sort students. Everyone who works hard and does well should be able to receive the highest evaluation.

- If the ability to work hard in an organized and disciplined fashion is one of the things we want students to learn, effort should count in an evaluation of students' work.

- If we want students to learn how to work collectively, take responsibility for group activities, respect the value and contributions of other people, and play leadership roles, performance on group activities should be factored into an evaluation of a student's work.

- Students with limited academic skills should be able to demonstrate their knowledge and understanding of a subject in ways that are appropriate to their skills. Imagine you are a chef being tested on your ability to cook a new dish, but the recipe is written in a language you cannot read. Would this be a fair assessment of your ability or knowledge?

- We are assessing knowledge and understanding of a subject and academic and social skills, not a student's qualities as a human being.

WHAT DOES A SOCIAL STUDIES PORTFOLIO LOOK LIKE?

Writing about assessment practices for the NCSS, Pat Nickell (1993) explains, "If our intended outcome is to enable all students to become competent citizens, we must give less emphasis to mere recall and low-level comprehension of facts and concepts, and more emphasis to applying knowledge to tasks that require high-level cognition. . . . 'Doing' social studies, like doing mathematics, science, or art is imperative. . . ."

Organizing project-based social studies classrooms where the primary method for evaluating student understanding is an evaluation of the products of their activity and research introduces a new dimension into social studies assessment: the *portfolio*. One group of West Coast educators defined the portfolio as "a purposeful collection of student work that tells the story of the student's efforts, progress, or achieve-ment in (a) given area(s). This collection must include student participation in selection of portfolio content; the guidelines for selection; the criteria for judging merit; and evidence of student self-reflection" (Arter and Spandel, 1992: 36–44).

Portfolio Assessment:

Student's performance evaluated based on a collection of their work assembled over an extended period of time. The portfolio demonstrates growth as well as final achievement.

A portfolio is not simply a collection of student work. For it to be a useful document that symbolizes a student's mastery of a subject area during a class or a whole course of study, it must be integrated into the instructional and assessment fabric of a school's social studies program. Effective portfolio programs need to provide students and teachers with specific guidelines for creating, assembling, and evaluating student work.

A multitude of questions must be addressed when a teacher or school establishes a social studies portfolio program:

- Who defines what goes into a portfolio: individual students and teachers, the social studies department, school or district administrators, or a state's regulatory body?
- Can portfolios accurately measure the full range of skills, attitudes, content knowledge, and conceptual understanding developed during a social studies course or multiyear program?
- Will students be involved in defining portfolio topics and projects, deciding on the products that will be evaluated, and the evaluation process itself?
- Are portfolios comprehensive documents showing the full span of a student's work, or do they contain a selection of typical, or perhaps exemplary, efforts?
- How much weight will be given to effort, the process of creation, and the final product in assessing student work?
- Does individual growth count, or only a student's final achievement?
- How will growth, the process of creation, and effort be measured?
- Can portfolios include group as well as individual work? If they can, how will a student's participation in a group project be evaluated?
- What standards should be used to evaluate the quality of work at different points in a student's secondary school career?
- Can evaluation be objective or even systematic?
- How do programs avoid the mechanical application of portfolio design and assessment?
- Will schools and districts sacrifice student experimentation and creativity as they try to ensure that minimum guidelines are met?
- Can portfolio assignments and even entire portfolios receive meaningful number or letter grades?

Grant Wiggins, formally affiliated with Center on Learning, Assessment, and School Structure addresses some of these questions in proposals for integrating portfolio creation and assessment into regular social studies classrooms (Wiggins and McTighe, 1998). Wiggins recommends involving students in clearly defined and guided multiple-step projects that are evaluated at different points in the creative process. He also recommends detailed assessment rubrics that examine both content and presentation. The following sample scoring rubrics can be used to evaluate student oral presentations and written work. To learn more about Wiggin's approach to teaching and assessment, check out the Relearning by Design web site at http://www.relearning.org.

Scoring Rubric for Oral Presentations/Demonstrations

Content (55%): Poor 0–3 pts., Average 4–6 pts., Good 7–9 pts., Excellent 10–11 pts.

Worthwhile and relevant information	
Sufficient information	
Ideas clearly explained	
Ideas logically explained	
Effective organization	

Delivery (35%): 0–1 pts., 2–3 pts., 4 pts., 5 pts.

Contact with audience	
Effective use of notes	
Confidence	
Articulation	
Projection	
Enthusiasm	
Avoids distractions	

Overall (10%): 0–4 pts., 5–6 pts., 7–8 pts., 9–10 pts.

Coordination with group	

Comments:

Grade (100%) (   )

Written Analysis or Critique Paper

Weak (0–1)   Satisfactory (2–3)   Strong (4–5)

Clear, interesting, and informative introduction, summary, and conclusion	
Provides main idea for each paragraph	
Identifies and explains social forces	
Explains different perspectives	
Clearly identifies author's views	
Presents appropriate information	
Uses details and examples effectively	
Includes connections with current issues	
Satisfies writing requirements	
Satisfies project requirements	

Total Points ( ) × 2 = Assignment Grade ( )

Jennifer Bambino (NTN) is a middle school social studies teacher who has worked in both urban and suburban communities and with diverse student populations. Projects and portfolio assessment have consistently been a major part of her approach to teaching. This is a sample guideline she gives to students and a portfolio check-off sheet students use to insure that they have completed the entire assignment.

Jennifer Bambino's Seventh Grade Social Studies Portfolios:

You are to keep a portfolio detailing your progress and personal achievements in social studies every marking period.

You are responsible for handing in your portfolio four (4) times this year.

Every portfolio should be your own unique creation.

Your portfolio will contain a minimum of 15 assignments each marking period.

Each marking period you **MUST** include:

- Three tests
- Five homework assignments (you choose which ones)

Continued

- Five journal entries (you choose which ones)
- Two required assignments

In addition, you will also include special projects, essays, or reports that you did during the marking period.

REMEMBER: These are **not** additional assignments. Your portfolio contains work that you have already completed during the marking period.

Portfolio Guidelines:

Each entry must be dated, and each area should be clearly defined (e.g., tests, homework, journal entries). You should use dividers to clearly mark the sections of your portfolio.

Entries should be in chronological order (in order of their dates).

All pages should be neatly arranged (no shredded paper) and written neatly in **PEN!**

Pages that are colorful and neat are more interesting and make a better impression on the reader.

There should be a title page with your name, school, grade, and class, an introductory page, a table of contents, and a "check-off" page.

Some of you may wish to write a narrative introduction indicating your progress, your personal learning style, and describing some of the talents you possess.

Entries should focus attention on your progress in social studies during the marking period and year. Your portfolio should provide visible signs that show your growth and development.

Include the things that you are most proud of, even if they are not all "A" or "B" papers. Things you worked hard on and gained personal satisfaction from, regardless of the grade, should be included.

At the bottom of each entry, you should write a brief paragraph explaining your reasons for including it. Ask yourself the following questions (include the answer to at least three of them for each entry):

Why did I select this item?

What makes this my best piece?

How does this work show what I learned?

If I could work on this assignment again, what would I do differently?

What do I think of the teacher's evaluation of my work?

What grade would I give this work? Why?

You should spend a **minimum of 1 hour per week** preparing your portfolio. When there is no other homework assignment, your assignment is to work on your portfolio.

There will be a "portfolio check" midway through the marking period so that I can check to see if you are making good progress. The due date for your portfolio will be at the end of the marking period.

You should come see me during extra help periods to ask questions and discuss your portfolio.

Your portfolio is worth two (2) test grades.

PORTFOLIO CHECK-OFF SHEET

Name _____

_____ included a title page?

_____ included a table of contents?

_____ included 3 tests?

_____ included 5 homework assignments?

_____ included 5 journal entries?

Continued

_____ included special assignments?
_____ checked to make sure all of your entries are in pen?
_____ checked to see if entries are dated and in chronological order?
_____ wrote a personal statement about each piece?
_____ wrote an introduction to your portfolio?

Signature _____

Portfolio Rubric:

Name:_____ Class: _____ Marking Period: _____

Quality	Possible Score	Your Score
Have you included 3 tests?	15	
Have you included 5 homeworks?	25	
Have you included 5 journals?	25	
Have you included special assignments?	5	
Are papers in chronological order?	5	
Is there a written reflection for each piece?	20	
Have you included an introduction?	5	
TOTAL	100	

The portfolio creation and assessment program at the Central Park East Secondary School (CPESS) in New York City, which is part of the Coalition for Essential Schools, is a more radical departure from traditional assessment. CPESS requires that seniors create and defend 14 portfolios to graduate. Each student selects seven major areas and seven minor areas for portfolio development. Four of the major areas are required of every student: Science/Technology, Mathematics, History and Social Studies, and Literature. Social studies subjects that can be used as electives for either major or minor area portfolios include Ethics and Social Issues and Geography (Meier and Scwartz, 1995).

Portfolios reflect cumulative knowledge and skills acquired by students while at CPESS. They demonstrate students' command of information about the subject, their ability to explain their own and other people's points of view, their ability to draw connections between different topics, their ability to think creatively about the subject, and their ability to explain the broader relevance of their work. Students work with staff advisors to prepare their final portfolios and present all 14 areas to a graduation committee for review and evaluation. The graduation committee members assess portfolios using an established scoring grid that weighs both the substance and style of the work. When portfolios need to be modified or expanded, students are given the opportunity to complete the necessary work and resubmit the portfolio for approval.

The majority of the material included by students in their portfolios is originally done as coursework. The inclusion of collaborative work is encouraged. Interdisciplinary projects can be submitted in more than one portfolio area. Because each student works at a different pace and in a different way and because students bring a diversity of academic, social, and cultural experiences with them to their work, CPESS has no single prescribed formula for completing the portfolio assessment process. To learn more about Coalition for Essential Schools, check out its web site at http://www.essentialschools.org.

In 1995, the State of New York began exploring ways to add a performance assessment or portfolio component to its standardized Regents global studies and U.S. history tests, much as laboratory experiences and practicums were added to chemistry and biology exams. The integration of portfolio assessment with more traditional unit and final examinations may be a key for maintaining both generalized curriculum goals and academic standards in diverse authentic assessment and portfolio assessment programs. Final student portfolios can contain a wide range of social studies projects, as well as their scores on different types of classroom and standardized tests.

The following are suggestions for activities to include in middle and high school social studies portfolios. Some of the activities can also be included as interdisciplinary items in portfolios for other subject areas. In their final portfolios, students should strive to show the increasing sophistication of their work over time.

Example: Portfolio Assessment

Sample middle school social studies portfolio (Grades 6, 7, 8):

- **Active reader/thinker**. Student develops a series of questions based on a primary source reading passage.
- **Outline of a textbook chapter**. Student demonstrates the ability to select and organize social studies information presented in a textbook.
- **Mapping, graphing, chart interpretation**. Student demonstrates the ability to interpret and create maps, graphs, and charts based on social studies and/or historical information.
- **Dramatic presentation**. Student participates in a dramatic presentation or role play that demonstrates an understanding of an historical era and the character and experiences of an historical figure. This is a group activity.
- **Narrative (expository) essay**. Student describes and explains an historical event.
- **Persuasive essay**. Student develops a position on an issue, supports the position with evidence, and tries to persuade the audience to accept this position.
- **Book report**. Student reads a work of historical fiction, summarizes the work, and analyzes it for historical accuracy.
- **Biography report**. Student reads the biography of an historical figure, summarizes the main events in the person's life, and explains the person's role in history.
- **Secondary source research report**. Student selects and researches a topic using multiple secondary sources. Report includes a bibliography. This can be an individual or group activity.
- **Interview**. Student develops a questionnaire and interviews a person or people about their involvement in local issues or major historical events. This can be an individual or group activity.
- **Social studies journal**. Student maintains a journal that includes comments on material studied in class and reports on progress on class projects.
- **Current events scrapbook**. Student collects current events newspaper and magazine articles and maintains a scrapbook and commentary on a specific subject.
- **Cultural art or craft project**. Student creates an art or craft project that represents the culture of a group studied in class. Student presents the project and background information in class. This can be an individual or group activity.

- **Class presentations**. Student presents different portfolio assignments to the class. This can be an individual or group activity.
- **Tests**. Traditional unit essay and short answer exams, quizzes, and standardized examinations.

Sample high school social studies portfolio (Grades 9, 10, 11, 12):

- **Active reader/thinker**. Student develops a series of questions based on a primary source reading passage.
- **Outline of a textbook chapter**. Student demonstrates the ability to select and organize social studies information presented in a textbook.
- **Outline of a lecture**. Student demonstrates the ability to select and organize social studies information presented in a class lecture.
- **Mapping, graphing, chart interpretation**. Student demonstrates the ability to interpret and create maps, graphs, and charts based on social studies and/or historical information.
- **Dramatic presentation**. Student participates in a dramatic presentation or role-play that demonstrates an understanding of an historical era and the character and experiences of an historical figure. This is a group activity.
- **Document summary**. Student demonstrates the ability to summarize the main points in a primary source historical document and explains the document's historical significance.
- **Comparison essay**. Student demonstrates the ability to summarize and compare the main points in two or more primary source historical documents or historical or social science monographs.
- **Analysis essay**. Student demonstrates the ability to summarize, compare, and analyze the main points in two or more primary source historical documents or historical or social science monographs.
- **Opinion essay**. Student demonstrates the ability to summarize, compare, and analyze the main points in two or more primary source historical documents or historical or social science monographs and develops an interpretation based on these sources.
- **Book review**. Student reads a full-length historical or social science monograph, summarizes the work, and comments on the study's implications.
- **Primary source research report**. Student selects and researches a topic using multiple primary sources and writes a report that includes a bibliography and footnotes. This can be an individual or group activity.
- **Interviews**. Student develops a questionnaire and interviews people about their involvement in local issues or major historical events. Information from the interviews is verified and expanded using published sources. Materials are integrated into an essay or essays. This can be an individual or group activity.
- **Social studies journal**. Student maintains a journal that includes comments on material studied in class and reports on progress as historians and social science researchers during class projects.
- **Current events scrapbook**. Student collects current events newspaper and magazine articles and maintains a scrapbook and commentary on a specific subject. Student develops a position on the issue and writes a persuasive essay that supports the position with evidence and tries to persuade the audience to accept this position.
- **Cultural art or craft project**. Student creates an art or craft project that represents the culture of a group studied in class. Student presents the project and background information in class. This can be an individual or group activity.
- **Cultural comparison project**. Student compares different aspects of cultures examined in the curriculum, including his or her own culture. Report can be written or oral. It should include examples of cultural similarities and differences. This can be an individual or group activity.
- **Creative display of social studies conceptual understanding**. Student creates one or more of the following: a book of the student's political cartoons and/or political poems; a poster display on an historical or contemporary topic; an audio- or videotape of social and political

music and songs, including the student's own compositions; a photo essay on an historical or contemporary topic that includes the student's own work; a museum exhibit on an historical or contemporary topic. This can be an individual or group activity.

- **Oral presentations and comments**. Student participates in panel presentations to class, both as a presenter and a commentator. This is a group activity.
- **Journal of civic responsibility**. Student maintains a journal in which she or he comments on involvement and learning as a community volunteer or in political or social action campaigns.
- **Tests**. Traditional unit essay and short answer exams, quizzes, and standardized examinations.

Teaching Activity: Constructing Social Studies Portfolios

Add your voice to the discussion:
Do you think portfolios or examinations provide more accurate assessment of student learning? Why?

It's your classroom:
1. Select one of the social studies–related portfolio areas (history and social studies, geography, or ethics and social issues) from the CPESS and develop guidelines for an acceptable (or an excellent) "major" portfolio.
2. What types of reports and projects would you require?
3. Would you allow students to submit group work to fulfill part of their individual requirements? Why?
4. Would you include unit and standardized test results as part of a portfolio requirement?

HOW DO TEACHERS DESIGN FAIR EXAMS?

I use multiple forms of assessment in my high school social studies classes, including standard short answer and essay tests geared to the academic level of my students. Most students find my tests challenging but not tricky. There is no simple rule for the frequency of tests, the number of questions on a test, the type of questions, the vocabulary level used in questions, the time allocated for a test, or the weight assigned to different kinds of questions. Much of test design is based on a teacher's judgments about her or his class and the points and skills stressed in a particular unit. I tend to give short tests on a more frequent basis to classes whose students have greater academic difficulty. I find that this gives more structure to their studying and allows me to target specific academic skills. Otherwise, I give full-period exams at the end of a unit as part of the process of pulling together what we have been learning.

One rule I have is that everybody gets to finish the test. If students need more time, they can come back later in the day during lunch or a free period. If necessary, a student can finish the test after school or the next day. I find that this takes some of the pressure off students who score poorly because they get anxious or because of academic difficulties.

My tests usually include multiple-choice questions and a selection of essays. I generally use matching questions only when I want students to identify places on a map or the people who said or wrote particularly important quotations that we examined in class. As a policy,

I do not use fill-in or true-false questions. I hated them as a student, and I am not convinced they tell teachers very much about what students know or understand.

I usually take the multiple-choice questions on an exam directly from the homework assignments and classwork activities. A typical homework assignment that could be adapted for a test would be to read "Wars in China and Korea," pp. 697–700 in

The Americans (Jordan, Greenblatt, and Bowes, 1985), and answer the questions from your homework sheet. If there are four questions to an assignment and 10 assignments to a unit, this gives me 40 questions from which to choose. Approximately 20 of them will be on the test. They will be supplemented by between 10 and 20 questions based on charts, graphs, quotes, or cartoons examined in class.

Homework Assignment:

A reading, writing, research, or thinking assignment that students complete after the lesson. It can be a review of the lesson, an introduction to a future lesson, background material that enriches student understanding, an exercise that improves student skills, or part of a long-term project.

The section "Wars in China and Korea" starts with a discussion of the impact of World War II on China, explores problems with the Nationalist government, and examines differences between the Communists and the Nationalists. It continues with a discussion of the post-World War II U.S. role in Asia and in the conflict in China and the U.S. response to the fall of the Nationalist regime. Increasing U.S. diplomatic and military involvement in Korea is explained as a response to Communist victory in China. The ability of the United States to enlist the United Nations in support of U.S. policy is credited to a Soviet boycott of the Security Council.

In its suggested homework assignment, the text recommends two activities: "Developing Vocabulary" and "Mastering Facts." In "Developing Vocabulary," students are asked to explain the following terms: *mediate, Long March, limited war,*

and police action. "Mastering Facts" asks students to answer four questions:

1. What were three reasons for the downfall of Chiang Kai-shek's Nationalist government?
2. How did the 38th parallel come to be the dividing line between North Korea and South Korea?
3. What was Truman's objective in Korea?
4. Why did the Soviet Union not veto the UN recommendation to send UN troops to Korea?

For an assignment such as this one, most students skim the chapter to locate the vocabulary words and facts that answer the homework questions. Instead of using the questions provided in the book, I ask homework questions that require students to draw conclusions based on the information in the chapter. I also try to provide context clues in the questions that help students focus on the chapter's main ideas. Students know that these questions will appear on the unit test in multiple-choice form. If they read the chapter and do the written assignment conscientiously, they should do well on the tests.

Sample homework questions for this reading from *The Americans* follow:

1. What were the main reasons for the downfall of Chiang Kai-shek's Nationalist government? In your opinion, which reason was most significant?

2. U.S. General Wedemeyer recommended that the United States send troops into China to support its Nationalist allies. President Truman was unwilling to commit U.S. soldiers. Do you agree with General Wedemeyer or President Truman? Why?

3. The Truman administration was bitterly attacked by conservatives for "losing China to the Communists." Do you agree with the conservatives? Why?

4. North Korea considered its government the legitimate ruler of all of Korea and considered the war in Korea a civil war. However, President Truman compared North Korean actions to those of "Hitler, and Mussolini, and the Japanese" during the 1930s. In your opinion, was the United States right to enter the Korean War? Why?

On the unit test, these homework questions become the following multiple-choice questions:

1. Why was Chiang Kai-shek's Nationalist government in China defeated by Communist forces?

a. Many people considered the Nationalist government dictatorial and corrupt.

b. Many Chinese peasants supported the communist program to redistribute land from the large landowners to the poor farmers.

c. Nationalist leaders used poor military strategy. Troops remained isolated in cities while their supply lines were cut.

d. Chiang Kai-shek was unwilling to change economic policies that favored the wealthy and his friends.

e. All of these reasons.

2. Why was the Truman administration bitterly attacked by conservatives for "losing China to the Communists"?

a. President Truman refused to send any financial support to U.S. allies in China.

b. President Truman was unwilling to use U.S. troops to support the Nationalist government.

c. President Truman sent thousands of U.S. soldiers to China without adequate weapons.

d. President Truman gave the Communist forces financial help so they could win their war against the Nationalists.

e. All of these choices.

3. In his memoirs, President Truman compared the actions of North Korea to those of Hitler, Mussolini, and the Japanese during the 1930s. Why did Truman believe U.S. troops had to be sent to Korea?

a. Truman thought North Korea would join with Germany and Japan to rebuild the World War II Axis alliance.

b. Truman believed that if communist aggression went unopposed in Korea, communism would keep expanding until there was a third world war.

c. Truman did not trust the U.N. or other countries to help defend freedom.

d. The North Korean army was the second most powerful army in the world and only the United States could effectively oppose it.

e. All of these choices.

Teaching Activity: Designing Homework and Test Questions

Add your voice to the discussion:
What do you think about these types of homework and test questions? Why?

It's your classroom:
Select a three- to five-page reading assignment from a standard secondary school text. Design four homework questions based on the selection. Rewrite the homework questions as multiple-choice questions for a unit test. In the chapters on unit and lesson planning, we discussed the development of document-based lessons. Reusing the documents on a test helps determine whether all of the students understand the material presented during lessons.

Example: Adapting Classwork to Create Test Questions

Wealth in the U.S.:
A sample document-based activity in an economics class might involve students in analyzing and discussing Figs. 9.1a, 9.1b, and 9.1c on the increasing disparity of wealth in the United States during recent decades.

1. Why is information in Figs. 9.1a and 9.1b shown in "constant dollars"?
2. What was the median income for men working full time in 1973?
3. What happened to the median income for men working full time between 1973–1993?
4. Whose earnings are included in "median household income"?
5. What happened to the median household income from 1989 to 1993?
6. What happened to the share of the nation's total net worth held by the top one half of 1 percent (0.005%) of the population from 1983 to 1993?
7. Describe the trend (pattern of change) in each figure.
8. What general conclusions can you draw based on these trends?
9. Based on your analysis of these figures, what further information would you want to know about the U.S. economy during this period?
10. In your opinion, what potential problems do these trends suggest for the United States?

On a short-answer test, these questions could appear "as is" or reappear in the following form:

1. Why is information in Figs. 9.1a and 9.1b shown in "constant dollars"?
   a. The value of money was constant from 1973 to 1993.
   b. The only people included are men who remained at the same jobs.
   c. Economists removed the impact of inflation on wages from the graph.
   d. All of these choices.
2. What was the median income for men working full-time in 1973?
   a. $34,048   b. $30,407   c. $33,585   d. $31,241
3. What happened to the median income for men working full time from 1973 to 1993?
   a. It rose by approximately 10 percent.   b. It declined by a little less than 10 percent.
   c. It rose by over 25 percent.   d. It declined by over 25 percent.

Source: The New York Times Magazine, November 19, 1995, 78–79.

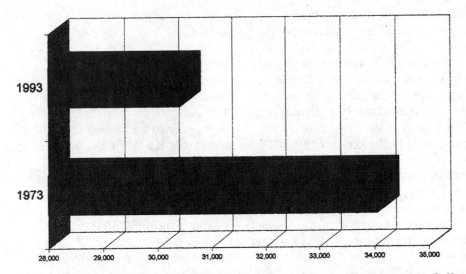

FIG. 9.1a   Median wage for all men working full time (shown in constant dollars).

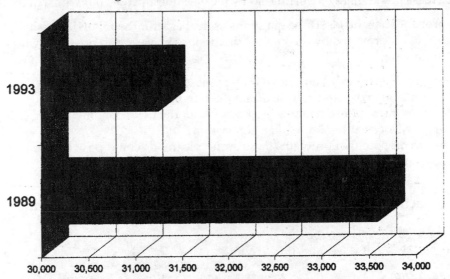

FIG. 9.1b   Median household income (shown in constant dollars).

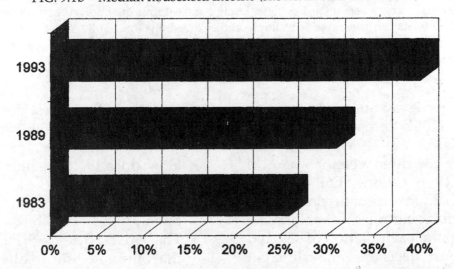

FIG. 9.1c   Share of the nation's total net worth held by the top one half of 1 percent (.5%) of the population.

4. What earnings are included in "median household income"?
   a. Income earned by only the head of the household.
   b. All income earned by people living in a household.
   c. Only the salaries of full-time wage earners living in a household.
   d. All income earned by the people or person who owns the house.
5. What happened to the median household income from 1989 to 1993?
   a. It rose by approximately 5 percent.   b. It declined by more than 5 percent.
   c. It rose by more than 25 percent.   d. It declined by more than 25 percent.
6. What happened to the share of the nation's total net worth held by the top one half of
   1 percent (0.005%) of the population from 1983 to 1993?
   a. It rose by approximately 35 percent.   b. It declined by more than 35 percent.
   c. It rose by less than 10 percent.   d. It declined by less than 10 percent.
7. Describe the trend in Fig. 9.1c. How does the share of the nation's total net worth held by
   the top one half of 1 percent of the population change from 1983–1993.
   a. A slow but constant increase in the share of wealth held by the wealthiest people.
   b. A slow but constant decline in the share of wealth held by the wealthiest people.
   c. An increase in the share of wealth held by the wealthiest people at a faster rate.
   d. An increase in the share of wealth held by the wealthiest people but with a decreasing rate.

I would probably use the last three questions as the basis for the following essay:
Use the information provided by the graphs, discussions in class, and other relevant sources to discuss the following:

- Trends in the U.S. economy you can identify in these graphs.
- General conclusions you can draw based on these trends.
- A list of further information you want to know about the U.S. economy during this period and the reasons you want to know this information.
- Your opinions on potential problems these economic trends could pose for the United States.

Teaching Activity: Creating Short Answer Test Questions

Add your voice to the discussion:
What do you think about these questions? Why?

It's your classroom:
Select a document (quote, graph, chart, picture, or cartoon) you would use during a lesson in a middle or high school social studies class. Design at least four questions based on the document. Rewrite the questions as multiple-choice questions for a unit test.

I try to design essay questions utilizing the same principles I employ in developing short answer tests. Generally, essay questions are rewritten versions of AIM or SUMMARY questions. For example, a unit in a U.S. government class might explore the changing role of the Supreme Court through an examination of selected landmark court decisions and different theories for interpreting the Constitution.

Sample lesson AIM questions during the unit could include the following:

- How does the Constitution describe the Judicial Branch?
- What was the origin of judicial review?
- The Dred Scott Decision: How did the Supreme Court attempt to resolve the debate over slavery?

- How did the Supreme Court redefine equal protection of the law in the *Brown v. the Topeka, Kansas Board of Education* decision?
- Why did the Supreme Court support abortion rights?
- Continuing the debate: Should Supreme Court Justices reinterpret the Constitution?

The three essay questions that follow are based on these AIM questions. The first question is a structured essay that tests whether students understand the main ideas examined during the unit and can recall and use specific information about cases discussed during the lessons. It also calls on students to formulate their own views and support them with evidence.

The second essay question is more open ended. Students are provided a quote that has been discussed in class and directions for answering the question. The third essay question is completely open ended and is taken directly from an AIM question. Based on earlier work, students understand that an effective essay must present a clear point of view, provide supporting evidence, and address arguments made by people who hold alternative viewpoints.

Essay 1

The U.S. Supreme Court has repeatedly reinterpreted the meaning of the Constitution during the last 200 years.

1. Explain the concept of judicial review. In your answer, discuss the origin of the idea of judicial review in the *Marbury v. Madison* decision.
2. Select three of the five cases listed next, and describe how the

Supreme Court's decision in each case changed our understanding of the Constitution.
   a. *Brown v. Topeka, Kansas Board of Education* (1954)—school segregation.
   b. *Engle v. Vitale* (1962)—school prayer.
   c. *Miranda v. Arizona* (1966)—Rights of the accused.
   d. *New York Times v. United States* (1971)—Freedom of the press.
   e. *Roe v. Wade* (1973)—Abortion rights.
3. Select one of the cases and discuss the legal, social, or political issues involved in that case.
4. Conclude with a discussion of your views on the role of the Supreme Court in the U.S. system of government. In your answer, provide specific examples to support your viewpoint.

Essay 2

Read the excerpt from a speech by former Supreme Court Justice William Brennan (*The New York Times*, October 13, 1985, p. 36), and then answer the question that follows it:

> We current Justices read the Constitution in the only way that we can: as 20th century Americans. We look to the history of the time of framing and to the intervening history of interpretation. But the ultimate question must be, what do the words of the text mean in our time? For the genius of the Constitution rests not in any static meaning it might have had in a world that is dead and gone, but in the adaptability of its great principles to cope with current problems and current needs.

Decisions by the U.S. Supreme Court have been criticized by citizens, including Supreme Court Justices, who hold different views of the way that the court should interpret the Constitution and decide particular cases. Explain and evaluate at least three different points of view of how the Supreme Court should interpret the Constitution. In your answer, discuss the ways that advocates of these views might (or did) view a particular issue.

Essay 3

Write an editorial expressing your views on the question, Should the U.S. Supreme Court Justices reinterpret the Constitution?

Teaching Activity: Designing Essay Questions

Think it over:
1. As a high school student, which essay would you have preferred to answer? Why?
2. As a teacher, which do you consider the most effective essay question? Why?

Try it yourself:
Write sample answers to the essay questions that you would consider appropriate for high school students.

It's your classroom:
Design a structured and a less structured essay question for a unit of your own design.

Generally, I use relatively structured homework and classwork assignments like the samples included here to direct students toward key information that they need to think about, analyze, and study. I also use these as the basis for test construction.

Assessment can also be based on more open-ended activities. Social studies teachers Bill Bigelow and Bob Peterson (1994) designed a project for Grades 5–12 that they call Students as Textbook Detectives. In this project, students research social studies topics and use their knowledge to examine classroom texts for biases, distortions, and omissions. Their goal is to make it possible for students to frame their own questions about the way knowledge received from textbooks shapes our understanding of the past and present.

I did a similar project in an advanced placement U.S. history class using the text, *The American Pageant*, by Thomas A. Bailey and David M. Kennedy (1983). Bailey and Kennedy are "consensus historians"; their text focuses on broad areas of agreement and continuing growth and development in U.S. history. They minimize points of conflict and tension and present injustices as unfortunate aberrations from the main democratic thrust of U.S. history. They dismiss demands for radical change as extremist, unnecessary, and disruptive. For example, in the chapter "The South and the Slave Controversy," Bailey and Kennedy argue that the U.S. Civil War was avoidable if extremists on both sides, especially among the northern abolitionists, had not undermined compromises and plunged the nation into catastrophic war.

Bailey and Kennedy believe that White southerners were "Slaves of the Slave System" (331) who would have eventually accepted calls by "reasonable" abolitionists for the gradual elimination of slavery. Unfortunately for the United States, "Garrisonian Militants" shattered "the atmosphere of moderation" by provoking violence until "The South Lashes Back." Garrison is described as "the emotionally high-strung son of a drunken father." The historians conclude, "Abolitionist extremists no doubt hastened the freeing of the slave by a number of years. But emancipation came at the price of a civil conflict that tore apart the social and economic fabric of the South." In addition, as a result of the Civil War, "bewildered blacks were caught in the middle. . . . Emotionalism on both sides thus slammed the door on any fair adjustment" (344).

During this unit, students examine the underlying causes of the Civil War in class using primary source documents. Their homework assignment is to read and outline the main ideas of the chapter and to compile a list of their questions and responses to the authors' ideas. At the unit's conclusion, students draw on their notes from the text and classwork to examine the different interpretations of the causes of the Civil War. As part of this discussion, they explore the ideological biases of the textbook's authors and the way these shape their interpretation of historical events.

On the unit test, students are asked to answer the following essay question:

ESSAY QUESTION

According to the authors of *The American Pageant*, extremists, especially northern abolitionists, were the primary cause of the U.S. Civil War. Explain why you agree or disagree with Bailey and Kennedy. Provide evidence from the text and from class document packets to support your position.

HOW CAN TEACHERS GRADE FAIRLY?

Even when tests are "fair" assessment devices, teachers must decide how much to weight different parts of a test and how to evaluate student answers on essay questions. Frequently, I assign a point value to questions after I see how students perform on a test. If many students do poorly on one part, I assume the problem was either in my teaching or with the test itself, and I count those questions for less. By being flexible, I get a more accurate measure of what students understand, I avoid demoralizing students with low test scores,

and I eliminate the practice of curving grades.

Evaluating essay answers requires a grading strategy. The three major approaches are "wholistic" grading of entire essays, assigning a specific number of points for each section of an essay, or using an assessment rubric that gives students credit for including different types of evidence and arguments and for the effectiveness of their writing. I have used all three strategies, and I do not think there is one correct approach. However, whatever approach you take, you need to be as consistent as possible so students know what to expect when they write essays.

Sample Rubric for Assessing an Essay Answer

15 Points Total	Weak	Satisfactory	Strong
Introduction **3 points**	**0–1 pts.** Confused and incomplete	**2 pts.** A clear but brief statement	**3 pts.** A clear and well-developed statement
Use of evidence to support argument **6 points**	**1–2 pts.** Insufficient or inaccurate evidence	**3–4 pts.** Sufficient evidence but not well developed or well developed but in need of additional evidence	**5–6 pts.** Sufficient information that strongly supports the position taken in the introductory statement
Conclusion **3 points**	**0–1 pts.** Insufficient; unclear. Not based on the evidence	**2 pts.** Some problems with either the clarity or logic of the argument	**3 pts.** A clear concluding statement that follows from the introduction and the evidence
Quality of writing **3 points**	**0–1 pts.** Serious problems with clarity, spelling, grammar, and paragraph structure	**2 pts.** Some problems with clarity, spelling, grammar, and paragraph structure	**3 pts.** A well-written essay with minimal problems

Teaching Activity: Grading Essay Questions

It's your classroom:

1. Select one of the essay questions suggested in this chapter or a question of your own design. If you were grading an answer to this question "holistically," what would you look for in an essay? Why?
2. If you were assigning a set point value to each part of this question, how many points would each part be worth? Why?
3. If you were developing a grading rubric, how much value would you place on the quality of writing? Why?

SHOULD STUDENTS BE INVOLVED IN ASSESSING THEIR OWN LEARNING?

For many teachers, involving students in the assessment of their own learning is a touchy subject. They worry about whether students are capable of objectivity in grading themselves or others and about the dangers of surrendering some of the teacher's authority in the classroom. However, instead of seeing student involvement in assessment as a problem of fairness or a question of classroom management, we need to view it as social studies teachers committed to developing critical thinkers and democratic citizens. Involving students in assessment can but does not necessarily mean they participate in deciding their own grades. It definitely means that students are involved in developing the parameters for class projects and deciding the criteria for assessing their performance in these activities. The benefits of this student involvement include a deeper understanding of historical and social science research methods, insight into the design and implementation of projects, a greater stake in the satisfactory completion of assignments, and a sense of empowerment because assessment decisions are based on rules that the classroom community has helped to shape.

Mike Pezone (NTN) discusses assessment with students as part of discussions of social justice (Pezone and Singer, 1997). Often he poses a problem for students to examine. For example, they own a plot of land that is covered by a forest and they hire two workers to harvest the timber. Worker 1 is a large, strong, experienced lumberjack. Worker 1 proceeds at a relaxed pace and takes extended breaks and is able to cut down and trim 50 trees a day. Worker 2 is on the small side and has never done this type of work before. Worker 2 gives a full effort from sun up to sun down but is able to harvest an average of only 35 trees a day. The class is asked to discuss how much a fair employer should pay each of these workers. During the course of the discussion, the issue of fair payment is connected to the question of how to fairly assess student performance in class. Mike uses this story and student responses to involve the class in establishing grading procedures for tests, projects, and class participation.

Writing in *Educational Leadership*, Walter Parker (1995) recommends the development of performance criteria and scoring rubrics for assessing "civic discourse" in social studies classes. The evaluation of these discourses makes it possible for teachers to assess a student's ability to put "democratic principles into action." I think student involvement in defining civic discourse, in establishing procedures and criteria for assessment, and in evaluating performance, as they did in Mike Pezone's class, is a particularly useful way to encourage and evaluate democratic "habits of mind." It also provides a model that can be adapted by programs that expect students to make presentations and assemble portfolios that demonstrate the depth and breadth of their work.

Teaching Activity: Should Students Assess Their Own Learning?

Add your voice to the discussion:
Do you believe that students should be involved in assessing their own learning? Why? How?

Essay 1: From Instruction to Assessment

As I have argued repeatedly, authentic assessment means testing what we taught. This essay follows two sets of documents as they move from activity sheet to unit examination. The first set, intended for high school, starts as part of a group project that can be organized in different ways, depending on your students. It has five documents. An entire team can examine and report to the class on one of the documents, or each member of a team can examine a different document and help prepare a team report. The level of difficulty of the documents varies, so the package lends itself for use in heterogeneous classes. The documents from the first package (Murphy and Singer, 2001) reappear along with multiple choice questions on the unit exam. Sometimes at the end of a lesson, I ask students, What questions are answered by the information in these documents?

Their questions and the document package can appear on the unit exam as a document based essay.

The second set of documents is designed for use in middle school. In this case, the activity and the exam are both more directive.

Document-Based Assessment:

Students are asked to act as historians and social scientists as they examine and explain individual or sets of documents and artifacts. It is a form of performance assessment.

HIGH SCHOOL LEVEL ACTIVITY SHEET: 19TH CENTURY IRISH IMMIGRATION TO THE UNITED STATES

Instructions: Examine your assigned document. What does the document tell us about conditions faced by Irish immigrants to the United States in the 19th century?

A. Letter from Michael Hogan, Albany, New York, to Catherine Nolan, Pollerton, County Carlow:

I take this opportunity of writing those few lines to you hoping to find you and your family in good health as this leaves us all in good health at present. I thank God for his mercies to us all. I received a letter from Patrick Kelly on the 24th of December '51 which gave us all great pleasure to find that all friends were well. We were sorry to hear of my grandmother's death but yet thankful to God for taking her out of this wicked world.

I got a situation [job] on the 12th of February 1851 which I occupy up to this time. My wages is 6 dollars a week from the 1st of April until the 1st of January. The following three months I get 4 dollars per week. I board myself. My work is but 10 hours in the day. Dennys is working at boot and shoe making since we came here with the exception of four months which he worked in a foundry last summer. Patrick is idle at present but I expect to get him work in a few days. As the girls, Mary and Ann and Margaret are in good situations in the city, and Eleanor is learning the tailoress trade.

I would not encourage any person to come here that could live middling well at home as they might meet with many difficulties by coming here but any boy or girl that has to labor for their living, this is the country for them. Winter is a bad time for any person to come here as it is almost impossible to get anything to do and expensive to travel.

B. Song—Paddy Works on the Railway:

In eighteen hundred and forty four, I landed on America's shore, I landed on America's shore, to work upon the railway. Filly-me-oori-oori-ay (3x), to work upon the railway.
In eighteen hundred and forty five, I found myself more dead than alive, I found myself more dead than alive, from working on the railway. Filly-me-oori-oori-ay (3x), to work upon the railway.
In eighteen hundred and forty six, they pelted me with stones and sticks, and I was in one hell of a fix, from working on the railway. Filly-me-oori-oori-ay (3x), to work upon the railway.
It's "Pat, do this!" and "Pat, do that!", without a stocking or cravat (scarf), and nothing but an old straw hat, to work upon the railway. Filly-me-oori-oori-ay (3x), to work upon the railway.

C. A Writer Describes Irish Immigrants in New Orleans, 1833:

One of the greatest works now in progress here, is the canal planned to connect Lac Pontchartrain with the city of New Orleans. I only wish that the wise men at home who coolly charge the

Continued

present condition of Ireland upon the inherent laziness of her population, could be transported to this spot. Here they subsist on the coarsest fare; excluded from all the advantages of civilization; often at the mercy of a hard contractor, who wrings his profits from their blood; and all this for a pittance that merely enables them to exist, with little power to save, or a hope beyond the continuance of the like exertion. The mortality amongst them is enormous. At present they are, where I have seen them working here, worse lodged than the cattle of the field; in fact, the only thought bestowed upon them appears to be, by what expedient the greatest quantity of labour may be extracted from them at the cheapest rate to the contractor. Slave labour cannot be substituted to any extent, being much too expensive; a good slave costs at this time two hundred pounds sterling, and to have a thousand such swept off a line of canal in one season, would call for prompt consideration.

D. Political Cartoon:

E. Immigration from Ireland to the United States, 1842–1854:

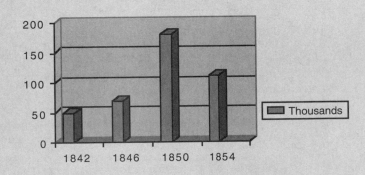

HIGH SCHOOL LEVEL UNIT TEST 19TH CENTURY IMMIGRATION TO THE UNITED STATES

Instructions: Examine each document and answer the questions that follow it.

A. Letter from Michael Hogan, Albany, New York to Catherine Nolan, Pollerton, County Carlow:

I got a situation [job] on the 12th of February 1851 which I occupy up to this time. My wages is 6 dollars a week from the 1st of April until the 1st of January. The following three months I get 4 dollars per week. I board myself. My work is but 10 hours in the day. Dennys is working at boot and shoe making since we came here with the exception of four months which he worked in a foundry last summer. Patrick is idle at present but I expect to get him work in a few days. As the girls, Mary and Ann and Margaret are in good situations in the city, and Eleanor is learning the tailoress trade.

I would not encourage any person to come here that could live middling well at home as they might meet with many difficulties by coming here but any boy or girl that has to labor for their living, this is the country for them. Winter is a bad time for any person to come here as it is almost impossible to get anything to do and expensive to travel.

1. Where is Michael Hogan writing from?
   a. Pollerton, County, Ireland.
   b. New York State in the United States.
   c. A ship crossing the Atlantic Ocean
   d. Breslin 018, Hofstra University.
2. Why did Michael Hogan settle in this place?
   a. It is the place he always dreamed of living.
   b. Irish immigrants are required to live in this town.
   c. He was able to find a job here.
   d. All of these choices.
3. What does Michael Hogan recommend to people in Ireland?
   a. He encourages everyone that he knows to move to the United States.
   b. He feels that people who are poor in Ireland will do better if they move here.
   c. He suggests that the Irish people would be better off if they remain in Ireland.
   d. He is sorry that he came to America and plans to return home as soon as possible.

B. Immigration from Ireland to the United States, 1842–1854:

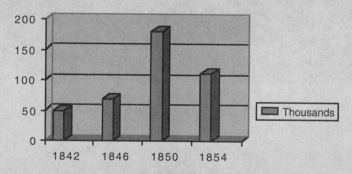

4. Approximately how many people migrated from Ireland to the United States in 1842?
   a. 50,000 b. 200,000 c. 50,000,000 d. 1 million
5. In which of these years did the most people migrate from Ireland to the United States?
   a. 1842 b. 1846 c. 1850 d. 1854
6. What was the "pull" that brought Irish immigrants to the United States?
   a. They liked the way they were treated by Americans and were immediately given citizenship rights.
   b. They were able to get high-paying professional jobs and live in luxury in the finest homes.

Continued

c. While jobs paid low wages and living conditions were harsh, the situation was better than in Ireland.

d. All of these choices.

MIDDLE-LEVEL ACTIVITY SHEET—THE SOUTH AFTER RECONSTRUCTION

Introduction: Conditions were very difficult for African Americans in the South after the end of Reconstruction. The four documents that follow describe one of the most unjust periods in United States history. Examine each document carefully and answer the questions at the end of the document. Be prepared. They are very upsetting.

Document A.   Mrs. Ida Wells-Barnett Writes a Letter to President William McKinley, 1898:

Source: Aptheker, H. *A Documentary History of the Negro People in the United States. New York: Citadel Press, 1968, 798.*

> Mr. President, the colored citizens of this country . . . desire to respectfully urge that some action be taken by you as chief magistrate of this great nation . . . for the apprehension and punishment of the lynchers of Postmaster Baker, of Lake City, S.C. . . . (W)e most earnestly desire that national legislation be enacted for the suppression of the national crime of lynching.
>
> For nearly twenty years lynching crimes . . . have been committed and permitted by this . . . nation. Nowhere in the civilized world save the United States of America do men, possessing all civil and political power, go out in bands of 50 and 5,000 to hunt down, shoot, hang or burn to death a single individual, unarmed and absolutely powerless. Statistics show that nearly 10,000 American citizens have been lynched in the past 20 years.

Questions:

1. What year is this letter from?
2. Ida Wells-Barnett writes President McKinley about the "colored citizens of this country." What term would we use to describe this group of people today?
3. What problem does Ida Wells-Barnett describe?
4. How many times has this happened in the last 20 years?
5. What does Ida Wells-Barnett demand of President McKinley?

Document B. Photograph of a Lynching:

1. Describe what you see in this picture.
2. Why is this picture so frightening?

Two men are lynched in Mario
Source: © Bettman/Corbis. Reprinted by permission.

Continued

Document C. How Many People Were Lynched in the South?:

Year	Total Victims	Whites	Blacks	Percent of Victims Who Are Black
1882	113	64	49	43%
1885	184	110	74	40
1890	96	11	85	88
1895	179	66	113	63
1900	115	9	106	92

Source: Adapted from Bailey, T. and Kennedy, D. *The American Pageant.* 7th edition. Lexington, Mass.: D.C. Heath 1983 p. 447.

1. How many years are shown on this chart?
2. How many people were lynched in the South in 1882?
3. How many of these people were White? How many were Black?
4. How many people were lynched in the South in 1900?
5. How many of these people were White? How many were Black?
6. What has changed from 1882 to 1900?

Document D.　Strange Fruit, a Song Sung by Billy Holiday in the 1930s:

Southern trees bear a strange fruit,
Blood on the leaves and blood at the root,
Black body swinging in the Southern breeze,
Strange fruit hanging from the poplar trees.
Pastoral scene of the gallant South,
The bulging eyes and the twisted mouth,
Scent of magnolias sweet and fresh,
And the sudden smell of burning flesh!
Here is the fruit for the crows to pluck,
For the rain to gather, for the wind to suck,
For the sun to rot, for a tree to drop,
Here is a strange and bitter crop.

Source: http://www.xs4all.nl/~ace/Literaria/Song-Holiday.html Strange fruit words and music by Lewis Allan. Copyright © 1939 (1939) (Renewed) by Music Sales Corporation (ASCAP). International Copyright Secured, All Rights Reserved. Reprinted by permission.

1. The lyrics to this song say that there is "Blood on the leaves and blood at the root" of the trees in the South. What is the "strange fruit" described in this song?
2. What images does the song use to create a picture in your mind?
3. Draw a picture or write your own poem, song, or rap about lynching in the South.

Middle-Level Document-Based Essay on Reconstruction:

A. Examine each of the documents in your package.
B. Make a list of three pieces of information you learn from each document.
C. Using this information, write a letter to your home town newspaper describing what is happening in the South.
D. Conclude your letter with your ideas on what should be done.

Essay 2: Assessing Our Teaching Practice

Overview:

Discuss reflective practice and action research strategies
Examine an action research project

Key Concepts:

Reflective Practice, Action Research

Continued

Questions:

Why Should Teachers Assess Their Teaching Practice?
How Does Action Research Improve Teaching Practice?
Can Teachers Assess Changes in Student Values and Ideas?

Why should teachers assess their teaching practice?:

One of the main reasons for social studies teachers to assess student learning is to understand our own performance. Examining student work makes it possible to evaluate the effectiveness of curricula and to decide whether individual lessons and activities connect to and scaffold on prior student understanding and experience. The assessment of students helps social studies teachers figure out how to better prepare, to more successfully present ideas in class, and to achieve goals. It makes possible what John Dewey and other educators have called *reflective practice*.

In *Reflective Practice in Social Studies* (Ross, 1994), the NCSS examines a number of school programs whose systematic effort to promote reflective practice has both enhanced instruction and supported comradery among teachers. For example, teachers at the Mifflin International Middle School in Columbus, Ohio, described how they "work hard to share their university level, inservice, and workshop learning with staff. . . . They exchange resources and instructional ideas gained

from these conferences during team meetings or special staff meetings. . . . Continued reflection . . . is helping them creatively plan and implement" the school's program (21).

Be careful about assumptions.
Used with permission of Pamela Booth.

Reflective Practice:

A process of professional self-examination through which classroom teachers, working individually or with colleagues, review and reconsider educational goals, strategies, classroom decisions, curricula, and school organization.

Action Research:

Part of reflective practice that entails testing assumptions about curricula, pedagogy, and student achievement through the systematic organization, observation, and examination of what takes place in our own classrooms.

How does action research improve teaching practice?:

John Dewey (1933) believed that human beings have "an innate disposition to draw inferences, an inherent desire to experiment and test. The mind . . . entertains suggestions, tests them by observation of objects and events, reaches conclusions, tries them in action, finds them confirmed or in need of

correction or rejection" (9). In my experience, what Dewey called an "innate disposition" can more accurately be described as a *potential*. Human beings have the capacity to reevaluate, draw connections, and learn, but that does not mean we always engage in reflective practice. The value of including action research in our teaching is that it encourages us to more systematically evaluate our ideas about history and social studies and our teaching methods. Using action research in class, teacher/researchers can identify particular issues or questions, develop strategies for addressing them, and, through recurring cycles of teaching, observation, and reflection, test and revise our teaching strategies.

Myles Horton (Horton and Freire, 1990) suggested an additional dimension for action research. He called on teacher/researchers to "Experiment with people, not on people.... They're in on the experiment. They're in on the process" (148). This is a valuable idea for a number of reasons. Involving students in action research projects adds to their sense of ownership over what goes on in social studies classes, and it helps teach them what it means to be an historian or social scientist. Additionally, when students are part of the research team, assessment of student learning becomes less a battle of wills and more a part of the learning process.

Can teachers assess changes in student values and ideas?:

As a high school social studies teacher, I was particularly concerned whether students were using academic learning from class to reevaluate their values and ideas. I decided to develop an action research project involving students in determining whether the study of struggles for civil rights and gender equity influenced attitudes about gender differences and bias (Singer, 1995). At the start of the semester, I explain the idea of action research and ask students to participate in an undefined experiment. If students agree, I explain that they will be informed of the details of the experiment after an activity is completed in class so that their participation will not be influenced.

Learning Activity: Cartoon Dialogue

Try it yourself:

1. Examine the cartoon panels. These female high school students are having a serious discussion.
2. Write a dialogue for their discussion.
3. Why did you decide to create this dialogue?

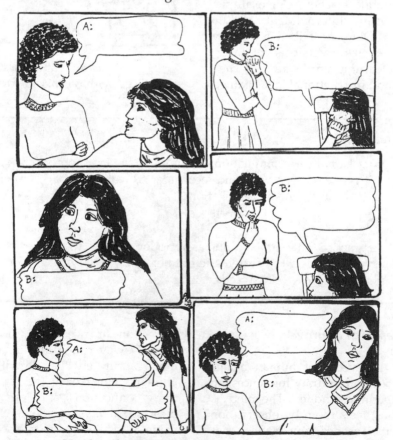

Used with permission of Pamela Booth.

The attitudes of young men toward young women, and of young women about themselves and toward each other, continually emerge in social studies classroom discussions and activities. As part of a unit on the changing role of women in the contemporary United States, I ask students to design "dialogues" between two female high school students who are having a serious discussion. Students can imagine any dialogue they choose; they have approximately 10 minutes to complete blank dialogue boxes on a cartoon. They are also asked to explain why they created a particular dialogue.

Later in the unit, I explain that the cartoon dialogues provide us raw data for an experiment measuring the impact of what we studied in class on student ideas and values. Cooperative learning teams examine the dialogues and sort them by topic and according to student explanations for why they created dialogues. After general results are discussed in class, cooperative learning teams meet to discuss (1) what students were trying to show in their dialogues, (2) why students chose particular topics, (3) why students felt that these female students were discussing these particular topics, and (4) whether gender stereotypes or biases influenced topic choices and dialogue content.

Generally, discussion in cooperative learning teams and later in the class as a whole is heated. Many students argue that some of the "cartoon dialogues," either by choice of subject or because of the content of the dialogue, express stereotypes about teenage women. Usually, however, students are divided over which dialogues and which explanations constitute gender bias.

Eventually, discussion of the "cartoon dialogues" extends into broader discussion of continuing gender bias in U.S. society and modern American youth culture. In general, female students react most strongly to the impact of stereotyping. Male students, with a few exceptions, are less vocal than female students. What is striking in these discussions, however, is the absence of flippant and derogatory remarks about women, which male students often make in class.

It is difficult for teachers to get students to express their opinions on issues that are important to them, especially when the experience of so many young people is one of being vulnerable and silenced by both adults and peer groups. Even when students speak up in class, much of their effort is aimed at presenting the answers they believe teachers want to hear or that other students will accept. I believe that action research projects, such as the one described here provide students opportunities to state and discuss what they are really thinking. Because of this, student choices on the "cartoon dialogues" and the discussions that followed helped me evaluate what was actually taking place in my classes.

From this action research project, I learned that I could not assume that students are making the intellectual connections I would like them to make. Academic knowledge by itself, even knowledge of social struggles against racial and gender prejudice, did not prompt students to reconsider their basic ideas and values. Knowledge remained compartmentalized until cooperative learning teams evaluated the student-created "cartoon dialogues" for potential gender bias. For me, the study suggests that if social studies teachers want students to make connections between school topics and life, we must find ways to make the parallels clear and help students make their understandings explicit.

REFERENCES AND RECOMMENDATIONS FOR FURTHER READING

Arter, J., and V. Spandel. "Using Portfolios of Student Work in Instruction and Assessment." *Educational Measurement: Issues and Practice*, Spring 1992, 36–44.

Bailey, T., and D. Kennedy. *The American Pageant*. 7th ed. Lexington, Mass.: D.C. Heath, 1983.

Bigelow, B., and B. Peterson. "Students as Textbook Detectives." In *Rethinking our Classrooms; Teaching for Equity and Justice*. Milwaukee, Wis.: Rethinking Schools, 1994, 158–59.

Dewey, J. *How We Think: A Restatement of the Relation of Reflective Thinking to the Educative Process*. Boston: Heath and Company, 1933.

Horton, M., and P. Freire. *We Make the Road by Walking*. Philadelphia: Temple University Press, 1990.

Jordan, W., M. Greenblatt, and J. Bowes. *The Americans: The History of a People and a Nation*. Evanston, Ill.: McDougal, Littell, 1985.

United States using either an e-mail address or the White House web site (http://President@whitehouse.gov or http://www.whitehouse.gov). Access to the Internet requires a modem, a phone or cable line, and a connection through a public (e.g., university) or commercial service provider. Some commercial providers offer forums designed to facilitate conversations between people who share common interests. Many special interest groups, or ListServs, will interest teachers. They focus on specific areas in history and the social sciences and on teaching at different levels. H-serv lists are described at (http://www.h-net.msu.edu).

4. Cooperation

The ability to merge files, transport disks, and send information electronically to different sites increases the possibility of students working together. A student can take a disk home, pop it into a computer, and work on a project begun by someone else in school, or everyone in the group can access information through e-mail or a web site.

5. Webquests and Simulations

Commercial simulation programs available on CDs such as Sim City and Sim Isle (Maxis Software, http://www.simcity.htmlplanet.com) require students to balance human needs with ecological concerns. The University of San Diego supports a webquest site with links to approximately 100 social studies–related problem-solving adventures for middle school and high school students. These are among the webquests linked to this site:

2030: Homesteading Mars, where students compare homesteading in the Midwest, United States, to homesteading Mars.

A Pilgrim's Tale, which introduces students to Medieval theatre.

China: Roots of Revolution, where students compete for a state department contract to produce a documentary on China.

Courtship and Marriage around the World, which has students analyze marriage and its impact on the role of women.

Creating the 8th Continent, where students design a utopian society on a new continent.

Diary of Anne Frank, which has students travel into the past in order to report on Ann Frank's world.

Global Challenges, where students participate in a U.N. simulation focusing on the issue of water scarcity.

Global Warming, a U.N. conference on climate control where students represent special interest groups and present their positions.

Imperialism in Africa, where correspondents for a British newspaper at the end of the 19th century report on imperialism in Africa.

PeaceQuest, which is designed to engage society in a dialogue to eliminate hatred and bigotry, to foster understanding and tolerance, and to bring peace to our world.

Seven Wonders of the Ancient World, where students travel back in time to visit the Seven Wonders and create an 8th wonder.

For the webquest, *Attack on Hiroshima* sixth- through eighth-grade students imagine they are members of a newsgroup writing a special magazine issue about the nuclear attack on Hiroshima, Japan. Each group member interviews someone with a different perspective on the events.

Subjects include an American soldier, a Japanese survivor, President Harry Truman, and an American Civilian (http://www.manteno.k12.il.us/drussert/WebQuests/JeremyFoster/attack.htm). The Quest Channel from Classroom Connect offers a number of webquests including *MayaQuest*, where students examine the collapse and disappearance of Mayan civilization (http://www.quest.classroom.com/maya2001).

6. Review/Practice

Individual students, working at their own pace, can review what they have learned and practice skills. Specific programs are designed to prepare students for standardized tests. Review programs also provide teachers with prepared testing materials that are geared to the level that students are expected to achieve. A search using the keyword *social studies* on Google (my preferred search engine) listed nearly 60,000 web sites. In addition, new sites are constantly being developed and older ones are abandoned. Clearly, there are too many places to just drop in and visit. Searches must be limited and directed.

7. Searches

Netscape is one of the many popular programs that allows students and teachers to search web sites. Using Netscape, a browser enters cyberspace at the home page of an Internet provider. At this point, a browser can either click on the open button and type in a specific web site address or begin a web search. To begin a web search, click on the Net Search button. A box opens and asks you to type in a keyword identifying the topic of your search. You may also be asked to select a search engine. Popular search engines include Yahoo, Excite, Google, Infoseek, and Lycos. Each engine offers specific advantages (e.g., larger database). Browsers can experiment with different engines to see which best meets their research needs.

8. New Problems

Students always seem to be at least one step ahead of teachers, and when it comes to the latest technology, the gap is probably wider. Downloading information and word processing have made copying reports easier. Some schools are investing in sophisticated search engines that help teachers uncover web-based plagiarism. Another solution, one that I prefer, is to have students hand in outlines, notes, and rough drafts of their work so that the process is an important part of their learning. A teacher has the right to reject finished student work when he or she has not submitted the preliminary assignments.

Because of the web, it has also become more difficult to monitor the sources students use to research and write reports. To address this problems, and the temptation by students to copy, many teachers are creating their own or school web sites with links to appropriate material. Students are required to conduct research using these sites. Students who want to use other sources must show them to their teacher for prior review. The following web site was developed for social studies teachers and students by Paula Trapani, a middle school librarian/media specialist. I strongly recommend it.

It is followed by a list of recommended web sites that students can use to research slavery in the United States. The list was put together by high school teachers Robin Edwards, Vonda-Kay Campbell, and Charles Cronin of the New Teachers Network. They also recommend these sites to teachers for preparing lessons.

SOCIAL STUDIES RESOURCES ON THE WEB

Paula Trapani, Lawrence Road Middle School, Uniondale, New York School District
(uniondale.k12.ny.us/lrms/socstudsites.htm)

General Topics

⊕ American Memory (Library of Congress)
http://www.memory.loc.gov/ammem/
collections/finder.html

⊕ The World Factbook (countries)
http://www.odci.gov/cia/
publications/factbook/index.html

⊕ History Online http://www.jacksonesd.
k12.r.us/k12projects/jimperry/colony.
html

⊕ Multicultural Resource Center
http://www.tenet.edu/academia/
multi.html

⊕ Foreign Embassies of Washington
D.C. (countries) http://www.embassy.
org/embassies

⊕ Background Notes on Countries
http://www.state.gov/www/
background_notes/index.html

Primary Sources & Historical Documents

⊕ American Memory:
Historical Collections
for the National
Digital Library http://www.
memory.loc.gov/ammem/
amhome.html

⊕ National Archives
and Records
Administration
http://www.nara.gov

⊕ AMDOCS: Documents
for the Study of American
History http://www.ukans.
edu/carrie/docs/amdocs_
index.html

⊕ The American Colonist's
Library http://www.
constitution.org/
primarysources/

⊕ America at War:
American Military
History (Revolutionary
War to WWII)
http://www.semo.net/
suburb/diswoff/
Documents.html

⊕ Archiving Early America
http://www.earlyamerica.
com/index.html

⊕ The Avalon Project: Major
Document Collections
http://www.yale.edu/
lawweb/avalon/avalon.htm

⊕ A Chronology of U.S.
Historical Documents
http://www.law.ou.
edu/hist

⊕ Douglas Archives of
American Address
http://douglas.speech.
nwu.edu/

⊕ Government Documents at
Yale http://www.library.
yale.edu/Govdocs/
gdchome.html

⊕ Documenting the
American South
http://www.ibiblio.
org/docsouth

⊕ Historic Audio Archive
http://www.webcorp.
com/sounds/index.htm

Adapted from P. Trapani, "Social Studies Resources on the Web," *Social Studies Docket* 2, no. 2 (2002).

⊕ Historic Documents of the United States http://www.ukans.edu/carrie/docs/docs_us.htm

⊕ Historical Text Archive http://www.msstate.edu/Archives/History/USA/usa.html

⊕ Documents that helped frame the Constitution http://www.lcweb2.loc.gov/glin/us-const.html

⊕ Hypertext on American History http://www.odur.let.rug.nl/~usa/usa.htm

Global Studies

⊕ Library of Congress Country Studies http:www.//lcweb2.loc.gov/frd/cs/cshome.html#toc

⊕ Explorers http://www.bham.wednet.edu/explore.htm

⊕ Background Notes on Countries http://www.state.gov/www/background_notes/index.html

⊕ Net Serf (Medieval History Resources) http://www.cua.edu/www/hist/netserf/home.htm

⊕ Latin American Studies http:www.//lanic.utexas.edu/

⊕ Primary sources from Vietnam http://www.vietvet.org/thepast.htm

Government

⊕ Government Information http://www.lib.utexas.edu/Libs/PCL/Government.html
U.S. Historical Census Data Browser http://www.fisher.lib.virginia.edu/census/

⊕ U.S. Census Bureau http://www.census.gov/

⊕ Census Data, 1790–1860 http://www.icg.harvard.edu/census/

⊕ Statistical Abstract of the United States http://www.census.gov/stat_abstract/

⊕ U.S. Supreme Court Decisions http://www.supct.law.cornell.edu/supct/

⊕ The Great American Website http://www.uncle-sam.com/

Geography

⊕ Atlapedia http://www.atlapedia.com/

⊕ Color Landform Atlas of the U.S. http://www.fermi.jhuapl.edu/states/states.html

⊕ Flags and Maps of the World http://www.plcmc.lib.nc.us/kids/mow/

⊕ How Far Is It? http://www.indo.com/distance/

⊕ Map Machine-National Geographic http://www.nationalgeographic.com/resources/ngo/maps/

⊕ MapQuest http://www.mapquest.com/

⊕ Great Globe Gallery http://www.hum.amu.edu.pl/~zbzw/glob/glob1.htm

⊕ 3D Atlas Online Home http://www.3datlas.com/

⊕ American Memory Map Collections http://www.memory.loc.gov/ammem/gmdhtml/gmdhome.html

⊕ Maps on the Internet http://www.byu.edu/ipt/vlibrary/curriculum.maps.html

⊕ The GIS Portal (Harvard Design and Mapping Co.) http://www.gisportal.com/

⊕ Cultural Maps http://www.xroads.virginia.edu/~MAP/map_hp.html

⊕ Oddens' Bookmarks: The Fascinating World of Maps and Mapping http://www.kartoserver.geog.uu.nl/html/staff/oddens/mapsat3.htm

⊕ Perry-Castañeda Library Map Collection http://www.lib.utexas.edu/LibsPCL/Map_collection/Map_collection.html

⊕ Working with Maps http://www.usgs.gov/Education/learnweb/MA/

SLAVERY ON THE WORLD WIDE WEB

African American History Sites

http://www.members.aol.com/donnpages/holidays.html Lessons, activities, biographies, and links related to Black History. Includes an interactive web treasure hunt and The Amistad Case: A Mock Trial.

http://www.nypl.org/research/sc/sc.html The Schomburg Center for Research in Black Culture. Digital images of slavery, lesson plans, and useful links.

http://www.kn.pacbell.com/wired/bhm/afroam.html Links to popular and informative sites on the African American experience.

http://www.blackquest.com/link.htm Alphabetical list of links to African American history, culture, and Black Studies resources. Includes slave narratives and the history of slavery in America.

http//www.africana.com/tt_145.htm Includes life in Africa before the transatlantic slave trade.

African Experience/Slavery in Ancient World/Middle Passage

http//www.usbol.com/ctjournal/Slavery2.html United States Black On-Line. Slavery in the Ancient World, Middle Ages, and the New World, The African Slave Trade, and Opposition to Slavery.

http://www.highseas.org/mpv_webpages/welcomepage.html Lessons about the Middle Passage.

R. Edwards, V. Campbell, and C. Cronin, "Slavery on the World Wide Web," *Social Science Docket* 1, no. 2 (2001). Used with permission.

http://www.pbs.org/wonders Hosted by Henry Louis Gates, Jr. Wonders of the African world and the legacy of the African slave trade.

http://www.africancultures.about.com/culture/africancultures Links to over 700 sites including a wide variety of documents about the trans Atlantic Slave Trade.

http://www.cocc.edu/cagatucci/classes/hum211 Notes for a college course. Includes timeline of events from before the Atlantic Slave Trade through 19th century European expansion in Africa.

Slavery in the Americas Sites

http://www.lcweb2.loc.gov/ammem/aaohtml/exhibit/aopart1.html African American Odyssey exhibit explores efforts to resist enslavement and achieve full participation in American Society.

http://www.pbs.org/wgbh/aia/ Africans in America. Includes images, documents, stories, biographies, commentaries.

http://www.spartacus.schoolnet.co.uk Slavery in the United States from 1750–1870 and the American Civil War. Excerpts from narratives of Olaudah Equino, Solomon Northup, and Sojourner Truth. Accounts range from 1,000 to 2,000 words.

http://www.web.uccs.edu/~history/index/afroam.html Links to primary source documents on the history of slavery, slave narratives, and the slave trade.

http://www.blackhistory.harpweek.com/2slavery/levelone.htm News articles and illustrations from *Harper's Weekly* on the slave trade, slavery, the Dred Scott case, John Brown's Raid, and abolitionists.

http://www.afroam.org/history/slavery/index.html Black resistance to slavery in the United States and a brief introduction to slavery, short stories, the role of women, and a chronology of revolts.

http://www.scriptorium.lib.duke.edu/slavery Limited number of pictures from the era of slavery.

http://www.eca.com.ve/wtutor/juli/gallery.htm Gallery of pictures on slavery gathered from the book "A Kidnapped Prince" by Olaudah Equino. Sponsored by the Equiano Foundation.

http://www.inform.umd.edu/arhu/depts/history/freedman/fssphome.htm Freedman and Southern Society Project at the University of Maryland. Primary sources on Emancipation and the Civil War.

http://www.amistadamerica.org/history/welcome.html A brief history of Amistad, links for Amistad research and primary source documents.

http://www.nationalgeographic.com/features/99/railroad National Geographic site that takes you on an interactive trip on the Underground Railroad.

http://www.undergroundrailroad.com/home.html The National
Underground Railroad Freedom Center. Features alphabetical list of major
participants in the Underground Railroad movement.

http://www.gliah.org and www.yale.edu/glc Primary source material from
the Gilder Lerner Institute includes documents on Amistad.

Slave Narrative Sites

http://www.vi.uh.edu/pages/mintz/primary.htm Edited versions of slave
narratives including Venture Smith and Olaudah Equiano. Documents
average 2,000 to 5,000 words.

http://www.xroads.virginia.edu/~hyper/wpa/wpahome.html American
Slave Narratives: An Online Anthology. Narratives and pictures from the
Works Progress Administration, 1936 to 1938.

http://www.newdeal.feri.org/asn/ Selections from the Works Progress
Administration American Slave Narratives. Seventeen narratives capture the
experience of former slaves.

http://www.io.com/~mjolly/ Vanderbilt University's site on slavery in
America includes edited narratives by Olaudah Equiano, Venture Smith,
Solomon Northup, Frederick Douglass, and John Brown. Includes
information on the Underground Railroad and the mistreatment of
slaves.

Slavery in the Contemporary World

http://www.antislavery.org Anti-Slavery International and Human Rights
Watch. Includes reports prepared by students at Immaculata High School in
Somerville, New Jersey.

http://www.unhchr.ch/html United Nations High Commissioner report on
human rights and slavery in the contemporary world.

Teaching Activity: Computers in the Social Studies Classroom

Add your voice to the discussion:
In your opinion, will computer resources revolutionize the study of history and the social
sciences, or will they end up being a temporary fad that gradually fades into disuse? Explain
the reasons for your answer.

Try it yourself:
Browse the web. Locate and list social studies–related sites you think will interest social
studies teachers and students.

Add your voice to the discussion:
Sign up for a social studies listserv.

WHO PROVIDES RESOURCES FOR SOCIAL STUDIES TEACHERS?

For this edition, members of the New Teachers Network compiled an updated list of regional and national professional organizations and advocacy groups, catalog companies that sell social studies materials, publications, curriculum guides, public service groups, and federal agencies that we find helpful. Some of the national organizations have local affiliates that provide classroom speakers (they are marked with an asterisk, *). When possible, we include a brief description of the social studies resources they provide. Denise Lutz coordinated creation of the original list for the 1997 edition. Brian Messinger performed a similar function for this edition.

American Association for State and Local History

1717 Church Street, Nashville, TN 37203, 615/320-3203, history@aaslh.org, http://www.aaslh.org

Works to preserve, interpret, and promote local history. Publishes *History News* and a monthly newsletter.

American Automobile Association

1000 AAA Drive, Heathrow, FL 32746-5063, 407/444-7000, http://www.aaa.com

Provides maps and guidebooks for members.

American Bar Association (*)

740 15th Street NW, Washington, DC 20005-1019, 312/988-5522, http://www.abanet.org

National organization of lawyers. Sponsors the Youth Education for Citizenship program.

American Civil Liberties Union (*)

125 Broad Street, New York, NY 10004, 212/549-2500, aclu@aclu.org, http://www.aclu.org

Supports legal cases to protect and expand constitutional rights. Publishes pamphlets on legal issues.

American Federation of Labor/Congress of Industrial Organizations (*)

815 16th Street, NW, Washington, DC 20006, 202/637-5000, feedback@aflcio.org, http://www.aflcio.org

George Meany Memorial Archives

10000 New Hampshire Avenue, Silver Spring, MD 20903, 301/431-5441, http://www.georgemeany.org

Umbrella organization that includes most of the labor unions in the United States. Meany Archives publishes *Labor's Heritage,* an historical magazine dedicated to the study of organized labor in the United States. Local union leaders and members provide speakers.

American Federation of Teachers

555 New Jersey Avenue NW, Washington, DC 20001, 202/879-4400, online@aft.org, http://www.aft.org

National teacher's union. Its publication, *American Educator,* frequently discusses issues for social studies educators. Sponsors Education for Democracy program.

American Forum for Global Education

120 Wall Street, Suite 2600, New York, NY 10005, 212/937-9092, globed120@aol.com, http://www.globaled.org

Promotes responsible citizenship and publishes a resource catalog.

American Heritage

60 Fifth Avenue, New York, NY 10011, 800/624-6283, http://www.americanheritage.com

Popular magazine with a focus on U.S. history.

American Historical Association

400 A Street SE, Washington, DC 20003, 202/544-2422, http://www.theaha.org

Primarily for university-based historians. Promotes history teaching in secondary schools. Publishes the *American Historical Review, Perspectives,* a newsletter, and a pamphlet series on historical ideas. Co-sponsor of the History Teaching Alliance and National History Day.

American Political Science Association

1527 New Hampshire Avenue NW, Washington, DC 20036, 202/483-2512, http://www.apsanet.org

National academic organization that organizes conferences and sponsors publications in its field of study.

American Social History Project

Center for Media and Learning, The Graduate Center, CUNY, 365 Fifth Avenue, New York, NY 10016, 212/817-1966, http://www.ashp.cuny.edu

Produces teaching videos, texts, and curriculum guides that focus on social history.

American Sociological Association

1307 New York Avenue NW, Suite 700, Washington, DC 20005, 202/383-9005, http://www.asanet.org

National academic organization that organizes conferences and sponsors publications in its field of study.

Amnesty International USA (*)

322 Eighth Avenue, New York, NY 10001, 212/807-8400, admin-us@aiusa.org, http://www.amnesty.org

International movement for the rights of the accused. Publishes *Amnesty Action* and *Student Action*.

Anti-Defamation League (*)

823 United Nations Plaza, New York, NY 10017, 212/885-7700, http://www.adl.org

Combats hatred and bigotry in U.S. society. Documents and publishes accounts of bias, promotes laws against hate crimes, and develops antibias programs.

Association for Supervision and Curriculum Development

1703 North Beauregard Street, Alexandria, VA 22311, 800/933-ASCD, http://www.ascd.org

Publishes *Educational Leadership*. Thematic issues frequently discuss topics relevant to social studies.

Association of American Geographers

1710 16th Street NW, Washington, DC 20009, 202/234-1450, gaia@aag.org, http://www.aag.org

National academic organization that organizes conferences and sponsors publications in its field of study.

Bread and Roses Cultural Project, Inc.

330 West 42nd Street, New York, NY 10036, 212/603-1186,
http://www.bread-and-roses.com

Sponsored by Local 1199, the National Hospital Workers Union. Provides educational posters and organizes exhibits and shows.

California Federation of Teachers Labor in the Schools Committee

1 Kaiser Plaza, Suite 1440, Oakland, CA 94612, 510/832-8812,
http://www.cft.org

Resource guide for teachers on bringing labor into the K–12 curriculum.

California History-Social Science Project

UCLA/CHSSP, Public Policy Building, Box 957101,
Los Angeles, CA 90095-7101, 310/206-5501,
resa@ucla.edu, http://www.sscnet.ucla.edu/ch-ssp

Active in developing history-based social studies curricula. Publishes *Primary Source*.

Center for Civic Education

5146 Douglas Fir Road, Calabasas, CA 91302-1467, 818/591-9321,
cce@civiced.org, http://www.civiced.org

Creates resources and curricula for civics education. Publishes a newsletter, *Center Correspondent;* a curriculum guide, *CIVITAS: A Framework for Civic Education;* and a book for middle school students, *We the People.*

Center for Research on Women

Wellesley Centers for Women, Wellesley College, Wellesley, MA 02481,
781/283-2500,
wcw@wellesley.edu, http://www.wcwonline.org

Sponsors research, publications, and conferences on issues related to women and gender bias.

Center for Responsive Politics

1101 14th St. NW, Suite 1030, Washington, DC 20005, 202/857-0044,
http://www.opensecrets.org

Studies and publishes pamphlets on the role of money in politics.

Center for the Study of Responsive Law

> P.O. Box 19367, Washington, DC 20036, 202/387-8030,
> csrl@csrl.org, http://www.csrl.org
>
> Promotes active citizenship. Publishes *Civics for Democracy: A Journey for Teachers and Students.*

Children's Defense Fund

> 25 E Street NW, Washington, DC 20001, 202/628-8787,
> http://www.childrensdefense.org
>
> Advocacy organization that conducts and publishes research on poor and minority children.

Church World Services Office on Global Education

> 475 Riverside Drive, New York, NY 10115, 212/870-2061,
> http://www.churchworldservice.org/resrcsht.html
>
> Provides resources for teaching about World Food Day and other global issues.

Close Up Foundation

> 44 Canal Center Plaza, Alexandria, VA 22314-1592, 800/CLOSE UP,
> http://www.closeup.org
>
> Nonpartisan organization that promotes citizen involvement in government and student trips to Washington, DC.

Cobblestone Publishing

> 30 Grove Street, Suite C, Peterborough, NH 03458-1454, 800/821-0115,
> http://www.cobblestonepub.com
>
> Publishes thematic magazines for classroom use, Grades 4–9: *Calliope* (world history), *Cobblestone* (U.S. history), and *Faces* (world cultures).

Common Cause

> 1250 Connecticut Ave. NW, #600, Washington, DC 20036, 202/833-1200,
> http://www.commoncause.org
>
> Nonpartisan group that campaigns for responsive and responsible government. Publishes *Common Cause.*

Concord Review

> P.O. Box 661, Concord, MA 01742, 800/331-5007,
> fitzhugh@tcr.org, http://www.tcr.org
>
> Publishes historical articles written by secondary school students.

The Constitution Papers

> Johnston & Company, Electronic Publishers, Bloomington, IN 47407,
> 812/339-9996,
> johnston@ansel.intersource.com
>
> Produces a CD-ROM for Windows that provides students primary source
> documents related to U.S. constitutional history.

Constitutional Rights Foundation

> 601 S. Kingsley Drive, Los Angeles, CA 90005, 213/487-5590,
> http://www.crf-usa.org
>
> Catalog of teaching materials on human and legal rights. Distributes *Bill of
> Rights in Action.*

Consumers Union of the United States

> 101 Truman Avenue, Yonkers, NY 10703, 914/378-2000,
> http://www.consumersunion.org
>
> Tests and reports on consumer products. Publishes *Consumer Reports* and
> *Consumer Reports for Kids.*

Council for the Advancement of Citizenship

> 44 Canal Center Plaza, Suite 600, Alexandria,
> VA 22314, 703/706-3361,
> http://www.apsa.com/CENnet/organizations/cac.cfm

Council on Interracial Books for Children

> 1841 Broadway, New York, NY 10023
>
> Develops materials designed to reduce racism and sexism in schools. Publishes
> a catalog.

Documentary Photo Aids

P.O. Box 597732, Lake Mary, FL 32795, 800/222-0763, docphoto@csof.net, http://www.computersol.net/DocumentaryPhotoAids/index.htm

Produces thematic sets of cartoons and photographs.

Educators for Social Responsibility

23 Garden Street, Cambridge, MA 02138, 800/370-2515, http://www.esrnational.org

Promotes active citizenship and conflict-resolution programs. Offers a resource catalog and curriculum materials. Publishes *Forum* and *Making History*.

Educators for Social Responsibility—Metro

475 Riverside Drive, Room 554, New York, NY 10115, 212/870-3318, staff@esrmetro.org, http://www.esrmetro.org

A local affiliate of Educators for Social Responsibility, ESR—Metro pioneers curriculum material on conflict resolution in the classroom and on a global scale.

Empak Publishing

P.O. Box 8596, Chicago, IL 60680, 800/477-4554, http://www.empakpub.com

Catalog of materials for teaching African American history.

Facing History and Ourselves

16 Hurd Road, Brookline, MA 02445, 617/232-1595, info@facing.org, http://www.facing.org

Produces curriculum material that uses the Holocaust as a starting point for understanding conflict and moral choices in the past and present.

Federal Reserve Bank

33 Liberty Street, New York, NY 10045, 212/720-6130, http://www.ny.frb.org

Provides materials for teaching about the U.S. economic and banking systems.

Feminist Press at CUNY

365 Fifth Avenue, 5th Floor, New York, NY 10016, 212/817-7920,
http://www.feministpress.org

Publishes material on women's history and lives.

Filmic Archives

The Cinema Center, Botsford, CT 06404, 800/366-1920,
http://www.filmicarchives.com

Source for historical videos and CD-ROMs. Catalog lists documentaries
such as *Eyes on the Prize* and *The Civil War* and commercial movies such as
Dances with Wolves and *Schindler's List*.

Foundation for Teaching Economics

550 Kearny Street, Suite 1000, San Francisco, CA 94108,
http://www.fte.org

Global SchoolNET

P.O. Box 243, Bonita, CA 91908, 760/635-0001,
helper@globalschoolnet.org, http://www.gsn.org

Links teachers and students around the world.

Greenpeace

702 H Street NW, Washington, DC 20001, 800/326-0959,
http://www.greenpeace.org

Campaigns against the dumping of toxic waste, in support of nuclear
disarmament, and to protect the environment. Publishes *Greenpeace
Magazine*.

Habitat for Humanity

121 Habitat Street, Americus, GA 31709-3498, 229/924-6935,
http://www.habitat.org

Organizes volunteer labor to combat housing shortages around the
world.

History Teaching Alliance

Department of History, Western Washington University, Bellingham, WA 98225-9056, 360/650-3096, compston@cc.wwu.edu

Clearinghouse for local content-based collaboration among teachers, public historians and museums, and university faculty.

International Institute of Minnesota

1694 Como Avenue, St. Paul, MN 55108, 612/647-0191, http://www.iimn.org

Promotes international pen pals program.

Jackdaw Publications

Division of Golden Owl Publishing, P.O. Box 503, Amawalk, NY 10501, 800/789-0022, http://www.jackdaw.com

Thematic primary source document packages from both U.S. and world history. Topics include atomic bomb, the Depression, votes for women, China, the Holocaust, Russian Revolution.

Joint Council on Economic Education

432 Park Avenue, South, New York, NY 10016, 212/730-7007

Knowledge Unlimited, Inc.

P.O. Box 52, Madison, WI 53701, 800/356-2303, http://www.ku.com

Catalog offers posters, videos, CD-ROMs, books, and filmstrips.

Labor Heritage Foundation

888 16th Street, NW, Suite 680, Washington, DC 20006, 202/974-8040, http://www.laborheritage.org

Catalog offers cassette and compact disc versions of labor and work songs. Publishes newsletter, *Art Works,* and sponsors an annual three-day conference.

League of Women Voters (*)

1730 M Street NW, Suite 1000, Washington, DC 20036, 202/429-1965,
http://www.lwv.org

Nonpartisan political group that supports voter registration and discussions of issues.

Library of Congress

101 Independence Ave. SE, Washington, DC 20540, 202/707-5000,
http://www.loc.gov

Source for reference works and government documents.

Metropolitan Museum of Art

Uris Library and Resource Center, 1000 5th Avenue, New York,
NY 10028, 212/570-3985,
http://www.metmuseum.org/education

Provides circulating audiovisual collection for teachers in the New York metropolitan area.

National Archives and Records Administration

Education Branch, 700 Pennsylvania Avenue NW,
Washington, DC 20408, 800/234-8861,
http://www.nara.gov

Preserves and makes documents available to the public. Sample documents and lesson plans are available at its web site. Publishes a newsletter, *The Record*.

National Archives Publications

1557 St. Joseph Avenue, Eastpoint, GA 30344, 404/763-7438,
http://www.nara.gov/publications/prologue/prologue.html

Source for documents from U.S. history. Publishes a quarterly magazine, *Prologue*.

National Archives Teaching Kits

SIRS Publishing, Inc, P.O. Box 272348, Boca Raton, FL 33427-2348, 800/232-7477
http://www.sirs.com

Topical documents packages include *World War I—The Homefront* and *The Great Depression*.

National Association for the Advancement of Colored People (*)

4805 Mt. Hope Drive, Baltimore, MD 21215, 410/521-4939,
http://www.naacp.org

Organizes young people for social action. Publishes monthly magazine,
The Crisis.

National Center for History in the Schools

Department of History, UCLA 6339 Bunche Hall,
405 Hilgard Avenue, Los Angeles, CA 90095, 310/825-4702,
http://www.sscnet.ucla.edu/nchs

UCLA/NEH program coordinates the National History Standards Project.

National Coalition of Education Activists

P.O. Box 679, Rhinebeck, NY 12572, 845/876-4580,
members.aol.com/nceaweb

Provides audiovisual materials. Lists speakers and activists involved with
school reform.

National Council for Geographic Education

Indiana University of Pennsylvania, 16A Leonard Hall,
Indiana, PA 15705, 724/357-6290,
http://www.ncge.org

Organizes conferences and sponsors publications.

National Council for History Education

26915 Westwood Road, Suite B-2, Westlake, OH 44145, 440/835-1776,
nche@nche.net,
http://www.garlandind.com/nche/main.html

Promotes the importance of history in schools and society. Publishes
Building a Curriculum: Guidelines for Teaching History in the Schools, and a
monthly newsletter, *History Matters.*

National Council for the Social Studies

8555 Sixteenth Street, Suite 500, Silver Spring, MD 20910, 301/588-1800,
http://www.ncss.org

National organization dedicated to the professional development of social studies
educators. Annual conferences and publications are available to members.

Annual membership dues include a subscription to the newsletter, *The Social Studies Professional*, and a choice between two magazines: *Social Education* and *Social Studies and the Young Learner*. Also publishes curriculum bulletins and a quarterly journal for university-based social studies educators, *Theory and Research in Social Education*. State and local chapter memberships support national efforts.

National Council on Public History

327 Cavanaugh Hall, IUPUI, 425 University Blvd, Indianapolis, IN 46202, 317/274-2716, ncph@iupui.edu, http://www.ncph.org

Publishes quarterly journal, *The Public Historian*, and newsletter, *Public History News*.

National Endowment for the Humanities

1100 Pennsylvania Avenue NW, Washington, DC 20506, 202/606-8400, http://www.neh.fed.us

Provides grants and sponsors institutes to promote humanities education. Publishes semimonthly journal, *Humanities*.

National Geographic Society

1145 17th Street NW, Washington, DC 20036, 800/NGS-LINE, http://www.nationalgeographic.com

National Geographic Society is well known for the *National Geographic* magazines and expeditions and research in geography, national history, astronomy, archeology, ethnology, and oceanography. Disseminates knowledge through magazines, maps, books, films, videotapes, educational materials, and television specials. Developed a geography education program.

National History Day

0119 Cecil Hall, University of Maryland, College Park, MD 20742, 301/314-9739, http://www.thehistorynet.com/nationalhistoryday

Sponsors annual student competition.

National Institute for Citizen Education in the Law (NICEL)

711 G Street SE, Washington, DC 20003, 202/546-6644, http://www.civnet.org/resources/teach/lessplan/nicel.htm

Publishes street law materials.

National Issues Forums

> 100 Commons Road, Dayton, OH 45459, 800/433-7834,
> http://www.nifi.org
>
> Sponsors public forums for adults and students. Publishes booklets
> presenting multiple views on controversial issues (e.g., poverty, social
> security, the U.S. international role).

National Museum of Natural History

> 10th Street and Constitution Ave NW, Washington, DC 20560, 202/357-2700,
> http://www.mnh.si.edu
>
> Publishes newsletter for teachers.

National Organization for Women (*)

> 1000 16th Street NW, Suite 700, Washington, DC 20036, 202/331-0066,
> http://www.now.org
>
> National organization that influences public issues of concern to
> women.

National Park Service

> 1849 C Street NW, Washington, DC 20240, 202/208-6843,
> http://www.nps.gov
>
> Promotes history education in national parks. Provides guided tours.

National Women's History Project

> 3343 Industrial Drive, Suite 4, Santa Rosa, CA 95403, 707/636-2888,
> nwhp@aol.com, http://www.nwhp.org
>
> Dedicated to including women in school curricula as equal participants in
> history. Research library for scholars and students. Publishes catalog of
> multicultural resources.

Network of Educators on the Americas (NECA)

> P.O. Box 73038, Washington, DC 20056, 800/763-9131,
> http://www.teachingforchange.org
>
> Works with schools to develop and promote teaching methods and
> resources for social and economic justice in the Americas. Publishes *Teaching
> for Change* and curriculum materials.

New York City Board of Education Curriculum Guides

Office of Instructional Publications 131 Livingston Street, Room 613, Brooklyn, NY 11201, 718/935-3985, http://www.nycenet.edu/publications

Excellent collections of edited primary source materials with teaching ideas for 7th- and 8th-grade U.S. history and 9th- and 10th-grade global history.

North American Congress on Latin America (NACLA)

475 Riverside Drive, Suite 454, New York, NY 10115, 212/870-3146, http://www.nacla.org

Concerned with political and economic development in Latin America.

Northern Sun Merchandising

2916 E. Lake Street, Minneapolis, MN 55406, 800/258-8579, http://www.northernsun.com

Catalog provides products for progressives, especially posters.

Organization of American Historians

112 N. Bryan Street, Bloomington, IN 47408, 812/855-7311, oah@oah.orgl, http://www.oah.org

Organization of U.S. historians and history educators. Publishes *Journal of American History, OAH Newsletter*, and *OAH Magazine of History*. Sponsors an annual Focus on Teaching Day.

Organization of History Teachers

19 Corie Court, Port Jefferson, NY 11777 umu.massed.net/~viceroy1/OHT.htm

Sponsors sessions for secondary school teachers at the annual conferences of the OAH and AHA and distributes a newsletter.

People for the American Way

2000 M Street NW, Suite 400, Washington, DC 20036, 202/467-4999, http://www.pfaw.com

Promotes voter education in secondary schools. Publishes newsletter, *First Voter*.

Phi Alpha Theta

> National Headquarters, University of South Florida, SOC 107,
> 4202 East Fowler Avenue, Tampa, FL 33620, 800/394-8195,
> http://www.phialphatheta.org
>
> National history honor society. Organizes conferences and publishes *The Historian* and a newsletter.

Physicians for Social Responsibility (*)

> 1875 Connecticut Avenue NW, Suite 1012, Washington, DC 20009,
> 202/667:4260,
> http://www.psr.org
>
> Campaigns for nuclear disarmament and for shifting national priorities to ensure that basic human needs are met.

Political Economy Research Center

> 502 S. 19th Avenue, Suite 211, Bozeman, MT 59718, 406/587-9591,
> perc@perc.org, http://www.perc.org
>
> Publishes curriculum on environmental issues.

Population Growth Education Program

> 1400 16th Street NW, Suite 320, Washington, DC 20036, 202/332-2200,
> http://www.zpg.org
>
> Organizes teacher education programs and K–12 curricula on population issues.

PBS Learning Link

> 1320 Braddock Place, Alexandria, VA 22314, 703/739-8464
>
> Provides database listing public television programs and lesson plans.

Pueblo to People

> 2105 Silber Road, Suite 101-80, Houston, TX 77055, 800/843-5257
>
> Catalog of clothing, ornaments, wall hangings, toys, foods, and books from Latin America.

Radical History Review

Tamiment Library, 70 Washington Square South,
New York, NY 10012, 212/998-2632,
rhr@igc.org, http://www.chnm.gmu.edu/rhr/rhr.htm

Journal with a radical focus on history and contemporary political issues.

Rethinking Schools

1001 East Keefe Avenue, Milwaukee, WI 53212, 414/964-9646,
http://www.rethinkingschools.org

Dedicated to reforming elementary and secondary schools with an emphasis on progressive values. Publishes newsletter, *Rethinking Schools*, which frequently includes social studies teaching materials and curriculum ideas.

Scholastic Inc.

555 Broadway, New York, NY 10012, 800/325-6149 or 212/343-6100,
http://www.scholastic.com

Publishes monthly magazines for students including *Junior Scholastic* (Grades 6–8) and *Scholastic Update* (Grades 9–12).

Sierra Club

85 Second Street, Second Floor, San Francisco, CA 94105, 415/977-5500,
http://www.sierraclub.org

Provides a free teachers' newsletter, a list of environmental education materials, filmstrips, slides, and videos.

Smithsonian Institution Office of Elementary and Secondary Education

A & I Building Room 2283, MRC 444, Washington, DC 20560, 202/357-1697,
http://www.si.edu

Publishes interdisciplinary curriculum guides on museum activities and *Smithsonian* magazine.

Social Science Education Consortium

P.O. Box, 21270, Boulder, CO 80308, 303/492-8154,
ssec@ssecinc.org, http://www.ssecinc.org

Develops lesson ideas integrating history, literature, the arts, and film.

Social Studies Development Center

ERIC Clearinghouse for Social Studies/Social Science Education, Indiana University, 2805 East 10 Street, Suite 120, Bloomington, IN 47405 812/855-3838, http://www.indiana.edu/~ssdc/ssdc.html

National information system. Provides access to education literature and curriculum material. Accessible from CD-ROM and the Internet. Publishes *The ERIC Review* and *ERIC Digest*.

Social Studies School Service

10200 Jefferson Boulevard, P.O. Box 802, Culver City, CA 90232 800/421-4246, access@socialstudies.com, http://www.socialstudies.com

Comprehensive catalog offers books about teaching social studies, activities, curriculum guides, reproducibles, transparencies, CD-ROMs, video and audio cassettes, documentaries and movies, posters, games, computer software, fiction for the social studies classroom, artifact kits, photograph displays, art prints, simulations, maps, and globes.

Society for History Education

California State University, Long Beach, CA 90840, 562/765-2205, http://www.theaha.org/affiliates/soc_his_education.htm

Reports on techniques, programs, curricula, and assessment. Publishes *The History Teacher*.

Southern Poverty Law Center

400 Washington Avenue, Montgomery, AL 36104, 334/956-8200, http://www.splcenter.org

Monitors and mounts legal challenges to racism. Publishes *Teaching Tolerance*.

Teachers' Curriculum Institute

P.O. Box 1327, Rancho, Cordova, CA 95741, 800/497-6138, info@historyalive.com, http://www.teachtci.com

Develops middle and high school activity-based curriculum guides that emphasize engaging all learners in diverse classrooms. Produces a teacher's guide, *History Alive*.

Teaching History

Box 4032, Emporia State University, Emporia, KS 66801
http://www.emporia.edu/socsci/journal/main.htm

Journal examines teaching methods in history and reviews history books.

Tom Snyder Productions

80 Coolidge Hill, Road Watertown, MA 02472, 800/342-0236, ask@tomsnyder.com, http://www.tomsnyder.com

Catalog offers educational software, videodiscs, videos, and CD-ROMs. The interactive program Decisions, Decisions places students in lifelike dilemmas based on historical and contemporary issues.

UMI (University Microfilms Inc.)—Great Events

300 N. Zeeb Road, P.O. Box 1346, Ann Arbor, MI 48106, 800/521-0600, http://www.umi.com/products/pt-product-NYTHistoricIndex.shtml

Six-volume Great Events history series is a package of *New York Times* articles on microfiche starting from 1851. Articles are arranged topically. Over 300 topics with more than 30 articles each. Topics include My Lai, the Brooklyn Bridge, the Scopes Trial, and the Moon Landing. Also volumes on Great Presidential Campaigns, Great Personalities, and Great Supreme Court Decisions.

UNICEF House

3 United Nations Plaza, New York, NY 10017, 212/759-0760, http://www.unicefusa.org/trickortreat/

Sponsors Trick-or-Treat for UNICEF. Publishes booklets and teaching materials on international issues and a catalog with multicultural educational materials.

United Nations Headquarters

United Nations Plaza, New York, NY 10017, 212/963-1234, http://www.undp.org

Supports refugees through UNESCO. Publishes booklets and teaching materials on international issues and a catalog with multicultural educational materials.

United States Public Interest Research Group

218 D Street SE, Washington, DC 20003, 202/546-9707,
http://www.uspirg.org

Lobbies for environmental and consumer protection. Publishes *Citizen Agenda.*

United States Holocaust Memorial Museum

100 Raoul Wallenberg Place SW, Washington, DC 20024, 202/488-0400,
http://www.ushmm.org

Books and materials for teaching about the Holocaust in Europe during World War II.

Veterans of Foreign Wars (*)

406 West 34th Street, Kansas City, MO 64111, 816/756-3390,
info@vfw.org http://www.vfw.org

Local chapters provide speakers for social studies classes.

World History Association

Department of History, 254 Upham Hall, Miami University,
Oxford, OH 45056, 513/529-3841,
http://www.thewha.org

Publishes *Journal of World History* and the *Bulletin of World History.*

Women's International League for Peace and Freedom

1213 Race Street, Philadelphia, PA 19107, 215/563-7110,
http://www.peacewomen.org

Works for social, political, economic, and psychological conditions necessary to ensure international peace and freedom.

Youth Action

2335 18th Street NW, Washington, DC 20009

Encourages teenagers and young adults to became active in campaigns on social, economic, and environmental issues. Publishes *Noise!*

Youth Peace/War Resisters League

339 Lafayette Street, New York, NY 10012, 212/228-0450, http://www.warresisters.org

Promotes nonviolence, justice, and an end to global militarization. Written and video instructional materials are available.

REFERENCES AND RECOMMENDATIONS FOR FURTHER READING

Braun, J., and F. Risinger. *Surfing Social Studies: National Council for the Social Studies Bulletin 96.* Washington, D.C.: NCSS, 1999.

Carnes, M. "Beyond Words: Reviewing Moving Pictures." *Perspectives: American Historical Association Newsletter* 34, no. 5 (1996), 1.

Demac, D. *Is Any Use Fair in a Digital World?* New York: Columbia University, The Freedom Media Studies Center, 1996.

Eakin, S., and J. Logdon, eds. *Twelve Years a Slave.* Baton Rouge, La.: Louisiana State University Press, 1968.

Littlefield, H. "The Wizard of Oz: Parable on Populism." *American Quarterly*, 16 (1964), 47–58.

Name Index

Subject Index